AFTERIMAGES OF GILLES DELEUZE'S FILM PHILOSOPHY

Afterimages of Gilles Deleuze's Film Philosophy

D. N. Rodowick, Editor

UNIVERSITY OF MINNESOTA PRESS
Minneapolis · London

Frontispiece: Mark Hansen and Ben Rubin, *Listening Post,* 2002.

See page 373 for information on previous publications.

Published by the University of Minnesota Press
111 Third Avenue South, Suite 290
Minneapolis, MN 55401-2520
http://www.upress.umn.edu

Library of Congress Cataloging-in-Publication Data

Afterimages of Gilles Deleuze's film philosophy / D. N. Rodowick, editor.
   p. cm.
Includes bibliographical references and index.
ISBN 978-0-8166-5006-4 (hc : alk. paper) —
ISBN 978-0-8166-5007-1 (pb : alk. paper)
1. Motion pictures—Philosophy. 2. Deleuze, Gilles, 1925–1995—Criticism and interpretation. I. Rodowick, David Norman.
   PN1995.A275 2009
   791.4301—dc22

                    2009034206

16 15 14 13 12 11 10   10 9 8 7 6 5 4 3 2 1

In memory of Marie-Claire Ropars-Wuilleumier (1936–2007),
who lived well the philosophical life

CONTENTS

Part III. Becomings

Part IV. Experiments

Part V. Futures

Acknowledgments

This book would not have been possible without the original thought and creativity of the contributors, who worked hard, individually and collectively, and accepted with good humor and grace the obsessive demands of its editor. Richard Morrison, senior editor for humanities and social sciences at the University of Minnesota Press, also gave his enthusiastic support throughout the process of bringing this book into print. Jason Weidemann took up the editorial baton and conducted the manuscript to publication with grace and efficiency, assisted by Davu Seru.

The colloquium celebrating the twenty-fifth anniversary of the publication of *The Time-Image*, and which brought the original speakers together, was sponsored by Harvard University's Office of the Dean of the Faculty of Arts and Sciences. Kind support was also provided by the Department of Visual and Environmental Studies and the Carpenter Center for the Visual Arts. I wish to thank, especially, Marjorie Garber, chair of the department and director of the center. Other institutions and individuals who contributed to the intellectual life of this event, and thus to this book, include the Humanities Center in the Faculty of Arts and Sciences; the Minda de Gunzburg Center for European Studies, Patricia Craig, executive director; French Cultural Services in Boston, Eric Jausseran, artistic attaché; Charles Stivale; and, of course, all the students and visitors in my spring 2005 seminar dedicated to the film theory of Gilles Deleuze. I am also very grateful to Melissa Davenport and Clayton Mattos for their untiring staff support. However, the conference coordinator, Allyson Field, was the person who really made things happen. During the preparation of the colloquium and the editing of the book, Matthew Lazen, Michael Sanchez, and Alina Opreanu provided invaluable help with translation and editing. Kasia Cieplak–Mayr von Baldegg did a wonderful job as my editorial assistant in the final stages of preparing the manuscript.

Several essays in this volume were seeded, tended, or otherwise transplanted from other people's gardens, although all are presented here in substantially new and revised versions. I thank all the editors and publishers of these works for their kind permission to reprint this material.

During the last stages of preparing the book for publication, I learned with deep regret of the passing of Marie-Claire Ropars-Wuilleumier in February 2007, after a long and valiant struggle with cancer. From my earliest days as a student in Paris, Marie-Claire was a formidable figure. Along with Gilles Deleuze and others, she was one of the founders of University of Paris VIII, with its political and philosophical experimentalism, and a profoundly original thinker who, by her example, showed me and many others the many points of contact between contemporary French philosophy and film theory. She was a fierce intellect, then, but also a person of great personal charm and elegance, always open to long discussions of film and philosophy. In homage to her long and distinguished career, and in sympathy with her husband, Jacques Ropars, this book is dedicated to her memory.

Introduction: What Does Time Express?

D. N. Rodowick

According to Gilles Deleuze, time is the Event defined as the ever-recurring possibility for the creation of the new. Cinema no doubt was birthed in time in that no one in 1895 could have imagined that it would develop as an art, much less as a philosophical machine. As Deleuze writes of cinema's origins, "the essence of a thing never emerges at its beginning, but only in the middle, in the course of its development when its powers are affirmed."[1] Only retrospectively do we recognize the emergence of the new.

"The essence of a thing never emerges at its beginning": the same might be said of Deleuze's two-volume study of cinema and philosophy, *Cinema 1: The Movement-Image* and *Cinema 2: The Time-Image*, published in France in 1983 and 1985, respectively. Although the books were quickly translated, appearing in the United States from University of Minnesota Press in 1986 and 1989, they had little impact on Anglophone film studies in the ten years following their translation. I first set out to write a review essay of the cinema books in Paris in 1991, at the height of the first Gulf War. Conceived as a small project, it consumed my life for the next five years, eventually becoming *Gilles Deleuze's Time Machine*.[2] Little did I know then to what degree Deleuze was becoming for me, as for so many others, a "philosophical friend," intercessor, or conceptual persona.

There is a phrase from Foucault that has gripped me from the first time I read it: that the reason for writing is to become other than I am, and to think other than I think. Variations on this phrase occur throughout Foucault's writings, and one of the most beautiful appears already in *The Order of Things*: "What must I be, I who think and who am thought, in order to be what I do not think, in order for my thought to be what I am not?"[3] *Penser autrement*, or to think otherwise, is the highest task of philosophy and for a critical mind—this is one of the fundamental lessons that Deleuze draws from Foucault, or at least one of the ideas that connects them. But, as Deleuze and Guattari show in *What Is Philosophy?*, to think, to perform philosophy, one needs conceptual personae, or more simply, philosophical friends. Foucault and Guattari were philosophical friends for Deleuze, intercessors who pushed his thinking to new creative acts. But there are others no doubt, "real before becoming actual, ideal without being abstract": Marcel Proust, Francis Bacon, Samuel Beckett, and all the great cineasts cited in the two books on cinema.

In the years before Deleuze's untimely passing in 1995, I met precious few film scholars in the Anglophone world who found the books interesting or important. I was even warned against devoting so much time to two books that many film scholars found marginal at best and incomprehensible at worst. Without the support of sympathetic friends, Dudley Andrew and Raymond Bellour foremost among them, I could never have completed this work. Thankfully, the new millennium has brought forth new possibilities for thought. The book you are now reading began in the realization that 2005 would mark the twentieth anniversary of the publication of *The Time-Image* in France as well as the tenth anniversary of Gilles Deleuze's disappearance from the theater of philosophy. These were events of such deep personal and intellectual importance to me that I was determined not to let them pass unacknowledged. With the generous support of Harvard University's Office of the Dean of the Faculty of Arts and Sciences and the Carpenter Center for the Visual Arts, I decided to organize a colloquium to evaluate the "afterimage" of Gilles Deleuze's film philosophy. Preceded by an extensive film series at the Harvard Film Archive, curated by Ted Barron and me, the colloquium Time@20: The Afterimage of Gilles Deleuze's Film Philosophy took place at Harvard on May 6 and 7, 2005. The idea was to bring together a group of internationally renowned scholars to evaluate the continuing influence of the cinema books on artists and scholars in film, video, photography, interactive media, and other time-based arts. Moreover, it was important to me that the continually renewed life of Deleuze's cinema books be accounted for, not just in the light of contemporary film studies and world cinema, but also in the contexts of philosophy, literature, the history of art, and the history of science.

A lot had changed in twenty years. Since 2000, there was an explosion of English-language scholarship on Deleuze's philosophy as well as his writing on cinema, which made more prescient than ever Foucault's oft repeated statement at the beginning of "Theatricum Philosophicum" (remarkably, written in 1970) that "perhaps one day, this century will be known as Deleuzian."[4] It was also more and more evident that the cinema books were having a profound impact on artistic practice in general, and on filmmaking in particular. Furthermore, as moving images became more and more electronic and digital, the destiny of the time-image and its immanent relation to duration, so closely tied to analogical and photographic materiality, was thrown into question. What might be the future of Time in the silicon era? And so on two rainy spring days in 2005, I convened eleven philosophical friends—Raymond Bellour (Centre National de Recherches Scientifiques, Paris), Ronald Bogue (University of Georgia), Ian Buchanan (Cardiff University), James Chandler (University of Chicago), Amy Herzog (Queens College, City University of New York), András Bálint Kovács (Eötvös Loránd University of Science), Timothy Murray (Cornell University), Dorothea Olkowski (University of Colorado), John Rajchman (Columbia University), Marie-Claire Ropars-Wuilleumier (University of Paris VIII), and Garrett Stewart (University of Iowa)—and five intercessors—Dudley Andrew (Yale University), Réda Bensmaïa (Brown University), Giuliana Bruno (Harvard University), Tom Conley (Harvard University), and Peter Galison (Harvard University)—to discuss the afterimage of Gilles Deleuze's film philosophy.

The eleven papers delivered at the colloquium form the core of this book. Rewritten and expanded, they are here joined by seven new, original essays. Despite the variety of their approaches and diversity of perspectives, all the essays pursue three convictions: that *The Movement-Image* and *The Time-Image* present a coherent and original philosophical exploration of cinema; that in Deleuze's approach to cinema, one can find a grand résumé of the most inventive concepts and arguments of his philosophical work through that time and after; and finally, that these concepts have a rhizomatic life that continually blossoms in the arts, literature, and philosophy. Thus the cinema books may be read as the linchpin of Deleuze's work of the 1980s, bringing out the major themes and points of contact between other important works such as *Foucault*, *Logic of Sensation*, and his last work with Félix Guattari, *What Is Philosophy?*

But there is yet another, deeper theme made apparent in the cinema books. Like Stanley Cavell, for Deleuze, cinema is the philosophy of our everyday life; it brings philosophy into contact with life, and for these and other reasons, cinema has defined the audiovisual culture of the twentieth century. Deleuze also teaches us that philosophy has an intimate relationship with art. However, philosophy's complex points of contact with both everyday life and art are often untimely, hence the historical ellipsis I described previously. Professional film, media, and cultural studies are still struggling to understand how to incorporate Deleuze's thought. Alternatively, Deleuze had a more immediate impact on arts practitioners. There are good reasons, I feel, for the visceral impact of Deleuze's concepts on visual artists and musicians especially. In 1987, Deleuze gave an important lecture at the FEMIS, the French national film and television school, an excerpt of which was published as "Having an Idea in Cinema."[5] What does it mean to have an Idea in art, and how do Ideas differ from concepts? Ideas are specific to a domain, a milieu, or a material. And so Deleuze writes that "Ideas must be treated as potentials that are already engaged in this or that mode of expression and inseparable from it, so much that I cannot say I have an idea in general. According to the techniques that I know, I can have an idea in a given domain, an idea in cinema or rather an idea in philosophy."[6]

Now, ideas in philosophy are already oriented by a certain kind of conceptual image, what Deleuze calls the *image of thought*, and so a connection or relation must link them. And indeed, artists also think, but through constructions of space and of time—their ideas are immanent to the materials with which they work. Despite the abstractness and difficulty of some of Deleuze's filmic concepts, they are immediately and intuitively graspable to those whose eyes and ears are sensitive to the materiality of cinematic expression. Moreover, Deleuze respected, better than any other philosopher of the twentieth century, the great partnership between philosophy and art: that philosophy could inspire Ideas in art, just as art could provoke philosophers to create concepts.

So far, I have emphasized the untimeliness of philosophy—always too early or too late, it pushes thought from behind or draws it forward in a slipstream. Nevertheless, perhaps the time is now propitious for a reexamination of Deleuze's philosophy of cinema as a new millennium presents new cinemas and new forms of art, electronic and digital as well as cinematographic. Film itself may be disappearing as digital imaging and the digital arts come more and more to supplant the analogical arts, and so Deleuze may help us to confront new questions. In what ways may cinema remain relevant, aesthetically and philosophically, in the twenty-first century? What new forms and what new subjectivities may it solicit? In what ways can cinema continue its century-long dialogue with philosophy on questions of space, time, image, and ethics? Will the time-image persist as a contestatory force in relation to what Deleuze called control societies, or will it be displaced, for good or ill, by a silicon-image? Can digital imaging and digital cinema express time and duration with the same qualitative powers as film and so find their own original "will to art"?[7]

To ask or answer these questions implies that the time-image has a historical sense, but there are good reasons why Deleuze insists that the cinema books do not present a history of cinema. In *Reading the Figural*, I suggest that the movement-image and the time-image are not historical concepts and that it is misleading to conceive of the latter as following the former along a chronological time line.[8] The two concepts do suggest, however, divergent philosophies of history, owing to their different relationships to the Whole and to their immanent logics of image and sign. The movement-image unfolds according to a Hegelian and dialectical conception of history, while the time-image is Nietzschean and genealogical. The movement-image has a history in a dialectically unfolding teleology. It progresses to a point where it logically completes its semiotic options in what Deleuze calls Hitchcock's relation-images. This does not prevent it, of course, from persisting and prevailing as a filmic regime, or even from adopting a postmodern form.

But the time-image pursues another logic altogether. Expressed as eternal return, the recurrent possibility in each moment of time for the emergence of the new and unforeseen, the appearance of direct time-images is unpredictable in advance. If the time-image occurs or recurs in the form of eternal recurrence, as soon as the cinema becomes possible, the direct time-image subsists within the logic of cinema as a pure virtuality, and this virtuality is not historical because it is unencumbered by the empirical or chronological forms of time.

Several conclusions may be drawn here. The transition from the movement-image to the time-image is neither complete nor distinct, and indeed even "primitive" time-images persist and insist from the very beginnings of cinema. Nonetheless, because the movement-image presents the whole as a dialectical totality, it defines the entirety of pre–World War II cinema and most of what comes after. Contrariwise, time-images are rare: here the whole is in relation with an Outside expressing a possibility or virtuality that has existed since the beginning of cinema but only rarely finds the right conditions for appearing as such, and then only infrequently in "pure" examples. Moreover, the movement-image and time-image are not opposed as negation or critique, for negation and opposition only count within the logic of the movement-image; rather, they are distinguished by two different logics, semiotics, values, and planes of immanence in relation to thought and time. As a genealogical force, the time-image has no history in the usual sense. Appearing as a nonchronological force, what it expresses is an Event wherein each passing present yields to the unforeseeable, the unpredictable, and the emergence of the new.

Just as the movement-image, though logically exhausted by the 1950s, persists in a postmodern form, the time-image continually seeks out new conditions and contexts of existence. We may still find these conditions in Europe, in the films of Claire Denis and others or in the extraordinary work of Béla Tarr in Hungary. We may even generate our list of favorite filmmakers in the United States: Jim Jarmusch or Gus van Sant. Yet more significantly, the new Iranian cinema of Abbas Kiarostami and the emergent (post)modernity of the Pacific Rim have been producing some of the most exciting, and most thought-provoking, world cinema today. Twenty years on, perhaps Deleuze can still help us to evaluate the future of cinema and of creative, filmic thinking in Wong Kar-Wai, Hou Hsiao-Hsien, or Tsai Ming-Liang. Let a thousand time-images bloom!

Inspired by the knowledge that time is always on the side of life—not only the thrown dice but also the casting itself and the pitch of the dice through the air—this book places its bets on the power of the time-image to return eternally, and in many different domains, but always as a force that expresses difference itself. Part I of the book, "Doublings," groups essays that place Deleuze in dialogue with other philosopher-artists. The authors chart a complex trajectory of concepts leaving, returning to, and passing across *The Movement-Image* and *The Time-Image* in ways that engage the books both directly and obliquely. Raymond Bellour begins by mapping out the vicissitudes of the "image of thought" in its fuguelike returns and variations across Deleuze's many books and essays, and places this concept in dialogue with the thought of art using the work of Henri Michaux as an example. Here the image of thought presents a new way of thinking thought and of qualifying philosophy. And because its indebtedness to the arts is so strong, inevitably, philosophy escapes itself on the line of flight of philosophy-as-art. Marie-Claire Ropars-Wuilleumier continues this evaluation of image and thought in discussion of the complex relation between Deleuze and Maurice Blanchot in the cinema books, especially with respect to problems of becoming and the Outside, as encountered in Deleuze's original reading of Foucault, casting new light on the arrangements between image and time. András Bálint Kovács then opens a debate between Deleuze and Umberto Eco on the "openness" of the work of art in asking, what is the relationship between the ideas of aesthetic openness as conceived by Eco, with his fundamentally structuralist approach, and an openness professed by Deleuze of a fundamentally poststructuralist inspiration? Is it possible to demonstrate the difference between structuralist serialism and another one resting on the ideas of infinity and chaos? In this way, a new context is forged for the time-image across the question of the inorganic series and postmodern art, with reference to key concepts from *Difference and Repetition*. While most readers of Deleuze place the cinema books in the orbit of Henri Bergson and Friedrich Nietzsche, in a highly original essay, Melinda Szaloky examines the concepts and thought of cinema in relation to Immanuel Kant's critical philosophy. In so doing, Deleuze's film philosophy is reaffirmed as a powerful practice of transcendental empiricism. Following the logic of Kant's aesthetic reflection, which magnifies the moment of linkage in the lingering play of the cognitive faculties, Szaloky presents the time-image as a presentation of a continuity in discontinuity, or the broken link that the brain is now believed to be. Through its automatic interstitial structure, film is uniquely suited to offer a mise-en-scène of the endless splitting that thinking both performs and is subject to, in line with the aberrant movement of the self-founding of time. Dorothea Olkowski's "Darkness and Light" concludes this section with a stunning exploration of the phenomenology of photography and photographic perception that renews the dialogue between Deleuze and Bergson. As Olkowski relates, in Deleuze's account of film's relation to philosophy, there is no opposition to the conception of images and knowledge organized on a plane of immanence, and no objection to the disappearance of any conception of interiority. Instead, Deleuze puts forth a concept of reality in which otherwise isolated and contingent elements encounter one another on a continuous spatial manifold. As a structure articulated by nonequilibrium thermodynamics that either refutes or ignores the idea of a discrete space and time, this is a position that appears to be much closer to Bergson's critique of cinematographic movement and that once again makes sense of interiority.

Part II, "Ethics," explores moral reasoning as a question central to Deleuze's interest in film and film philosophy. In an essay titled "The World, Time," I present an overview of Deleuze's cinematic ethics as it bridges between *The Movement-Image* and *The Time-Image*. Suggesting links both to Deleuze's Nietzscheanism and to Stanley Cavell's interest in cinema as the moral accompaniment to our everyday lives, I outline Deleuze's ethical thought as the force of time as eternal recurrence as well as the power of choosing. Both find expression in the lyrical abstraction and virtual conjunctions of the movement-image and in the time-image's "im-powers" of thought, which demand a revaluation of our perceptual disjunction from the world that makes of it the possibility for a new faith, and a new thought. Ronald Bogue both broadens and deepens these arguments in his essay "To Choose to Choose—to Believe in This World." As Bogue argues, in *The Movement-Image* and *The Time-Image*, ethics is addressed directly when Deleuze says that we have need of an ethic or a faith that makes idiots laugh. This is an ethic of choosing to choose and a faith that allows belief in this world. In the philosophy of Pascal and Kierkegaard and the cinema of Bresson and Dreyer, Deleuze thus produces a set of invaluable relations linking philosophy and cinema to each other and to our everyday lives.

Part III, "Becomings," explores the possibilities of schizoanalysis for differential accounts that place image, desire, and subject(s) on a single plane of immanence. Not just Deleuze, but Deleuze *with* Guattari, is crucial to the three essays in this section, each of which examines cinema's multiple potentialities for intensive spectatorship and new tactics of becoming. Ian Buchanan launches this discussion in asking "Is a Schizoanalysis of Cinema Possible?" Here Buchanan highlights delirium as a regime of signs linking the two cinema books to *A Thousand Plateaus*, while demonstrating that key concepts of the latter—the body without organs, assemblages, and abstract machines—transform and evolve across Deleuze's characterization of image and sign in *The Movement-Image* and *The Time-Image*. In what may be the most provocative and original work included in this book, Patricia MacCormack offers a feminist manifesto on embodied spectatorship as "Cinemasochism: Submissive Spectatorship as Unthought." Cinemasochism describes the openness of the spectator to images. Especially in cases of "extreme cinema," MacCormack argues, affect rises to a level of intensity at which the immanent relation between image and spectator demands submission before comprehension, taking the viewer outside of metonymy, meaning, and time toward a spatial ecstasy or folding of form, film, and flesh. MacCormack is concerned to show how the philosophy of difference in Deleuze, and especially Guattari, expresses forces for becoming in an embodied spectatorship that over-flows any binary logic of sexual differentiation. In "Unthinkable Sex," I continue this line of thought by developing *What Is Philosophy?*'s characterization of conceptual personae as the unthought of sexual dif-ference in the time-image. Looking at three exemplary cases of postwar French cinema—Godard from Anna Karina to Anne-Marie Mièville, Agnès Varda, and Chantal Akerman—I show that when the interstice or irrational interval passes within the subject, there is no longer an identity that returns to itself, nor is there the possibility of sustaining a binary logic that opposes femininity to masculinity. This is a question of comprehending how relations of sexual difference, rather than op-position, are expressed through conceptual personae as constructions of the direct time-image as series or becoming, or as nomad identities open to new constructions of subjectivity.

Part IV, "Experiments," brings together four deeply original ex-aminations of film form and materiality inspired by the two cinema books. In "The Strategist and the Stratigrapher," Tom Conley presents the stratigraphic image as a new way of mapping the "geological sense" of the image as the embedding of different strata of time. Drawing from the book that is undoubtedly closest to *The Time-Image*, both chronologically and conceptually, Deleuze's *Foucault*, Conley mobilizes the concepts of "archive" and "diagram" as elements of a strategy in which, instead of making an inventory of history in the manner of an archive, the auteurs of the time-image open an interstice between the visible and the expressible. Here the diagram unfolds onto a horizon of unforeseen and unheard creativities, mapped across cinema's actual and conceptual landscapes. In her essay "Pleats of Matter, Folds of the Soul," Giuliana Bruno reconsiders Deleuze's concept of the fold as a "moving" filmic fabric. For Deleuze, Bruno argues, the fold is something that moves in us. It is also something that moves in matter, which itself is a projection of our inner activation, our inner motion. But how does an object of material culture fold and unfold? Bruno explores these questions across a "textural" journey from the fashions of Issey Mi-yake to the fabrication of moods in Wong Kar-Wai's cinema. Similar ideas of movement become emotion are examined in James Chandler's study of "The Affection-Image and the Movement-Image." In this fascinating essay, which ranges across the philosophical and literary as well as cinematic contexts of the movement-image, Chandler traces the deep epistemological history of "sensibility" as an anticipation of the "motion/emotion" that Deleuze attributes to the reflexive work of the affection-image. In "Becoming-Fluid: History, Corporeality, and the Musical Spectacle," Amy Herzog examines two filmic practices that challenge notions of interiority and exteriority in transforming the temporal and spatial planes along which they unfold: Tsai Ming-liang's *The Hole* and Esther Williams's musicals of the 1940s. Deeply attentive to the gendering of music, embodiment, and place, Herzog argues that the aqueous spaces invoked by Williams and Tsai each forge a historical image. This image is not a passive reflection of its historical conditions, but rather, like a tune that enters us from outside, acts as a provocation that generates thought and, as such, may contain a transformative potential.

In his conclusion to *The Time-Image*, Deleuze himself occupies a curious temporal perspective, both retrospective and prospective. On one hand, Deleuze evinces nostalgia for a certain kind of art cinema, a cinema of Bergsonian duration and Nietzschean recurrence, closely tied to philosophical thought, that has longed struggled for its right to existence, succeeding only intermittently. No doubt Deleuze imagines the fate of his own philosophy as well as the struggle against alienation and capitalism as closely tied to the fate of the cinema. Yet in 1985, with the emergence and increasing power of electronic and digital images in "control societies," Deleuze also imagined that the struggle for cinema would be a conflict in which the "life or afterlife of cinema depends on its internal struggle with informatics."[9]

The five essays comprising the concluding part of this book, "Futures," take more complex and nuanced views, imagining new relationships to time, or even a "silicon-image," that Deleuze might never have anticipated in contemporary art. John Rajchman opens this section with a philosophical overview of how Deleuze's conception of the cinematic has changed our contemporary views of art. How, Rajchman asks, does the time-image lead to new thinking about figure and narration, violence and memory, image and reality, fiction and documentary, movement and time? How does it form part of a larger "interference" among many arts and disciplines not based in a medium or modernism (or their "posts") and yet opposed to the present of information? In attempting to pose and answer these questions, the cinema is renewed as a *dispositif*, or machine for thinking and sociablility, that continues to impact the larger domain of the visual and temporal arts.

The contributions that follow all respond to these questions in provocative and complex ways. In "Immanent Images: Photography after Mobility," Damian Sutton explores the transformation of personal photography by digital representation and transmission. Personal images—taken, saved, and sent—are now mobile sections of time in a manner different from the film shot, as they create a narrative in their movement through time and space to the screens of others. Such images are also immanent as shared actualizations, a cinema created by every viewer. As such, photography is now closer to the virtual insistence of pure recollections in time than the recollection-images, memory-images, and dream-images that form the materials of the so-called Kodak moments of everyday life. With Garrett Stewart's essay "Cimnemonics versus Digitime," we move from photography back to the cinema, or rather, forward to what Stewart terms a millennial postrealist and postfilmic cinema in recent European and American productions. Such Hollywood films of the ontological gothic (in either digital or spectral modes) throw into relief the epistemological twists of European plots turning on less overt forms of paramnesia, telepathic intersubjectivity, and temporal recursion (from *The Double Life of Veronique* through *Lovers of the Arctic Circle* to *He Loves Me . . . He Loves Me Not*), many of which depend on the drastic refaceting of memory's "crystal image." Here, in what might be called a time-space image, we find an impossible mode of temporality returned to a function of movement, not indirectly but directly, where time is rendered planar and mobile in itself, shuffled and reversible. Timothy Murray's essay "Time @ Cinema's Future: New Media Art and the Thought of Temporality" concludes this volume in examining the rebirth of the time-image and its new forms of expression in contemporary digital art. Murray asks, how might the Deleuzian frontier of cinematic temporality articulate itself now into the digital future? How might Deleuze's thinking about cinematic futures inform a philosophy of the new media interface? Examining a broad selection of contemporary new media art, Murray charts time's relation to the futuristic expressions of the digital archive across thematics of future cinema, archival intensity, interactivity, and coded automatons. Here, as in many other areas, the time-image asserts its new virtual life in often unanticipated ways, offering new directions and possibilities of thought.

Philosophy is a voyage of self-invention, or of "thinking to become other than I am," in Foucault's fine phrase. Philosophy is also a pragmatism—the invention or creation of concepts—and one does not speak or write philosophy to discover or incorporate the thought of an other, but rather, to think for one's self in an act of creation. As you join us here to celebrate the thought of Gilles Deleuze, dear reader and virtual member of our pack or nomadic horde, it is important to remember not just to listen or to read, but to *make* philosophy, and to make it ours for today. In 2009, the afterimage of Gilles Deleuze's film philosophy continues to recur and to reignite new thinking. Welcome to the new Deleuzian century!

Notes

1   Gilles Deleuze, *Cinema 1: The Movement-Image*, trans. Hugh Tomlinson and Barbara Habberjam (Minneapolis: University of Minnesota Press, 1986), 3; translation modified. Gilles Deleuze, *Cinema 2: The Time-Image*, trans. Hugh Tomlinson and Robert Galeta (Minneapolis: University of Minnesota Press, 1989).

2   D. N. Rodowick, *Gilles Deleuze's Time Machine* (Durham, N.C.: Duke University Press, 1997).

3   Michel Foucault, *The Order of Things* (New York: Vintage Books, 1973), 325.

4   Michel Foucault, "Theatricum Philosophicum," in *Language, Counter-Memory, Practice: Selected Essays and Interviews*, ed. Donald F. Bouchard (Ithaca, N.Y.: Cornell University Press, 1977), 165.

5   Gilles Deleuze, "Having an Idea in Cinema," in *Deleuze and Guattari: New Mappings in Politics, Philosophy, and Culture*, ed. Eleanor Kaufman and Kevin Jon Heller (Minneapolis: University of Minnesota Press, 1998), 14–19. This lecture was videotaped and published as *Qu'est-ce que l'acte de création?* (Paris: FEMIS and Ministère de la culture et la communication, 1987). A French transcript was published in *Deux Régimes de Fous* (Paris: Editions de Minuit, 2003).

6   Ibid., 14.

7   Deleuze, *Time-Image*, 266.

8   See D. N. Rodowick, "A Genealogy of Time," in *Reading the Figural, or, Philosophy after the New Media* (Durham, N.C.: Duke University Press, 2001), 170–202.

9   Deleuze, *Movement-Image*, 270.

Part I. Doublings

1. The Image of Thought: Art or Philosophy, or Beyond?

Raymond Bellour

1964. Gilles Deleuze concludes the first version of his book *Proust and Signs* with several incisive pages titled "The Image of Thought," taking up again the essential points of chapter 2, "Sign and Truth." Through his search for truth as the truth of time, expressed by signs to be interpreted, Proust's work "rivals philosophy. Proust constructs an image of thought opposed to that of philosophy."[1] Deleuze adds, "Philosophy, with all its method and its good will, is nothing compared with the secret pressures of the work of art."[2] But he also makes clear, "It may be that Proust's critique of philosophy is eminently philosophical."[3]

1968. Deleuze titles "The Image of Thought" the great third chapter that is at the heart of *Difference and Repetition*. With a relentless passion, he deploys here the eight postulates that compose the Image of thought in philosophy, an "Image in general which constitutes the subjective presupposition of philosophy as a whole."[4] So much so that the first condition of an alternative philosophy supposes a "radical critique of this Image and the 'postulates' it implies," in favor of "thought without Image."[5] Image equals representation here, as seen again in the conclusion of the book (without doubt the most condensed pages ever written by Deleuze); but the term *Image* remains itself targeted as an "Icon" to be destroyed: "The theory of thought is like painting: it needs that revolution which took art from representation to abstraction. This is the aim of a theory of thought without image."[6]

There would be a history to write, spanning the twenty-six books written by Deleuze alone and in collaboration, augmented today by a final volume of his scattered texts: a precise, tangled history of this term

Translated by Alina Opreanu with Michael Sanchez

and idea of the Image of thought, especially in its ambiguous relation to the key words *image, figure,* and *concept.*[7] What follows is only a schematic indication of such a history.

In the books Deleuze wrote with Guattari over a span of ten years ("My encounter with Félix Guattari changed many things"), it seems that this new thought then brought into play depends above all on a general polemical capacity for reaffirmation and positivity, with the abrasive effects inherent to the happy yesterdays of political utopia. *Generalized constructivism*: this means rewriting the history of the world according to the principle posed in "Rhizome": "Arrive at the magic formula we all seek—PLURALISM = MONISM—via all the dualisms that are the enemy, an entirely necessary enemy, the furniture we are forever rearranging."[8] Thought with or without image no longer seems a concern as such—images flood in from everywhere as thought(s), pressing and plural visions whose reality as art (then mostly literary and musical) could be the surest line of flight. (We did not see this enough in the anthropologic–psychoanalytic–political torment of *Anti-Oedipus.*)

With *The Logic of Sensation*, everything changes with an inflexible smoothness. At the very end of his study of Proust, later expanded by half, Deleuze already proposed an image: opposing "thought to philosophy," Proust becomes "the spider–Narrator whose very web is Remembrance *[La Recherche]* in the process of making itself . . . an enormous Body without Organs."[9] Never has Deleuze been closer, I think, to a self-image of his art as he imagines it, of an uncanny self-portrait whose image, real or virtual (it all becomes one), Bacon allows him to realize to his advantage. To Hervé Guibert, Deleuze said of this book, about which he spoke little, "I hardly ever had such pleasure writing a book." When Proust inevitably comes up, it is to better qualify Bacon's approach and that which Deleuze looks for in him: "Bacon, when he refuses the double way of figurative painting and an abstract painting, is put in a situation analogous to that of Proust in literature. Proust did not want an abstract literature that was too voluntary (philosophy), any more than he wanted a figurative, illustrative, or narrative literature that merely told a story. What he was striving for, and what he wished to bring to light, was a kind of Figure, torn away from figuration and stripped of every figurative function: a Figure-in-itself, for example, the Figure-in-itself of Combray. He himself spoke of 'truths written with the aid of figures.'"[10]

In a word, this book devoted to Bacon's gesture, which hardly invokes a single philosopher, works persistently at capturing, as pure sensation, the Figure, "which is the improbable itself"[11] and precisely "the body without organs."[12] Deleuze releases his renewed philosophical method across these painterly images. He erects his own good image of philosophy as art, a philosophy whose dimension only art can open. Such is the case on pages 76–79 of the chapter "The Painting before Painting," at the beginning of which Deleuze reminds us that for D. H. Lawrence, "Cézanne's apple is . . . more important than Plato's Idea"[13]—pages on probabilities, conceived or seen, the injunction of chance where, through the painter's gesture, the Figure becomes like the model for the new qualifications of the concept which are nonetheless proper to philosophy.

The two great works on cinema extend this construction of a philosophy for which art provides at once the material depth and the surface of projection. These are above all concepts of images that Deleuze extracts from cinema to make of it, let us say, a philosophy—from the modalities of the movement-image to those of the time-image, where the crystal-image becomes, with its characteristic virtuality, that which affects the concept itself. Between cinema and philosophy, two movements in tension overlap each other in these books. The first begins at the end of the nineteenth century, with the crisis of psychology and the invention of cinema, a rebirth of the world as a world of images, to which Nietzsche and Bergson respond with a new way of thinking philosophy. The second movement, internal to the first, links the two major modes of the image, qualified as classical and modern cinema— two ways, old and new, to relate to philosophy and conceive of concepts such that the split between image-thought and thought without image posed in *Difference and Repetition* gets reframed purely in terms of differences between images.

From there, it is captivating to see how the apparent return to pure philosophy operates throughout *Foucault*, and especially in *The Fold*. Indeed, in Leibniz Deleuze finds the most extraordinary conceptual machine to feed his own, without risking, as with Nietzsche and Spinoza, too much philosophical proximity. Finally, it is enough for him to overturn Leibniz's Baroque classicism, taken to its limits in the modern Baroque, to give full effect to the numerous more or less contemporary artistic references that, throughout the book, support his construction of a thought of the fold (from Tal Coat to Boulez, from Stockhausen to Dubuffet, from Cocteau to Hantaï, from James to Kleist or De Quincey). Thus, "because what always matters is folding, unfolding, refolding," as works of art endlessly show us,[14] "we are all still Leibnizian, although accords no longer convey our world or our text."¹⁵ And so perhaps we have become, by this very torsion, Deleuzian.

In fact, this involuted tension between philosophy and art finds two modes of expression. On one hand, it is philosophy's repeated affirmation as an activity in itself, qualified by the invention of concepts, that Deleuze intends to distinguish from art's sensations and fabrications *(fabulation)*, despite their troubling proximity. This is the thesis of *What Is Philosophy?*, with its distinctions and its interferences between disciplines, as fragile as they are sharply divided. Deleuze's revealing use of a writer like Michaux, who is often brought up, against all apparent logic, alongside philosophers, seems like the intentionally blurred marker of an excess of clarity. (His strategic role has already been articulated in *Foucault, The Fold,* and *Negotiations.*)

On the other hand, the overlap and fusion of art and philosophy, begun so long ago, later extends to the point of indiscernability. The short essay on Beckett, "The Exhausted," written just after *What Is Philosophy?*, reiterates in a pointed and stunning way the gesture previously begun thanks to Bacon. Through Beckett's works for television, Deleuze lays out his own vision of space and pure image, thus bringing language to the point of dissolving into thought, thereby refinding its own being, which would be vision or music: "Like a new style, finally."¹⁶ In *Essays Critical and Clinical*, writers and philosophers are treated in terms of a game of constant amalgamations and reversals, to the point of Deleuze positing, in "Spinoza and the Three 'Ethics,'" percepts, intervals of space, and light beyond concepts, which thereby bring together painters, filmmakers, and musicians in a supreme ambiguity.

Michaux as Example

The most troubling suggestion comes from the unique place Michaux occupies in the philosophy of Deleuze, or of Deleuze–Guattari. This becomes evident in the book Deleuze devotes to Foucault, especially the third chapter of the part titled "Topology: 'Thinking Otherwise': Foldings, or the Inside of Thought (Subjectivation)." The important thing is that to qualify the concepts of thought and unthought, inside, outside, and the fold in the work of Foucault, Deleuze first uses one of Michaux's titles to support his principal argument: "an *inside-space* that will be completely co-present with the outside-space on the line of the fold."¹⁷ But then, at the end of his journey to attempt to "tell the great fiction of Foucault," whose terms he has just set out, suddenly, Deleuze concentrates, strangely and absolutely, on Michaux, combining three of his titles in a single stream ("inside-space," "faraway interior," "life in the folds"). Mixing references to *Elsewhere* and to *Great Ordeals of the Mind*, he extracts "Michaux's line": a savage singularity expressing, beyond the relationship between forms and forces attached to knowledge and power, the seething outside as a "zone of subjectivation," just above the fissure that separates the visible from the expressible, Light and Language. Why this book of philosophy, then, on a philosopher confronting himself as much as the painters and writers who shaped his thinking (like Raymond Roussel opening in Foucault the "hallucinatory theme of Doubles"[18])? Why does this book end on a writer–painter, on this image of a central chamber where "one becomes master of one's speed, relatively master of one's molecules and one's singularities"?[19] After passing through Leibniz, where Michaux becomes one of the modern heroes of the fold and of the Baroque,[20] a response, in itself enigmatic, emerges in *What Is Philosophy?*

Deleuze and Guattari thus gather material for a book whose objective is to qualify philosophy, science, and art by their respective differences, each field being ultimately conceived as an exercise and a production of thought without privilege in relation to the others: "plane of the immanence of philosophy, plane of composition of art, plane of reference or coordination of science; form of concept, force of sensation, function of knowledge; concepts and conceptual personae, sensations and aesthetic figures, figures and partial observers."[21] Now it happens that Michaux is cited five times in this book: once as would be expected, four times much less so. He appears logically when, taking up the relationships between conceptual personae and aesthetic figures, Deleuze and Guattari emphasize how much "the plane of composition of art and the plane of immanence of philosophy can slip into each other to the degree that parts of one may be occupied by entities of the other."[22] Such is the particular situation of certain writers who draw up new images of thought:

These thinkers are "half" philosophers but also much more than philosophers. But they are not sages. There is such force in those unhinged works of Hölderlin, Kleist, Rimbaud, Mallarmé, Kafka, Michaux, Pessoa, Artaud, and many English and American novelists, from Melville to Lawrence or Miller, in which readers discover admiringly that they have written the novel of Spinozism. To be sure, they do not produce a synthesis of art and philosophy. They branch out and do not stop branching out. They are hybrid geniuses who neither erase nor cover

over differences in kind but, on the contrary, use all of the resources
of their "athleticism" to install themselves within this very difference,
like acrobats torn apart in a perpetual show of strength.[23]

However, it so happens that Michaux, and he alone, is cited four
times with philosophers: first at the initial qualification of the plane of
immanence—"From Epicurus to Spinoza (the incredible Book 5) and
from Spinoza to Michaux the problem of thought is infinite speed"—
then, "We head for the horizon, on the plane of immanence, and we
return with bloodshot eyes, yet they are the eyes of the mind. Even
Descartes had his dream. To think is always to follow the witch's flight.
Take Michaux's plane of immanence, for example, with its infinite wild
movements and speeds." Michaux is later associated with Blanchot and
Foucault in a note that makes the characterization of the plane more
precise: "intimacy as the Outside" or "distant interior." This is a strong
reference—such a suggestion, incessant, of the plane of immanence
could be "the supreme act of philosophy," which makes Spinoza "the
Christ of philosophers."[24] In the conclusion, Michaux appears once
more as science, art, and philosophy are again put into play together
("From Chaos to the Brain") to show that for philosophy, "conceptual
variation" is the particular form of a battle against chaotic variability,
allowing one to reach "*as quickly as possible* at mental objects deter-
minable as real beings." To highlight what Spinoza or Fichte proved
so well, why return, then, to the opposition that Michaux indicates
between "current ideas" and "vital ideas"?[25] No doubt it is to show,
in this most delicate final opening, how much Michaux is in a position
to incarnate, to bring to life the problem.

Exactly what is it about then? It is to reaffirm and to relativize the
relationship between science, art, and philosophy with as much precision as possible. Here there are three types of interference supposed
between the disciplines, or "between the planes that join up in the
brain."[26] The first are said to be extrinsic, when each discipline, being
inspired by the internal dimensions of another, "remains on its own
plane and utilizes its own elements. But there is a second, intrinsic type
of interference when concepts and conceptual personae seem to leave
a plane of immanence that would correspond to them, so as to slip in
among the functions and partial observers, or among the sensations
and aesthetic figures, on another plane; and similarly in other cases.
These slidings are so subtle, like those of Zarathustra in Nietzsche's

philosophy or of Igitur in Mallarme's poetry, that we find ourselves on complex planes that are difficult to qualify."[27] Such is the delicate level where Michaux finds himself with other writers and thinkers, half of them philosophers and much more than philosophers. Finally, there are unlocatable interferences, which delineate the obscure ending of this book. For each discipline finds itself entering in its own way into an essential relationship with a No, at the point at which its own plane confronts chaos, and where the various planes "are no longer distinct in relation to the chaos into which the brain plunges."[28] Deleuze and Guattari then write that philosophy, art, and science could share "the same shadow that extends itself across their different nature and constantly accompanies them."[29] The particular and very enigmatic fate accorded to Michaux all the way through this book is due to the fact that he, certainly more than the others, and perhaps the only one on this count, gives body, voice, and horizon to this shadow, projecting and reprojecting what was the "philosophy" of *Plume* into the "space of the shadows."[30] This is what Michaux, in this fictive place of transition, alluded to with an irreplaceable formula: "Knowledge, another knowledge here, not *Knowledge* for information. *Knowledge* to become a musician of Truth."[31]

How can one understand this unique and almost inexpressible position of Michaux inside of a philosophy that is itself in search of a transformation for which this might be a means of suggesting the way? There are thus, in the work of Deleuze, two key moments when philosophy, still reaffirmed as ever, according to its own reality, is returned to a similar oscillation between the intrinsic and unlocatable interferences. The first instance occurs in the preface to *Difference and Repetition*, where the use of concepts is related from the start to "dramas," as to an exercise of "cruelty." Here the relationship between knowledge and ignorance, each one passing and passing again into the extreme of the other (in terms very close to those of the afterword to *Plume*[32]), founds the possibility of writing, in a manner more intimate than its supposed relationship to silence and death, and finally, there is a reference to the new means of philosophical expression inaugurated by Nietzsche, announcing that a "time is coming when it will be hardly possible to write a book of philosophy as it has been done for so long."[33] The second instance occurs in Deleuze's last book, *Essays Critical and Clinical*, where, as if indifferently, philosophers and writers are caught up in a single stream, having become creators of many languages within language, all bearers of nonlinguistic visions and sounds that, through their words, also make them colorists and musicians. This movement culminates in a final text, where Deleuze, returning to Spinoza one last time, overturns the distinctions previously made between art and philosophy, to the point of causing, in a "third *Ethics*," through "the prodigious Book V," a reversal analogous to the one that made it necessary to introduce Michaux alongside Spinoza to better qualify the plane of immanence and speed of concept proper to philosophy.[34]

It would be false to object that such shifts apply more here to Deleuze than to Michaux, and to the uncertitudes of philosophy rather than to the transformations of literature and poetry. A single movement—the same one that traverses the nineteenth century from the romantics of Jena, from Schlegel and Novalis, to Kierkegaard, then to Nietzsche— becomes the affair of the century that emerges from it, in France, for example, through Breton, Artaud, or Bataille. Such a movement affirms the necessity of confronting thought directly and without division as style and art, violence and search for the unknown. This was a confrontation that became proper to philosophy—in France anyway, in some great works, in Merleau-Ponty, Foucault, Deleuze, even if at the mercy of a classical need for specificity—if only by the force of an obligatory and ever closer relationship with the arts and literature, to the point where philosophy induces here the active image of its own displacement.[35] It is this obsession, for example, that impels Deleuze to find in Proust the forces with which he opposes philosophy, to draw inspiration for a new way of treating philosophy itself.[36] Such is the sense of a certain identity assumed here between Michaux and Deleuze (Deleuze and Guattari). It is not a question of believing, as one so often does, that one justifies the reality of a literary work in philosophical concepts that permit, from the outside, the designation of a more objective truth, one that the work is powerless to express. Even less is it a question of one of these haughty conjunctions, reality lacking here as much as metaphysical desire, by which one celebrated, through the mythic encounter between Char and Heidegger, the marriage of philosophy and poetry, each in communion with the other from the height of its mystery. More simply put (the influence, if it exists, of the writer on the philosopher), one recognizes through the proximity of terms (*flux* and *multiplicity*, for example,[37] but also *fold* or *passage*, *shadow* or *speed* or *line*), and more generally, of thought, a concern common to poetry–literature and philosophy: to enter into a collusion, a confusion of still unknown limits, perhaps mutually contaminating, to the point of finding in this movement, not a response or an obscure illumination, but at least a way of coming to terms with the univocity of being, whose joyous torment is common to them both.[38]

We can thus understand the question posed by Jacques Rancière: "Is there a Deleuzian aesthetic?"[39] But no matter how well we respond to this question, it could be a trap. For to postulate an aesthetic, no matter how much the idea behind it is reworked, is to suppose an order to which it refers, and this order belongs fatally to philosophy, to something of its old image. This is the entire paradox, perhaps untenable, of Deleuze's thought: it at once confirms philosophy, as such and forever, yet tears from it down to the roots that which makes it into something other than art.

In the last words that we exchanged, in the summer before his death, Deleuze evoked, with the playful frankness that he maintained until the end, the difficulties he was having with his book on the virtual, of which only a few pages exist. He said he was looking for a form. To this end, he listened to music (Ravel). And then he said, "I am not going to write fragments after all." No, not fragments, as this had been done so inventively by Nietzsche, but something new, to go beyond, beyond the shares that had already been touched. Simply beyond.

Notes

1   Gilles Deleuze, *Proust and Signs*, trans. Richard Howard (New York: George Braziller, 1972), 159; translation modified. Originally published as *Proust et les signes* (Paris: Presses Universitaires de France, 1964).

2   Ibid., 163.

3   Ibid., 165.

4   Gilles Deleuze, *Difference and Repetition*, trans. Paul Patton (New York: Columbia University Press, 1994), 132.

5   Ibid., 132.

6   Ibid., 276.

7   In the contents of Gilles Deleuze, *Desert Island and Other Texts*, we find, e.g., an essay titled "On Nietzsche and the Image of Thought," trans. Mike Taormina (New York: Semiotext(e), 2003).

8   In Gilles Deleuze and Félix Guattari, *A Thousand Plateaus: Capitalism and Schizophrenia*, trans. Brian Massumi (Minneapolis: University of Minnesota Press, 1987), 20–21.

9   See Deleuze, *Proust et les signes*, 218–19.

10 Francis Bacon, *The Logic of Sensation*, trans. Daniel W. Smith (Minneapolis: University of Minnesota Press, 2003), 56.

11 Ibid., 76.

12 Ibid., 39.

13 Ibid., 72; translation modified.

14 Gilles Deleuze, *The Fold: Leibniz and the Baroque*, trans. Tom Conley (Minneapolis: University of Minnesota Press, 2003), 137.

15 Ibid.

16 Gilles Deleuze, *Essays Critical and Clinical*, trans. Daniel W. Smith and Michael A. Greco (Minneapolis: University of Minnesota Press, 1997), 173; translation modified.

17 Gilles Deleuze, *Foucault*, trans. Seán Hand (Minneapolis: University of Minnesota Press, 1988), 118. Originally published in Paris by Éditions de Minuit, 1986. (Modified translations will give the French page numbers in italics.)

18 Ibid., 112.

19 Ibid., 123, *130*; "an inside space but coextensive with the whole line of the outside. The most distant point becomes interior, by being converted into the nearest: *life within the folds*. This is the central chamber" (123). Borrowed first from Melville, the image of the central chamber also belongs to Henri Michaux, *Life in the Folds*: "it's the blood of memories, of the pierced soul, from the delicate central chamber, struggling in the packing, it's the reddened water of useless memory"; see Henri Michaux, *Darkness: An Henri Michaux Anthology, 1927–1984*, trans. David Ball (Berkeley: University of California Press, 1994), 155. See also the passage in Gilles Deleuze, *Negotiations*, trans. Martin Joughin (New York: Columbia University Press, 1995), 111–13, where Deleuze grants Foucault a proximity to, and a concern for, Michaux that has solely to do with a projection from one through the other that he makes for his own ends.

20 Deleuze, *The Fold*, 33–34, 93. This passage, in which Deleuze notes numerous "Leibnizian reminiscences," is a turning point in the chapter "Perception in the Folds," opening "the sum of the theory of the fold" (98–99).

21 Gilles Deleuze and Félix Guattari, *What Is Philosophy?*, trans. Hugh Tomlinson and Graham Burchell (New York: Columbia University Press, 1994), 216.

22 Ibid., 66. "*Igitur* is just such a case of a conceptual persona transported onto a plane of composition, an aesthetic figure carried onto a plane of immanence: his proper name is a conjunction" (67).

23 Ibid., 67.

24 These three mentions, ibid., 36, 41, 59–60, appear inside the section "Philosophy" in the chapter "The Plane of Immanence."

25 Ibid., 207.

26 Ibid., 216.

27 Ibid., 217.

28 Ibid., 218.

29 Ibid.

30 "The Space of the Shadows," in *Facing the Locks*, Michaux, *Darkness*, 181–91. Such a movement of interference between art and philosophy also affects science, of course, which explains the interest of scientists in the work of Michaux, e.g., Stéphane Lupasco. See Robert Bréchon, *Michaux* (Paris: Gallimard, 1959), 217–20. Also see the recent and remarkable book by Anne-Elisabeth Halpern, *Henri Michaux: le laboratoire du poète* (Paris: Séli Arslan, 1998).

31 "Space of the Shadows," 189.

32 "Any progress, every new observation, every thought, every creation, seems to create (at the same time as light) a zone of darkness./All knowledge creates new ignorance"; Michaux, *Darkness*, 78–79.

33 Deleuze, *Difference and Repetition*, xxi.

34 See "Spinoza and the Three 'Ethics,'" in Deleuze, *Essays Critical and Clinical*, esp. 148–51. Deleuze thus distinguishes in the three ethics signs or affects, notions or concepts, and essences or percepts. These last are then the only ones to possess the absolute speed attributed to the concept in Deleuze and Guattari, *What Is Philosophy?*, whereas in this text from *Essays Critical and Clinical*, the concept becomes endowed with a relative speed. Percept is, on the other hand, one of the two terms used (with affect) to express, in opposition to concept, the plane of artistic composition in *What Is Philosophy?*

35 Although in terms that still suggest a strict division of fields, this relationship was underscored by André Pierre Colombat in "The philosopher–critic and poet: Deleuze, Foucault, and the work of Michaux," *French Forum* 16 (1991): 209–25. The "vitesse-Michaux" was also proposed as the most certain mode of reading Deleuze by Patrice Loraux in his contribution to the conference on Deleuze, "Immanence et vie," Paris, January 25–27, 1997.

36 Here note the close correlation between Deleuze, *Proust et les signes*, and "The Image of Thought," the central chapter of Deleuze, *Difference and Repetition*. On the relationship between Proust and Michaux, the first having been an important reference for the other, see Luc Fraisse, "Proust et Michaux: assonances profoundes," *Revue d'histoire littéraire de la France* 2 (1995): 218–38.

37 These two central terms from the *Anti-Oedipus* (Minneapolis: University of Minnesota Press, 1983) and Deleuze and Guattari, *A Thousand Plateaus*, appear together in the afterword of *Plume* (Paris: Gallimard, 1938): "The true, deep thinking flux no doubt happens *without conscious thought*"; "False simplicity of first truths (in metaphysics) followed by extreme multiplicity—that's what he's trying to get accepted" (Michaux, *Darkness*,

78). Or "the expatriation" of Michaux becoming the "deterritorialization" of Deleuze-Guattari.

38 See Deleuze, *Difference and Repetition*, 303–4. This univocity, which is in accordance with the "individuating difference" ("A single and same voice for the whole thousand-voiced multiple, a single and same Ocean for all the drops, a single clamor of Being for all beings" [304]), is self-evident in Michaux.

39 "Existe-t-il une esthétique deleuzienne?"; *Gilles Deleuze, une vie philosophique*, ed. Eric Alliez (Le Plessis-Robinson, France: Les Empêcheurs de penser en rond, 1998), 525–36.

2. Image or Time? The Thought of the Outside in *The Time-Image* (Deleuze and Blanchot)

Marie-Claire Ropars-Wuilleumier

A Strange Attractor

The grand narrative of the cinema that Deleuze proposes is, we know, ruled and turned on its head from the inside by the eternal return of sameness-in-difference *(l'éternel retour du même différent)*. Many film-makers who we thought modern—such as Jean-Luc Godard and Pier Paolo Pasolini, as well Robert Bresson and Orson Welles—have a place in both of the work's two volumes, reappearing not only in *Cinema 2: The Time-Image*, but also in *Cinema 1: The Movement-Image*, along-side those greats of the silent era, Buster Keaton, Jean Epstein, or F. W. Murnau. Thus the cinema plunges into itself, digging within itself its own time, more than it develops linearly.

Nonetheless, volume 2, that *Time-Image* that preoccupies us today, sees the appearance of auteurs that are its exclusive domain: not only Alain Resnais and Alain Robbe-Grillet, who take their place alongside the return of Welles, but also Philippe Garrel and Marguerite Duras, accompanied by Youssef Chahine, Pierre Perrault, Carmelo Bene, Hans-Jürgen Syberberg, and Jean Eustache, who join the eternally returning Pasolini and Godard. In this way, volume 2 turns the system of the books in a new direction, placing it officially under the heading of time and not movement (with, nonetheless, the always possible dual affiliation that I have just indicated). But above all, it incorporates a reflection, and filmmakers who do not deal with time, or deal with it differently.

Still, in the last chapters, this slippage is precipitated by the oblique but recurrent eruption of a point of reference relatively foreign to Deleuze—Maurice Blanchot, who he rarely calls on in his earlier books.

Translated by Matthew Lazen with D. N. Rodowick

Anticipated simply by an obscure reference in volume 1,[1] Blanchot's sudden appearance is particular to volume 2. Although localized, it plays a systematic role there, thanks to a slanted reading by Deleuze, who alters the interpretation of Blanchot according to his own objectives. But this intrusion of Blanchot also designates a difference within the text itself that causes Deleuze's book to change course.

I want to show that Deleuze's use of Blanchot helps him to seal off a line of flight that, in reality, traverses the entire organization *(dispositif)* of the time-image and calls into question the possibility of inscribing the image in time. But, similarly, I will outline an astonishing convergence between the thought of Blanchot and the becoming of thought in *The Time-Image*. In this sense, Blanchot intervenes as a "strange attractor," who invites us to shift our evaluation of *The Time-Image*'s place in cinematic analysis as well as in the work of Gilles Deleuze.[2]

Blanchot's Emergence and Treatment in *The Time-Image*

Taken on the whole, Blanchot's intervention introduces a movement from the outside that affects thought and its relation to perception. Appearing relatively late, it finds a place in the last three chapters of *The Time-Image* and punctuates almost the entire second half of the book. This begins in chapter 7, titled "Thought and Cinema," with the rise to power of a new cinema (Garrel and Godard) specifically represented by Pasolini's *Teorema*, which reveals a "crisis of cinema" understood by Deleuze as cinema's crisis of confidence in thought, or, more precisely, in the rationality and the power of logical mastery attributed to thought.

The first mention of Blanchot takes place in this context, invoking him first for his study of Artaud and the "im-power *[impouvoir]* of thought," to use the terms initially employed by Deleuze. This is an "impossibility of thinking" (Blanchot's exact formula in *The Book to Come*), which is part of thought, and which is also, according to Deleuze's gloss on Blanchot, "what forces us to think."[3]

Once introduced, the nonpower of thought embodies little by little the crisis of belief confronted by Deleuze; it designates a crack in the Whole of cinema and thought at the same time and therefore indicates "the inexistence of a whole which could be thought,"[4] thus placing in question the totalizing project that presides over the organization of the two volumes of *The Movement-Image* and *The Time-Image*. It should be noted here that reference to Bergson, the great regulator of the system, has disappeared since chapter 5, with the fourth and last promised commentary.

Moreover, this perilous upheaval, which affects the thought of cinema and the very possibility of thought itself, takes very quickly, in chapter 7, the name of "thought of the outside," explicitly borrowed from Foucault.[5] It is a matter of a veritable reversal of terms: "the outside of thought," that "event" sweeping up the movement of thought, is transformed into a formulable, speakable act of thought, whatever may be the "force of dispersal" that governs it.[6]

Thinking the outside already entails controlling it by assigning it a place. This much is indicated by the equivalence Deleuze establishes between Blanchot's "outside" and the "interval" that characterizes the discontinuity internal to Godard's films; placed "between two images," the outside becomes by extension the constitutive in-between of every image.[7]

Thus channeled and made thinkable in its very irrationality, the "outside" becomes the other name for the Whole ("the whole is the outside"[8]). It replaces "the open" of *The Movement-Image* ("the whole was the open"[9]) and starts the project of the set anew, to the extent that it can be circumscribed at the heart of an "interstice." If the totalization of images is hereafter obliterated, it is "in favor of an outside which is inserted between them."[10] Such is the particularly ambiguous, final articulation of chapter 7: the outside has found its place, even if it is between places, and it is henceforth located at the frontier between the visible and the invisible, thereby warding off the disruption that characterizes it.

The next two chapters accelerate the regulation. In chapter 8, where thought is incorporated into the brain ("Cinema, Body and Brain, Thought"), the return of the "outside" is from now on linked to the proximity of an "inside" that it attracts. Thus, in *Why Alexandria?* Chahine proposes "an immediate putting into contact of the outside and the inside," of the world and the I, even though the two poles remain asymmetrical.[11] As for chapter 9, the last, it closes with the now fully visible reappearance of the most "distant" outside coexisting with the "deepest" inside at the heart of an "audiovisual image," like the ones embodied by Marguerite Duras's divided images.[12] According to Deleuze, this is a question of a new time-image, in which visibility is located in the disjunction between the visual and the auditory. The originary crack that came from the outside thereby finds itself reincorporated into the image's inside, thus proposing a sort of visibility of the invisible itself.

This ultimate restoration can only be realized thanks to another text by Blanchot—the chapter "Speaking Is Not Seeing" in *The Infinite Conversation*, which Deleuze radically inverts into a "to not speak (or a speaking at the limits of sound) is to see." To do this, he draws on Blanchot's critique of the power of speech but robs it of the critique of vision that Blanchot associates with it when, in the same motion, he calls into question the possibility of seeing the visible.

What should we retain of this trajectory sketched out in broad strokes? In the first place, this—the thought of the outside, which is a force of exclusion and upheaval—has become, through the strange use Blanchot makes of it, a power for including an exteriority that burrows inside the image. It is a matter of saving the image of the whole *[image-tout]* and its visibility at the heart of a system that vacillates beneath the force of a rift. Equating the whole-cracked and the outside-inside preserves the imaging totality by joining two faces that are certainly heterogeneous and disjunctive, but that touch at the heart of a single perception working in favor of the visible. Here speech itself can be seen in the interval opened by Duras's off-screen, observational voices *[les voix* off *et voyeuses]*. Thus is maintained a general system unsettled by a cinematic breakthrough that places this system in danger, while causing speech to be heard against the image. The recourse to the outside, and its overturning, therefore assures a kind of aesthetic counteractualization of an event that sweeps up the system, and which it would be art's function, if one believes *The Logic of Sense*, to make "present" as a pure operation that is always repeatable and thus perceptible each time.[13]

Still, a question arises: what image is in question? Deleuze repeatedly insists on making this audiovisual image into a final form of the time-image. It is necessary to note that it is no longer a question of time, but of speech, or more precisely, of the rapport between speech and thought, under whose auspices the last three chapters are opened. Henceforth, what is at stake is enunciation, as evidenced by the unexpected reference to Benveniste.[14] And the problem this implies is to know how cinema could assume a sensible and counterlinguistic enunciation of thought itself. A new event is outlined here that doubles from the interior the event of the outside—a thought to come that no longer concerns cinema directly, but for which cinema's aesthetic development serves as a beacon.

In this sense, the end of *The Time-Image* develops against the current of time—hence the passage from Bergson, philosopher of temporality, to Blanchot, critical analyst of thought in speech. It only remains to ask if this contretemps is not already at work in the whole of the time-image, a question that we will examine by tracing the genesis of this notion back through the book that bears its name.

Reverse Shot: Blanchot–Deleuze–Foucault

Before broaching this new step in my analysis of *The Time-Image*, I would like to pinpoint the diversion that Deleuze works on Blanchot.

Blanchot–Deleuze

It is clear by now that Deleuze's use of Blanchot is hardly Blanchotian. In *The Space of Literature*, as in *The Infinite Conversation*, the outside is never formulated as a "thought," but rather, as an "attraction" *[attrait]* that is also a "passion," that is, the force of an attraction whose particularity is due to the fact that it strips the subject of all reference to being. More radically, the outside, according to Blanchot, exteriorizes the categories that serve as reference points to conceptual thought, whether it is a question of speech or the person, of time, or of being itself. Consequently, the outside obstructs the interiority of the inside and removes all spatial anchoring from exteriority itself. Not only is there no juncture (even disjointed) between the outside and the inside, but the outside has no place of being because it is carried away by its own exteriorization.

However, Blanchot links this strangeness of the outside, provoking fear and vertigo, to a deficiency of time, a lacking of the present that makes presence impossible. In *The Infinite Conversation*, the passion of the outside is the "dispersion of a present that, even while being only passage does not pass."[15] The present thus becomes "exterior to itself"; even more, it is defined as "the exteriority of presence."[16] In this way, the "intimacy with the outside"[17] to which Deleuze refers in order to plunge the outside into the inside is, for Blanchot, in reality, "intimacy as the outside"[18] and thus an uprooting beyond all intimacy.

One could easily conclude from this that Deleuze has barely read Blanchot because he distorts his terms, does not retain what concerns time, and rejects the radical logic that places ontology into question. Alternatively, Deleuze does his utmost to found anew an ontology of the image in *The Time-Image*.

Foucault–Blanchot

This misunderstanding of Blanchot hardly matters, and in reality, it is extremely interesting. Deleuze reads Blanchot through Foucault, about whom he is already preparing his 1986 book.[19] And in *The Time-Image*, he focuses on the text that Foucault devotes to Blanchot in 1966 under the title "Maurice Blanchot: The Thought from Outside."[20]

In its time, this long article appeared to be one of the most innovative studies of Blanchot. Credit goes to Foucault for having highlighted this notion of the outside, "toward which, and outside of which" discourse speaks.[21] For Foucault, the outside is characterized by the paradox of attraction-exclusion, but he links it to "the very being of language"[22] as it is embodied through an "I speak."[23] Good archaeologist that he is, Foucault is interested here in the outside for what it says about and contradicts in discourse: it is necessary to study the "forms," the "categories," and the genealogy (from pseudo-Denys to Bataille or Artaud) to clarify their impact on the "positivity of our knowledge" and "the interiority of our philosophical reflection."[24] As Blanchot suggests in an ambiguous eulogy that also dates to 1986, Foucault works to isolate statements that he formulates negatively, and by so doing, he might very well miss what constitutes the *value* of the statement, that is to say, the statement's relationship to its own exteriority.[25]

Following Blanchot, by definition, the reference to the outside is infinite. In Foucault's embodiment of Blanchot, thought from the outside exorcises the paradox of enunciation it bears because it gives body to a speech in which only language speaks, a language "freed from all of the old myths by which our awareness of words . . . has been shaped."[26] It is understandable that Deleuze retained this interpretation of the outside to confer on it the paradox of thought that the crisis of cinema conveys. Here it is the outside of Foucault's reading that is incorporated into the final enunciative posture, where "seeing" excludes "speaking" by including it in a purely visible statement.

Deleuze–Foucault

However, in his *Foucault*, Deleuze profoundly modifies his reading of the outside and of the relationship between Blanchot and Foucault. The disjunction between seeing and speaking no longer occupies any more than a relative place alongside Deleuze's invention of an imaginary encounter between Foucault's essay on Magritte, "This Is Not a Pipe," and Blanchot's text (which Foucault never cites because he does not speak of Blanchot in this essay).[27] In his chapter on "The Visible and the Speakable (Knowledge)," the fictive application of "speaking is not seeing," to the dissociation that Foucault constructs serially between the linguistic statement and Magritte's figurative design, allows Deleuze to use Foucault to verify his own reading of Blanchot by imputing to him an "irreducibility of the visible" that is the stake of *The Time-Image*. But the relation has shifted. What is essential appears in the following chapter, "The Thought from the Outside (Power)," when Deleuze, in a very attentive reading, shows to what extent Foucault's outside represents a play of forces (or diagram) opposed to forms and develops in this way the force of a counterpower. This movement of multiple expansion, which ruins from within established forms and machines of power, is ultimately embodied for Deleuze by Foucault's "vitalism,"[28] which, inspired by Nietzsche, carries against history the dynamism of a pure becoming. Rereading Foucault broadly, for Deleuze, "forces are in a perpetual state of becoming *[devenir]*, there is a becoming *[devenir]* of forces that doubles history."[29]

The cards have been redealt for Blanchot as well as for Foucault. Deleuze juxtaposes "exteriority," which pertains to form, and the "outside," which is nothing but force.[30] Even if he still ties the act of thinking to the disjunction between seeing and speaking, Deleuze underlines emphatically how "thinking addresses itself to an outside that has no form,"[31] and this new thought of the outside liberates, with this reduced Foucault, an uncontrolled "becoming" that is obviously not foreign to Deleuze himself.

Grafting becoming onto the outside does not go in the same direction as the incorporation of the outside into the inside that I have insisted on so far. Retroactively, it leads us to illuminate an inverse movement at work throughout *The Time-Image*—becoming is projected into this movement, while undoing the relation between time and image. I will now outline the terms of this reversal. It will be a matter of applying to the Deleuzian time-image, and the question of thought that extends out from it, the outside-becoming that comes to the foreground in the aggregate reading of Foucault, even while remaining tied to the thought of Blanchot, which is, in turn, given new depth through the light Foucault casts on it. This coming and going was no doubt necessary to remain faithful to a Deleuzian reflection which, once again, does not develop linearly, but rather, in a spiral and in opposing lines. In this last step, I will attempt to tie together the impossibility of the present, which distinguishes Blanchot's outside, with the crisis of the time-image itself, carried away by a current that leaves no place for either the present or presence, but that precipitates in the same gesture the advent of thought as the sole distinctive feature of time.

The Becoming-Outside of *The Time-Image*

Let us work our way backward through *The Time-Image*. In chapter 6, "The Powers of the False"—thus at the turning point between the end of Bergson (chapter 5) and the arrival of Blanchot (chapter 7)—a rupture breaks out in the thought of time. It arises with the emergence of a "third time-image,"[32] placed under the auspices of Orson Welles and the simulacrum, that ruins the "truth of time"[33] by making the image enter the orbit of the false. The rupture consecrates, in Deleuze's terms, the end of the *order* of time, until then regulated by the succession or by the simultaneous coexistence of different temporal relations. This regime of chronological time gives way to the *series of time*, which no longer allows us to distinguish the before and the after because they are joined in a becoming "that digs the interval into the moment itself."[34] Thus, on one hand, with the preceding time-images, there is the ordering and distinction of moments, and on the other, with the new time-image, there is serialization in discontinuous becoming, in which every moment slips away *[se dérober]*. Naturally, in this becoming that interrupts the present, one recognizes the return in force of Aion as it appears in the twenty-third series of the *Logic of Sense*—that work entirely dedicated to the serial division of signs and, in particular, time. Whereas Chronos is nothing but the present, there is no present possible in Aion, which tends simultaneously toward the past and the future and thereby traces a formidable straight line oriented in two inverse directions. In the opposite spirit of this paradoxical and unlimited becoming, the present is impossible because it is infinitely divided between the past and the future. It may be said, therefore, that time is no longer visible because it has become pure becoming, loosed from presence and thus from the image, as is, precisely, Blanchot's outside, which will later serve as relay and recourse.

Moreover, serialized becoming already undermines the first two time-images, whose order totters beneath this force's impulsion. In chapter 5, "Peaks of Present and Sheets of Past," the second time-image is unsettled by the discontinuity of the past and the present in Bergson, for whom the past takes two different guises, depending on whether it is a stock of memories, from which the present draws using its proper means, or to the contrary, the actualization of memories that erupt into the heart of the present. There are two inverse temporal movements in Bergson—from the present toward the past and from the past toward the present that it modifies. Deleuze then refers to St. Augustine to characterize the multiplicity of presents—presents of the future, of the present, and of the past.[35] He thus founds Robbe-Grillet's multiple and contradictory presents by inscribing them on a single straight line with inverse directions. But the present is saved only by being divided, thereby escaping its proper measure, as Augustine already stressed at the beginning of chapter 7 of his *Confessions*.

As for the first time-image—in chapter 4, "The Crystals of Time"— it constitutes, as we know, the foundation of visible time in the very Bergsonian fabrication of the crystal-image. Actual and virtual "at the same time,"[36] it guarantees, thanks to Bergson's linked circuits, "the indivisible unity"—visible in the crystalline image—"of an actual image and 'its' virtual image."[37] But this image, too, is traversed by the double inverse movement of two heterogeneous directions, "one of which is launched towards the future while the other falls into the past."[38] Becoming, as lack of the present, is already at work in the first time-image; the present depends only on the crystal, which shows to what extent it is fragile. And if one *sees* time in the crystal, it is an originary secession of a time that flies in and by the time-image.

Like a thought of the outside, becoming overcomes, head on or underground, the entirety of a system in which the present would always be lacking if the image did not guarantee presence by guiding exteriority back toward the intimacy, crystalline or fissured, of visibility itself. In *The Time-Image*, the image is there to save us from time, this endless line of flight. And when Bergson's continuous circuits have exploded in Godard's short-circuits, then Blanchot takes up where Bergson leaves off by responding to the advance of the outside by inserting it into the very inside of the image. In this sense, the outside serves as a backfire to the becoming that traverses all time-images and makes the presence of the present in the present image ungraspable. If time is becoming, there is an antinomy between the image and time in *The Time-Image*, hence the transfer of time toward thought, declared in chapter 7, that quietly accompanies the reflection on Bergson (for whom the time-image extends naturally into a thought-image[39]), as well as the formation of time-images themselves. Isn't Thought Resnais's only character since his very first films?

One last word on the complex articulation of becoming and the outside. Becoming is only force, but Deleuze's outside, which follows on its heels, oscillates between form and force. We have seen how Foucault-Deleuze's reading evolves on this subject. And this wavering determines the double game of *The Time-Image*, which turns to Blanchot to find, at times, a new impulsion of becoming toward thought alone, and at other times, the embodiment of a linguistic paradox that gives form to the thought of the outside by tying it back to a speakable and thinking audiovisual image, although it is named "time-image" one last time.

Numerous ambiguities remain, then, regarding the relationship between time and thought in becoming, according to Deleuze, as well as the ambivalence of a thought of the outside that sometimes takes the form of an image, said to be time or thought, and at other times is nothing but the force of exteriorization of thought itself. I will come back to this in conclusion, after a detour through a filmic example that best illustrates the power of rupture that the attraction of the outside puts to work when it drives the free play of becoming outside of any perceptual field. In a recent film by Godard, *In Praise of Love* (2001), inspired simultaneously by Blanchot and Deleuze, time finds itself implied everywhere, but nowhere graspable, because it is delivered from its own exteriority. The film thus gives to the interaction of Deleuze-Blanchot the full range implied by Deleuze in *The Time-Image*, even though Deleuze strives to suppress it by summoning the simulacra of time-images against the sweeping away of a becoming in which time escapes itself.

An Emblem: The Time of the Outside in *In Praise of Love*

In Praise of Love is entirely constructed around the inverse logic of becoming, as underscored by the film's division into two parts separated by an intertitle ("two years earlier"). Each filmic element manages this double constraint in its own way. The story advances by moving backward, leading from a second amorous meeting, which evolves across Paris and terminates in the death of the young woman, to the steps of the protagonist toward the anterior moment (two years ago) and the distant place (a Breton port) of a first encounter, unaware of what precedes it, yet charged with its memory. The omnipresent reference to history plunges what is extremely contemporary (a lecture on the war in Kosovo; the resurrection of the Aubrac affair, with Jean Lacouture and Françoise Vierny, for a scriptless project to remake *Schindler's List* by "Spielberg Inc.") into the return of a past that does not pass (the German occupation, the despoiling of the Jews, the dispersed network of a resistance to be rediscovered in a treason to be dispelled).

Above all, the very form of the film heightens the permanent inversion of time in changing the classical black and white of the first part, bearing Bresson's signature and heralding Vigo, for the completely modern colors of the second part, whose landscapes saturated with Fauvist pictorial citations hearken back to a time before cinema. Thus everything in the film, moving at once toward the past of a future and toward the future of a memory, impels each filmic instant into a temporal circuit that is incomplete because it is simultaneously carried away by two contradictory aims. To take charge of this temporality it harbors, the image must respond to this double circuit, which it projects simultaneously toward and outside of time, which the image hails as if to come, yet assumes to be already past to be understood. This is a perfect vicious circle that transforms the very sight of the film, in memory of a transpired vision that must ceaselessly begin again, in just the same way as the second part of the film runs back up the course of the first part.

Therefore, to the extent that the legibility of each image depends on an overall trajectory working in contrary senses, no image is a time-image. *In Praise of Love* is a Deleuzian film in its organizing principle, but only Blanchot's outside takes into account the impossibility for the spectator of perceiving it without having already come to the end. The before comes after, the after was before, but this is only known after the fact. The film can only be viewed in the present by re-viewing it as already past, and thus in the memory-forgetfulness of a passage that is outside itself by definition. This is the time of the outside, without beginning or end, that Blanchot calls the *vertigo of spacing.* Here it affects the visibility of the film because, at the limit, it submits the comprehension of the image to the only memory of itself where it is forgotten.

> And then
> the first moment . . .
> Do you remember the names?
> No, no.
> Maybe one didn't say them.
> No, I don't know at all.

These are the first spoken phrases "drawn from the film," which will repeat in another way at the end:

> OK, now we have a project,
> and it recounts something
> about history.
> And this something is one of those
> moments.

> And then,
> the first moment ...
> You remember the names
> Perhaps
> One didn't say them, etc.

The text begins with forgetting and ends with the project. Thus Godard, in the book made from the film, where nothing more of the image exists, tirelessly repeats the purely memorial flux of a film that remains to come again.[40]

In Praise of Love figures the emblem of a desired time as the fault in being. This passage to the outside crossing the film turns the image and inverts its signs. Far from crystallizing into time-images, the image becomes the vector of an idea, which is itself completely carried away by the exteriority it attends. This idea of time, both a becoming and a breaching [*rupture de ligne*], gives Godard's film a troubling intensity, following which the outside, all at once, impedes time and declares it the eventual event.

From the Percept to the Concept

I want to conclude by addressing the stakes of Deleuze's path as well as my own reasoning such that it might clarify an emblematic illustration, committed to showing the driving force that the outside exerts on the thought of becoming.

1. Let it first be said (and this will be my first conclusion) that cinema does not make time visible, contrary to a widespread vulgate on *The Time-Image* rehearsed by Alain Badiou at the beginning of a recent special issue of *Critique*, titled "Cinéphilosophie."[41] In reality, cinema makes perceptible, with and against the time-image, the movement whereby time escapes the image at the very moment when the image aims for it. Such is the constitutive aporia of time, which assumes and removes the present in an incessant short circuit, where the instant slips away by advancing backward.

2. A second conclusion extends the preceding one. The attraction of the outside, even withdrawn into the visibility that comes from a relationship to the inside, is not limited to the modern cinema inventoried by Deleuze in 1985. The attraction of the outside operates on the whole of the Deleuzian apparatus, which situates, as we know, the paradox of movement—both visible and nonvisible, continuous and continually discontinuous—as the very principle of cinematographic

imaging. In this way, the projection toward the outside announced in the last chapters of *The Time-Image* could well guide obliquely Deleuze's very conception of cinema.

3. I will emphasize the hypothesis that flows from this and that finds support in a third remark: issuing from the movement-image, the time-image is traversed by the movement of a becoming that, in taking the name of "thought of the outside," puts into play thought itself through an intrication that remains to be unraveled. "Thinking belongs to the outside": this firm affirmation by Deleuze in *Foucault*[42] retroactively illuminates the genesis of a new stake in *The Time-Image* and, more broadly, in *The Movement-Image* and *The Time-Image* as a whole. Playing a double game, Deleuze designates on the outside both the visual embodiment of disjunction in an aesthetic *percept* and the virtual approach of a thought whose vocation is conceptual. The particularity of this thought derives from the exteriority that impels it and makes it think by the sole force of its becoming—without presence to itself and thus "without body and image," as Jean-Louis Schefer puts it.[43] Declared along with Blanchot, "the absence of image"[44] draws, for Deleuze, the dividing line between the becoming of time through the image and thought conceived as a pure becoming outside of the image.

"The impossibility of thinking that is thought," according to Blanchot's exact expression, can thus be reversed by Deleuze as a prefiguration of the concept, defined in *What Is Philosophy?* as both the entanglement that links it to the percept and by the fact that, unlike the percept, which perceives itself in its present actualization, the concept remains always to come: "the concept is the contour, the configuration, the constellation of an event to come."[45]

Here results a series of consequences that must be made explicit. This becoming of an alternative event, which is proper to philosophy and to it alone, is active in Deleuze's recourse to Bergson as well as in his replacement of Bergson with a Foucault-Blanchot responsible for making possible the advent of the concept in a thought that is speakable, yet open to its own exteriority. The defeat of time in *The Time-Image* is bound to the idea's becoming. Because it is movement before being time, cinema serves as a laboratory for the invention of a thought that concerns less the cinema than the future of Deleuze's philosophy in its relationship to art.

The ambiguous use of Blanchot, both repairer of the crack and element of flight, thus designates in the thought-cinema of Deleuze a blind spot of the image, where philosophy attempts contradictorily to preserve the percept in the interior of an ultimate time-image and to precipitate the concept's becoming by the eruption of movement at the heart of a temporality that toys with the image and can only subscribe to the visible by signaling its proper invisibility.

According to Deleuze's contradictory logic, the primary role of cinema, as time and, first, as movement, would be to turn the image-percept against itself by making it, indefatigably, the impetus of thought and the index of thought's resistance to its own actualization. Thought remains forever outside the formulation where it takes on form. The force of the cinema invented by Deleuze would be to embody this double gesture of exclusion and attraction of a thought that is only to come, but that will come to be, by leaps and discontinuity, always ready to break with its own trajectory. The astonishing meeting of becoming and the outside here finds its effectivity (which is not, all things considered, foreign to Blanchot), providing that we rigorously apply the exigent demand for exteriority that comes from Blanchot to the ambivalence of the Deleuzian spirit, which aims in a contradictory fashion at both the effective presence of the perceptible image, where the concept is still only contour, and the effacement of the image in the very process of uprooting by which we think. There can be no resolution.

A concept is a chaos become thought, Deleuze concludes at the end of *What Is Philosophy?*,[46] which is to say that thought plunges into chaos to extract itself. In playing the role of a strange extractor that detours the trajectory of a reasoning it is supposed to guide, Blanchot participates in this paradoxical constraint assigned by Deleuze to philosophy. The resolution of chaos proceeds from chaos itself, which provides simultaneously the remedy and the return of the illness *[le remède et la relance du mal]*. "Nothing is more distressing than a thought that escapes itself"[47]—a ready *pharmakon*, the attraction of the outside, coming from Blanchot, haunts a reflection that is at once a programmed function and a detonator of unexpected effects. Suddenly appearing in an analytical detour, Blanchot's attraction quickens the strangeness of a Deleuzian text that does not follow its own declared program—thought-cinema—in taking the risk of thought's escaping the conceptual frame where it attends. But is this not the particularity of Deleuze's gamble, which makes the im-power of thought the drive augmenting the principle of thinking?

Notes

1   Gilles Deleuze, *Cinema 1: The Movement-Image*, trans. Hugh Tomlinson and Barbara Habberjam (Minneapolis: University of Minnesota Press, 1986), 106.

2   This term, borrowed in an analogical way from chaos theory (or the theory of dissipative systems), is meant to take into account the at once programmed and unforeseeable Deleuzian trajectory of Gilles Deleuze, *Cinema 2: The Time-Image*, trans. Hugh Tomlinson and Robert Galeta (Minneapolis: University of Minnesota Press, 1989). Nor is it a stranger to the shift in orientation inflecting research where becoming unsettles the measure of objects it investigates.

3   Maurice Blanchot, *The Book to Come*, trans. Charlotte Mandell (Stanford, Calif.: Stanford University Press, 2003), 35; Deleuze, *Time-Image*, 168.

4   Deleuze, *Time-Image*, 168.

5   Ibid., 311n37.

6   To use Blanchot's terms in *The Infinite Conversation*, trans. Susan Hanson (Minneapolis: University of Minnesota Press, 1993), cited in Deleuze, *Time-Image*, 80.

7   Deleuze, *Time-Image*, 180.

8   Ibid., 179.

9   Ibid.

10 Ibid., 187.

11 Ibid., 221.

12 Ibid., 260.

13 Gilles Deleuze, *The Logic of Sense*, trans. Mark Lester (New York: Columbia University Press, 1990), 161, 168.

14 Deleuze, *Time-Image*, 226.

15 Blanchot, *Infinite Conversation*, 45.

16 Ibid., 46.

17 Maurice Blanchot, *The Space of Literature*, trans. Ann Smock (Lincoln: University of Nebraska Press, 1982), 24.

18 Blanchot, *Infinite Conversation*, 46.

19 Gilles Deleuze, *Foucault*, trans. Seán Hand (Minneapolis: University of Minnesota Press, 1988).

20 Michel Foucault, *Maurice Blanchot: The Thought from Outside*, trans. Brian Massumi (New York: Zone Books, 1987).

21 Ibid., 25.

22 Ibid.

23 Ibid., 10, 58.

24 Ibid., 16.

25 Maurice Blanchot, *Michel Foucault as I Imagine Him*, trans. Jeffrey Melman (New York: Zone Books, 1987), 74.

26 Ibid., 55.

27 Michel Foucault, *This Is Not a Pipe*, trans. James Harkness (Berkeley: University of California Press, 1983).

28 Deleuze, *Foucault*, 93.

29 Ibid., 85.

30 Ibid., 86.

31 Ibid., 87.

32 Deleuze, *Time-Image*, 155.

33 Ibid., 143.

34 Ibid., 155.

35 Ibid., 101.

36 Ibid., 69.

37 Ibid., 78.

38 Ibid., 81.

39 Ibid., 99.

40 Jean-Luc Godard, *Éloge de l'amour* (Paris: P.O.L., 2001).

41 Alain Badiou, "Du cinéma comme emblème democratique," *Critique* 692–93 (January–February 2005): 4–13.

42 Deleuze, *Foucault*, 93.

43 As cited in Deleuze, *Time-Image*, 220.

44 Ibid., 260.

45 Gilles Deleuze and Félix Guattari, *What Is Philosophy?*, trans. Hugh Tomlinson and Graham Burchell (New York: Columbia University Press, 1994), 32–33.

46 Ibid., 208.

47 Ibid., 201.

3. Notes to a Footnote: The Open Work according to Eco and Deleuze

András Bálint Kovács

In a footnote to *Difference and Repetition*, Deleuze notes, "Eco shows that the 'classical' work of art can be considered from different perspectives and can be judged according to different interpretations, but to not every interpretation or point of view corresponds an autonomous work contained in the chaos of a great work. The characteristic of the 'modern' work of art appears to be the absence of a center of convergence."[1] This reference to Eco is a small detail in Deleuze's work; it never returns in the rest of the book. And the fact that Deleuze attributes to Eco the idea of the "absence of a center of convergence" in the interpretation of modern works of art does not represent a very important argument. So why deal with it?

To be faithful to the Deleuzian spirit, one has to pay attention to very small differences hidden in very little details. Now, that is what I will do here: single out a little detail to find the small difference that makes all the difference between two approaches to the "openness" of the work of art. One approach, which I would call the idea of *structural openness*, could be considered as the last attempt to save the classical conception of the organic nature of the work of art, thus reconciling it with the increasing indeterminism appearing in the modern art of the middle of the twentieth century. The other, which I call the idea of the *serial openness*, is an attempt to liberate aesthetic quality from the requirement of classical organicity. As represented by Eco, the first strives to save the idea of the "organic work," while the other, represented by Gilles Deleuze, abandons completely the idea of the *organic* for that of the *infinite and inorganic series*, with regard to which Deleuze uses the word *orgique*. Eco claims that the modern work of art is organic *and* open at the same time; Deleuze claims that the modern work of art is

31

not organic, and therefore it is open. Eco's goal is to construct the idea of an organic open system in the arts; Deleuze's goal is to construct the idea of a system that contains no unity, only multiplicity. First, I would like to show the difference between these two conceptions of openness: the first one conceived in the beginning of the 1960s by a fundamentally modernist and structuralist thinker such as Eco, and the second theorized by one of the most prominent figures of poststructuralist philosophy and aesthetics at the end of the 1960s. Then I will comment briefly about how to attribute the explanatory value of each of these concepts.

Eco wrote his book *The Open Work* at the beginning of the 1960s to explain a phenomenon in late modern art, namely, the tendency in an increasing number of works to deliberately leave large portions of the work unfinished.[2] Eco felt it necessary to prove that even these works of art respect traditional aesthetic notions of organic completeness. The requirement of organic aesthetic coherence states that rules forming the work of art must have a logical connection between them, and elements of the work must be integrated into an overall logical structure of the work. Essentially, this is a requirement of the classical aesthetic tradition formulated in the eighteenth century. What provides formal coherence? It is provided, in classicism, by the ideal of artistic antiquity; in romanticism, by all the positive and negative spiritual contents that can be deduced from Christian faith in the individual's yearning for transcendence; and in modernism, by various scientific and philosophical ideas, logical principles, and ideologies of the period concerning the relation between the individual and the outside world. The underlying idea behind the requirement of the organic work of art is that art creates a *model* of the completeness of the world, or more than that, a model of its ideal existence. This modellike logical cohesion—*organicism*—has been a basic requirement of works of art since the end of the eighteenth century, when aesthetics emerged as a domain in modern philosophical thinking. But even in a nontheoretical form, the conception of art as an ideal model is traceable to the seventeenth-century novel—think only of *Don Quixote* by Cervantes or *Tom Jones* by Fielding.[3] The first serious critique of this requirement occurs in late modern art and, in a theoretical form, in poststructuralist aesthetic thinking.

The most important attempt to demonstrate the basic principle of the modellike coherence in the milieu of late modern art is Umberto Eco's analysis of what he called the *open work*. There was a slight ambiguity as to the real meaning of *open work* in the first edition of this book. On one hand, Eco says that art is by definition "open" to different interpretations: "in this sense, a work of art, this form *enclosed* into the perfection of the finished and perfectly calibrated organism is also *open*."[4] On the other hand, he claims that in a certain tendency of modern music, one can discover a conscious effort by the author to leave the work clearly unfinished. So in the first case, openness means only the possibility of different interpretations of a completed, finished structure. In the second case, openness is the absence of structural completeness.

Now, Eco had to show that even in the latter case, we are talking about the work of art in "organic totality," which is why he claims that with regard to such modern works, we are talking only about a "more tangible openness" than in the case of classical works. Here there is no substantial difference between classical completeness and the unfinished character of modern works of art. To avoid misunderstanding arising from this ambiguity, in the preface to the second edition, Eco unambiguously formulates what he means by the concept of the open work. He considers the open work as an *organic form*, just like traditional, closed works: "we are going to talk about the work as a form, i.e. as an organic totality, which is born from the fusion of the different levels ... preliminarily provided by experience."[5] How is it possible to reconcile the organic and the unfinished character of the modern work? Eco's response is a coherent structural *model* that can be unfolded from this "fusion" and that can be used to describe the general structure not only of a single work, but also of a whole type of work. This model is "independent from the actual existence of the works defined as open."[6]

The principle of logical coherence means universality of the principles forming the work; that is, aesthetic principles can and should be made universally valid. As Eco writes, "we reduce the form to its system of relations to shed light on the fact that this system is general and transferable, so that we can demonstrate in a specific object the structure that is present in other objects, too.... After all, a work's structure in a proper sense is what it has in common with other works, i.e. what is illustrated by a *model*."[7] The possibility of generalization, on one hand, means a teleological organization, which in a way limits interpretative options: "[the artist] in fact offered rationally organized, oriented opportunities that contained already the organic need for development."[8] On the other hand, it means that the organizing principles of the work of art somehow correspond to the principles organizing *reality*, so that the work of art and reality are in interaction. The structural logic of the work of art reflects the way reality is, or at least the way we think of reality: "that gives rise to the open art as the function of the epistemological metaphor: in the world where discontinuity of phenomena prevents us from forming a uniform and closed picture of it, art puts forward a proposal how to perceive what we are living in the midst of and after having seen it how to accept and integrate it into our own sensibility. An open work completely undertakes the task to provide a picture of discontinuity.... As an almost transcendental pattern, it helps to understand the new aspects of the world."[9] Hence Eco supposes that the modern open work of art plays a more serious role in society than the classical work of art as it contributes to the spreading of the new scientific approach to the world: "poetics of the work in motion ... establishes a new kind of relation between the artist and its audience, develops a new mechanism of artistic perception, alters the art's role in society; and can be regarded as a new initiative beyond the history of art, in sociology and pedagogy."[10] Nevertheless, the open work in fact does not deviate from the romantic paradigm in which art is reality's "transcendental model" or "improved version." As an aesthetic model, this open art is a theoretical generalization of reality conceived of as discontinuous and probabilistic.

Eco's open work is in fact not a new concept of the work of art. He indicates, rather, a specific aesthetic apparatus whereby the composition of the work becomes definite only in the course of the reception on the basis of some optional alternatives and, as a consequence, of the audience's mental activity. Eco keeps insisting that the open work of art is created in the same traditional artistic universe as the closed one, and for this reason, among others, it is not a critical category that can be used to judge certain works, but rather, it is a specific trend of modern art that reflects a certain philosophical and scientific conception of reality: "so after all, we examine the characteristics by which contemporary art takes disorder into consideration. It is not about the blind, irremediable disorder that foredooms each ordering attempt to failure. It is rather about the fertile disorder, which is in fact a breach with the traditional order thought to be unalterable and definite and considered as identical with the objective structure of the world.... [Art] did what it had to do by its mission: it adopted the new situation and tried to *give it a form*."[11] Thus it is by taking the apparent "disorder" of the modern world into consideration that the open work takes the modern world as a model, while continuing to seek out structurable, overall order within it. This is an order that gives a logical structure to the feeling of randomness of the world through the variation principle, the permutation, and *critically* confronts this new order with traditional, "petrified" or "stereotyped" aesthetic forms. By emphasizing the critical component, Eco tries to keep open works away from the precipice that the breakup of the idea of the work-of-art-as-a-world model represents for the concept of art. Hence openness means nothing else but a simple tradition-breaking procedure whereby, at certain points of the composition, the artist provides alternative solutions and accepts the simultaneous realization of more than one option at a time. That is why Eco can say that openness is indeed a simple "increase of information."[12] This information surplus is created in the interaction between the artist and the audience. The artist composes by specifying some forming principles, and their relation or concrete realization is more or less determined by the current reception or presentation of the work. Thus the concrete, material form the given work of art takes on is different from time to time. However, Eco leaves no doubt about the fact that this type of composition can only be considered artistic if there is a limit set to this variation principle: "the *work* is open so long as it is a *work* and beyond this limit openness becomes a *noise*."[13] Authorial intention limits the reader's license to fill in the missing parts and sets a direction to this "creative" process: "so the author offers for the user a work *to be finished*. He doesn't know exactly how it would be finished, but he does know that the finished work continues to be his work and nothing else; that at the end of the interpretative dialogue the form that is created is one of his own even if it is organized by someone else, in an unforeseeable way."[14]

However, concrete "unforeseeability" in this wording is nothing else but a synonym for a general foresight. In Eco's view, the open work is prepared assuming that there are some premises from which one cannot draw an infinite number of conclusions, thus making the form of the work interminable and inorganic. The creator of the open work leaves his work unfinished because he strongly believes that the audience cannot do just *anything* with it, and indeed, that they are going to finish the work in the context of the same logical and aesthetic "universals" as those from which he is working. The reason why the artist leaves his work open is not to allow *any* kind of ending, but because the number of *rationally possible* endings is finite—all of them will originate from the same artistic universe. This is how the open work avoids chaos.

Here is a concrete example. No matter how open *Klavierstück XI* by Stockhausen is, the Beatles' song "Ob-La-Di, Ob-La-Da" will be very unlikely to ever be involved in any of its interpretations. Logically, the open work is indeed a strictly *closed* "structure." Right in the first chapter, Eco states that the authors of open, unfinished works are only "seemingly" not interested in "how the thing is going to get to an end," and that all of this is only a "paradox and imprecise interpretation," which gives reasons for "misunderstanding."[15] Nevertheless, this is a fertile misunderstanding because it provokes us to deeper scrutiny of these kinds of work. After all, the theoretical basis of the open work's closedness—and here we have returned to our starting point—is the idea of the work of art's individual organic nature. The theoretically infinite character of seriality is restricted, closed by the work of art's final, individual isolation as well as its unique character based on a rationally organized organic structure. "The infinite entrenches itself in the middle of finite," Eco argues, "but does not dominate the work conceived as an organic whole and existing as a closed model."[16] So the seriality of the open work is in the end a closed series of options deductible from a finite number of premises.

Now, let us see how this approach can be confronted with another one, which basically starts from the same artistic experience yet comes to a substantially different conclusion. This is the principle of *open seriality* that Gilles Deleuze formulated only a few years after Eco in his work *Difference and Repetition* and that he later developed in more detail in connection with modern cinema.[17] Because this concept is not developed in the context of aesthetics or the history of art, it does not try to reconcile the modern seriality of the work of art with a traditional, individual, work-centered conception. We can make the general remark that Eco describes the current reality of the modern art of the period more precisely, yet Deleuze had a presentiment as to the future consequences of modern art. Eco draws his examples primarily from music and literature, whereas Deleuze's main examples come from cinema. And while Eco's concepts are inspired by artistic experience, Deleuze's concept of seriality is more general and ontological, and he only extends it to art. This comparison remains reasonable because, on one hand, Deleuze quotes Eco, and on the other, because here we are dealing with a single process in modern and postmodern art grasped in its two different phases.

There is no need to spend too much time discussing the differences between modern structuralism and Deleuzian philosophy in general. It is more interesting to note how close Eco seems to be to Deleuze in their respective understandings of modern art. And yet the small difference that exists between them separates two entire philosophical universes. For Eco and structuralism, a system is a structure, and a structure is organized according to a unifying principle—understanding and interpreting a system amounts to understanding the unifying principle. In my understanding, the big challenge Deleuze faced in *Difference and Repetition* was to explain what a system is like that does not exclude the one, the same, or the similar, but rather, contains them only as a partial aspect: "multiplicity need not mean a combination of the multiple and the one, on the contrary, it is the organisation of the multiple as such, which does not need unity at all to be a system."[18]

Deleuze opposes *seriality* to *regularity*. *Regularity* means a series composed according to a *rule that is one and the same* all over in the series. *Seriality* means a series composed according to an infinite series of rules, where every element of the series obeys a different rule and yet belongs to the same system. With respect to art, the principle of open seriality means that a work of art is a series of several not necessarily connected forming principles, whose serial nature does not, therefore, constitute an organic whole or totality. Nor does the modern work of art transform the world into another medium according to certain unifying rules. In this way, the work is neither inorganic, nor is it a *representation of reality*. Right at the outset, Deleuze gives up the ideal of organicism and the model structure that had been valid in aesthetics since the seventeenth century. He thus replaces the requirement of *organicism (organique)* with the idea of *infinity (orgique)*.[19] Seriality occupies an absolutely different conceptual level for Deleuze than for Eco. If Eco says that in serial art, "infinite entrenches itself in the middle of finite," for Deleuze, finite and infinite are identical things. Seriality is not based on the logic of permutation of a closed set of elements; it is the way the work of art exists, namely, that it is not a copy, but an equal part, a *repetition* of reality. The name Deleuze gives this mode of existence is— as opposed to representation—*simulacrum*, the highest-level *repetition*. Deleuze uses the term *repetition* to emphasize that a work of art is not a copy, imitation, or representation of an "original," "real," "existing" thing, but rather, the work of art is as "real," "original," and "genuine" as the thing that is in another—namely, *practical*—position.

The concept of the simulacrum, as opposed to the concept of the copy or representation, leads to a more fundamental opposition, namely, the one between Plato and Deleuze. In Platonism, the idea of the image is defined by the concept of the imperfect copy. Things that exist are imperfect copies of Ideas, and works of art are imperfect copies of things that exist. Imperfection is a lack of adequacy to the original in similarity. Difference or imperfection of similarity becomes an error, something that has to be done away with. This error makes the difference between the real thing and its appearance. There are differences between appearances, too, according to their proximity to Ideas. Something that appears to be something else, but in fact is an opposite of what it appears to be, is a dangerous or bad appearance. Since all images are appearances, how, then, is it possible to distinguish between good and bad appearances? The Platonist Church Fathers, says Deleuze, constructed the idea of the "image without similarity," referring to the sinful man who had lost his likeness to God, but at the same time continued to be the "image of God." The distinction between similarity and image is important for Platonism to exclude "wrongful appearances," and this is obviously a moral distinction. Deleuze accepts the moral characterization and calls the "image without similarity" the "demonic image" that exists by virtue of its difference, rather than by virtue of its similarity. The "simulacrum" is the demonic image, in which similarity is only an appearance, a repetition, rather than an "essence," and in which difference is not subdued to the same—it is absolutely free and anarchic.[20]

Here is the essential difference between two contradictory approaches: very simply put, according to poststructuralist philosophy in general (in Derrida and Deleuze, at least), when one focuses on similarity, rather than difference, at the end of the day, one speaks of unity and the integration of differences into the "same" and downplays the importance of identity. The essence of identity is singularity, which can only be grasped by placing difference into focus. How, then, can the relationship between singularities be explained? What is the rule of a system consisting of singularities? And especially, how can the fatal isolation of identity be suppressed, as it stems from the metaphysical concept of individuality? Two of Deleuze's categories have been highly enlightening in this respect, especially for many artists after the high modernist period—rhizome and repetition. *Rhizome* explains the structure and the dynamics of proliferation of the system; *repetition* is the cohesive force in the chaos of differences that makes the series a system, while connecting singularities.

In contradistinction to Plato, Deleuze claims that instead of being an inferior imitation, a work of art is, on the contrary, the highest-level

repetition. Art raises things to their highest form, to the form of a simulacrum, where the only real factor of their coherence is repetition in the
form of Nietzsche's eternal return. The substance of the simulacrum
is *repeatedness*, and for Deleuze, this is also an ontological fact. It is
the nature of the simulacrum–work of art that, with regard to reality,
it is on the same level as so-called real things: "the difference lies not
between the thing and the simulacra; it is not between the original and
the copy."[21] The difference between reality and the simulacrum is of
the same nature as the difference among certain things of reality. The
identity of things in reality is provided by their final singularity (there
are no two identical hammers, says Deleuze), just as in the case of works
of art. A masterpiece is no more individual than a pissoir manufactured
in series: that is why any of them can become exhibition objects. Then,
in general, what is the difference between real things and simulacra?
In a simulacrum, *repeatedness*, the fundamental ontological status of
all things, becomes manifest.

Now, Deleuze does not think, for example, that you could smoke
with the pipe seen in Magritte's painting *(This Is Not a Pipe)* in the same
way as with the one you can buy at a tobacco shop; rather, he thinks
that the pipe bought at a tobacco shop is from the same series as the
one painted by Magritte, and the common feature of the things involved
in the series is that each of them is a difference-based repetition of a
former thing representing some kind of singularity, which is repetition
itself. Therefore a "net" of identities gets created, which is "open but
not to the 'real' pipe missing from these pictures and words but to all
the other elements, including each 'real' wooden, clay or meerschaum
pipe that falling into this net becomes the medium and function of the
simulacrum."[22] However, while we do not, or only unintentionally,
realize this character of repeatedness in the pipe bought at a tobacco-
nist's (because the only thing we focus on is whether we can smoke it),
with Magritte's pipe, nothing else can be seen but the fact that it is a
repetition, although no smoke will ever come out of it.[23] The paradox
of Magritte's work of art (which arises from the fact that the author
wrote on it, "This is not a pipe") seems to be a paradox only from the
point of view of a representational logic. What Magritte repeated was
not the pipe's practical function, but the pipe itself as *repetition*, drawing special attention to the difference of the repetition, by which his
painting became a *real* pipe, not *one* real pipe but *the pipe as a series,
as a simulacrum*.

As regards the work of art–simulacrum, there is no need for logical consistency according to one rule, as opposed to the traditional closed or open works of art. What the work of art imitates or represents is not the "original" thing's identity; rather, it repeats its *difference* from other things in the series by another difference. (This particular difference is being-a-work-of-art, i.e., simulating "real existence," or according to Plato, manifesting the "wrong appearance," which reveals to us the fact that every thing's identity rests on a small difference through which it repeats previous things.) There is no "original thing," says Deleuze. The only "original thing" is the small difference in repetition. And in this sense, it is not the original thing that becomes repeated; it is rather originality understood as a basic difference that is repeated infinitely. Thus modeling or restoring some original coherence or organic character will not be the task of a work of art, not even by representing multiple aspects at the same time. For Deleuze, the crucial issue is to know whether the work of art converges toward a principle of superior identity. The openness and undefinedness of representation alone are not sufficient for open seriality: "infinite representation can multiply aspects and arrange them in series; these series will still be subject to the requirement of the convergence towards the same object and the same world. The infinite representation can multiply the formations and elements, it can organize them into circles capable of self-movement; these circles will still bear the same centre as the big circle of consciousness."[24] Or, conversely, "when the modern work of art develops the permutation series and their concentric structures, it points at a way for philosophy that leads to the rejection of representation."[25] Multiplication of different aspects of the same falls back to repeating the same, while rejecting the idea of the same in the relationship between art and reality leads us to the recognition of real uniqueness and the real diversity of reality.

Eco thought it important to emphasize the organic character of the open work to avoid having to face chaos, as if the open work domesticated or structured chaos. Deleuze anticipates chaos. If the work of art's coherence is given by repetition or the eternal return, then it is (says Deleuze, citing Nietzsche) just identical with chaos. This means that elements do not converge into a single logical center or model, but constitute, rather, a pile of smothering, conflicting, controversial series. The work of art, as a repetition-series without a convergence center, does not avoid chaos or give it a form, but rather absorbs it, so to speak. This is not to say that the modern art reckons with disorder and tries to provide it with a coherent form; instead, it perceives this coherence in a different way than traditional art. The only way to understand real openness is to face chaos.

It is interesting that at this point, Deleuze mentions the same works of art as Eco, *Book* by Mallarmé and *Finnegans Wake* by Joyce, and what is more, he also refers to Eco. It is even more interesting that in his reference, he puts his own conclusion into Eco's mouth, although Eco thinks just the very opposite of these conclusions. For Eco never stated in his work that "the lack of convergence centre would be one of the characteristics of the modern work of art."[26] On the contrary, what Eco emphasized with regard to *Finnegans Wake* was that "the reason why Joyce provided clues was that he wanted us to read according to a certain direction of sense."[27] Moreover, he states that the multiplicity of possible readings indeed intends to involve the whole cosmos, and he compares this form with postdodecaphonic music. In this respect, he cites Pousseur, according to whom the important thing in this kind of music is that listeners place themselves into the work's center, and it is from this center that they capture the infinity of interpretative options.[28] However, from Deleuze's point of view regarding seriality, the universality of the work of art is impossible: "It isn't enough to multiply perspectives ... what is necessary is each perspective to have an adequate, separate work with sufficient sense: what counts is the deviation of the series, the lack of centres of the circles, the 'beast.'"[29] But the separate works gain their real coherence only "in the big work of the chaos of their series." This is the reason for the difference between Deleuze and Eco regarding their respective interpretation of the form of *Finnegans Wake*: while for Eco, the reader is in the "center" of the work, for Deleuze, the reader's identity, due to the several reading variants, "dissolves" in the decentered circles.[30] Therefore we can say that Deleuze's conclusions go beyond Eco's modernist open work toward the eclecticism of postmodern art, which allows conflicting formal principles to prevail over the same work of art, without the possibility of integrating them into some kind of common model. The work of art–simulacrum is a chaotically arranged series of logics of different nature, from which no coherent or rounded whole is possible, but only a *catalog* can be created. All things of life are situated on the same level; features and appearances of things are determined by the milieu and the series we meet them in. This logic, how the organic work of art becomes an infinite catalog, is very well illustrated by Peter Greenaway's works—not only his films, but also his exhibitions, especially his great exhibition in Vienna: "100 Objects to Represent the World."

This is also how banality becomes an aesthetically relevant concept. A commonplace thing becomes a work of art by changing the context—that is, the paradigm or catalog—without changing its physical form. Deleuze is confirmed in this by the same artistic phenomena indicating the end of modernism, as those leading Arthur Danto to formulate the aesthetic relevance of the commonplace.[31] However, Deleuze draws this conclusion merely by analyzing the repetition-logic:

> Art doesn't imitate, it does repeat and repeats every repetition by an internal capacity. . . . Even the most mechanic, most common, most regular and most stereotypical repetitions find their places in the work of art, since they are always removed compared to other repetitions, provided we emphasize their difference from other repetitions. For there exists no other aesthetic problem than art's integration into everyday life. The more standardized, the more stereotypical our everyday life is, the more it is subject to the faster and faster reproduction of consumer goods, the more art has to connect with it, so that it can pick out the slight difference that can be seen between the levels of repetitions simultaneously, and it has to make the two extremes of usual series of consumption and the instinctive series of destruction and death.[32]

Using banality as banality, pop art launches art toward the direction where every universal principle ceases to exist. No hierarchy exists here, but only series of different arrangements that give sense both to the material world and to events. It is not "reality" that is hidden behind the work of art, of which it is a dim or clear picture, but the work of art itself is a constituent part of reality—not a mirror, not a picture, not a representation, but a given particular position of the material world. There is no such hierarchical level in referring to which the work of art becomes a higher quality than life. Nothing is hidden, everything is visible, everything is direct and identical with itself.

We have seen that there is a slightly perceptible difference between Eco's open work and Deleuze's open seriality. (Clearly not even Deleuze himself noticed it, or rather preferred using Eco as an antecedent to entering into a controversy with him because of a nuance.) But this difference is still decisive. It determines the future of modernism itself. Stylistically, the difference between modern and postmodern art is, of course, more obvious. However, the question is whether there is a real, deeply seated difference behind the surface. Reading Deleuze confirms my conviction, and so much so that it sheds light for me on the transition through which the postmodern developed from the modern paradigm. This transition is called conceptual art.[33] Here the aesthetic form of the individual work of art breaks away from conventional meanings to such an extent that its aesthetic interpretation is possible nearly only through conceptual analysis. In other words, this art reduces conventions of representation to the level of linguistic metaphor. It is not by chance that metaphor is at the center of aesthetic analysis in the age of conceptual art. This is why it may appear as if art were integrated into philosophy, which would, at the same time, mean the "end" of art. The fine arts have undoubtedly exceeded modernism's presuppositions, desires, and illusions relating to totality and organicism, as inherited from romanticism. However, the extreme reduction of aesthetic form that takes place here is only in the context of the individual modellike work of art; it does not concern the whole of aesthetic art production activity. The sensuous reduction of the conceptual work of individuals is compensated for by the colorful diversity of the series of art creating gestures, and this reduction forms a transition to a concept of art in which the internal, organic totality of the individual work is replaced by the *orgique*, or the serial logics of partially valid works. Hence conceptual art is probably the first artistic paradigm in which, to use Arthur Danto's phrase, art "disenfranchises" philosophy (and not the other way around) by broadening and reversing the concept of art developed in philosophy.[34]

Conceptual art leads to an artistic world in which the theoretically unlimited proliferation of aesthetic forms is possible because they are opposed to the formerly prevailing need for totality, inherited from romanticism. Owing to conceptual art, local-mindedness, partial explicability, and seriality gained civil rights in the modern art world. From this point of view, Deleuze's statements on late modern art are really profound and historic from the perspective of postmodern art.

However, we have to recognize the limit that Deleuze transgressed in the interpretation of modern art. This is not easy because the postmodern approach, in a peculiar way and precisely due to the principle of partiality, does not *replace or invalidate* modernism, but rather, preserves it as an artistic principle of limited validity. From this perspective, it is true that the modern, in Habermas's words, is an "unfinished project." However, from another perspective, this is not true, as modernism's need for universality was irrevocably *relativized* by the postmodern. The postmodern did not abolish modernism, but rather, integrated it as *one style*—purist, minimalist, structuralist, constructivist, cubist, and so on—among many. The postmodern did not invalidate the two-hundred-year-old romantic-modern concept of art as a whole; it invalidated it only in a *political* sense, that is, in its aspiration to philosophical and political universality and exclusivity. The postmodern's great opponent is not modernity as such, but rather, modernity as a political program, which transforms art into a model of society—that is, the *avant-garde*. Modern universalism can be integrated into the postmodern only insofar as it does not refer directly to a concrete social reality as its own model and does not contain a concrete social program or utopia. In other words, modernism can live on in the postmodern as much as it can represent its own universalism as a *partial* aspect. This is a situation that seems to correspond to the way Deleuze thinks about the concept of organic totality. To think about something as a whole is like picking one of the thing's attributes among many.

Notes

1   Gilles Deleuze, *Difference and Repetition* (New York: Columbia University Press, 1994), 69, 313n23; translation modified. Originally published as *Différence et répétition* (Paris: Presses Universitaires de France, 1997), 94. Subsequent references will be my translations of the original French, followed by corresponding pages in the English translation in italics.

2   Umberto Eco, *The Open Work* (Budapest: Európa, 1998); all translations are my own. [Editor's note: An English translation was published by Harvard University Press in 1989, though it does not contain all the chapters of the original Italian edition. Pages corresponding to the English translation, where they exist, are indicated in italics.]

3   What I mean by modellike coherence is not identical with the requirements of harmony and proportionality raised for art already in ancient times. As the concept of the *work conceived as an organic whole* set against reality did not exist before the eighteenth century, the previously mentioned formal requirements focused on working out details and making connections among the elements but did not become a norm regarding the whole of the separate work. An initial sign of the appearance of individual works of art is when, e.g., general descriptions on dramas become norms in the French classicist dramaturgy of the seventeenth century.

4   Eco, *Open Work*, 74, *4*.

5   Ibid., 60.

6   Ibid., 62.

7   Ibid., 61.

8   Ibid., 101, *19*.

9   Ibid., 207.

10   Ibid., 105, 22–23.
11   Ibid., 55.
12   Ibid., 137, 43.
13   Ibid., 222.
14   Ibid., 101, 19.
15   Ibid., 75, 4.
16   Ibid., 97, 16.
17   See esp. Gilles Deleuze, *Cinema 2: The Time-Image*, trans. Hugh Tomlinson and Robert Galeta (Minneapolis: University of Minnesota Press, 1989). Originally published as *Cinéma 2: L'Image-temps* (Paris: Editions de Minuit, 1985).
18   Deleuze, *Difference and Repetition*, 236, 182.
19   Ibid., 337, 262.
20   Ibid., 168, 128; 341, 265–66.
21   Ibid., 93, 67.
22   Michel Foucault, *This Is Not a Pipe* (Budapest: Athaeneum, 1993), no. 1/4 158–59.
23   Here it is important to remark that following Hume, Deleuze, *Difference and Repetition*, 96, 70, interpreted difference as differentiation: "repetition changes something not in the repeating object but in the spirit of the one contemplating the repetition."
24   Ibid., 94, 68.
25   Ibid., 94, 68–69.
26   Ibid., 94, 69.
27   Eco, *Open Work*, 85, 10.
28   Ibid., 85, 14.
29   Deleuze, *Difference and Repetition*, 94, 69.
30   Ibid., 95, 69.
31   See Arthur Danto, *The Transfiguration of the Commonplace* (Cambridge, Mass.: Harvard University Press, 1981).
32   Deleuze, *Difference and Repetition*, 375, 293.
33   As Géza Perneczky, *The Net* (Budapest: Héttorony), 30, explains it, "the name of the door that belonged to the building of the avant-garde, but through which the way led outwards, was concept. It was the last section of the constant reduction process that drove fine arts from one ism to the other. . . . The concept was the door through which we could step out to a world beyond art, passing over the process of reduction." This idea concerning the character of the transition character between conceptual art and the postmodern is also formulated by Habermas; however, he called it "post avant-garde." Cf. Jürgen Habermas, "An Unfinished Project of Modernity," in *The Post-modern State* (Budapest: Századvég, 1993), 151–78.
34   Arthur Danto, *The Philosophical Disenfranchisement of Art* (New York: Columbia University Press, 1986).

4. Mutual Images: Reflections of Kant in Deleuze's Transcendental Cinema of Time

Melinda Szaloky

Prolegomena

In *Critique of Pure Reason*, Immanuel Kant describes the philosophical climate of his day in terms of trepidation and "indifferentism," brought about by the futility of attempts to bridge the rift between a despotic "dogmatic metaphysics" and the half-baked skepticism of inquisitive but uncouth intellectual "nomads."[1] Dissatisfied with the taste of his "*syncretistic* age" for an insincere and shallow "*coalition system* of contradictory principles,"[2] Kant refocuses his attention and power of reflection on the symptom of indifference and disaffection, which he perspicaciously considers to be the effect "not of the heedlessness but of the matured judgment"[3] of his time. Nourished by a lack of discipline, vigor, and inventiveness in metaphysics, and offset by an unprecedented outpouring of creativity in the other sciences, this indifferentism prompts Kant's "call to reason to take on once again the most difficult of all its tasks, namely, that of self-cognition."[4] The resulting transcendental critique—a thoroughgoing diagnostic mapping and recalibration of the Enlightenment mind—"was to define future philosophy," Gilles Deleuze claims.[5]

As a self-declared nomadic thinker and a chief architect of the powerful antifoundationalist, posthumanist trend in contemporary thought, Deleuze may strike us as an afterimage of the skeptical nomads of philosophy addressed by Kant, whose avatar, David Hume, was reportedly instrumental in awakening Kant from his "dogmatic slumbers." A more intimate association of Kant and Deleuze may appear counterintuitive, given Kant's reputation as the emblematic thinker of Enlightenment rationalism, the crisis of which has brought into play the poststructuralist critique launched by Deleuze and his peers. A closer look, however, reveals a remarkable affinity concerning the constellations that prompted these two thinkers to act within the stratigraphic time of philosophy. Kant's effort to rescue ontology and reinvigorate metaphysics through a peculiar transcendental dualism responds to the "historical crisis of psychology," manifest as the confrontation of materialism and idealism, and in general to a historical moment "at which it was no longer possible to hold a certain position," as Deleuze puts it in *Cinema 1: The Movement-Image.*[6] (Significantly, at this phase of his *Cinema* text, Deleuze makes an "absent-minded" leap to Husserl and Bergson, neglecting the Kantian intervention.[7]) In his turn, and in an equally transcendental, even Platonic vein, Deleuze labors to fight off inertia and suffocation by rekindling a belief in something possible amid the "exitless nothingness" of the "global zone" to which the West has given birth, according to Jean-François Lyotard.[8] As a philosopher of a synthetic and syncretic age, one that has declared the death of affect, metaphysics, and history, Deleuze finds himself reliving the conundrum of spiritual indifferentism, of lacking "*resistance to the present,*" and the shortage of inventiveness and creativity that Kant felt compelled to address.[9]

The kinship of the two philosophers becomes more prominent once we remind ourselves of their shared commitment to the "zeroness" of the idiosyncratic Socratic process of philosophizing. Kant's "method of watching, or rather of occasioning on one's own a contest *[Streit]* of assertions," seeks not "to finally decide in favor of one or the other half of our dialectical mind, but . . . to inquire whether the contest's object is not perhaps a *mere deception.*"[10] The transcendental way of thinking does not aim to confirm a transcendent synthesis through conflict, in contrast to Hegel, or, Deleuze tells us, an enthusiastic Eisenstein, a "cinematographic Hegel."[11] Rather, the transcendental critic seeks to attain certainty by discovering "the point of misunderstanding"[12] and by uncovering the "logic of illusion"[13] that grounds the objective claims of our dialectic reason.[14] This critic labors to freely nourish the "seed of the challenges, which lies in the nature of human reason,"[15] unearthing in the process an empty form of law—time—as the absolute measure of rational action as well as a nature inseparably intertwined with randomness and chaos.[16]

Deleuze's transcendental empiricist explorations of the powers of the false, his persistent concern with the unrealizable "eternal aspect" of the event (manifest, e.g., in his fascinating study of masochism and

Freud's pursuit of the pleasure principle), and finally, his grasp through cinema of the "perpetual foundation of time"—that is at once a "powerful non-organic Life" and "a *female gest* which overcomes the history of men and the crisis of the world"[17]—are in perfect resonance with Kant's transcendental search and aesthetic reflection of the "supersensible principle of nature (nature outside as well as within us),"[18] envisioned as an ineffable *"mother wit"* *[Mutterwitz]*, surreptitiously weaving its schematic art in and out of human time.[19]

Equally enlightening is to consider Deleuze's nomadism in light of the careful distinction that Kant draws between "skepticism" and the "skeptical method." While the skeptic (the Kantian nomad), in his "technical and scientific ignorance ... undermines the foundations of all cognition,"[20] the practitioner of the skeptical method is engaged in a rigorous thought experiment, ever mindful of loose threads, missing links, and anomalies. To my mind, Deleuze represents such a principled, (de)constructive nomadism. As Alain Badiou reminds us, "contrary to the commonly accepted image," Deleuze's fundamental problem is "not to liberate the multiple, but to submit thinking to the renewed concept of the One."[21] For Deleuze, "a single voice raises the clamour of being."[22]

Obviously, the exploration of the intricate connections between the Kantian system and Deleuze's oeuvre is beyond the scope of this chapter. My aim here will be to trace some key Kantian moments of inspiration in Deleuze's momentous *Cinema* books, whose power to intrigue, provoke, and enliven appears to be unchecked by the passage of time. I will pay special attention to the notion of the time-image, which D. N. Rodowick tells us makes manifest "a certain Kantianism of the cinema, a *foundation of thinking in the form of time*, or a *Critique of Pure Reason* in images."[23] I will argue that Deleuze's ostensibly Bergsonian conception of an intermediary, bireferential cinematic movement-image, complete with an aberrant interstitial moment waiting to be set free as time's infinite opening, constitutes an inspired reelaboration of the baffling balance of Kant's transcendental inquiry, played out in the *Critique of Judgment* between the beautiful and the sublime.

A Problematic Transcendental Topic

A remarkable feature of Deleuze's work on cinema is the relationship the books establish between the persistent concern of Western thought with the incommensurability of movement and its spatial extension, on one hand, and the emergence and development of an industrial art of moving images, on the other. Indeed, in sketching out a brief history of the problem of analyzing what "cannot be divided without changing qualitatively each time it is divided,"[24] Deleuze appears to be merely setting the stage for the dramatic entry of cinema as modernity's inventive response to the age-old philosophical problem of how to measure and represent a complexly evolving, constantly changing reality.

Cinema, Deleuze argues, does more than simply reproduce the illusion of movement by appending to immobile sections cut out of movement "the abstract idea of a succession, that of a time which is mechanical, homogeneous, universal, and copied from space, identical for all movements";[25] rather, cinema gives us "an *intermediate* image" [*l'image moyenne*] to which movement "belongs as immediate given."[26] Cinema, Kant might say, comes complete with synthetic a priori principles, or immanent criteria of assemblage, which for Kant constitute what Adorno calls "the curious imaginary realm of the transcendental,"[27] where the human world is constructed through the mutual interpenetration of the subjective and the objective.

Deleuze's intermediate cinematic movement-image responds to and mediates a dually referential signaletic movement, one that is equally beholden to, and endlessly passes between, absolute and relative, objective and subjective measures. Furthermore, this dual system of reference proper to the movement-image and manifest in a semisubjective camera consciousness pivots on an interval or interstice of movement. Deleuze describes this movement as "a gap or disproportion between a received movement and an executed one"[28] that constitutes "a profoundly aberrant and abnormal movement" of "non-localizable relation." However, it also tends to be normalized by assuming the role of a center within the sensory-motor schema of a perceptive-active consciousness.[29] Ultimately, such intervals of movement, recreated through the intermittent, spliced up procession of the cinematic image, hold the key to a new, increasingly unpredictable, and indeterministic notion of reality in which Deleuze envisions the cinema as becoming an "organ for perfecting the new reality."[30]

Remarkably, Deleuze's foundational claim that the cinematic shot "immediately gives us a movement-image"[31] as well as an immanent time-image appears vague, marking a point that "resonates problematically throughout the cinema books," as Rodowick perceptively notes.[32] I believe that this problematic foundation holds the key to Deleuze's dazzling and perplexing cinema project, whose strange fascination we may find hard but all the more desirable to discern. To pursue this pull, however, we need to submit to the problem, the "illness," the passion, and the "im-power," that, in Deleuze's view, the lived brain has come to pose to itself. Moreover, in the eyes of a prominent tradition, this problem has assumed a cinematic incarnation and imaginary focus.

The key premise of Kant's critique of Enlightenment reason is the Idea to consider consciousness, or transcendental subjectivity, problematically as a *focus imaginarius* outside of *and* constitutive of experience—a point of convergence and commerce between absolute (noumenal) and relative (phenomenal) realms.[33] In general, Deleuze reminds us, Kant treats reason as "the faculty of posing problems," where "problems are Ideas" and "Ideas are essentially 'problematic.'"[34] The intuition of an analogy between Deleuze's problematic, vague notion of a camera consciousness (as immediate and "intermediary" movement-image and inherent time-image) and Kant's problematic and vague principle *(principium vagum)* of a transcendental *focus imaginarius* of consciousness beyond, yet paradoxically within, sensible experience, justifies the desire to treat Deleuze's vibrant cine-philosophy as a summons for a transcendental, even transcendent, exercise.[35] Yet, as Deleuze himself admits, a transcendental inquiry follows a sinuous self-regulating logic— what Kant might call *heautonomous*, that is, neither autonomous nor heteronomous, but somewhere in between.[36] This, Deleuze claims, is an inquiry that we cannot break off when we please, and where every attempt at grounding will hurl us "headlong beyond to the absolutely unconditioned, the 'ground-less' from which the ground itself emerged."[37] I trust that my brief and necessarily incomplete foray into transcendental logic will be considered with this warning in mind.

How are we, then, to construe in transcendental terms Deleuze's problematic claim that the diffuse and pliable consciousness evident in the semisubjective cinematic perception-image is also "already deeply affected by injections of time,"[38] that it is inherently a time-image? There seems to be no simple answer to this question. As a marker and method of an incommensurable ratio, an infinitesimal, ungraspable difference in the relation between the sensible and the intelligible, Kant's curious transcendental dimension emerges as a hermeneutics of puzzlement.[39]

And yet there is a remedy at hand. In fact, all we need to do to orient ourselves in the force field of Kantian thought, and in the Deleuzian plane of immanence, is to follow the Kantian admonition to suspend knowledge and make room for a rational, skeptical belief. We, in other words, need to assume the stance of a simultaneously absent-minded (i.e., ordinary empirical and dual-minded), dialectically reflexive *and* speculative, transcendental-ideal consciousness, one that is at once limited to, and is operating beyond, sensible experience. Little wonder that Kant will end up diagnosing a "splitting of the way of thinking"[40] amid the mutual limitations imposed by reason's sensible and conceptual sources, theoretical and practical interests, and subjective and objective bases. To be more precise, Kant's qualification of knowledge as the cognition of mere appearances in a sensible yet phenomenal experience allows for the suspension or the disavowal of the certainty of empirical knowledge and makes room for a transcendentally extended as-if mode of reflection. This is a visit through the imagination to the unconscious mechanisms and forms of thought, or synthetic a priori processes, that for Kant are both independent of and constitutive of experience. This suspension of knowledge—which also places a block on knowledge, limiting it to the empirically knowable—gives Kant license to posit a supersensible substrate—a transcendental imaginary and ideal dimension beyond the empirically and intuitively limited, causally determined phenomenal experience that is the sensibly inaccessible, spontaneously operating condition of possibility of this very experience.

Already at this point, a remarkable resemblance may be detected between, on one hand, the Kantian superimposition of a sensible moment of perception and the transcendental and supersensible procedural dimensions of its production, and on the other, Deleuze's distinction of a dual perception-image, one that is both preassumed and general (a priori) and emergent and special (a posteriori), and which Deleuze considers as "the degree zero in the deduction which is carried out as a function of the movement-image."[41] Equally, Kant's basic synthetic act of perception, in which appearance is combined with consciousness through the inseparable transcendental imaginary act of apprehension and associative reproduction, brings to mind what Deleuze calls the witnessing of "the birth of memory, as function of the future which retains what happens in order to make it the object to come of the other memory."[42] In fact, as I am about to show, the initial Kantian moment of knowledge-suspension eventually clears room for a reflective, rather than cognitive, causal, perception in aesthetic reflection. This is an instance of immediate intermediacy, which, as Elizabeth Rottenberg observes as a "'res vacua' ... makes the line between the 'not yet' and 'no longer' of all empirical transfers passable (and impassable—except by recourse to this 'res vacua')."[43] This liminal moment of becoming of transcendental subjectivity, suspended at a standstill and evoked in the "smallest circuit" of the Deleuzian time-image,[44] will come into its own, will come to life, in Kant's conception of aesthetic reflective judgment. As Deleuze tells us, this first ascertains the deep-level "free and indeterminate accord" of the mental faculties, without which reason would be unable to pursue its speculative and practical interests.[45] It is this transcendentally conceived, intermediary synthetic a priori that is reanimated in the Metzian instance of "I am the camera," described as "a unique mixture of two contrary currents," a simultaneity of reception and release, pointing and recording.[46]

It is important to note here that Kant's ingenious dilation and stratification of the moment of (self-)consciousness reveals the proclivity of our dialectic reason to masquerade as itself, pretending to be able to make material and sensible what is noumenal and only intelligible. This inevitable fundamental fallacy of subreption is, if recognized as an objective or instrumental illusion, a useful and in fact indispensable tool of the transcendental inquiry aimed at the exploration of the sensible as well as merely thinkable bounds and grounds of possible experience.[47] Projecting objects in themselves (intelligible objects that lie behind our back, far from the phenomenal ones before our eyes), as if they were objects "seen behind the mirror's plane,"[48] is a Kantian idea that has certainly caught on (or has been reinvented) in cinematic thinking. This is manifest in Jean Cocteau's filmed mirror crossings into fantasmatic zones as well as in a variety of theories of the screen as the locus of projections of unconscious, imperceptible mental processes and content.[49] Deleuze's claim that cinema's simulation of unknown bodies that "we have in the back of our heads" is a projection of a cerebral dimension squarely within this tradition.[50]

Similarly, the routine conception of cinematic mediation in terms of illusion and mis(re)cognition may owe a debt to Kant's effort to grasp, even simulate, the dynamism of our dually biased reason through the illusion of subreption. Consider, for example, Metz's inspired notion of the imaginary cinematic signifier, which represents the "absent in detail," possessing "unaccustomed perceptual wealth, but at the same time stamped with unreality to an unusual degree."[51] Subreption in Deleuze becomes "a 'theft of thoughts' of which thought is a constant agent and victim."[52] This productive theft is traced through the ceaseless, imperceptible passage of the cinematic perception-image from the subjective to the objective (and vice versa), which "sometimes reveals itself in certain striking cases"[53] and which, I would add, becomes consistently self-conscious in the two-sided crystalline image, which is actual and virtual at the same time.

We can hardly linger any longer over Kant's momentous "ceremonial" gesture of suspending knowledge to make room for belief—a move that can be fittingly described, with Deleuze, as "a 'spectacle,' a theatricalization or dramatization which is valid for all plots."[54] However, it is worth noting that this initial priming (followed by multiple variations, elaborations, probings, and twists and turns of the original vacuous theme) appears to describe both the logic of classical narrative (as elegantly demonstrated in Roland Barthes's *S/Z*) and that of the defamiliarizing, distancing, and distracting concept of modern art that suspends the moment of associative (re)cognition to allow a series of randomly ordered, free perceptual-formal reflections on this moment in the hope of getting a better or fuller perspective. Equally, the Kantian call to suspend and reflect on our mental habits can be named as a key inspiration behind the neo-Marxist "transcendental" social criticism pursued by Althusser, Bourdieu, and Foucault. Needless to say, Freud's Oedipal *horror vacui* and Lacan's mirror stage constitute further influential reenactments of the drama of subjectivation, which Freud conceives in terms of disavowal and fetishistic displacement. It is precisely this complex scenario of disavowal and fetishism that Christian Metz and Jean-Louis Baudry adopt as the model of cinematic spectatorship.[55]

Deleuze, too, draws a parallel between the practice of cinema that seeks "to bring *the unconscious mechanisms of thought* to consciousness"[56] and the fuzzy transcendental logic of Kant's thought experiment.[57] Similar to the Kantian transcendental critic, cinema "spreads 'an *experimental* night' or a white space over us; it works with 'dancing seeds' and a 'luminous dust'; it affects the visible with a fundamental disturbance, and the world with a *suspension*, which contradicts all natural perception [indeed, cinema promotes a *reflective* inner perception]. What it produces in this way is the genesis of an 'unknown body' which we have in the back of our heads, like the unthought in thought, the birth of the visible which is still hidden from view."[58] Not only has cinema succeeded in faithfully reproducing the general premises of a transcendental scenario, but it has also followed Kant's lead in releasing time, the ultimate medium and form of thought, from its subordination to apparent movement. For Deleuze, the direct time-image has always been present as a phantom that haunted the cinema as a suppressed possibility waiting to be articulated. This aberrant, centerless, and nonlocalizable movement of the mental mediation through and in time of the irreconcilably different (outside and inside, sensible and intelligible) is inherent to cinema. A similar story, Deleuze claims, can be traced in philosophy, in which "we have to wait for Kant to carry out the great reversal: aberrant movement became the most everyday kind, everydayness itself, and it is no longer time that depends on movement, but the opposite."[59]

Through these comparisons, Deleuze establishes what may seem to be an absurdly close connection between the Kantian reversal and time-image cinema. That such a connection is indeed what Deleuze has in mind is confirmed at the end of *Cinema 2: The Time-Image*, in which Deleuze calls the modern cinema of the time-image "'transcendental' in the sense Kant gives this word: time is out of joint and presents itself in the pure state."[60]

The Kantian Reversal

It has been argued that the Kantian reversal, also called *Kant's Copernican revolution*, is constituted by a change of perspective whereby human experience and knowledge are no longer considered as derived from an independent objective reality existing outside of the observer; rather, they are thought to be the product of an anticipatory objectifying consciousness, a coordinated interplay of purely formal and assumedly timeless, transcendental, synthetic a priori principles. These forms of intuition and combinatory operations are all endemic to subjectivity. Although they are inseparably tied to material sensation, these invariant subjective criteria of objectivity are thought to constitute the limit and ground of all possible experience. This, again, implies that reason (which, for Kant, is dual or dialectic in nature, being at once speculative and practical, naturally causally determined and free, or spontaneously active) places a block on the empirically knowable through its hardwired formative habits. Kant's dual reality consists of a humanly constructed, sensible, phenomenal (i.e., variable, changing) world and a noumenal realm of absolutely unknowable things in themselves.

The examination of "the mode of our knowledge of objects insofar as this mode of knowledge is to be possible *a priori*" is what Kant terms a transcendental inquiry. The seminal insight of Kant's transcendental philosophy is that subjective, but at the same time universal (not simply individual and particular, but general), formal conditions lie at the base of objective knowledge and self-consciousness, thus making them possible. As Adorno reminds us, *reflexivity* is introduced into modern thought here. In fact, for Adorno, Kant's Copernican revolution lies in the realization that reason can reflect on itself, and more important, that the realm of synthetic a priori principles is not only the object of direct investigation, but is, at the same time, involved in the process of reflection.[61] This Kantian insight implies that as a process thought cannot catch up with itself, and this necessitates an aesthetic lingering—"a moment of becoming at a standstill," in Adorno's parlance—for disinterested self-contemplation.[62] In Kant, thinking appears to be close to the cinematic experience described by Georges Duhamel and revisited by both Benjamin and Deleuze: "I can no longer think what I want, the moving images are substituted for my own thoughts."[63]

A basic tenet of the Kantian reversal is the stunning idea that objects perceived outside us are not objects in themselves, but rather, the outward projected, spatially and temporally articulated, phenomenal appearances of our intuitive and conceptual inner organization of sensory material of a totally unknowable (noumenal) objective cause. One cannot help but marvel at the uncannily cinematic passage in which Kant describes outer presentations as ones that "belong just as much merely to the thinking subject as do all other thoughts, except for having the delusive feature that, because they present objects in space, they detach themselves—as it were—from the soul and seem to hover outside it; and yet the space itself wherein they are intuited is nothing but a presentation whose counterpart cannot in the same quality be encountered outside the soul at all."[64] (Again, the mind's creation of phenomenal reality is uncannily reminiscent of cinematic projection.) Thus the outside is really our inside turned outside, complete, so to speak, with the abysmal gap in knowledge marked by the "boundary concept" of the noumenal, which concerns the sheer possibility of an outer intuition (that of space and the filling of space with shape and motion) in a thinking being as such.[65] Deleuze's reference to "an irrational proper to thought, a point of outside beyond the outside world" appears to echo this Kantian insight.[66]

Significantly, in Kant, the soul is conceived in empirical terms as a continual flux whose form is time, with "nothing enduring, except perhaps (if one insists) the *I*."[67] The ineffable inner movements of thought united by the "I" as transcendental unity of apperception, which project an outside world of extensive bodies and their relative motions in space, including the empirical subject, have among themselves no "relation of place, or motion or shape—or any determination of space at all."[68] (We seem to be roaming the realm of Bergson's two-faceted movement-image and Deleuze's nonlocalizable relation.) Kant goes on to illustrate the kinship and coherence of the relational whole of the transcendental and ideal, supersensible domain of thought through the analogy of the principle of conic sections traced by gravitational celestial motion. In his fascinating mental cartography, or rather topology, where relations are considered in themselves, Kant even includes hyperbolic paths. This, I would argue, lends his mind-model a non-Euclidean slant that is ahead of his time but in line with the spherical geometrical and hyperbolic trigonometric discoveries of his age.[69]

When Deleuze describes the new cinematic time-image of thought as topological, probabilistic, and irrational (as, e.g., in the films of Alain Resnais), he may well be evoking Kantian ideas of transcendental thought configurations. Also, the "Riemannian spaces in Bresson, in neo-realism, in the new wave, and the New York school"—"where the connecting of parts is not premeditated but can take place in many ways"[70]—appear to share the relative freedom of transcendental thought acts. It is, again, this involuntary mental spontaneity—experienced as a "resistance against incentives of sensibility" and a restriction of "all inclinations"[71]—that is reanimated through the unstoppable procession of moving images, to the dismay of Duhamel and to the excitement of Benjamin and Deleuze.

Given all this, when Deleuze credited Kant with the unhinging of time from its subordination to movement, he may have had in mind the important distinction Kant draws between the simultaneity in time of supersensible spontaneous thought acts and "motion taken as the describing of a space," which is the "pure act of successive synthesis, by productive imagination, of the manifold of outer intuition as such."[72] Deleuze's claim that Kant put time into the cogito may be read with Adorno as an acknowledgment that Kant "perceives, like no one before him, that time is a necessary condition of knowledge, and hence of every instance of allegedly timeless knowledge, and that it exists as a form of intuition."[73] Ultimately, Deleuze's dictum that Kant recognizes aberrant movement as "the most everyday kind, as everydayness itself"[74] may be construed as a reference to Kant's curious empirical–imaginary–ideal "I think," which is at the same time present and passing, being simultaneously an ideal, free, and spontaneous self-regulator and a naturally causally determined temporal process, a transcendental systematic unity (or *focus imaginarius*) of consciousness and a sensible thinking being.[75]

This fragile intermediary "I" or "I think" constitutes the keystone of the Kantian edifice and ultimately makes itself sensibly manifest through the disinterested pleasure, displeasure, and momentary self-loss of aesthetic reflection. Kant finds in the purely formal, ideal-imaginary unity of consciousness of the "I think," which is able to accompany both intuitions and concepts, the "third something" that makes possible "the thoroughgoing and necessary time determination—without which even empirical time determination would be impossible—of all existence *in* [the realm of] *appearance*."[76] Without the intricate temporal intermediacy and mediation of the "I think"—which is "nothing more than *our way* of presenting the existence of things (in appearance)"[77]—appearances would "refer to two different times wherein existence would be flowing by concurrently," which Kant claims "is absurd."[78]

Needless to say, in Kant's *reductio ad absurdum* (which is the ultimate, if perhaps undeclared, trajectory of transcendental reflection), anything labeled as "absurd" and "impossible"—and at times also the simply transcendentally distinct, as, for example, the relationship between reason and history—carries a special weight and will serve as key pointers for (post)modern thought.[79] In Deleuze and Bergson, this "absurd" splitting of time into two confluent, dissymmetrical jets (sequence and simultaneity) constitutes not only the "most fundamental operation of time"—a time that "has to split itself at each moment as present and past," a present that passes and a past that is preserved—but also the basic moment, or "smallest circuit": a simultaneously actual and virtual consciousness, which Deleuze, with Bergson, envisions as the "vanishing limit between the immediate past which is already no longer and the immediate future which is not yet ... [a] mobile mirror which endlessly reflects perception in recollection."[80] This vanishing limit is, of course, quite similar to Kant's lingering imaginary focus, appearing beyond the limit of experience as an object behind the mirror's plane.

Given all this, it comes as no surprise that Deleuze acknowledges Kant as the architect of the "I is another," the splitting of the subject by time that moves into it as a form of interiority. Due to the Kantian intervention, Deleuze claims, "the subject can henceforth represent its own spontaneity only as that of an Other," always deferred from its sensible self, divided and delayed by time.[81] The new Kantian subject combines a passive empirical self, constantly changing in time, and an active, spontaneous transcendental "I," which "carries out a synthesis of time, and of that which happens in time, by dividing up the present, the past and the future at every instant."[82] This redefinition of consciousness by the notion of time as a form of interiority—which Deleuze claims brings Kant much closer to Bergson than Bergson himself thinks—is highly paradoxical, given that time is not so much the interior in us, but rather, "the interiority in which we are, in which we move, live and change."[83] For Deleuze, Kant's consideration of time as the form of the inner sense carries the important implication that "our interiority constantly divides us from ourselves, splits us in two: a splitting in two which never runs its course, since time has no end."[84]

Ultimately, then, the Kantian reversal may be summed up by Kant's opening up of a third, transcendental reflexive dimension, through which the empirically grounded, sensible, and thus only phenomenally knowable subject is provided with an imaginary-ideal extension of its speculative power. Adorno likens this move, motivated by a logical necessity, to the mathematical invention of the concept of the imaginary number, which has no correlatives in the series of natural numbers but which performs an important conceptual function.[85] The Kantian transcendental sphere answers the need to trace the nonsensible but assumedly objective (universal and necessary) immanent forms and processes of thinking subjectivity that make possible, and which delimit, knowledge of the world and self as phenomena.[86] The imaginary focus and unity of this vague, intermediary, and mutually reflexive dialectical transcendental zone—which probes into and redefines the limits and bounds of object and subject, outside and inside, empirical and metaphysical—is the curious transcendental subject as "mere form of consciousness . . . that can accompany both kinds of presentations," but which in itself is neither an intuition nor a concept.[87] Nor is the transcendental "I" simply the same as the noumenal self, Slavoj Žižek claims, arguing that this subject of transcendental apperception is the gap or void between and beyond the opposition of phenomenal and noumenal.[88] Thus the transcendental "I" is a veritable boundary concept marking the irreducible discrepancy between a subjective formal finality and a rationally ungraspable, unfinalizable objectivity, or thingness within and without, rather than, as Kant might have wished, a bridge cementing the unity of his dual reason and reality.

Finding a proper formulation of this structuring disproportion and nonidentity of signification has been a key preoccupation of poststructuralism. Deleuze's cinematic conception of the time-image as an aesthetic practice stands as a reminder that the problem may be susceptible to elaboration in aesthetic terms. Seeking to trace the "'affection of self by self' as definition of time," Deleuze pays tribute to Kant's fascinating transcendental self-reflection expounded in the complementary aesthetic reflective judgments of the beautiful and the sublime.[89]

Learning to Like the Symptom: Aesthetic Reflection as Time-Image

Given that the synthetic act and unity of consciousness is neither an intuition nor a concept, but a transcendental imaginary medium or act of mediation that is compatible with both, it makes perfect sense that Kant seeks to express the essence of subjective formal purposiveness through a disinterested (neither sensibly nor morally cued) feeling of pleasure in the beautiful as well as through the complex emotion of a painful pleasure tied to "a momentary inhibition of the vital force" in the sublime.[90]

We may say that Kant's transcendental psychology is summed up by a "psychology of pure feelings," which, for Deleuze, is a leading concern of Alain Resnais's time-image cinema.[91] It is feelings, Deleuze tells us in a Kantian vein, that "plunge into the past," the past, that is, of invariant a priori pure forms of thought. Moreover, Deleuze argues that feelings are in a continual exchange and transformation and come loaded with a simultaneity of mental functions (e.g., recollection, imagination, planning, judgment—as well as disavowal, I might add). In the special case, when "transformations themselves form a sheet which crosses all the others"—when, in other words, they realize the thoroughgoing connection sought in the Kantian "I"—feelings are able "to set free the consciousness or thought with which they are loaded," revealing thought to itself.[92] This is exactly what Kant had envisioned in aesthetic reflective judgment, where feelings are sensations of a basic and thoroughgoing mental connectivity—the transcendental subject.

The feeling of pleasure that, for Kant, accompanies the beautiful is the marker of the subjective, self-given principle or maxim of all reflection (and judgment), which Kant optimistically (yet self-critically) defines as the possibility of the specification of nature by human cognition. This principle of compatibility between nature and mind, registered as pleasure in the beautiful, is made manifest by a free and indeterminate accord or free play between sensible intuition and the cognitive faculties, to wit, the power of presentation, which is the imagination, and the understanding, or the power of concepts. Aesthetic reflection foregrounds the spontaneity of the synthetic imagination, which, in this type of judging, is not restricted to the temporal schematism of appearances according to a given concept of the understanding, as happens in empirical determining judgment. Rather, in aesthetic reflective judgment, the imagination is allowed to schematize freely in an "unstudied, unintentional" manner.[93] Here judgment accords solely with the subjective principle of a formal harmony between intuition and concept, which is the precondition of empirical knowledge and which Kant has previously pinned to the psychological idea of the transcendental "I" as synthetic unity of consciousness. Thus aesthetic pleasure is the sensible signal of a supersensible idea, that of an intermediary, focal, yet in itself vacuous subjectivity.

The only causality of this contemplative, indefinite mental play of the beautiful (which constitutes a reflection on mental reflexivity itself) is, in Kant's words, to "*keep* [us in] the state of [having] the presentation itself, and [to keep] the cognitive powers engaged [in their occupation] without any further aim. We *linger* in our contemplation of the beautiful, because this contemplation reinforces and reproduces itself. This is analogous to (though not the same as) the way in which we linger over something charming that, as we present an object, repeatedly arouses our attention, [though here] the mind is passive."[94]

Resonances of this rich Kantian passage are easily detectible in Deleuze's Bergsonian meditations on recollection-images and their role in the formation of the crystalline image of time. Consider, for example, the affinity between Kant's distinction of empirical determining and transcendental reflective modes or uses of judgment, and Bergson's dichotomy of an automatic or habitual and an attentive mode of recognition. Bergson's automatic recognition, tied to a "first subjectivity," works by sensory-motor extension that retains from the thing only what interests it, very much in the fashion of Kant's schematically organized determining judgment, cued by the logic of effective causes and preassigned universals. In distinction, attentive recognition is coupled with a new sense of subjectivity, "which is no longer motor or material, but temporal and spiritual: that which is 'added' to matter, not what distends it; recollection-image, not movement-image."[95] This is compatible with the rationale of Kant's aesthetic reflection, the aim of which is to bring into play, and make palpable, the a priori added pure form of the transcendental "I," which, again, can accompany both intuitions and concepts, but which is neither of those.

Kant's analogy between the indefinitely extended mental lingering in aesthetic reflection and our lingering over "something charming that, as we present an object, repeatedly arouses our attention" corresponds neatly to Deleuze's summary of Bergson's attentive recognition, which "calls up" recollection-images produced by an "added" new subjectivity. In attentive recognition, my perceptive movements "revert to the object, return to the object, so as to emphasize certain contours," beginning over again "when we want to identify different features and contours."[96] The descriptive handling of the object in attentive recognition, which makes the object remain the same but pass through different mental planes, is eminently compatible with the nonconscious spontaneity of the imagination in aesthetic reflection that can reproduce an object's image by recalling "a vast number of objects of different kinds or even of one and the same kind."[97]

A related technique, with evident cinematic overtones, is the imagination's superimposition of a large number of images of the same kind to find their congruence. This unconscious process of projecting "one image onto another" (perhaps even "a thousand") constitutes an aesthetic standard idea by abstraction.[98] Little wonder that Deleuze considers the cinematic technique of superimposition—together with dissolves, complex camera movements, and special effects—as a reference to a "metaphysics of the imagination."[99] The complementary technique of restraint, montage cuts, and a perpetual unhinging is, in turn, a reminder of the break in imagination, the lack of intuition, which Kant envisions in the sublime.

It is equally noteworthy that the physical-geometrical, inorganic description constituted as the pure optical and sound image of a thing in attentive recognition evokes the singular reflective perception (in distinction to a sensible, organic reception), which, for Kant, may be triggered by the uniformly sequenced, regular temporal vibrations of the ether that give us color, as well as such vibrations of the air, which give rise to sound. The "signaletic" material of (what we register as) pure or simple colors and tones allows the mind to perceive reflectively "the regular play of the impressions (and hence the *form in the connection* of different presentations)."[100] In other words, in aesthetic reflection, we directly perceive the vibrations, modulations, and movements that for Bergson constitute true reality—that of a universal movement-image—and that, he thinks, ordinary human perception immobilizes. Such pure optical and sound situations, to use Deleuze's parlance, provide an impetus or a ready-made pattern-rich playground for the facilitated free, indefinite play of the two cognitive faculties that Kant considers to be the expression of the subjective unity in the relation required by cognition, that is, the transcendental subject. It appears, moreover, that the measured intermittence of the automatic movement of cinema reproduces the regular vibrations of "ether" and air (or pure optical and sound situations) that for Kant induce an inner reflective, rather than an outer sensuous, perception—a feeling, that is, of an inner form of time. Deleuze's insistence that the cinema is a "flickering brain" working with "dancing seeds" and a "luminous dust," which communicates *vibrations* to the cortex, touching the nervous and cerebral system *directly*,"[101] appears to answer to, and contest, Bergson's consideration of cinema as a model of ordinary human perception, which cannot represent the mobile nature of reality, but rather, cuts things out of their temporal and spatial continuity.[102] This is, I believe, Deleuze's explanation of how cinema "immediately gives us a movement image."[103]

Similar to the Kantian mental lingering in the contemplation of the beautiful—the heterogeneous yet mutually compatible terms of which continually reinforce and reproduce their free indefinite relationship—Bergson's pairing of an optical and sound image with a recollection-image brings into play two related terms, which differ in nature "and yet 'run after each other,' refer to each other, reflect each other, without being possible to say which is first, and tend *ultimately* to become confused by slipping into the same point of indiscernibility."[104] It is quite apparent that the two-sided crystalline description organized around a point of indiscernibility (or should we say, internally reflexive *focus imaginarius*) as its "smallest circuit," or internal limit, is modeled on the Kantian dynamic of free and indeterminate aesthetic play of the faculties, which is grasped and made to linger, almost as a freeze-frame, in its barely discernible duality and continuous reciprocity between "perception and recollection, the real and the imaginary, the physical and the mental."[105]

Incidentally, Deleuze's characterization of the indiscernibility of the crystalline image as an "objective illusion" again points us toward the Kantian concept of subreption: the fundamental, inevitable, yet productive fallacy of the dialectic mind, which has been given a "body" in cinema's imaginary signifier and fetishistic technique. As mentioned earlier, Metz conceives of the cinema's imaginary signifier in Freud's terms of fetishism, as an arrangement based on the "absence of the object, replaced by its reflection" (while rendering this absence forgotten *and* remembered as forgotten).[106] In this respect, the imaginary signifier is in every way consistent with the Kantian dynamic of transcendental apperception (or subjectivity), whose avowedly purely subjective yet surreptitiously (subreptively) universal and objective reflective perception is uncovered, so to speak, in aesthetic reflective judgment.

Reading Kant's aesthetic reflection as a blueprint for Deleuze's time-image may appear as a bold move. Consider, however, the following passage from the *First Critique*, in which Kant anticipates the free indeterminate aesthetic lingering in terms that befit a time-crystal situation:

> Suppose that the event is not preceded by anything that it must succeed according to a rule. Then all succession of perception would be determined solely by apprehension, i.e., merely subjectively; but this would not at all determine objectively which item in fact precedes in perception and which follows. We would in that way have only a play of presentations that would not refer to any object whatever; i.e., our perception would not at all distinguish one appearance from all others in terms of time relation. For the succession in apprehending is in that case everywhere the same, and hence there is in appearance nothing determining this succession so that a certain succession is, as objective, made necessary by it.[107]

The notion of an indefinitely, unboundedly apprehending imagination plays a central role in Kant's aesthetic reflection. An imagination unhindered in its apprehension by the natural law of association, but focalized directly through the subjective *principium vagum* of the synthetic unity of consciousness (as happens in the beautiful), seeks a completeness beyond experience. Therefore, as Jean-François Lyotard asserts, "the time of aesthetic lingering is also the pause of diachronic time: the sensation provided by the free play of the faculties institutes a manner of being for time that cannot involve an inner sense."[108] Kant's acknowledgment of this violation of the inner sense in aesthetic reflection (by canceling the condition of time and making simultaneity intuitable) comes in his discussion of the sublime, which often reads today as a critique, an avowal, and perhaps a flattening out of the intricacies of suspense and pleasure woven by the operations of disavowal that sustain the beautiful.

Nothing illustrates better the fragile equilibrium of the beautiful than the ease with which it shifts from a relative (imaginary) to an absolute (supersensible) focus, assuming the attributes of the sublime and marking, in the process, an empty space and an irreducible and irrevocable time of "absolutely no intuition" within the subject's self-reflection.[109] This may well be the core of the transcendental subject as a void or pure form (on a par with time) and ineffable medium, which brings together and plugs up the discontinuities, the incompossibility of sensible intuition and intelligible concept. Not only is the beautiful the pleasure of a hypothetical, dispossessed permanence—that of a transcendental apperception, for which, Kant says, we "feel the need"[110]—but it also involves a curious aesthetic reflective liking, but sensible dislike, for "counterpurposive," irregular, asymmetrical, "misshapen," and even grotesque forms.[111] Kant appears to be equivocating between his conception of the beautiful as "the purposiveness of objects in relation to the subject in accordance with the concept of nature" and a sublime described as "the purposiveness of the subject with regard to objects in terms of their form, or even their lack of form, in conformity with the concept of freedom."[112] Freedom, after all, is an attribute of the productive imagination in the beautiful, whose formal play creates "something that surpasses nature."[113] Equally puzzling is the discrepancy between Kant's consideration of the beautiful as the mind's "*restful* contemplation"[114] and his vivid description of a "quickened," agitated imagination aspiring to reach for a maximum and go "beyond the limits of experience."[115]

Obviously, beauty shares the sublime's "liking for the expansion of the imagination itself,"[116] which, I could add, is the essence of the transcendental method. Likewise, both poles of aesthetic reflection appear to have their share of the violence inflicted on the subject of nature by the imagination (and vice versa), whose effort "to take up into a single intuition the measure for magnitude requiring a significant time for apprehension" is subjectively counterpurposive, but nevertheless "purposive *for the whole vocation* of the mind."[117] The time of aesthetic lingering is, after all, that of a mind in suspension, one searching itself for (and as) a missing universal—a new speculative construct, perhaps. This might be a moment "when we cannot remember" and when "sensory-motor extension remains suspended," as Deleuze has it, for whom such instances of "disturbances of memory and . . . failures of recognition" constitute "the proper equivalent of the optical-sound image."[118] The Kantian lingering of reflective perception, feasting on and quickened by the vibrations of pure and simple color and sounds (found in free or "vague" beauty), might just be such a gap in memory, forgetting, and recalling as forgotten, a fork in time.

Such forks in and of time—which, for Deleuze, lend recollection-images an "authenticity, a weight of past without which they would remain conventional"—"are very often so imperceptible that they cannot be revealed until after their occurrence, to attentive memory."[119] It is quite conceivable that the momentary self-loss and painful pleasure of the sublime commemorate such a shockingly compounded temporal experience, one of becoming one with time as well as being in time, and one, moreover, that Deleuze and Guattari construe as the coexistence of the accident and the event.[120] In fact, Deleuze acknowledges the "open and changing totality" of time as the agency, the motor force behind the mental devastation of the sublime. Time, however, remains tied to an indirect (negative) presentation in the sublime[121] that intimates the spiritual-energetic flow of the supersensible force field captured in Bergson's generic movement-image. The time-image, however, gives us time as pure difference between indiscernible terms, assuring us that there is still mediation, that we are not brain-dead.

Ultimately, Kant's bipolar aesthetic reflection appears to form mutual images, in Bachelard's sense of the term. The beautiful and the sublime complement each other in making apparent an instance of indiscernible difference in inherently dual images, bearing witness to an interstitial dimension, a modicum of nonidentity in an otherwise self-enclosed human experience. In *The Time-Image*, Deleuze's interest is clearly invested in the beautiful, which he considers as the "fourth dimension," that of time, and more important, "time *regained*."[122] With this, Deleuze may wish to remind us that the imagination's ungraspable act of superimposing a multitude of images in aesthetic reflection is not only a process of abstraction, but also, and at the same time, the projection of dead times or meanwhiles, irrecoverable interstices, onto one another.

Deleuze seeks to revisit such lingering moments of absentmindedness—filled with extinction as much as recollection, with jump cuts as well as "free" association—in his new aesthetic of the time-image. Here we are looking for the breaks in continuity, the between of movements (actions, affections, perceptions, images, and sounds), rather than for a relative or an absolute whole. Instead of reflecting fantasmatic objects, Deleuze's cinema foregrounds its "flickerings [which] multiply the interstices like irrational cuts."[123] This cinema thrives on a method of spacing in which "each image is plucked from the void and falls back into it."[124] In a hopeless, exitless age, Deleuze turns to the practice of the interstice to rekindle belief, not in a different world, but in "a link between man and the world, in love or life" as the impossible and unthinkable,[125] in other words, in a transcendental, and transcendent, dimension immanent to thought. Deleuze puts his faith neither in the image nor in reality, but rather, in an ungraspable link, an irrational, indeed, transcendental ratio shown as endlessly vanishing through the imaginary focus of a cinema that saves time for us.

Envoi

"There are times," Deleuze and Guattari write, "when old age produces not eternal youth, but a sovereign freedom, a pure necessity in which one enjoys a moment of grace between life and death, and in which all the parts of the machine come together to send into the future a feature that cuts across all ages."[126] In philosophy, Kant's *Critique of Judgment* is such an "unrestrained work of old age, which his successors have still not caught up with: all the mind's faculties overcome their limits, the very limits that Kant had so carefully laid down in the works of his prime."[127]

Although Deleuze disclaims such a status, his *Cinema* books reflect his desire to catch up with and reassess the consequences of the Kantian speed. And he did more: in a moment of tiredness of waiting, he chose the choice of "sovereign freedom," the simultaneity of "before and after" between life and death. Through his performance of disavowal, and his leap of faith, Deleuze may have left a legacy of "something to incommunicate": the "'unthought,' life."[128]

Notes

I am grateful to Edward Branigan and D. N. Rodowick for their cogent and inspiring commentary and their patience. I also owe a debt to Janet Bergstrom's close reading of the text. My thanks, and love, to Nicholas, my ten-year-old son, for making room for Kant in our lives. Merci à Clothilde Buisine et à Bernard Garrofé pour leur amitié et leur amour du cinéma.

1   Immanuel Kant, preface to *Critique of Pure Reason*, trans. Werner S. Pluhar (Indianapolis, Ind.: Hackett, 1996), 7.
2   Immanuel Kant, *Critique of Practical Reason*, trans. Werner S. Pluhar (Indianapolis, Ind.: Hackett, 2002), I, I, I, §3, Comment I, 37.
3   Kant, *Critique of Pure Reason*, 7.
4   Ibid., 8.
5   Gilles Deleuze, *Kant's Critical Philosophy: The Doctrine of the Faculties*, trans. Hugh Tomlinson and Barbara Habberjam (Minneapolis: University of Minnesota Press, 1984), xiii.

6   Gilles Deleuze, *Cinema 1: The Movement-Image*, trans. Hugh Tomlinson and Barbara Habberjam (Minneapolis: University of Minnesota Press, 1986), 56. Theodor Adorno refers to this as Kant's effort to "salvage fundamental spiritual realities." See his *Kant's Critique of Pure Reason*, ed. Rolf Tiedemann, trans. Rodney Livingstone (Cambridge: Polity Press, 2001), 85.

7   Deleuze, *Movement-Image*, 56. Deleuze's "jump" in the history of thought becomes obvious if we remember that Kant's transcendental idealism was expressly designed to address the problem of duality, which caused what Deleuze calls "the historical crisis of psychology."

8   Jean-François Lyotard, "The Zone," in *Postmodern Fables*, trans. Georges Van Den Abeele (Minneapolis: University of Minnesota Press, 1997), 23.

9   Gilles Deleuze and Félix Guattari, *What Is Philosophy?*, trans. Hugh Tomlinson and Graham Burchell (New York: Columbia University Press, 1994), 108.

10   Kant, *Critique of Pure Reason*, A 424, B 452, 456.

11   Gilles Deleuze, *Cinema 2: The Time-Image*, trans. Hugh Tomlinson and Robert Galeta (Minneapolis: University of Minnesota Press, 1989), 210.

12   Kant, *Critique of Pure Reason*, B 452, 456.

13   Ibid., B 170, 205.

14   In brief, the Socratic method proceeded along a left-hand and a right-hand path, the former being a myth, the latter the dialectic examination of the myth, its breaking down into axioms and going beyond what is taken for granted. This is, in other words, a method of separation or reduction that leads to enlightenment. The "mock battle" that Kant institutes between the warring minds of reason is a reference to the Socratic method. See, e.g., *Critique of Pure Reason*, A 747/B 775, 693; A 777/B 805, 714. On the "strict division between fact and right," between the principles of *quid facto* and *quid juris*, see also Deleuze and Guattari, *What Is Philosophy?*, 37.

15   Kant, *Critique of Pure Reason*, A 778/B 806, 715.

16   Ibid., A 697, B 725, 658. On Kant's candid views concerning the unpredictable, "all-powerful forces of a nature working in a state of chaos," see Immanuel Kant, *Critique of Judgment*, trans. Werner S. Pluhar (Indianapolis, Ind.: Hackett, 1987), II, §82, 315–16.

17   Deleuze, *Time-Image*, 81, 196.

18   Kant, *Critique of Judgment*, II, §82, 316.

19   Kant describes "mother wit" as a "secret art residing in the depths of the human soul" that makes possible, through the transcendental time determination of schematism, the mutual commensurability of intuition and concept, aesthetic and logic, and thus judgment. Kant, *Critique of Pure Reason*, B 181, 214; A 133/B 172, 206; B 178/A 139, 211.

20   Ibid., B 452, 456.

21   Alain Badiou, *Deleuze: The Clamour of Being*, trans. Louise Burchill (Minneapolis: University of Minnesota Press, 1994), 10.1.

22   Gilles Deleuze, *Difference and Repetition*, trans. Paul Patton (New York: Columbia University Press, 1994), 35.

23   D. N. Rodowick, *Gilles Deleuze's Time Machine* (Durham, N.C.: Duke University Press, 1997), 83; my emphasis.

24   Deleuze, *Movement-Image*, 1.

25   Ibid.

26   Ibid., 2.

27   Deleuze, *Kant's Critique of Pure Reason*, 220.

28   Deleuze, *Time-Image*, 40.

29   Ibid., 40, 36, 41.

30   Deleuze, *Movement-Image*, 8.

31   Ibid., 2.

32   Rodowick, *Time Machine*, 22.

33   On Kant's notion of an ideal point of convergence, or *focus imaginarius*, of the "directional lines" of the understanding's concepts, see Kant, *Critique of Pure Reason*, A 645/B673, 619.

34   Deleuze, *Difference and Repetition*, 168.

35   Deleuze's description of a "transcendent exercise" in ibid., 144, constitutes a paraphrase of the Kantian rationale of aesthetic reflection, especially that of the sublime.

36   *Heautonomy* is Kant's neologism to denote the complex self-legislation of aesthetic reflective judgment, and reflection in general. See, e.g., "First Introduction to the *Critique of Judgment*," in Kant, *Critique of Judgment*, 414. Deleuze uses the term *heautonomous* to denote the mutually distinctive and reflexive relationship between visual and sound images in time-image cinema. See, e.g., Deleuze, *Time-Image*, 252.

37   Gilles Deleuze, *Masochism: An Interpretation of Coldness and Cruelty*, trans. Jean McNeil (New York: Georges Braziller, 1971), 99.

38   Deleuze, *Time-Image*, 42.

39   Slavoj Žižek calls this Kant's parallactic conception of the transcendental. See Slavoj Žižek, *The Parallax View* (Cambridge, Mass.: MIT Press, 2006), 25, 21.

40   Kant, *Critique of Pure Reason*, B 694/A 666, 636.

41   Deleuze, *Time-Image*, 31.

42   Ibid., 52. In *Critique of Pure Reason*, A 121, 168, Kant clearly invests the transcendental imagination here with a memory function, which can summon "up a perception from which the mind has passed to another [and brings it over] to the subsequent ones." Indeed, we find Kant, *Critique of Pure Reason*, A 649/B677, 623, ponder "whether imagination combined with consciousness is not [the same as] memory, ingenuity, discrimination, or perhaps even understanding or reason."

43   Elizabeth Rottenberg, *Inheriting the Future: Legacies of Kant, Freud, and Flaubert* (Stanford, Calif.: Stanford University Press, 2005), 41. Rottenberg's lucid discussion of the Kantian rationale of the "legacy"—which she calls "'the 'keystone' *(Schlußstein)* and the 'stumbling stone' *(Stein des Anstoßes)* of the whole system of pure reason" (p. 38)—offers a useful model for grasping the significance of Kant's suspension of knowledge to make room for faith.

44   Deleuze, *Time-Image*, 68.

45   Deleuze, *Kant's Critical Philosophy*, 24, 23.

46   Christian Metz, *The Imaginary Signifier*, trans. Celia Britton, Annwyl Williams, Ben Brewster, and Alfred Guzzetti (Bloomington: Indiana University Press, 1982), 51; my emphasis.

47   According to Kant, "we may call *fallacy of subreption* . . . the intellect's trick of slipping in a concept of sense as if it were the concept of an intellectual characteristic." See Kant, *Critique of Judgment*, I §27, 114. See also Kant, *Critique of Pure Reason*, A 643/B671, 618.

48   Kant, *Critique of Pure Reason*, A 644/B 672, 619.

49   See ibid., A 644/B 672—A 645/B 673, 619.

50   Deleuze, *Time-Image*, 201, 215.

51   Metz, *Imaginary Signifier*, 61, 45.

52   Deleuze, *Time-Image*, 166.

53   Deleuze, *Movement-Image*, 72.

54   Deleuze, *Time-Image*, 192, 191.

55   Metz's discussion of cinematic spectatorship in terms of disavowal and fetishism constitutes a sensitive—if phallocentric—rendering of Kant's "transcendental" dialectic. See, e.g., Metz, *Imaginary Signifier*, 69–78.

56   Deleuze, *Time-Image*, 160.

57   In fact, Deleuze's reference to the "unconscious mechanisms" of thought recalls Adorno, who equates these with Kant's transcendental sphere. Deleuze, *Kant's Critique of Pure Reason*, 207.

58   Deleuze, *Time-Image*, 201; my emphases.

59   Ibid., 39.

60   Ibid., 271.

61   Deleuze, *Kant's Critique of Pure Reason*, 32.

62   Theodor Adorno, *Aesthetic Theory*, ed. Gretel Adorno and Rolf Tiedemann, trans. Robert Hullot-Kentor (Minneapolis: University of Minnesota Press, 1997), 71.

63   Duhamel's adage is reproduced in Walter Benjamin, "The Work of Art in the Age of Mechanical Reproduction," in *Illuminations*, ed. Hannah Arendt, trans. Harry Zohn (New York: Schocken Books, 1968), 238, as well as in Deleuze, *Time-Image*, 166.

64   Kant, *Critique of Pure Reason*, A 386, 412. See also A 780/B 808, 716 as well as the famous conclusion of Kant, *Critique of Practical Reason*, II, 203.

65 See Kant's discussion of the gap in human knowledge, which we can never fill, in Kant, *Critique of Pure Reason*, A 393, 416.

66 Deleuze, *Time-Image*, 181.

67 Kant, *Critique of Pure Reason*, A 381, 409.

68 Ibid., A 386, 413.

69 For Kant's description of gravitational celestial motion in terms of conic sections, see ibid., A 662/B 690, 633. It is justified to call Kant's treatment of mental relations in themselves a topological study, given that topology is established—among others, by Leonhard Euler, Kant's contemporary and correspondent—as a field of study considering connectivity properties alone and in themselves. Kant's awareness of hyperbolic trigonometry can be traced back to his friendship with Johann Heinrich Lambert, who has received recognition not only for his introduction of hyperbolic functions into trigonometry, but also for his work on conic sections and light. Lambert has also been credited for coining the word *phenomenology*, which, for him, referred to the way that objects appear to the human mind.

70 Deleuze, *Time-Image*, 129.

71 Kant, *Critique of Practical Reason*, 103, 102.

72 Kant, *Critique of Pure Reason*, B 155n283, 193.

73 Deleuze, *Kant's Critique of Pure Reason*, 11.

74 Deleuze, *Time-Image*, 39.

75 Kant's description of the "dual personality of human beings" in *The Metaphysics of Morals* is quoted by Rottenberg, *Inheriting the Future*, 48.

76 Kant, *Critique of Pure Reason*, B 264/A 217, 282; my emphasis.

77 Ibid., A 648/B 676, 622; original emphasis on "projected"; A 186, 256; my emphasis on "our way."

78 Ibid., B 232, 258; my emphasis.

79 The stunning idea that "the general root of our cognitive power divides and thrusts forth two stems, one of which is *reason*"—the other being *history*—has no doubt given an impetus to Marxian and neo-Marxian forms of criticism of ideology and culture, including the output of the Frankfurt School, Althusser, Foucault, and Bourdieu. See ibid., A 835/B 863, A 836/B 864, 757–58. Adorno confirms my proposition that Kant, *Critique of Practical Reason*, 25, follows the reductive method in his search for invariant features of consciousness. Adorno also notes that the most interesting features of Kant's system are the ruptures, the antinomies, the expanded "stammering," which can almost be said to constitute his philosophy. See Deleuze, *Kant's Critique of Pure Reason*, 178.

80 Deleuze, *Time-Image*, 81.

81 Deleuze, *Difference and Repetition*, 58.

82 Deleuze, *Kant's Critical Philosophy*, viii.

83 Deleuze, *Time-Image*, 82.

84   Deleuze, *Kant's Critical Philosophy*, ix.

85   Deleuze, *Kant's Critique of Pure Reason*, 218.

86   Deleuze's, *Movement-Image*, 17, discussion of a fourth dimension, which is time, opening onto a fifth, which is Spirit, as well as the possibility of further new dimensions waiting to be uncovered chimes with Elizabeth Rottenberg's argument that the Kantian turn is constituted in "*a shift in the notion of possibility itself.*" Kant opens up a condition of possibility that is a passage between and beyond the theoretical and the practical. This passage is an empty (but not blank) space for future explorations. See Rottenberg, *Inheriting the Future*, 22, 23.

87   Kant, *Critique of Pure Reason*, A 379, 408.

88   Slavoj Žižek offers an intriguing analysis of the Kantian transcendental subject, claiming that freedom is the attribute of the transcendental "I," which cannot be identical with the noumenal "I," a "mere mechanism." See Žižek, *Parallax View*, 21–23.

89   Deleuze, *Time-Image*, 83.

90   Kant, *Critique of Judgment*, I, §14, 72.

91   Deleuze, *Time-Image*, 124.

92   Ibid., 125.

93   Kant, *Critique of Judgment*, I, §49, 186.

94   Ibid., I, §12, 68.

95   Deleuze, *Time-Image*, 47.

96   Ibid., 44.

97   Kant, *Critique of Judgment*, I, §17, 82.

98   Ibid., I, §17, 82.

99   Deleuze, *Time-Image*, 56.

100 Kant, *Critique of Judgment*, I, §14, 70–1; my emphasis.

101 Deleuze, *Time-Image*, 156; my emphases.

102 For a cogent summary of Bergson's notion of perception and his comparison of perception with cinematography, see Malcolm Turvey, "Epstein, Bergson, and Vision," in *European Film Theory*, ed. Temenuga Trifonova (New York: Routledge, 2008), 172–75.

103 Deleuze, *Movement-Image*, 2.

104 Deleuze, *Time-Image*, 46.

105 Ibid., 69.

106 Metz, *Imaginary Signifier*, 74.

107 Kant, *Critique of Pure Reason*, A 194, 264.

108 Jean-François Lyotard, *Lessons on the Analytic of the Sublime*, trans. Elizabeth Rottenberg (Stanford, Calif.: Stanford University Press, 1994), 64.

109 Kant, *Critique of Judgment*, I, §59, 226.

110 Kant, *Critique of Pure Reason*, A 195, 255.

111 Kant, "General Comment of the First Division," in *Critique of Judgment*, I, 92, 93. The significant overlap of the beautiful and the sublime has been

noted, e.g., by Lyotard, for whom the "sublime feeling can be thought of as an extreme case of the beautiful." See Lyotard, *Lessons on the Analytic of the Sublime*, 75.

112 Kant, introduction to *Critique of Judgment*, VII, 32. Note that for Kant, *Critique of Judgment*, I, §59, 230, "taste enables, as it were, to make the transition from sensible charm to a habitual moral interest without making too violent a leap."

113 Ibid., I, §49, 182.

114 Ibid., I, §24, 101.

115 Ibid., I, §49, 183.

116 Ibid., I, §25, 105.

117 Ibid., I, §27, 116.

118 Deleuze, *Time-Image*, 54, 55.

119 Ibid., 50.

120 See Deleuze and Guattari's, *What Is Philosophy?*, 158, discussion of the relationship of accident and event.

121 Deleuze, *Time-Image*, 239.

122 Deleuze, *Movement-Image*, 17; Deleuze, *Time-Image*, 97; my emphasis.

123 Deleuze, *Time-Image*, 215.

124 Ibid., 179.

125 Ibid., 170.

126 Deleuze and Guattari, *What Is Philosophy?*, 1–2.

127 Ibid., 2.

128 Deleuze, *Time-Image*, 189.

5. Darkness and Light

Dorothea Olkowski

Sitting before the computer screen, we gaze at the display of digital photographs, souvenirs of summer. A few of the images appear to have a sequential or serial character. I am trying to make you laugh, so I click, click, click, one image after the next. We throw them up on the screen, viewing them at first simultaneously, then one at a time, but quickly. Your shoulders jerk back and forth; the laughing mouth lights up the image then quickly evaporates as we move forward, then backward, forward and backward again, symmetrically, through the series, replacing one image with the next as quickly as possible. It is so awkward; still, we exclaim, "Look! It's like a movie!" Yet, it is not quite like a movie because the movement is too slow, too jerky. It is not true animation, not a continuous sequence of moving images. It remains a set of discrete images, images that influence one another, images that have their effect on us, but not quite like a film, whose continuity is made possible by the minutely differentiated, sequential attitudes of the frames that make it up: twenty-four immobile frames per second. Moreover, as we click through the photographs, one or another in the array stops us. "Ah," you proclaim, "that one is you." The slideshow stops abruptly; you survey the image, a pure contingency, and one that does not interest me at all. Thus, in the midst of our display of discrete moments and halfway attempts to produce continuity, something else emerges. As photographs, individually and devoid of attempts to re-constitute movement, a few, a very few of the discrete images *engage* either me or you; one or the other of us cannot stop looking. Later, you, too, stop the slideshow at one photograph in particular. It is the social, historical, and cultural *discontinuity* of this image that seems, at first, to be so jarring, so improbable. It is the image of the seemingly impossible coexistence of you and the vacant, decaying shell of the once unknowable and menacing Palace of the Republic, in front of which, on this day, crowds are gathered to watch the Brazilian and Italian women play beach volleyball on sand courts splayed out over the former parade grounds of the dark empire. Although this profusion is surprising, even to we who have posed for and taken this photograph, it is not this discontinuity, but only the lopsided stance of your torso, that arrests my attention. This is the detail, this is the personal attitude reflected in the image that captures me as I gaze at you, your eyes shielded by dark glasses.

But mostly, these are just pictures, reminders of a place; a day; the cloudy sky; the rebuilt, fallen capital. The unsuccessfully serial images of you or me from grimace to grin, from grin to grimace, are so discretely separated from one another that running through them in reverse order absolutely reveals their individual character. Our attempt to bring movement to these images from outside ultimately fails, and they do not seem to attract us, except as information, most lacking even the discontinuity implicit in the photograph where I stand, in colorful attire, with my hand clasping that of the giant Marx, who sits, placidly, next to an equally giant standing Engels. To make a movie, to produce the illusion of mobility, we need something else. We need thousands of frames that exist as immobile states, this frame and that; we need minutely sequential frames and much more movement.[1] This is possible with film, for which movement is *within the apparatus*. For traditional filmmaking, cinematographic movement consists in bringing together many sequential images, many successive attitudes to reconstitute mobility. Yet our experiment with stringing together discrete, photographic images leaves behind some uncertainties. What if we do not want merely to constitute movement from outside, by means of an external and awkward apparatus? What if we would like in some manner to exist in the midst of multiple combinations of images and influences, at the very interior of things, as you once existed in that dark world in the midst of coercion and uncertainty, threats and promises? If this is what we mean by "animation," not just the stringing together of a sequence of behaviors, then making use of the cinematographic apparatus, we will necessarily fall short; we will fail. The reasons for failure, however, are far from clear.

The filmmaking and film-projecting apparatus, it has been claimed, abstracts from visible figures some movement that is impersonal, abstract, simple. It has been characterized as movement in general, featureless movement, empty, silent, and dark, without the light that

emanates from your figure in the photograph, the light that *impels* me
to look, to see you, so familiar, yet a completely new and strange being,
a revelation. If we attempt to recombine this general, abstract movement, twenty-four frames per second, with the average and mundane
images among the still photographs, or even with the discontinuities or
the absolutely unique and remarkable individual attitudes, the results
are bizarre. In fact, do not the discrete photographs, because they will
never be able to be made into a film, do they not have an influence, an
impact, unknown in film? Is it possible that I will never see a film that
I love, a film that "*fills the sight by force*," that influences and recre-
ates my sensibilities as certain luminous photographic images do?[2]
How has this happened in spite of our good intentions, in spite of all
the attempts to make film real, to make it come alive? How has this
happened, not only for our ad hoc, amateur productions, but also for
the finest, high-production-value film showing at a theater near you?
How have we managed merely to juxtapose proximate realities, placing
ourselves outside the light that sears our eyes and goes to the heart of
things? How have we missed the reality of motion and, in its place, left
a string of abstract, uniform, invisible motions, a weak and pathetic
approximation of the existences we sought to capture, devoid of any
temporal articulations of their own? Is it possible that all our vision,
and even all our knowledge, is like this? That to know *anything*, we
place ourselves outside of it, and thereby lose it?[3]

Perhaps we have been led to believe that what is at issue here is the
distinction between continuity and discontinuity, and that all our attempts to bring mobility to discrete photographic images are centered
around the transformation of discontinuities into continuities. If so, then
we are misled. Discrete images are simply not able to be transformed
into continuous images. Even discontinuous images are unable to be
transformed into continuities. Let us begin with the latter, to follow the
implications of these statements. For mathematics, the relation between
continuity and discontinuity is asymmetrical. *Discontinuity* may be
defined as a discontinuous transformation of a continuous series. It
is a break, a gap, which implies the impossibility of remaining within
the existing system and the absolute necessity of escaping it. Moreover,
there is no going back; it is impossible to run the tape of discontinuity
forward, then backward. In this sense, a discontinuity is catastrophic,
not because it is destructive, but because, like the break between the
dark empire and the social and cultural mix that has irrupted out of
that break, it is final. Once a discontinuous transformation occurs, you

are elsewhere; you exist on another space-time trajectory, and another set of affects, percepts, procepts, and concepts constitutes your reality.

The cinematographic apparatus cannot string together discontinuities; this is an impossible act. What, then, does it do? We learn from Immanuel Kant that understanding and reason are limited with respect to what can be known. What can be known must be able to conform to the spatiotemporal manifold of our faculties. Beyond this lies a nearly unlimited realm, the realm of what can be done. It is no exaggeration to say that intellect is almost wholly interested in what can be done and in the results of its activities. This is the point of the *Critique of Practical Reason*.[4] Moreover, given its limitations, intellect is only able to represent its actions in terms of their ends and to represent ends as points of rest on a given manifold. Thus our actions are represented to ourselves as movement from one point of rest to another. Most important, "in order that our activity may leap from an *act* to an *act*, it is necessary that matter should pass from a *state* to a *state*," an unmovable, material surrounding, the frame of our acts.[5] And the frame of our acts is continuous.

The role of perception is to serve the intellect, to assist in carrying out actions. For intellect to succeed, prior to grasping any objects, perception must be simply the perception of qualities—color, sound, touch—each persisting in an immobile state until replaced by the next quality. Yet further analysis allows us to postulate that even the most immobile quality consists of trillions of oscillations, and that it is their repetition that leaves us with the sense of permanence. This is why perception condenses: "the primal function of perception is to grasp a series of elementary changes under the form of a quality or of a simple state, by a work of condensation."[6] Moreover, there must be continuity between those entities that oscillate impassively, with few oscillations, and those for which every perception is a gestaltlike consumption of trillions of such oscillations dedicated to action. Thus, for every gestalt, for every stable view, there are a trillion instabilities. And although every body is changing at every moment, and what is real is movement or change, perception nonetheless perceives form, a "snapshot view of transition," potential motion only, thereby solidifying into immobilities what is otherwise nothing but movement and change. Changes in situation reflect the profound changes accomplished within the whole, changes hidden in the shadows, hidden in the *penumbra*. In this aspect of our sensibility, we fail completely as narcissists. For most people, alcohol and entertaining distractions are evidence of the extreme discomfort and tedium we would suffer were we to attend to the complex relations of even our simple acts, with their myriad motions. Perhaps this is why we overlook the motions and imagine the meaning, which we suppose will be discoverable at the end point as the form of each act.[7]

Yet the limitations imposed by cinematographic movement and the knowledge we derive from it remain mired in confusion. Given the vast variety of interactions that are encompassed by change, given that, on a certain scale, all is change, a single account of becoming, a single, general abstraction, an abstraction posited from outside, can, at best, represent changes of state. Thus the Bergsonian argument perplexes us. How can it be that we may grasp *change itself*, myriad complex interactions, along with the successive states in which these complexities might potentially, at any moment, become immobilized? That is, what structure might allow us to grasp change from within, rather than from the outside, from inside and not from the situation of a dynamical system, a pure exteriority, a trajectory assembled from contingent affects, percepts, procepts, and concepts? The apprehension of change itself, in all its complexity, makes it possible to conceive of immobility in the same way that the apprehension of what is, what exists, makes it possible for us to conceive of "nothing" and the "void." "Nothing" is conceivable only as the annihilation of what is.[8] Immobility, this state or that, is similarly the imaginary annihilation of motion. But from outside, such states are taken to be real, individual states, no longer merely potentially immobile, but really or actually immobile, and all efforts on our part to reconstitute change out of real or actual states, which is to say, immobilities, lead to paradox.[9] Multiple expressions of the paradoxes of motion exist: the dichotomy, Achilles and the tortoise, the flying arrow, the stadium. It is likely that these paradoxes, attributed to Zeno, form a group addressing a multiplicity of questions: motion between given limits, limits of indeterminate and indifferent lengths, one single mover realizing a motion, a comparison of two movers in motion, the impossibility of relative motion as well as of absolute motion, the impossibility of motion in space or in time when either are conceived of as indivisible points, and that the first pair of arguments combats the idea of the indefinite divisibility of the continuous, while the second pair opposes indivisibility.[10]

For our purposes, let us work through just one paradox, that of the flying arrow, as emblematic of the problem at hand. Its argument is as follows: (1) anything occupying a place just its own size is at rest; (2) in the present, what is moving occupies a place just its own size; (3)

so, in the present, what is moving is at rest; (4) what is moving always moves in the present; (5) so what is moving is always—throughout its movement—at rest. In other words, "time" is composed of moments or instants; it is a series of *immobile* "nows." Stated in terms of space and motion, since the arrow is at rest at any given point, the arrow is motionless at each point, motionless during all the time it is moving.[11] The moving arrow is "never moving, but in some miraculous way the change of position has to occur between instants."[12] "Every attempt to reconstitute change out of states implies the absurd proposition, that movement is made of immobilities"; it forms the basis of the "cinematographic" mechanism of our ordinary knowledge, a mechanism that makes motion an illusion.[13] This is an old problem, one for which Bergson's concerns are illuminating. Can the arrow ever *be* in a point? Can a moving arrow *be* in a position that is motionless? Can we say anything more than that a moving arrow *might* stop at some point in its course, but if it did, would it not be at rest, and would there be any further movement? Is not a single movement just a movement between two stops? What happens in this paradox? What is the source of the illusion? Is it that "the movement, *once effected*, has laid along its course a motionless trajectory on which we can count as many immobilities as we will?"[14] If so, it is a count that can proceed to infinity. Are we to simply dismiss the moving arrow as the misconception of mathematical physics inappropriately applied to nature, or can some sense be made of this paradoxical model? Perhaps we have assumed too quickly that we understand the paradox when, in fact, we do not. Take, to begin with, the concept of a motionless trajectory: what, really, are we referring to? Although the paradox is ancient, modern mathematics continues to conceptualize it.

Mathematical idealization posits a geometrical model, called *state space*, for the set of *idealized* states of any phenomenon—thus our first possible misconception. According to the mathematicians, "the relationship between the actual states of the real organism and the points of the geometric model is a fiction maintained for the sake of discussion, theory, thought, and so on."[15] Within state space, changes in position can be represented by points that, when connected, form a curved line. Each point is an implicit record of the time at which an observation is made within the geometrical model. This is the definition of a *trajectory*. A time series may also be represented across multidimensional space, meaning a series of state spaces, with each one situated vertically at a unique designated time. Representations of trajectories in geometric state space or of the time series (called a graph) of the trajectory were already in use in the Middle Ages. The modern innovation, introduced by Newton, was the addition of velocity vectors, that is, the ability to calculate, using differential calculus, the average speed and direction of any change of state. Trajectories determine, calculate, and accurately predict velocity vectors, or the average speed and direction of a change of state. Velocity vectors may be *derived* at any point, that is, at any *time* along the curve. Inversely, velocity vectors can also determine, calculate, and accurately predict trajectories using the process of calculus known as integration. Thus, if every point in a given state space were to be mapped in this manner, the state space would be filled with trajectories. Over time, which is to say, at many different given points, points that are connected and represented as trajectories, each point will have the exact same velocity vector (the average speed and direction of any change of state) as the vector specified by the dynamical system. There will be no surprises. The system determines velocity vectors. Second, and equally important, the space that is being described here, the space of a dynamical system, is smooth space; it is continuous, without jumps, breaks, leaps, or corners, as trajectories are smoothly curved. Thus, if a dynamical model is called for to describe some observable behavior, the model will consist of a *manifold* or state space and a vector field; it is a model for the habitual tendencies of the situation as it *evolves* from one state to another. This charting of evolution is what makes the model dynamic. But insofar as the system yields qualitative predictions of long-term behavior, its evolution is deterministic. This is what makes it useful.

It is precisely trajectories and velocity vectors that are at stake in the acknowledgment that our ordinary knowledge has become cinematographic, and that cinematographic motion is an illusion. Bergson seeks precisely to limit this view of reality to its appropriate sphere, to separate it from other views of reality, views that take seriously the words *creative* and *evolution*, especially when they are characterized by an explosive evolutionary force, a *grand éclat*, which is not possible in continuous, smooth space, but rather requires, minimally, a discontinuous transition onto another manifold and, maximally, a discrete transition, which would be an emergent event, unpredictable and unknown. Nevertheless, Bergson's hesitations concerning the continuous, dynamical manifold have been criticized as "overhasty," and the idea of a creative explosion has been covered over by a vast, articulated "encounter" between movement, the physical reality in the external world, and the image, the so-called psychic reality in consciousness, between these two and the cinematographic image is a dynamical model of observable behavior.[16] Like the dynamical model, the cinema may be said to consist of a manifold and a vector field. It is a model for the habitual tendencies of the situation as it moves from one state to another. Yielding long-term predictions, it is useful for action. And although such dynamical systems have been contrasted again and again with the phenomenological view, they are utterly commensurate with the position expressed by Maurice Merleau-Ponty in "The Film and the New Psychology," for whom objects and lighting form a system—not through any operations of intelligence, but rather, through the configuration of the field that organizes itself in front of me. Henceforth, it has been declared, philosophy will be in harmony with cinema; thought and technical effort are said to be heading in the same direction.[17] Or, as this has been more recently expressed, a theory of the cinema is not about cinema, but about concepts, concepts that are every bit as practical, effective, or existent as cinema, and we are admonished that "there is always a time, midday-midnight, when we must no longer ask ourselves, 'What is cinema?' but 'What is philosophy?'"[18] Indeed, that is the question. What is philosophy? What is the relation between cinema and philosophy? Cinema and the real? Philosophy and the real?

Hoping only to entertain ourselves by gazing at some photographs, we have instead become mired in problems. But we might wish to attempt to sort through some of these questions so as to return to those photographs. If two such outwardly different philosophies as phenomenology and the philosophy of difference are in agreement that dynamical systems provide a model for cinema, and that cinema provides concepts for philosophy, then perhaps we need to pay a bit more attention to these systems. We said that dynamical systems consist of two principal ingredients: first, a manifold, that is, a playing field or space on which the motion of the system takes place; and second, a vector field, which is simply a set of rules that tell us where to go on this space from where we are now. If we follow the rules, beginning with the system's initial state and moving from space to space, from location to location, this route is our trajectory. Once the manifold, the initial state, and the rules are given, our trajectory is completely fixed. We will unquestionably reach the end point of the trajectory, called the *attractor*. So important is this end point that the behavior of dynamical systems is largely fixed by the number and character of the attractors, and so it is precisely with the attractors that dynamical systems become interesting, insofar as many attractors are unstable and allow for some unpredictability, even while deterministically following the established rules.[19] Everyone has seen films whose characters, plots, and ending are, if not absolutely predictable, nonetheless hardly surprising. *Romantic comedy, horror film, film noir, chick flick, action film,* even *art film* or *independent*: each of these terms seems to describe a well-known genre of film, many films of which ultimately offer few surprises. So many films move inexorably from a particular starting point, consisting of characters, plot, and visual and sound effects, to a particular end point (attractor)—the particular story line (trajectory) is little more than an effect of the starting point. In most cases, we are merely grateful that sequels are usually limited to two; otherwise, we would find ourselves trapped forever in a limit cycle, a cyclic orbit in which the same or similar characters and events are repeated over and over, the true formula for pornography. In every case, something is happening, but mostly, it is excruciatingly predictable and repetitive.[20]

In *Phenomenology of Perception*, Merleau-Ponty opposes this model for perception in his discussion of the phenomenal field. "For centuries," he argues, "perception appeared to be quasi-teleologically directed to an end; every instant could be coordinated with the previous and the following instants, and every perspective could likewise be coordinated with every other in an orgy of monadic and intersubjective experience constituted as a single unbroken text."[21] The continuous manifold of dynamical systems used to observe the body yields a notion of geometrical space indifferent to content—a pure movement, a setting of inert existence in which each event could be clearly related to physical conditions producing changes of location. It matters little if the object is never completely constituted, for the natural object is still an ideal unity. Moreover, the gestures, expressions, and acts of a subject had now to be resolved into a series of causal relations, thereby bringing experience "down" to the level of physical nature and converting the living body into an interiorless thing. Nor are emotional and practical attitudes of living beings spared. They, too, are able to be mixed into the vat of psychophysiological mechanisms, namely, elementary impressions of pleasure and pain bound up with nervous system processes. Intentions are converted into the objective movements of the nervous mechanism; sensory experience becomes a quality traceable from nerve endings to nervous centers, as the body is transformed into an object, a machine among machines, both one's own body and that of others.[22]

Merleau-Ponty is right to argue that this view of the world was already collapsing, even as he was writing *Phenomenology of Perception*, but only insofar as it was globally applied to all observable phenomena. Nature is geometrical only within a certain macrocosmic system. The experience of "chaos," he believes, changes everything.[23] In the face of this chaos, Merleau-Ponty demands a return to philosophy and to the philosophical *act* of returning, returning to a world in which *actual* experience precedes the objective world and somehow serves as its basis. Of course, if we stop with classical science, which, after all, begins with Newton and Leibniz, the deterministic causal world it describes does indeed appear to have long ago collapsed, or at least to have been circumscribed to a limited field of stable behaviors. That phenomenology, rushing in to fill the void, may appear to be an appropriate corrective. But what is it that Merleau-Ponty proposes in place of deterministic, dynamical systems, and is it any different than the corrective that mathematics itself proposes? Has phenomenology, along with certain other enormously influential contemporary philosophies (and here I am thinking of nothing else than the philosophy of Gilles Deleuze), been caught up in what can be called a *limit cycle*, an attractor that arises when the rules of the system cause a given trajectory to repeat itself cyclically, to pass through the same series of points forever? Is this the meaning of cinematographic movement? Is this the true consequence of what Bergson refers to as the view from outside?[24] Acknowledging that it would be difficult for life to emerge and survive in a structurally unstable world, where no situation and no pattern could be counted on to repeat itself with any regularity, mathematics also recognized that not all phenomena are structurally stable, nor are they continuous. Not only are dynamical systems open to contingent factors, but discontinuities abound. Moreover, from the perspective of some other structure, one that might be said to take its view from within, on microscales, nothing is continuous, nothing is stable; space and time are themselves discrete.

Let us begin with the simplest of these ideas: the idea that some things are not stable, even though they are continuous, a system that is accurately named *deterministic chaos*. Simply stated, "Newtonian determinism assures us that chaotic orbits exist and are unique, but they are nonetheless so complex that they are humanly indistinguishable from realizations of truly random processes."[25] Sufficiently complex dynamical systems require as much informational input as they can provide informational output; in other words, strictly speaking, nothing can be predicted if the input information has to be equivalent to the output information. Under these conditions, if the rules of combination do not alter, in this sense, determinism remains, but predictability is lost. In other words, there is rule-following behavior, but the elements entering into it appear to be contingent insofar as they cannot be predicted.

The cinematographic illusion relies on the failure to understand deterministic chaos as well as the failure to distinguish the continuity of dynamical systems from movement itself. A moving body that would remain the same throughout its motion returns us to the moving arrow, to motion as a series of continuous but separate positions successively occupied in a series of continuous but separate instants, a cinematographic illusion. The cinematographic illusion has less to do with the successive occupation by a moving body of every position (something cinema in no manner can achieve) than with the continuity of deliberate, successive snapshots that are virtual immobilities, frames in a given manifold. That movement cannot be accurately described as a system of relations external to an object in motion without leading to paradox in no way implies that movement cannot be described as a system of relations period. It is entirely a matter of scale. Most of the time, it appears that when we say movement, we mean continuity, so when implied continuity disappears for us, so does movement. Thus the discrete transition of an object from one room to another does not intuitively constitute movement for us because we assume that movement can only take place within a continuous system whose rules do not allow either discontinuous or discrete transitions. This, however, may be our error.

This intuition may be as mistaken for perception as it is for film. In film, the succession of scenes creates a new reality that is not merely the sum of its parts. In film, there is a certain order of shots, and a certain duration for each in that order, cinema being a system of measurements. Music, sound, and noise also contribute to the expressive force of this montage. Characters are created out of vocal and visual components, parts that add up to more than a whole, not simply through expository dialogue, but through tone of voice and the dramatic interactions between characters, scenes, lighting, and sounds, each of which consists of myriad components. In all this, it is the ensemble that produces the expression. Here, understanding serves imagination, and the idea that is the film emerges from its many component parts, parts that emerge into a whole, pushed forward by the rhythm, that is, the temporal structure of the film, the temporal and spatial arrangement of its elements. But by this means, cinema produces a world that is more exact, which is to say, more predictable than the real world, but a world like the real world, in which we do not have the thoughts of its inhabitants; rather, we have only the conduct or behavior, a world in which dizziness, pleasure, grief, love, and hate are ways of behaving, visible only from the outside.[26] In short, what is the difference between the phenomenological world and the Deleuzian acknowledgment that there are material flows, the expressed as mind and body, body and world, self and others, love and hate?

No doubt, between the phenomenology of the visible and the invisible and the philosophy of differenciation–differentiation, there is a greater gap than this comparison allows for, but insofar as this is the case, it is a gap that yields the structural similarities all the more compelling. In the philosophy of difference, "the model would be rather a state of things which would constantly change, a flowing-matter in which no point of anchorage nor center of reference would be assignable. . . . It would be necessary to show how, at any point, centers can be formed which would impose fixed, instantaneous views. It would therefore be a question of 'deducing' consciousness, natural *or* cinematographic perception."[27] Seen through the eyes of phenomenology, the new psychology does view the world from outside, through conduct and structures of behavior. Yet it does form centers by asking, again and again, what does the film *signify:* what does it mean? This incessant question is given the strange answer that "the film does not mean anything but itself"; the idea emerges from the structure of the film, from the temporal and spatial arrangement of elements.[28] Were Merleau-Ponty able to give up the power to tacitly decipher the world, there would be much less distinction between his position and that of his critic, who argues that the cinema lacks a center of anchorage and horizon, and thus nothing prevents it from moving away from perception, away from a centered state of affairs to an acentered state, suppressing the subject's anchorage along with the world's horizon.[29] What is at stake here begins with the new psychology. It begins when images could no longer be placed in consciousness and movement no longer separated in the world; the qualitative and intensive world opposed to the quantitative and intensive, overcoming the duality of image and movement, consciousness and thing. Or, as Merleau-Ponty articulates this, movement does not presuppose a moving *object*, a collection of determinate properties; it is merely something that moves. And, if not an object, then why not simply *something*, something colored, something luminous, something in between the object that moves and pure movement. This color, this luminosity, is the excluded middle. Between the propositions that there is an object that moves and that there is not an object that moves, there is something, rather than nothing, but something excluded by binary logic. Yet, in the same breath, he takes this back. If motion must either have or not have a moving body, then let us not dare to deny the logic of the excluded middle, and let us posit a prelogical, preobjective world that foregoes the unity of a Kantian actor but nevertheless unifies.[30] And so we have not an alternative ontology, but rather, the classical dynamical system in relation to which philosophy both cowers and preens as its preobjective condition or its emancipated but deterministic chaos. Phenomenology will not make the leap into non-sense and contradiction, but this is the very foundation of the philosophy of difference, whose Kantian subject knows nothing but does all or is done to by the infinity of affects, percepts, procepts, and concepts. However, this philosophy, too, will not take the risk of the excluded middle. Its encounter with non-sense and contradiction is merely the encounter or the incitement sending the acentered, fragmented subject into the flux of deterministic chaos—the dynamical system or the plane of immanence, whose contingencies are infinite but whose *rules are fixed.* So have we articulated something new if we claim that matter and movement are identical, but in a manner that foregoes temporalization and makes of every matter-movement a "bloc of space-time," part of an infinite series of such blocs corresponding to the succession of movements in the universe, the universe transformed now into an infinity of cinematographic movements, where in place of movement, there are states, bodies (both subjects and objects), and action, everywhere action, in all possible directions and dimensions, always tearing apart whatever has connected itself, whatever habits have formed, then conjoining these fragments into a shattered universe on a single plane of immanence.[31] For these ontologies, as for Kepler and Galileo, time has no natural articulations; we can and ought to divide it as we please. If no moment has the right to set itself up as a privileged or essential moment, the one that represents all the others and is retained in memory as the essential moment, then like the succession of film frames, time isolates any moment whatsoever, putting them all in the same rank. As in film, the successive states of the world could be spread out all at once, without having to alter the ontological conception.[32]

We can still speak about time as units of time because for modern science, as for cinematographic knowledge, time is an independent variable, a parameter of the spatial manifold useful for calculating the positions of real elements of matter at any moment whatsoever if their current positions are given. Time is then a "mobile T on its trajectory ... [so that] to consider the state of the universe at the end of a certain time t, is to examine where it will be when T is at the point T_t [to the power of t], of its course."[33] From this point of view, events do not happen; rather, events are already mapped on the trajectory. We simply encounter them along our way; the emergence of events, spatialization, and temporalization would be an illusion. Events are then nothing more than snapshots—successive images, indifferent, insofar as the partitioning of space and time must be given equal rank. Thus their succession is the illumination of points on a line given all at once.[34] But alternatives can and have been offered. Unlike the snapshot, a successive image in a determined trajectory, as a virtual immobility, the photograph is an effect of an "uncertain art," a science of desirable or detestable bodies that *animate* the spectator by means of discontinuous elements and discrete effects. If film photography is the invention of chemists, then digital imaging is the invention of physicists. What does not alter is the role of light. The photographed body is expressed by the action of light; its luminescence touches the viewer with its own rays, so that the photograph is a literal emanation of light. Light-sensitive silver halogens make it possible to recover and print the luminous rays emitted by a lighted object. Image sensors sample light coming through the lens, converting it into electrical signals. Its grid of electrodes, exploiting the photoelectric effect, release electrons when exposed to light—the light that emanates from objects. Voltages are measured, amplified, converted, stored, but sensitivity to light ensures that the photographed body touches you with its own rays.[35]

In a dynamical system, every trajectory is defined by laws that specify the movement and interaction of particles. The rules are given; what may be contingent are the particular particles themselves, that is, particles entering into a given trajectory. Which affects? Which percepts? Which concepts? Which prospects? This cannot be predicted, and thus every configuration of particles produces a different world. But what does not alter are the rules themselves, rules that specify the movement and interaction of particles. Moreover, in these systems, space and time are given, not emergent—they are the preexistent manifold. And time is a fourth dimension, a means for differentiating different spaces, but it is not a temporalization. But what if it were possible to theorize a world in which different observers "see" partly different, partial views of the universe, partial views that nonetheless overlap? Would this imply a dependence on the location of the observer, on the observer's unique duration, not the flow that constitutes her, but the information that constructs her perspective—her spatio-*temporalization*? Recall the image of a cone, so intimately identified with Henri Bergson's concept of ontological memory, that memory created by the imperceptible influences of events in the world on a vulnerable sensibility. Under the sign of this cone, in a system that affirms relativity, the entire past coexists with each new present in relation to which it now past. "Memory, laden with the whole of the past, responds to the appeal of the present state by two simultaneous movements, one of translation, by which it moves in its entirety to meet experience, thus contracting more or less, though without dividing, with a view to action; and the other of rotation upon itself by which it turns toward the situation of the moment."[36]

All this occurs as if these memories were repeated a vast but not infinite number of times in the many possible contractions of any past life, but always altering, altering in each so-called repetition under the influence of intersecting networks of events. These *different planes* are myriad in number, but not infinite. They stand in relations of simplicity and contiguity, influencing one another and influencing the present for the sake of action or *restraint*. For any present, for any perspective emerging from this past, there is the influence of the many layers of the past and of many interactions, networks of interacting events. How similar this is to what theoretical physics calls *the past light cone of an event*. "The causal past of an event consists of all the events that could have influenced it. The influence must travel from some event in the past at the speed of light or less. So the light rays arriving at an event form the outer boundary of the past of an event and make up what we call the *past light cone of an event*."[37] But what if, rather than a single cone, every perspective and every event consists of a multiplicity (not an infinity) of cones linked to one another, "combinatorial structures" that have been called "spin networks," networks giving rise to self-organized, critical behavior? Keep in mind that the causal structure of events evolves, and the motion of matter is a consequence of evolution. This brings forth the following conjecture. What if smooth or continuous space-time are useful illusions, and what if, from the perspective of a different system, the world can be said to be composed of discrete events, events on a very small scale, but nevertheless, events that are discrete with respect to both space and time on that very small scale? Under such conditions, what would be observed, what would be discerned? "The photograph does not call up the past," it does not restore the past, it is not a memory, not a reconstitution; it is at once past and real.[38] It is a spatiotemporalization that fascinates me, that attracts me, that makes me the reference, that generates my astonishment. It evokes not only the question, why is it that I am alive here and now to see, to sense this light radiating from your body to mine? but also, what is this world, this universe, that intertwines its events, that spatiotemporalizes itself, radiant and diffusive in myriad directions, making it possible, one again, for beauty to emerge?

The continuum of differenciation–differentiation is the field of pure immanence. As a system, its primary processes are not the same as those under consideration here. These processes involve the construction of a vulnerable duration, a sensitive contingency, an ontological spatiotemporalization, an ever-changing perspective in the heterogeneity of space and time. Such a perspective, if it is thinkable, if it is real, could manifest itself as a sort of history—not a linear, causal chain, but a complex causality, layers and layers of events, always susceptible to realignment, to patterns and particles resolving their scintillation and constructing an ontological memory below the speed of light. These primary processes, imperceptible, ephemeral, evanescent, influence one another, and in this, they influence the sensibility of human beings. This is not perception, for it does not yet imply typical perceptual prerequisites, thoughtlike mental processes such as description, inference, and problem solving, no matter how unconscious or nonverbal.[39] Nor is it a preperceptual hovering at the edges of dynamical systems, mysteriously tied to their logic, the logic of excluded middle. Rather, given that this is something much more difficult to situate, it is much more likely to be overlooked. It is the manner in which states (including very tiny states) influence and alter one another and so influence and alter human sensibility, all sensibility. These influences are not the objects of perception nor of consciousness; they cannot be experienced as increases or decreases of power, as the raising or lowering of intensities. They are, in some sense, receptive and primary. If they are noticed at all, it is insofar as they are *felt*: felt as pleasure, felt as pain, as expansion and dissolve, as distress. Their influence on sensibility comes via the sensory system, but as ontological, not personal, memory. It is manifest in the exceptional absorption and emission of each event-organism—purely contingent, subject to alteration, but circumscribing what is characteristic of each sensibility as an original spatiotemporalization. So it is the way you emerge in the photograph, in the midst of multiple combinations of images and influences, at the very interior of things, as you once existed in that dark world in the midst of coercion and uncertainty, threats and promises. It is an absolute, immediate, nonconscious consciousness, an ontological unconscious whose existence no longer refers to an individual or to a being, but is unceasingly suggested in the reflection, refraction, and dispersion of light.

Notes

1 See Henri Bergson, *Creative Evolution*, trans. Arthur Mitchell (New York: University Press of America, 1983), 304–6, where Bergson argues that for photographs to be animated, there must be movement.
2 Roland Barthes, *Camera Lucida*, trans. Richard Howard (New York: Hill and Wang, 1981), 91. Perhaps Barthes is mistaken that photographers are "agents of death"; instead, they may be agents of life, the life of the spectator (cf. p. 92).
3 "Instead of attaching ourselves to the inner becoming of things, we place ourselves outside them in order to recompose their becoming artificially"; and "All moments count.... Consequently we know a change only when we are able to determine what it is about at any one of its moments." Bergson, *Creative Evolution*, 306, 332.
4 This is the subject of chapter 2 of my book *The Universal (in the Realm of the Sensible)* (New York: Edinburgh University Press/Columbia University Press, 2007). See also Bergson, *Creative Evolution*, 299.
5 Bergson, *Creative Evolution*, 308. Bergson's analysis of action implies the Kantian one but does not refer to it.
6 Ibid., 300–1. This is precisely what Merleau-Ponty will protest.
7 "Perception of movement can be perception *of movement* and recognition of it as such, only if it is apprehension of it with its significance as movement, and with all the instants which constitute it and in particular with the identity of the object in motion." Maurice Merleau-Ponty, *Phenomenology of Perception*, trans. Colin Smith, rev. Forrest Williams and David Guerrière (London: Routledge, 1989), 271.
8 Bergson, *Creative Evolution*, 308, 279, 283. Moreover, the nothing is implicated in desire or will because it involves a comparison between what is and what could or *ought* to be.
9 Ibid., 308.
10 Paraphrased from Patricia Glazebrook, "Zeno against Mathematical Physics," *Journal of the History of Ideas* 62 (April 2001): 205. Reproduced in H. D. P. Lee, *Zeno of Elea: A Text, with Translation and Notes*, trans. Patricia Glazebrook (Amsterdam: A. M. Hakkert, 1967), 103.
11 Bergson, *Creative Evolution*, 307. Also see Glazebrook, "Zeno against Mathematical Physics," 201. I have substituted the concept "discontinuous"

for Glazebrook's "discrete" insofar as discrete space and time are quantum concepts, an entirely different structure from that of continuous or discontinuous space and time. Glazebrook argues that Zeno meant these paradoxes to be an indictment of mathematical physics. She cites G. S. Kirk, J. E. Raven, and M. Schofield, *The Presocratic Philosophers* (Cambridge: Cambridge University Press, 1983), 273, for this version of the arrow.

12   Bertrand Russell, "The Problem of Infinity Considered Historically," in *Our Knowledge of the External World* (London, 1914), 175–78, 179. Russell is cited in Glazebrook, "Zeno against Mathematical Physics," 202. Glazebrook also refers to Bergson, but I have not utilized her reading as I am seeking greater precision.

13   Bergson, *Creative Evolution*, 308.

14   Ibid., 309.

15   Ralph H. Abraham and Christopher D. Shaw, *Dynamics—the Geometry of Behavior, Part I: Periodic Behavior* (Santa Cruz, Calif.: Aerial Press, 1984), 13, 19–20, 21.

16   Gilles Deleuze, Preface to the French edition of *Cinema 1: The Movement-Image*, trans. Hugh Tomlinson and Barbara Habberjam (Minneapolis: University of Minnesota Press, 1986), xiv.

17   Maurice Merleau-Ponty, "The Film and the New Psychology," in *Sense and Non-sense*, trans. Hubert Dreyfus and Patricia Allen Dreyfus (Evanston, Ill.: Northwestern University Press, 1964), 51, 59.

18   Gilles Deleuze, *Cinema 2: The Time-Image*, trans. Hugh Tomlinson and Robert Galeta (Minneapolis: University of Minnesota Press, 1989), 280.

19   These are John Casti's wonderful explanations, not mine. I hope I have not misrepresented these ideas, fueling the fires of Alan Sokal and other muckrakers. See John Casti, *Complexification, Explaining a Paradoxical World through the Science of Surprise* (New York: HarperCollins, 1994), 26–28.

20   Ibid., 28–32. See Linda Williams, *Hard Core: Power, Pleasure, and the "Frenzy" of the Visible* (Berkeley: University of California Press, 1989), for an account of the dynamics of pornography.

21   Merleau-Ponty, *Phenomenology of Perception*, 54.

22   Ibid., 54–55. Merleau-Ponty's adaptation of behaviorism has generally been evaded by the contemporary philosophical community.

23   Ibid., 56. One wonders how well or what Merleau-Ponty understood by the term *chaos*.

24   Casti, *Complexification*, 28. Although there are numerous extrinsic and intrinsic differences between the phenomenology of perception and Deleuze's philosophy of difference, nonetheless, in relation to cinema, they are each drawn by the same attractor.

25   Joseph Ford, "What Is Chaos, That We Should Be Mindful of It?," in *The New Physics*, ed. Paul Davis (Cambridge: Cambridge University Press, 1989), 350–51.

26 Merleau-Ponty, "Film and the New Psychology," 51, 59. These remarks are an amalgamation of the analysis given by Merleau-Ponty on these pages.

27 Deleuze, *Movement-Image*, 57–58. Deleuze says of both Merleau-Ponty and Bergson that for each, cinema is an ambiguous ally. While this is clearly the case for Bergson, this is not commensurate with Merleau-Ponty's own claims.

28 Merleau-Ponty, "Film and the New Psychology," 57, 58.

29 Deleuze, *Movement-Image*, 57. Deleuze still assumes the intentional consciousness of Husserl, but the tacit cogito produces a similar, if less constrained, effect.

30 Merleau-Ponty, *Phenomenology of Perception*, 274. Merleau-Ponty comes right to the edge of insight but backs off. His faith in meaning is problematic.

31 Deleuze, *Movement-Image*, 59. The extent to which Bergson's analysis of modern science is simply not acknowledged by this view is startling.

32 Bergson, *Creative Evolution*, 332, 339. Thus the concept of the frame as "any moment what ever."

33 Ibid., 335–37. Thus modern science is, as Bergson says, the child of astronomy, a matter of knowing the respective positions of the planets at a given moment and knowing how to calculate their positions at another moment.

34 Henri Bergson, *Duration and Simultaneity*, trans. Leon Jacobson (New York: Bobbs-Merrill, 1965), 148–49.

35 The digital process does not alter this. In place of film, an image sensor samples the light coming through the lens and converts it into electrical signals, boosted by an amplifier and sent to an analog-to-digital converter that changes the signal to digits. A computer processes the digits to produce the final image data, which are stored on a memory card. Ben Long, "Framed and Exposed: Making Sense of Camera Sensors," August 25, 2004, http://www.creativepro.com/article/framed-and-exposed-making-sense-of-camera-sensors.

36 Henri Bergson, *Matter and Memory*, trans. N. M. Paul and W. S. Palmer (New York: Zone Books, 1988), 168–69. Contraction and rotation refer to the translation of motion from one inertial frame of reference to another, in accordance with the theory of special relativity, in which motion is relative to an inertial point of view. I have attempted to render the operations of affectivity and ontological memory in all their complexity in my *Gilles Deleuze and the Ruin of Representation* (Berkeley: University of California Press, 1999), 109–15.

37 Lee Smolin, *Three Roads to Quantum Gravity* (New York: Basic Books, 2001), 58–65. I owe much here to Smolin's simplified explanations of quantum gravity as well as to discussions with Marek Grabowski, who guided me through the more complicated mathematical aspects of these

concepts. Misinterpretations of these concepts are entirely my own doing. I have tried to stretch these concepts without distorting them. This can be difficult because, in mathematics, context is everything, and implications beyond very precise contexts can easily be disputed. These final pages are adapted from Olkowski, *The Universal*, chap. 1.

38 Barthes, *Camera Lucida*, 82. Barthes calls the photograph a resurrection, but I am unwilling to make use of such an overdetermined term.

39 See, e.g., Irvin Rock, "The Intelligence of Perception," in *Perception* (New York: Scientific American Library, 1984), 234–35. Rock differentiates between experience and perception (rightly so) and even proposes that perception may precede conscious reasoning in evolution, making thought a modification of perception.

Part II. Ethics

6. The World, Time

D. N. Rodowick

At the beginning of the epilogue to his *Theory of Film*, Siegfried Kracauer asks, "What is the good of film experience?"[1] The phrasing of the question clarifies what it means to bring ethics and cinema together as a philosophical problem. Kracauer does not want to know if a particular film or filmmaker is "ethical," nor is the question the basis for making moral judgments of artworks and their makers. His asks, rather, how do we evaluate our *experience* of the movies, meaning, in what ways do the movies offer themselves as a medium for an interrogation of ourselves, of our relationship to the world, and to other beings? In other words, how do movies solicit and sustain the possibility of ethical thought?

Aesthetics and ethics do not make an obvious pairing, much less film and moral reasoning. In 1960, Kracauer was among the first to offer an explicitly ethical question to film theory. In so doing, he placed the study of film along some of the most ancient lines of philosophical reasoning. From at least the fifth century B.C., the activity of philosophy has been characterized by two fundamental questions: how do I know, and how shall I live? The latter is the most self-evidently ethical question. Yet how can the quality of one's thought be separated from the choice of a mode of existence? Both questions demand a reflexive examination of self, in its possibility of knowing itself and others and in its openness to change or not. What links philosophy today to its most ancient origins are the intertwining projects of evaluating our styles of knowing, and examining our modes of existence and their possibilities of transformation. In this way, an ethics is distinct from the usual sense of morality. Morals refer ordinarily to a transcendental system of values to which we conform, or against which we are found lacking. An ethics is an immanent set of reasoned choices. In ethical expression, we evaluate our current mode of existence, seeking to expand, change, or abandon it in the effort to achieve another way of living and another form of community. Inspiring an individual to choose a mode of existence embodied in a community, real or imagined, philosophy thus entails the expression and justification of this existential choice and its representation of the world. Therefore *philosophein* is, simultaneously, expression and existential choice—the medium and idiom of a life.

Gilles Deleuze never devoted a book exclusively to ethics. Yet the two philosophers with whom he felt the closest allegiances, Baruch Spinoza and Friedrich Nietzsche, are importantly connected to the history of moral reasoning, and his books and repeated references to these philosophers mark his frequent examination of ethical questions. Deleuze's most provocative comments on ethics, however, appear late in his work, specifically in the two books on cinema, *Cinema 1: The Movement-Image* and *Cinema 2: The Time-Image.*[2]

Here an interesting question detours our path. Why is film so important as the companion or exemplification for ethical self-examination? Indeed, the idea that art should inspire ethical inquiry marks the greatest distance between ourselves and the philosopher-citizens of Periclean Athens. At the same time, it is also one of the clearest signposts of philosophical modernity. In twentieth-century philosophy, especially in its Anglo-American and analytic incarnations, ethics has taken a back seat; indeed, it has been sent to the back of the bus by the more strident emphasis on logic and epistemology—an attitude forcefully summarized in Quine's insistence that the philosophy of science is philosophy enough.

The turn to film as an important site of ethical interrogation is thus doubly curious. And if there is something that can be called "film philosophy" today, moral reasoning persists as one of its most powerful, defining activities. Undoubtedly, this is due to the influence of Stanley Cavell as the contemporary philosopher most centrally concerned with the problem of ethics in film and philosophy, above all through his characterization of an Emersonian moral perfectionism. However, in Cavell's Emersonian ethics, there are also curious and powerful echoes with Gilles Deleuze's Nietzschean and Bergsonian perspectives on cinema, wherein concepts of movement and time are related as the expression of belief in the world and its powers of transformation. This may appear to be an odd couple. But I am haunted by the idea of a dialogue, as if in a real conversation, but between partners who seem only dimly aware of one another, where Deleuze's cinema books, published in 1983 and 1985, respond to Cavell's *The World Viewed* (1971) and *Pursuits of Happiness* (1981), and where *Contesting Tears* (1996) and *Cities of Words* (2004) echo some of the most provocative thinking in *The Movement-Image* and *The Time-Image*.

Both space and time are lacking here to develop all the implications of this missed philosophical friendship.[3] It is worth noting, though, that one important bridge between Deleuze and Cavell's thought on cinema and moral reasoning is their mutual interest in Nietzsche. Another is their original way of asking ethical questions in ontological contexts. Though Cavell uses the word frequently, and Deleuze rarely, both evaluate ontology as a particular approach to Being. This is not the being or identity of film or what identifies film as art, but rather, the ways of being that art provokes in us—or more deeply, how film and other forms of art express for us or return to us our past, current, and future states of being. Also, in both philosophers, the ethical relation is inseparable from our relationship to thought. For how we think, and whether we sustain a relation to thought, are bound up with our choices of a mode of existence and our relations with others and to the world.

There is also an important contrast with Cavell. Part of the difficulty of Deleuze's thought has to do with his choice to ignore or circumvent the dilemmas of skepticism and its characterizations of the self in relation to being, the world, and others. These are central features of the philosophical culture most familiar to us, and it is disarming to consider seriously a thinker for whom the great difficulties of relating subject and object seem to have been completely dispelled or overcome. Indeed, throughout his career, Deleuze turned consistently to philosophers for whom the division of the thinking subject from the world was ontologically irrelevant, hence his recovery of a path alternative to Descartes, leading from Spinoza and Nietzsche to Henri Bergson.

In Deleuze, the fundamental ethical choice is to believe in this world and its powers of transformation. How does his avoidance or circumvention of the history of skepticism and Cartesian rationalism inform this question? Although Deleuze was not known for his love of philosophical systems, Alberto Gualandi has astutely recognized his commitment to two principles, which may be considered the basis of his ethics as well as his more general philosophy. The first is Spinoza's "pure ontology," or doctrine of the *univocity of Being*. For Spinoza, there is no division between humanity and nature, but only one absolute and unique substance for all that exists—all attributes and identities are only different manners of being for this substance, or different modalities of its expressiveness. As Gualandi explains, "the principle of univocal Being affirms the absolute *immanence* of thought in the world as it exists, as well as the categorical refusal of any form of thought *transcending* the Being of things in whatever form of the supersensible. For Deleuze as well as Spinoza, the intuition of the univocity of being is the highest intellectual expression of love for all that exists."[4] This doctrine of a single expressive substance inspires a first ethical principle: the choice to believe in *this* world, the world in which we exist now, alive and changing, and not some transcendent or ideal world. This is also an affirmation of thought's relation to the world, as the movements of thought in relation to those of matter differ only in their ways of expressing a common being or substance.

The second principle is that of *Becoming*, wherein the univocity of Being is characterized by its relation to movement, time, and change. Here substance is connected to force as self-differentiation, producing a universe of continual metamorphosis characterized by Bergson as "creative evolution." Becoming is the principle of time as force, and time is the expressive form of change: the fact that the universe never stops moving, changing, and evolving, and that no static picture could ever be adequate to this flux of universal self-differentiation. In this, time is something like a metaphysical constant in Deleuze, characterized in *Kant's Critical Philosophy* as "the form of that which is *not* eternal, the immutable form of change and movement."[5] All that moves or changes is in time, but time itself never changes or moves. The highest expression of this force is not Kantian, however, but what Nietzsche called *eternal recurrence*.

Deleuze offers an original reading of the concept of eternal recurrence. In fact, it is the key element of his philosophy of difference as well as his ethics, linking the univocity of Being and the force of Becoming. In *Nietzsche and Philosophy*, Deleuze asks, "What is the being of that which becomes, of that which neither starts nor finishes becoming? *Returning is the being of that which becomes.*"[6] What does Being speak of in one voice? It does not sing of identity, but rather, of recurrence as change and differentiation, of a "returning itself that constitutes being insofar as it is affirmed of becoming and of that which passes. It is not some one thing which returns but rather returning itself is the one thing which is affirmed of diversity or multiplicity. In other words, identity in the eternal return does not describe the nature of that which returns but, on the contrary, the fact of returning for that which differs."[7] What returns eternally is not the identity of the same, but the force of difference or differentiation. What Being speaks of recurrently is difference from itself.

Welles, Nietzsche, and the Powers of the False

The ethical stance in the cinema books is fundamentally Nietzschean. (The ontological passes through Spinoza and Bergson.) Deleuze characterizes a Nietzschean ethics as encompassing two related activities: interpretation and evaluation. "To interpret," Deleuze wrote earlier, "is to determine the force which gives sense to a thing. To evaluate is to determine the will to power which gives value to a thing."[8] "Interpretation" would relate here to Deleuze's theory of film semiotics, which is too complex to address here. Alternatively, evaluation is central to the ethical project of Deleuze's cinema books.

What philosophy must evaluate in any expression, including aesthetic expression, are its possibilities for life and experimentation in life. This is another important link between Nietzsche, Spinoza, and Bergson in Deleuze's account. Both Spinoza and Nietzsche distinguish between morality and ethics. Morality involves sets of constraining rules that judge actions and intentions against transcendent or universal values. An ethics evaluates expression according to the immanent mode of existence or possibilities of life it implies. The ethical choice for Deleuze, then, is whether the powers of change are affirmed and harnessed in ways that value life and its openness to change, or whether we disparage life in *this* world in fealty to moral absolutes. Do we affirm life and remain open to its powers of continuous, qualitative self-transformation, or do we maintain an image of thought whose movements are stopped or frozen?

To evaluate is to ask, *what mode of existence is willed in a given expression?* One must go beyond the transcendent moral opposition of good and evil, but this does not mean relinquishing judgments of good and bad as ethical distinctions. Life should not be judged. But the will to power that informs or characterizes a mode of existence may be evaluated as good or bad, noble or base. From Nietzsche's vitalist perspective, all is a question of force, and ethics involves characterizing forces by evaluating the qualities of their will to power. For example, there are fatigued or exhausted forces that can be quantitatively powerful but that no longer know how to transform themselves through the variations they can affect or receive. Deleuze finds this will to power often expressed in the films of Orson Welles—Nietzschean filmmaker par excellence—where characters such as Bannister in *Lady from Shanghai* or Hank Quinlan in *Touch of Evil* are the bodily expressions of a certain impotence: "that is, the precise point where the 'will to power' is nothing but a will-to-dominate, a being for death, which thirsts for its own death, as long as it can pass through others."[9] Here force finds a center that coincides with death. These are characters who only know how to destroy or kill, before destroying themselves. This is the mode of existence of *ressentiment*, characteristic of the men of vengeance. And no matter how great the forces these characters exercise or represent, they are exhausted and incapable of transformation. This spirit of revenge is often paired in Welles's films with a blind will to truth as transcendent moral judgment. Thus Quinlan is paired with Vargas, or Iago with Othello. The latter are "truthful men," who judge life in the name of higher values:

> They . . . take themselves to be *higher men*; these are higher men who claim to judge life by their own standards, by their own authority. But is this not the same spirit of revenge in two forms: Vargas, the truthful man who invokes the laws for judging; but also his double, Quinlan, who gives himself the right to judge without law; Othello, the man of duty and virtue, but also his double, Iago, who takes revenge by nature and perversion? This is what Nietzsche called the stages of nihilism, the spirit of revenge embodied in various figures. Behind the truthful man, who judges life from the perspective of supposedly higher values, there is the sick man, "the man sick with himself," who judges life from the perspective of his sickness, his degeneration and his exhaustion. And this is perhaps better than the truthful man, because a life of sickness is still life, it contrasts life with death, rather than contrasting it with "higher values" . . . Nietzsche said: behind the truthful man, who judges life, there is the sick man, sick of life itself. . . . The first is an idiot and the second is a bastard. They are, however, complementary as two figures of nihilism, two figures of the will to power.[10]

Ethics, however, is not a question of passing judgment on these figures, as if from some higher moral ground. Following Nietzsche, Deleuze (and Welles) want to do away with the system of judgment to evaluate, rather, modes of existence in their relation to life. "It is not a matter of judging life in the name of a higher authority," Deleuze writes, "which would be the good, the true; it is a matter, on the contrary, of evaluating every being, every action and passion, even every value, in relation to the life which they involve. Affect as immanent evaluation, instead of judgment as transcendent value."[11]

Going "beyond good and evil" does not mean renouncing ideas of good and bad, or in Nietzsche's parlance, noble and base. What is base is an exhausted, descendent, and degenerating life, especially when it seeks to propagate itself. But the noble is expressed in a blossoming, ascendant life, capable of transforming itself in cooperation with the forces it encounters, composing with them an ever growing power, "always increasing the power to live, always opening new 'possibilities.'"[12] There is no more "truth" in one life than the other: there is only becoming, descendant or ascendant, and life's becoming is "the power of the false," a noble will to power. "False" here is not opposed to the "true," but rather, allied to an aesthetic or artistic will, the will to create. The base will to power is the degenerative becoming of an exhausted life, with its destructive and dominating will. But the noble will to power is characterized by a "virtue that gives"; it is an artistic will, the becoming of an ascendant life that creates new possibilities and experiments with new modes of existence. If becoming is the power of the false, then the good, the generous, or the noble is what raises the false to its highest creative or transformative powers—a becoming-artist. If there is exhaustion in this aesthetic life, it is put in service to what is reborn from life through metamorphosis and creation. "It makes of becoming a protean Being," Deleuze writes, "rather than hastening it, from the height of a uniform and fixed identity, towards non-being. These are two states of life, opposed at the heart of an immanent becoming, and not an authority that would pose itself as superior to becoming in order to judge or dominate life, thus exhausting it. What Welles sees in *Falstaff* or *Don Quixote* is the 'goodness' of life in itself, a strange goodness that carries the living toward creation. It is in this sense that one can speak of an authentic or spontaneous Nietzscheanism in Welles."[13]

Choosing to Choose: Virtual Conjunctions and Any-Spaces-Whatever

The Nietzschean moral universe defines an ontology of descent and ascent, destruction and creation, a base will to power fueled by *ressentiment* and the will to truth, and a creative or artistic will that affirms life and its powers of transformation, while seeking out possibilities for enhancing these powers and this life. Between these two wills lies the deepest ethical problem: the problem of choosing a mode of existence defined by the possibility of choice.[14]

The problem of the choice of a mode of existence first occurs in the pages of *Cinema 1: The Movement-Image*, devoted to "lyrical abstraction," a style found principally in the films of Robert Bresson and Carl Theodor Dreyer. Deleuze is writing here, first, of the qualities and powers of affect in the image, especially in the treatment of light. This affection-image is distinguished from other types of cinematic movement-images through its virtuality or potentiality. In this, the affection-image is unlike action-images. The latter are caught up in chains of causality—or what Deleuze calls "real connections"—and are always expressively related to succession as well as sets of actions and reactions rebounding between objects and persons. The action-image is thus characterized as a sensorimotor whole, bound up in an organic representation that believes in the representability of the world for a perceiving subject as well as the unity of subject and world. Related to C. S. Peirce's category of "Firstness," or pure presignifying quality, affection-images present, instead, "virtual conjunctions": "there one finds pure qualities or singular potentialities—pure 'possibles,' as it were."[15] These qualities are luminescent and affective. They are possibilities for meaning and emotion expressed not in a determined and meaning-laden space, but in an "any-space-whatever" *(espace quelconque)*. They are ready to act or to signify, but one does not yet know in what direction or with what meaning. They are the virtual expression of choices yet to be accomplished.

How does the expression of choice correspond to the compositional logic of lyrical abstraction? Deleuze contrasts this style to German expressionism, whose approach to chiaroscuro defines a gothic world in which the struggle of shadow and light submerges the contours of things in a nonorganic life. Light and darkness collude here, prolonging the anticipation of a universal dread. But in lyrical abstraction, light and darkness alternate, thus expressing "an alternative between a given state of things and a possibility or virtuality that overtakes them. . . . In effect, what is essentially spiritual to lyrical abstraction is to be in search of an alternative, rather than being caught up in a struggle."[16]

What lyrical abstraction exemplifies in the construction of any-space-whatevers are scenarios of undetermined choice. Deleuze turns here to Pascal and Kierkegaard as emblematic of a new approach to ethics in modern philosophy, where moral dilemmas are less a matter of selecting from a limited set of alternatives—the lesser evil or the greater good—than the expression of the mode of existence of the one who chooses. The first case means persuading oneself of the absence of choice or to remain in ignorance of the power to choose, either because one believes in moral necessity (this is my duty, or this conforms to an ideal of the Good) or the situation presents no viable alternatives, or one is condemned by an inescapable drive or desire. What Deleuze calls *spiritual determination*, however, presents the possibility of choosing a way of life along with the philosophical reasoning that accompanies it. Here the essence of moral reasoning is awareness of the choice between choosing or not choosing. Deleuze characterizes this awareness as an extreme moralism that opposes morality and a faith that opposes religion, exemplified by Pascal's wager:

> If I am conscious of choosing, there are, therefore, already choices I can no longer make and modes of existence I can no longer pursue, which are all of those I followed in convincing myself that "I had no choice." Pascal's wager says nothing else: the alternation of terms is either the affirmation of the existence of God, its denial, or the suspension of doubt and uncertainty. But the spiritual alternative is something else—it is between the mode of existence of one who "wagers" that God exists and the mode of existence of one who gambles on nonexistence or who does not want to bet. According to Pascal, only the first is conscious of the possibility of choosing; the others are only able to choose in ignorance of the choices confronting them. In sum, choice as spiritual determination has no other object than itself: I choose to choose, and in this act I exclude every choice made in the mode of not having a choice.[17]

From Pascal to Bresson, and Kierkegaard to Dreyer, Deleuze identifies an ethical typology of characters whose moral choices typify different modes of existence that swing from belief in the inescapability of a moral path to the possibility of choice. Of the former, Deleuze characterizes three types of characters and modes of existence. First there are the "white" men of moral absolutes, of God and Virtue—the perhaps tyrannical or hypocritical guardians of religious or moral order, as in the priest-judges of Dreyer's *Jeanne d'Arc*. There are then the gray men of uncertainty or vacillation, as in the protagonists of Dreyer's *Vampyr*, Bresson's *Lancelot du lac*, or *Pickpocket*. Third, there are creatures of evil and the blackness of drives: Hélène's vengefulness in *Les Dames du bois de Boulogne*; Gérard's wickedness in *Au hasard Balthazar*; the thievery of *Pickpocket* and Yvonne's crimes in *L'argent*. These are all instances of false choice or decisions made from denying that there is or may still be a choice.

Here, Deleuze's reading of lyrical abstraction is close to the ethical interpretation of Nietzche's eternal return. We are not caught by the absolute values of darkness and light, or even the indecisiveness of gray; rather, the possibility of "spiritual determination," indeed, what Cavell might call *moral perfectionism*, is a choice not to be defined by what is chosen, "but by the power choosing possesses of being able to start again at each instant, to restart itself, and to affirm itself of itself, by putting all the stakes back into play each time. And even if this choice means sacrificing the character, this is a sacrifice made in full knowledge that it will recur each time, and for all times."[18]

This is an image figuring an authentic choice in and of consciousness of the power to choose. To each character and image, there corresponds an affect. For the white, the dark, and the gray, affects are actualized in an established order or disorder (moral absolutism, indecisiveness, or tragic destiny). But authentic choice "raises affect to its pure power or potential, as in Lancelot's courtly love, but also embodies or carries out this potential so powerfully as to release in it that which will not let itself be actualized, and which overwhelms its realization (eternal recurrence)."[19] (And there is yet a fifth type: the innocent embodied by the donkey in *Au hasard Balthazar*: the holy fool who is not in a state of choosing and who cannot know the effect of humanity's choosing or not choosing.)

The problem of choice is presented in the affection-image by a certain relationship to light, a fluctuation of light. It is an image that solicits thought and draws us to a space of moral reasoning. Expressionism thus conveys, for Deleuze, a space determined by the alternation of terms, each of which compels an inescapable choice, in fact, a nonchoice—White–Black–Gray:

> White marks our duty or power; black, our impotence or thirst for evil; grey, our uncertainty, restlessness, or indifference.... But only one other implies that we choose to choose, or that we are conscience of choice.... We have reached a philosophical space [*espace spirituel*] where what we choose is no longer distinct from choice itself. Lyrical abstraction is defined by the adventure of light and white. But the episodes of this adventure mean, first, that the white that imprisons light alternates with the black that stops it, and then white is liberated in an alternative, which restores to us the white *and* the black. We have traveled, without moving, from one space to another, from a physical to a philosophical space of experimentation (or metaphysics).[20]

From Classic to Modern Cinema: The Crisis in Belief

This passage already anticipates the problems raised by modern cinema in *Cinema 2: The Time-Image*. The organic representation of the movement-image is based on connections that are rational as well as real. The term *rational* indicates a formal relation that ensures the continuity of shots within each segment, the spatial contiguity of one segment to another, and the dialectical unity of parts within the whole of the film. But these rational connections also have an ethical dimension—they are expressive of a will to truth. They express belief in the possibility and coherence of a complete and truthful representation of the world in images, and of the world in relation to thought, that is extendible in a dialectical unity encompassing image, world, and subject—hence Sergei Eisenstein's belief in the utopia of an intellectual cinema and of a direct relation between image and thought.

In Deleuze's account, however, modern cinema is inaugurated by a crisis in the action-image and a corresponding crisis in belief. This crisis is profoundly related to the dilemma of skepticism, though Deleuze's conception of the history of cinema in relation to ontological and moral reasoning differs significantly from Cavell's. In its purest form, the movement-image—or what Deleuze calls the plane of immanence—defines a world where skepticism is absent or irrelevant. This is a world defined by Spinoza's pure ontology of one unique substance, or Bergson's world of universal change and variation, based on the equivalence of matter and light, and memory and matter, in a world of open creation. But from this world, there emerges the *cinematic* movement-image, which, in believing itself to have overcome skepticism in the form of an identity between image and thought, nonetheless perpetuates the division of subject and object as a problem. Thus the organic form of the cinematic movement-image believes in the representability of the world for a knowing subject, but in the form of a will to truth—a separation and rejoining of subject and object. Sergei Eisenstein's theories remain the most powerful visions of a cinematic movement-image that forges a dialectical unity of subject and world through cinematic representation—the utopia of a truthful representation founded on the laws of a "non-indifferent nature."[21] And indeed, this is a "white" theory, in which all is subsumed to the dialectics of nature and choice is no longer a possibility.

It is important to emphasize here that the purest form of the cinematic movement-image is rare. The logic of affection-images and the expressiveness of any-space-whatevers demonstrate that the action-image is, rather, in a continuous state of crisis or struggle with the essential movements of the world and of cinema, where time is defined not as space, but rather, as force, the Open, or the virtual—the eternally recurring potentiality for new creation in each passing present. Similarly, there is no clear historical break between the movement-image and the time-image, for the direct-image of time is an ever renewable possibility recurring throughout the history of cinema, like an underground river that swells and recedes unpredictably, gushing up in springs or receding still and hidden beneath deserts.[22]

Therefore the recurrence of Bresson and Dreyer in the second volume demonstrates a deep connection across the two cinema books. There is less a break between the modern and classic cinema than a shift in the concept of belief, where the direct image of time restores or gives new expression to a potentiality always present, always renewable, within film's expressive movements. If the ethical stance of the cinematic movement-image is expressive of a will to truth, then that of the direct image of time is given in powers of the false that challenge the coherence and unity of organic representation. Indeed, for Deleuze, modern cinema emerges from a profound and global crisis of belief, experienced as a traumatic gulf between humanity and the world. With neither causality nor teleology directing the unfolding of images, nor a given totality in which they can be comprehended as a Whole, the powers of nondetermined choice anticipated by affection-images are raised here to a new power. Consequently, there arises within the universe of modern cinema a new moral type defined by their sensitivity to "pure optical and acoustical situations" and their susceptibility to "wandering forms" (la forme-balade)—affective situations in which characters stroll or stray without obvious goals, destinations, or motivation. Best exemplified by Ingrid Bergman in Rossellini's great postwar trilogy—Voyage in Italy, Europa 51, and Stromboli—the protagonists of modern cinema wander and observe. They transmit sights, rather than motivating movements and actions: "the character becomes a kind of spectator. She may move, run, or stir restlessly, but the situation in which she finds herself overflows her motor capacities on all sides, making her see and hear what no longer justifies a response or an action. She registers more than reacts. She surrenders to a vision, which she pursues or which pursues her, rather than engaging in an action."[23]

Finally, this modern cinema is subject to a generalized paranoia, sensitive to conspiracy and suspicious of all forms of totality. In this, Deleuze writes, "The pure optical and acoustical situation does not extend into action, any more than it is induced by an action. It makes us grasp, or it is supposed to make us grasp, something intolerable, unbearable. . . . It is matter of something too powerful or too unjust, but sometimes also too beautiful, that henceforth exceeds our motor capacities."[24] In sum, the time-image produces characters and affective situations marked by a perceptual sensitivity to the intolerability of a world in which faith and confidence in representation have disappeared, and in which we are consumed by "the idea of one single misery, interior and exterior, in the world and in consciousness."[25] Or, as Ingrid Bergman exclaims in *Europa 51*, "Something possible, otherwise I will suffocate."

The Subtle Way Out

Both Cavell and Deleuze assert a special connection between cinema and the concept of belief. The movement-image as plane of immanence is the most direct expression of a link between being and the world, or matter becoming luminescent, and thought emerging in relation to the movements of the world. The *cinematic* movement-image and time-image, however, appear as two ethical directions across this plane of immanence: one is a transformation of the world by humanity, or the Eisensteinian belief that one can construct an image that makes thought happen; the other is Antonin Artaud's intuition of an interior, deeper world, "before man," as it were, produced from a shock to thought or by thought's confrontation with what is unthinkable. This is a confrontation with a time that is not that of Being, identity, or teleology, but rather, an anticipatory time—of contingency, the purely conditional, the nondetermined or not yet.

The dilemma of modern cinema is, in many respects, that of skepticism as Cavell describes it. But Cavell describes belief in the mode of credibility and a potential overcoming of skepticism. In contrast, a European pessimism pervades Deleuze's account. As in Kracauer's late theory, the confrontation with postwar destruction, genocide, and the collapse of the grand narratives of ideology and utopia mark the decline of belief, expressed as a crisis in the action-image and the collapse of the sensorimotor schema. For Deleuze, modernity is experienced as a kind of traumatism. The break in the sensorimotor whole and the emergence of pure optical and acoustical situations

> makes man a seer who finds himself struck by something intolerable in the world, and confronted by something unthinkable in thought.

Between the two, thought undergoes a strange fossilization, which is as it were its powerlessness to function, to be, its dispossession of itself and the world. For it is not in the name of a better or truer world that thought captures the intolerable in this world, but, on the contrary, it is because this world is intolerable that it can no longer think a world or think itself. The intolerable is no longer a serious injustice, but the permanent state of daily banality. Man *is not himself* a world other than the one in which he experiences the intolerable and feels himself trapped.[26]

The problem, then, becomes how to restore belief in a world of universal pessimism, in which we have no more faith in images than we do in the world?

In the pure optical situation, the seer is alienated both within herself and from the world, but she also sees farther, better, and deeper than she can react or think. This augmentation of the powers of sight and of sensitivity to the injustices of the world may give the appearance of passivity, or an impotence of thought before that which is intolerable to consider. But for Deleuze, the solution is not to quail before the thought that there is no alternative to this or any other situation. What Deleuze calls the "im-powers of thought" demand a revaluation of our perceptual disjunction from the world that makes of it the possibility for a new faith, and a new thought. The problem of skepticism is here radically reconfigured. It is not that we are perceptually disjoined from the world, but rather, that self, sight, and thought are divided from within and from each other by time, or by the force of time's passing. What is outside of thought, which thought must confront as the unthought, is our existential and ethical relationship to time as an infinite reservoir of nondetermined choice, which is also an ontology where life and thought are inseparable.

What Deleuze calls the "subtle way out" of this dilemma has already been introduced through the concept of lyrical abstraction—to commit to a mode of existence in which one chooses out of faith in the link between world, thought, and life. An arc must be drawn between the movement-image and the time-image, where new thought is generated by experiencing the powerlessness to think, just as new alternatives emerge in confrontation with the inability to choose:

Which, then, is the subtle way out? To believe, not in a different world, but in a link between man and the world, in love or life, to believe in this as in the impossible, the unthinkable, which none the less cannot but be thought: "something possible, otherwise I will suffocate." It is this belief that makes the unthought the specific power of thought, through the absurd, by virtue of the absurd. Artaud never understood powerlessness to think as a simple inferiority which would strike us in relation to thought. It is part of thought, so that we should make our way of thinking from it, without claiming to be restoring an all-powerful thought. We should rather make use of this powerlessness to believe in life, and to discover the identity of thought and life.[27]

For Deleuze, the basic fact of modernity is that "we no longer believe in this world." However, much is explained by emphasizing that "we no longer believe in *this* world," that is, the world present to us, in which we are present and which comprises the present time we occupy as a constant becoming:

> We no longer even believe in the events that happen to us, love or death, as if they hardly concern us. We do not make cinema; rather, the world looks to us like a bad film. . . . It is the link between man and the world that has been broken. Henceforth, this link must become an object of belief, as the impossible that must be given back in faith. Belief is no longer addressed to another world, or a transformed world. Man is in the world as if in a pure optical or acoustical situation. The reaction of which man is dispossessed can only be replaced by belief. Only belief in the world can reconnect man to what he sees and hears. Cinema must not film the world, but rather, belief in this world, our only link. One often questions the nature of cinematographic illusion. To give us back belief in the world—this is the power of modern cinema (when it stops being shoddy). Christians or atheists, in our universal schizophrenia *we need reasons to believe in this world.*[28]

From Eisenstein to Artaud, the ethical problem for Deleuze is to understand that the traumatic unlinking of being from the world is yet more powerfully a leap toward faith in life, in *this* life or this world and its powers of self-transformation. The time-image's powers of the false do not show that the image is an illusion, nor do they replace a false perception with a true one; rather, the powers of the false release the image from the form of identity and restore to it the potential for Becoming or eternal recurrence. From the cinematic movement-image to the time-image, from Pascal to Nietzsche, and in the cinema of

Rossellini and Dreyer, a great shift occurs in philosophy, replacing the model of knowledge with that of belief, as if in a conversion from piety to atheism, and moralism to morality—thus the turning points represented in the history of moral reasoning by Deleuze's pairing of Pascal and Hume, Kant and Fichte, or Kierkegaard and Nietzsche. One should emphasize that knowledge is based on faith no less than belief, namely, the will to truth and a belief in humanity's technological domination of nature. But even among the "pious" philosophers here, belief no longer turns toward another, transcendent world, but is directed, rather, to *this* world, the one in which we exist. In Deleuze's account, what Kierkegaard or even Pascal assert in the concept of faith is something that returns to us humanity's link with the world and with life. Hence belief only replaces knowledge when it elicits belief in this world and its future-oriented powers.

Deleuze's ethics, then, is a moral reasoning that wants to give back to us a belief capable of perpetuating life as movement, change, becoming—the eternal recurrence of difference. And rather than yearning for another transcendent or transformed world, we must believe in the body and the flesh, to believe in the substance of the world and the world as substance, returning to them all their one and unique voice. "We must believe in the body as in the germ of life, a seed that splits the pavement, that is conserved and perpetuated in the holy shroud or mummy's wrappings, and which bears witness to life and to this very world such that it is. We need an ethic or a faith that makes idiots laugh, not a need to believe in something else, but a need to believe in this world, of which fools are a part."[29] Belief must then be reconnected to the two principles of Deleuze's system. Skepticism is the sign of a thought disconnected from Life comprised of a single substance and a time of constant becoming. But Being and thought are in Life; they speak with a single voice and become in the same time, such that skepticism must be overcome with another will to power, which draws its energy from Life's potential for self-differentiation, and moralism overcome by choosing to believe in the ever renewable possibility of beginning again—eternal recurrence.

Notes

1. Siegfried Kracauer, *Theory of Film* (New York: Oxford University Press, 1960), 285.
2. Gilles Deleuze, *Cinema 1: The Movement-Image*, trans. Hugh Tomlinson and Barbara Habberjam (Minneapolis: University of Minnesota Press, 1986), and Gilles Deleuze, *Cinema 2: The Time-Image*, trans. Hugh Tomlinson and Robert Galeta (Minneapolis: University of Minnesota Press, 1989). The original editions were published in Paris by Éditions de Minuit in 1983 and 1985, respectively. I have modified most of the translations cited here. When this is the case, page numbers from the original French editions are cited in italics. The ethical arguments of especially *Time-Image* are taken up in interesting ways in Gilles Deleuze and Félix Guattari's final published work, *What Is Philosophy?*, trans. Hugh Tomlinson and Graham Burchell (New York: Columbia University Press, 1994). I comment on this relation in the concluding chapter of *Gilles Deleuze's Time Machine* (Durham, N.C.: Duke University Press, 1997), 194–210.
3. The relation between Deleuze and Cavell as the two most compelling voices in contemporary film philosophy is a central feature of my forthcoming book from Harvard University Press, *An Elegy for Theory*.
4. Alberto Gualandi, *Deleuze* (Paris: Les Belles Lettres, 1998), 18–19; my translation. Also see Alain Badiou, *Deleuze: La clameur de l'Être* (Paris: Hachette, 1997).
5. Gilles Deleuze, *Kant's Critical Philosophy*, trans. Hugh Tomlinson and Barbara Habberjam (Minneapolis: University of Minnesota Press, 1984), viii.
6. Gilles Deleuze, *Nietzsche and Philosophy*, trans. Hugh Tomlinson (New York: Columbia University Press, 1983), 48.
7. Ibid.
8. Ibid., 54.
9. Deleuze, *Time-Image*, 140–41, *183–84*.
10. Ibid., 140–41, *184*.
11. Ibid., 141, *184–85*.
12. Ibid., 141.
13. Ibid., 142, *185–86*.
14. This problem is explored in depth in Ronald Bogue's contribution to this volume, "To Choose to Choose—to Believe in This World" (chap. 7).
15. Deleuze, *Movement-Image*, 102, *145*.
16. Ibid., 112–13, *158–59*.
17. Ibid., 114, *161*.
18. Ibid., 115, *162*.
19. Ibid., 115–16, *163*.
20. Ibid., 117, *165*.

21 See Sergei Eisenstein, *Nonindifferent Nature: Film and the Structure of Things*, trans. Herbert Marshall (Cambridge: Cambridge University Press, 1987).

22 On the historical relation between the cinematic movement and time-images, see my essay "A Genealogy of Time," in *Reading the Figural, or Philosophy after the New Media* (Durham, N.C.: Duke University Press, 2001), 170–202.

23 Deleuze, *Time-Image*, 3, 9.

24 Ibid., 18, 29.

25 Deleuze, *Movement-Image*, 209.

26 Deleuze, *Time-Image*, 169–70, 220–21.

27 Ibid., 170.

28 Ibid., 171–72, 223.

29 Ibid., 173, 225.

7. To Choose to Choose— to Believe in This World

Ronald Bogue

Though one might argue that all of Deleuze's work deals with ethics, the topic itself does not arise frequently in his writings. In *Cinema 1: The Movement-Image* and *Cinema 2: The Time-Image*, however, ethics is addressed directly when Deleuze says that "we need an ethic or a faith, which makes idiots laugh,"[1] an ethic of choosing to choose and a faith that allows belief in this world.[2] In the philosophy of Pascal and Kierkegaard and the cinema of Bresson and Dreyer, Deleuze finds "a strange thought," an "extreme moralism that opposes the moral," a "faith that opposes religion."[3] This conjunction of Pascal, Kierkegaard, Bresson, and Dreyer, says Deleuze, "weaves a set of invaluable relations between philosophy and cinema."[4] Striking is the fact that this "strange thought" is usually articulated in terms of the transcendent—specifically, the transcendent terms of Roman Catholicism in the case of Pascal and Bresson, and those of Protestantism in Kierkegaard and Dreyer— whereas Deleuze consistently maintains that his thought is above all a philosophy of immanence. One might ask, then, by what means and for what purposes Deleuze appropriates this transcendent thought for an immanent ethics, and in what ways he delineates a specifically cinematic dimension of that ethics. And beyond these issues, one might ask of this meeting of philosophy and cinema the larger question of Deleuze's conception of the basic relationship between these two enterprises. In *What Is Philosophy?* Deleuze insists on the separate vocations of philosophy and the arts, but in *The Time-Image* he suggests a more intimate relationship between philosophy and cinema, and perhaps it is in the domain of this immanent ethics that cinema serves a privileged function for philosophical thought.

The first task in exploring this "strange" philosophical-cinematic thought is to determine the manner in which Deleuze reads the philosophers Pascal and Kierkegaard. Deleuze's earliest engagement with Pascal and Kierkegaard comes in *Nietzsche and Philosophy*, during his analysis of Nietzsche's sense of the tragic and its relationship to chance.[5] Deleuze notes that Pascal and Kierkegaard are often labeled "tragic philosophers" and that both formulate an ethics of risk and the aleatory: Pascal with his wager of God's existence, Kierkegaard with his leap of faith. Pascal's wager and Kierkegaard's leap of faith prefigure Nietzsche's cosmic throw of the dice, but in Deleuze's view, Nietzsche's Christian antecedents remain trapped in a tragedy of guilt and dread, whereas Nietzsche embraces a tragedy of joyous affirmation. Pascal and Kierkegaard are poets of the "ascetic ideal,"[6] who oppose conventional morality and reason, but only via "interiority, anguish, groaning, culpability, all the forms of discontent."[7] What they lack is Nietzsche's "sense of affirmation, the sense of exteriority, innocence and play."[8] The Pascalian wager especially reveals a mentality of *ressentiment* in that Pascal's gambler tries to overcome chance and hedge all bets, to transcend the insecurity of the aleatory and escape to a providential beyond. The Nietzschean throw of the dice, by contrast, is an affirmation of each aleatory cast, whatever its specific outcome.

In subsequent references to Pascal, Deleuze, for the most part, simply reiterates his assessment of the Pascalian wager, but his engagement with Kierkegaard is somewhat more detailed in later works. His most extended treatment of Kierkegaard is in *Difference and Repetition*, in which he parallels the concepts of repetition developed by Kierkegaard and Nietzsche. The two Kierkegaardian texts on which Deleuze concentrates are *Repetition* and *Fear and Trembling*, published the same day in 1843.[9] Kierkegaard's chief aim in these works is to challenge the reigning Hegelianism of his day and assert the primacy of religion and the personal over philosophy and the collective.[10] In Hegel's terms, Kierkegaard's position might be characterized as that of the Unhappy Consciousness, that phase of the dialectic traced in *Phenomenology of Mind*, in which consciousness recognizes itself as at once finite and infinite (or delimited and undelimited), yet without any means of overcoming this fundamental contradiction. In this basically religious consciousness, spirit (or mind) is aware of itself as a finite entity, yet also as a faculty capable of determining all natures through thought, and hence capable of comprehending the infinite. But the unhappy consciousness cannot grasp itself as being both a limited entity and an unlimited capacity of mind, and as a result, it attributes that unlimited capacity to an eternal and infinite God, from which consciousness is separated, despite its sensed affinities with that God. To overcome this division, says Hegel, consciousness must make a "movement" *(Bewegung)* of thought, whereby spirit understands itself as the medium of the infinite coming to awareness of itself in time. In this higher form of consciousness, or absolute mind, the finite spirit recognizes itself as the necessary manifestation of the infinite. A religious unhappy consciousness thus gives way to a superior philosophical absolute mind; the individual spirit transcends its finitude and discovers itself as one with the infinite and undelimited. The ethical and political consequences of this movement beyond unhappy consciousness are that the individual comes to comprehend itself in its universal humanness, to recognize its own goals and purposes in the communal purposes of all humanity, and to find freedom and ultimate fulfillment through the rational coordination of action within social institutions.

Kierkegaard rejects the Hegelian elevation of philosophy over religion and its valorization of the collective over the individual, arguing instead that the religious and the individual (in a certain guise) represent the highest form of experience and thought. The movement of thought that Kierkegaard traces is not one from Unhappy Consciousness to Absolute Mind, but rather, a three-stage movement from what Kierkegaard labels the "aesthetic," through the "ethical," to the "religious." The aesthetic, by which Kierkegaard means the consciousness inherent in immediate sensual experience, is a form of consciousness that is surpassed by the ethical, another word for Hegelian universal philosophical reason, but what Kierkegaard calls the religious is a mode of being beyond reason, ethics, and the universal, in which the ethical may be suspended and the individual enters into "an absolute relation to the absolute."[11]

In *Difference and Repetition*, Kierkegaard initially frames the difference between the ethical and the religious in terms of contrasting conceptions of time, the one manifesting a temporality of recollection, the other a temporality of repetition. "Repetition and recollection," he says, "are the same movement, except in opposite directions, for what is recollected has been, is repeated backward, whereas genuine repetition is recollected forward."[12] Obviously, with the term *recollection*, Kierkegaard is invoking Platonic *anamnesis*, that re-memoration whereby the mind recalls those universal, eternal truths that it once knew but has since forgotten. But Kierkegaard insists as well that the Hegelian movement of thought is no alternative to Platonic *anamnesis*; rather, it is simply another version of recollection, despite its terminology of "movement" and "mediation." In Platonic *anamnesis*, the true, the eternal, the nonfinite, the Whole, has always been, and thought is merely a present recalling of that totality. In the Hegelian movement of mediation, the true, eternal, nonfinite Whole becomes manifest through history, but once revealed, it remains the same unchanged Whole as in Plato, and the process of its temporal revelation ultimately affects that Whole in no meaningful way. For Kierkegaard, by contrast, the infinite is beyond full comprehension and containment, a Whole that is genuinely open to change in the future and hence an unbounded Whole. Kierkegaard's point is roughly the same as that made later by Bergson: in Plato and Hegel, the Whole is *given*; that is, the Whole is presupposed as a closed, complete, and knowable entity, whereas for Kierkegaard and Bergson, the Whole is open, a genuinely *becoming* Whole that is constitutively unknowable in any permanent sense. To engage such an open Whole, thought must abandon the backward movement of recollection and embrace the forward movement of repetition. Kierkegaard's concise, though somewhat cryptic, formulation of the recollection–repetition opposition is that "when the Greeks said that all knowing is recollecting, they said that all existence, which is, has been; when one says that life is a repetition, one says: actuality, which has been, now comes into existence."[13] What repeats in repetition is life (not knowing, as in recollection), and that vital repetition consists of a manifestation of an open, ungraspable Whole in a concrete instant (an "actuality"), which is followed by a subsequent instant in which the open, ungraspable Whole yet again "now comes into existence."

What is at stake in Kierkegaard's reflection on time is the status of the future in recollection and in repetition. In recollection, the Whole is closed and knowable. Whether it is suddenly recollected in Platonic *anamnesis*, or slowly revealed through the Hegelian movement of mediation, once that Whole is fully comprehended, the future is empty. At that point, the Whole, as completed entity, has exhausted its possibilities, and the future can be only a reiteration of that selfsame set of possibilities. In repetition, by contrast, the Whole is open and ungraspable, as yet undetermined and undeterminable. The instant in which this open Whole comes into existence is always full of unknowable possibilities. The future is a genuine future, in which time matters, that is, in which the forward surge of time makes a difference. To engage the time of repetition, one must go beyond the domain of the "ethical," which belongs to a time of recollection, and enter the domain of the "religious."

In *Difference and Repetition*, Kierkegaard's chief exemplar of the movement beyond the ethical to the religious is Job, but perhaps his most illuminating example of the religious consciousness is Abraham, the central figure in *Fear and Trembling*. Abraham is called to commit an incomprehensible act, one that, by the standards of universal morality, must be condemned as murder. He has various rational means of avoiding the dilemma of his situation, but he declines them all. He makes a leap of faith, moving beyond the human community into an immediate and personal relationship with God. As he prepares to sacrifice Isaac, there seems no possible outcome other than Isaac's death, but Abraham trusts, despite all reason, that his son will be fully restored to him in this life. For God, all things are possible, which means that for Abraham, the future is genuinely open. Unlike the tragic hero, who subordinates one ethical norm to another (such as Agamemnon, who subordinates his duty as a father to his duty as a king in sacrificing his daughter), Abraham enters a domain in which the ethical is suspended altogether. He goes beyond universal humanity to become a specific individual in an absolute relationship with the absolute. He is what Kierkegaard calls a "Knight of Faith," and his leap beyond rational comprehension and ethical norms brings him into a cheerful enjoyment of this world. "He finds pleasure in everything, takes part in everything,"[14] and seems no different from the average well-fed burgher. But for him, all has been transformed because the world now is replete with possibility.

In *Difference and Repetition*, Deleuze identifies four elements common to Kierkegaard's and Nietzsche's conceptions of repetition. First, both "make of repetition itself something new" in that both regard repetition as the reiteration of unpredictable possibility, a repeated coming into being of an open Whole in Kierkegaard, a repeated cosmic throw of the dice in Nietzsche.[15] Second, both "oppose repetition to the laws of Nature"[16] in that they reject the deterministic, mechanistic model of a nature regulated by linear causality and hence subject to total predictability (at least in theory). Third, they "oppose repetition to moral law,"[17] Kierkegaard by positing an ultimate suspension of the ethical, Nietzsche by advocating a thought beyond good and evil. Finally, both "oppose repetition not only to the generalities of habit, but also to the particularities of memory";[18] that is, both reject a thought that looks backward via memory (be it Platonic *anamnesis*, Hegelian mediation, or a Humean association of ideas through habit) and embrace a thought that forgets what it thinks it knows and thereby becomes an active power capable of engaging an emergent future.

Deleuze does not minimize the differences between Kierkegaard and Nietzsche, and he makes it clear that his own concept of repetition is much closer to that of Nietzsche than that of Kierkegaard. Indeed, if we now consider the question of how Deleuze appropriates Kierkegaard's transcendent thought of the leap of faith for his own philosophy of immanence, we might say that it is primarily by reading Kierkegaard through Nietzsche. Kierkegaard's emphasis on the transcendent is part of his rejection of Hegel's ontology of immanent absolute spirit coming to consciousness of itself through time. The domain of the religious emerges as a transcendent disruption of the continuities, regularities, and inevitabilities of communal ethics and universal reason. The religious enters existence in the "moment," a transcendent rupture in historical time, and it defies rational comprehension as well as assimilation within human morality. What Nietzsche's concept of repetition allows Deleuze to do is to make Kierkegaard's transcendent force of disruption a part of a new, non-Hegelian ontology of difference. One might say, with a great deal of caution, that what was God in Kierkegaard becomes, through Nietzsche, difference in Deleuze. Put another way, the Kierkegaardian religious force that disrupts the Hegelian cosmos of immanent absolute spirit becomes the operative force immanent within a cosmos of self-differentiating difference.

A key element of Deleuze's ontology of difference is Nietzsche's concept of the eternal return, which Deleuze presents as a perpetually repeated cosmic throw of the dice. In Deleuze's ontology, however, this repetition is not purely chaotic; rather, the series of dice throws is like a Markov chain, a formal model in which a discrete set of possibilities produces a second set of possibilities, which in turn produces a third, each set in the chain of events being affected and partially determined by the preceding set, yet with each set's potential for subsequent differentiation always being multiple and undeterminable.[19] The relationship between events is at once contingent and necessary, unpredictable yet nonarbitrary. Each set, in its multiple possibilities, exceeds any identity. It is a difference in itself, unfolding into further states of self-differing difference. The cosmos, as repeated dice throws, then, may be seen as an open Whole of interconnected Markov chains, each a contingent and necessary sequence of throws of the dice, any given result of a throw having immanent within it the potential for multiple outcomes in the next throw.

In *Difference and Repetition*, Deleuze distinguishes Kierkegaard's repetition from Nietzsche's by saying that Kierkegaard leaps, whereas

Nietzsche dances,[20] by which he means that Kierkegaard's leap is a one-time cosmic wager, whereas Nietzsche's dance is a perpetually repeated series of dice throws. But what is essential to the two thinkers, says Deleuze, is that they produce movement within thought, in the sense both of going beyond the false movement of Hegelian mediation and of inventing new means of philosophical expression. Rather than represent concepts, they "dramatize Ideas."[21] They create a theater within philosophy, each complete with its "heroes of repetition: Job-Abraham, Dionysus-Zarathustra,"[22] a theater that exceeds representation through "vibrations, rotations, turnings, gravitations, dances or leaps that directly touch the mind."[23]

"I pay attention only to the movements," says Kierkegaard,[24] and in *Difference and Repetition*, Deleuze identifies that principle as the source of Kierkegaard's theater of repetition. But when Deleuze comments on this "marvelous motto" in his analysis of movement in *A Thousand Plateaus*, he says that Kierkegaard "is acting astonishingly like a precursor of the cinema."[25] It comes as no surprise, then, that Kierkegaard appears in both *The Movement-Image* and *The Time-Image*. In each volume, Kierkegaard is invoked as a guide toward an ethics of "choosing to choose" and a faith that induces "belief in this world." What Deleuze finds interesting in Pascal, but especially in Kierkegaard, is that a genuine choice "does not bear on the terms one might choose, but on the modes of existence of the one who chooses."[26] One mode of life, for example, is that of the ideologue, or the true believer, for whom the answers are already given and there is nothing to choose. Another is that of the indifferent or the uncertain, those who lack the capacity to choose or who never know enough to be able to choose. A third is that of the fatalists and devotees of evil, those who make a single choice that commits them to an inevitable and unavoidable sequence of actions that afford no further choice. And finally, there is the mode of existence of those who choose to choose, those who affirm a life of continuous choosing. The choice in this last mode of existence, in short, "has no other object than itself: I choose to choose, and by that means I exclude every choice made according to the mode of having no choice."[27]

Those who choose to choose affirm the possible. Like Kierkegaard's Knight of Faith, they leap beyond rational and ethical certainties into an open Whole, their leap being an act of trust in possibilities beyond their present comprehension. Choosing to choose is crucial for Deleuze because contemporary men and women have lost faith with this world;

that is, they no longer believe in the possibility of anything new. The world is a bad movie, an endless series of banalities and clichés, platitudes and vacuous opinions. But this does not mean simply that the world is insipid and boring; it can also be an insidious and coercive film. Deleuze says that for modern directors, the world as bad film constitutes the "intolerable," but in his study of Foucault, he also treats all Foucault's work as a response to the "intolerable."[28] In *Discipline and Punish*, for example, the present prison system is the intolerable. As Foucault shows, within the first forty years of its existence, the prison's drawbacks and failures are evident, and within those forty years, one hears the same calls for reform and recommendations for more prisons, better prisons, stricter prisons, and so on, that one hears today. The penal system is a bad movie, an endless recycling of practices and discourses that seem unavoidable, inescapable, devoid of real alternatives, emptied of all genuine possibility.

The only viable response to the intolerable is to think differently, to disconnect the world's networks of certainties and pieties and formulate new problems that engender as yet unmapped relations and connections. For modern film directors, thinking differently, at its most fundamental level, is a matter of disconnecting and reconnecting images. The world as bad movie consists of myriad chains of association, which, in strictly visual terms, may be conceived of as images linked to other images to form natural, predictable, redundant sequences. The first task of thinking differently in images is to "disenchain" the chains, to dissolve the links of habitual association that tie images to one another (all of which links are embedded in the commonsense spatiotemporal regularities of the sensorimotor schema). The second task is to take a given image and "choose another image that will induce an interstice *between* the two."[29] Such a choice will be contingent, but not arbitrary, the choice of image being the result of a search for productive juxtapositions such that the sequence of images becomes a self-differentiating series, but one in which the gaps between images retain their primacy. Each gap in such a series, then, is the site of a choice, a throw of the dice, a leap, an experimentation in a zone of possibilities. The gap itself is off the map of the known world; it is a pure Outside uncharted by external spatial or internal psychological coordinates. The series of images formed by such choices "re-enchains" the images, but such that they form Markov chains, contingent but necessary iterations of possibilities differentiating themselves into further possibilities. In this regard, the choice of images is an ontological choice, the process of choosing constituting a mode of existence that is inseparable from the becoming of the cosmos as an open Whole of self-differentiating differences.

In *The Time-Image*, Deleuze discusses the Pascalian and Kierke-gaardian theme of choosing to choose through the films of Rohmer, Dreyer, and Bresson, the choice of directors obviously being guided in part by their frequent treatment as filmmakers concerned with religious themes. Certainly in the work of Bresson, if we limit our attention to that director, the religious dimension is incontestable. Besides dealing with explicitly religious subjects *(Journal d'un curé de campagne, Le Procès de Jeanne d'Arc)*, Bresson constructs what might be considered parables of grace, the grace that, like the wind, blows where it will in *Un condamné à mort s'est échappé*, or the grace that miraculously brings Michel to Jeanne at the end of *Pickpocket*. *Au hasard Balthazar* and *Le Procès* may be regarded as studies of sainthood, *Mouchette* and *Une femme douce* as films about suffering and the problematic redemption of suicide, *Le diable probablement* and *L'argent* as Jansenist essays in the bleakness of a world deprived of saving grace. Yet, if religious concerns are patent in Bresson's films, they are handled in a way that allows nonreligious interpretations as well. If the influence of a transcendent deity or a providential grace may be regarded as shaping events in his films, it is always by invisible means. No numinous clouds, transverse shafts of light, or surging strains of angelic choirs signal the presence of the divine; rather, the workings of grace shape a consistently sober, often grim, and insistently material world whose atmosphere, especially in the black-and-white films of the 1950s and 1960s, has some affinities with that of Italian neorealism. Bresson's ascetic reduction of compositional elements, his focus on isolated objects, his separation of elements from their usual contexts (especially hands, feet, and torsos), his spare use of camera movement and contrasting angles, all suggest a derealizing formalism consistent with a certain monastic sensibility, but the same techniques may be seen as a means of enhancing the intensity of sensual experience and focusing the viewer's attention on the life of the lived body. The result is that Bresson's cinema has lent itself to multiple, contradictory interpretations, especially as regards the status of the transcendent in his work. Paul Schrader, for example, considers Bresson to be the quintessential practitioner of the transcendental style in film, whereas Jonathan Rosenbaum counters that Bresson is the ultimate materialist.[30] Those who stress the formalist aspects of

Bresson's films do so often to emphasize the invisible presence of the transcendent, whereas those who focus on the centrality of sensation and the inseparable conjunction of perception and emotion in his films tend to call attention to the insistent corporeality of any reputedly immaterial forces. Hence Keith Reader can say of *Un condamné* that it is a "spiritual realist" film, open at once to a transcendental and a nontranscendental interpretation, and Ayfre can say of the transcendental in Bresson that "we are dealing with immanent transcendence, or even, one might say, with radical invisibility" in that "the invisible world remains invisible, or rather appears only as invisible."[31] Clearly, if Deleuze must read Kierkegaard through Nietzsche to transform a philosophy of transcendence into a thought of immanence, no such interpretive labor is required with Bresson because the transformation of transcendence into immanence may be regarded as having already taken place in his films.

Deleuze touches on the element of choice in the narratives of Bresson's films, and he alludes to Bresson's persistent dramatization of the theme of grace or chance, but Deleuze's interest in Bresson is largely formal, rather than diegetic or thematic. Deleuze stresses the principle of "fragmentation" in Bresson's practice, especially as it is brought to bear in the construction of an *espace quelconque*. In the famous Gare de Lyon sequence of *Pickpocket*, for example, the conventional spatiotemporal connections between elements are broken and the space is fragmented into components capable of being reconnected in diverse ways. "It is a perfectly singular space," says Deleuze, "which has simply lost its homogeneity.... It is a space of virtual connection, grasped as a pure place of the possible."[32] Deleuze also cites Bresson as one of the great innovators in the handling of sound. Bresson treats the sonic and the visual as separate strata, thereby introducing a gap between sight and sound that complements the gap between images that structures the visual. Bresson says that he seeks in his films a "*sort of relay*" between sight and sound, and Deleuze says that a "coming-and-going" between the visual and the sonic "defines the modern cinema."[33]

In his *The Time-Image* discussion of choosing to choose, however, Deleuze concentrates on a third aspect of Bresson's cinema—that of Bresson's selection, training, and manipulation of actors, or as Bresson prefers to call them, "models." Bresson observes that "nine-tenths of our movements obey habit and automatism. It is anti-nature to subordinate them to the will and to thought."[34] Traditionally trained actors are incapable of performances informed by such natural automatism, so he works largely with nonprofessionals. He forces his "models" to rehearse repeatedly until their gestures and words become automatic, and he demands that his models eliminate all overt signs of expressivity or intentionality during filming. Through the suppression of thought and will in his models, Bresson aims at a kind of naturalness, yet he also seeks the unexpected and the unknown, that which is beyond either the model's or the director's intentions but which the camera alone can capture. Models, says Bresson, are *"automatically* inspired, inventive,"[35] for it is "a mechanism [that] makes the unknown come forth."[36] The result of this practice is a cinema inhabited by hyperalert sleepwalkers, curiously doubled presences that seem separated from themselves, often apparently flat and unemotional, yet suddenly traversed by intense and unexpected affects.

Deleuze argues that in Bresson's models, we see a manifestation of the thinker within modern cinematic thought, which Deleuze labels the *spiritual automaton* (a term borrowed from Spinoza and Leibniz). If our contemporary dilemma is that of a loss of faith in this world, the dilemma of an "intolerable" bad-movie world devoid of genuine possibility, the only means of overcoming this dilemma is to think differently, and indeed, only such a different kind of thought constitutes genuine thinking. To think differently, however, is in a sense to exceed our present thought, to go beyond what we know and hold certain. Only by injecting into thought something uncharted and incomprehensible, a pure Outside, can genuine thinking begin. When this occurs, another thinker arises within thought, a thinker that is a function of the breakdown of ordinary thought, and hence, one might say, a thinker that is a perpetual product of the "impotence of thought." In the modern cinema, thinking differently consists of unchaining the image-chains of received opinions and beliefs and then reenchaining images through the gaps between them. Each gap is a locus of the Outside, within which conventional thought stutters and collapses, while in that same gap, another thinker within thought begins to arise, an alien, nonhuman (or ahuman) thinker, an automaton produced by and productive of the Outside.

Bresson's screen models, then, are both manifestations of the spiritual automaton and figures of that alien thinker within thought that is generated in the modern cinema. The spiritual automaton, finally, is not something limited to embodiment in the humans on the screen, but rather, a function distributed across a given film through its gaps as well as a function generated within spectators when the film succeeds in meeting its ends. Such a function arises through a practice, that of unchaining conventional chains of images and reenchaining, each new juxtaposition being a throw of the dice, a choice to trust in the possibilities of the unpredictable and unknowable. The modern cinematic practice of unchaining and reenchaining via the gap of the Outside is a practice of choosing to choose, a mode of existence that generates the spiritual automaton. We should note as well, however, that choosing to choose is not entirely a matter of will and personal decision. Kierkegaard's leap of faith is a leap beyond reason and into the absurd, but it remains a leap of the individual thinker possessed of an identity and a will. In appropriating Kierkegaard for his immanent ethics, Deleuze might be suspected of simply repeating Sartre's existential modification of Kierkegaard, but choosing to choose is not a matter of authenticity or a personal commitment to freedom; rather, it is a matter of generating an alien thinker within thought, one that only emerges at the limits of will and reason. The spiritual automaton is such a thinker, one proper to the modern cinema, and in Bresson's handling of his models, we find an instance of the practice of choosing to choose. Bresson "radically suppress[es] the *intentions* of [his] models,"[37] and he frees their movements from any subordination "to the will and to thought."[38] Once they "become automatic, protected against all thought,"[39] they become "*automatically* inspired, inventive,"[40] instances of "a mechanism [that] makes the unknown come forth."[41]

Bresson's cinematic models may be regarded as figures of the spiritual automaton, but in one specific sense, they may also serve as guides to an understanding of Deleuze's conception of cinema's relationship to philosophy. Bresson's models deliver their lines as if their words were someone else's. As they speak, linguistic signs begin to separate from visual signs; the verbal and the visual diverge into separate strata of sound and sight. This splitting of seeing from speaking, and this assimilation of language within a sonic continuum, are fundamental to modern cinema and to its potential for inducing new thought.

What does Deleuze find most appealing about cinema? Deleuze is fascinated by the visual, and especially by the possibility of seeing differently. The basic obstacle to seeing differently is conventional narrative, and by extension, language. In his study of Francis Bacon, Deleuze identifies Bacon's primary aim as that of rendering images devoid of narrative connotations. In his essay on Beckett's television plays, Deleuze argues that Beckett attempts to move beyond words, to dry up the voices that incessantly tell their mundane stories, and to bring forth pure images, both visual and sonic, which are freed from all narrative associations. Even in his many writings on literature, Deleuze pays little attention to narrative per se, and in his book on masochism, he shows that Sacher-Masoch's fictions are mere stagings of frozen visual tableaus. And in his last book, *Essays Critical and Clinical*, Deleuze asserts that one of literature's primary functions is to create within language what he calls Visions and Auditions, visual and sonic images at the limits of language that arise within the verbal like hallucinatory presences looming between or floating above the words.

For Deleuze, thinking differently is fundamentally a matter of seeing differently, and for him, cinema is above all a visual medium. What distinguishes cinema from painting is, first, that movement and time are directly rendered within the visual cinematic image, and second, that cinema immediately engages the problem of vision's relation to language and conventional narrative. With the collapse of the sensorimotor schema in modern film, detached, "unchained" visual images arise, while at the same time, commonsense narratives fall apart. Language is cut loose from its network of conventional associations with visual images, and it becomes part of a sonic continuum. Language enters into a back-and-forth relay with visual images, but as a component of the sonic continuum, it also tends toward its own aural limit as a-signifying affective sound. Cinema's distinction among the arts, then, is that of being the art that most fully and most directly engages the crucial philosophical problem of thinking differently by seeing differently.

The cinematic agent of this new mode of seeing is the spiritual automaton, a strange kind of agent in that it is less the cause of a new seeing than the produced locus within which such seeing arises. In this regard, it has as its analog in philosophy what Deleuze and Guattari call the "conceptual persona," the similarity between the spiritual automaton and the conceptual persona, suggesting one final aspect of cinema's privileged relationship with philosophy. In *What Is Philosophy?* Deleuze and Guattari approach philosophy as the invention of concepts, arguing that such invention requires three elements: concepts, a plane of immanence, and a conceptual persona. The conceptual persona "is not the representative of the philosopher, but the reverse: the philosopher is only the envelope of his principal conceptual persona."[42] The conceptual persona at once precedes and follows the plane of immanence, in this regard both producing and being produced by thought. It is "the becoming or the subject of a [given] philosophy"[43] that arises within the philosopher as a separate, "other" thinker. And above all, it is a locus of movement in thought. "In the philosophical enunciation," say Deleuze and Guattari, "one does not produce something by saying it, but one produces movement by thinking it, through the intermediary of a conceptual persona."[44]

In *What Is Philosophy?* Deleuze and Guattari assert that the conceptual persona is a component of all genuine philosophical thought, but it is clear that their inspiration for the notion comes primarily from such "philosophers of the future" as Kierkegaard and Nietzsche. In *Difference and Repetition* Deleuze says that Kierkegaard and Nietzsche are the first philosophers to put movement within thought, and they do so by fashioning a theater of philosophy, with its heroes being Abraham and Job in the one theater, and Dionysus and Zarathustra in the other. Those actors are the conceptual personae of Kierkegaard's and Nietzsche's thought, vectors that arise within thought as apersonal agents of movement. Given the similarity between the conceptual persona and the spiritual automaton, perhaps, then, we should rephrase Deleuze and say that Kierkegaard and Nietzsche create not a theater, but a cinema of philosophy, with conceptual personae that function like spiritual automata, generating and being generated by different ways of thinking.

In *What Is Philosophy?* Deleuze and Guattari outline the fundamental elements of philosophy and then differentiate philosophy first from the sciences and then from the arts. The domain of the arts is said to be that of sensation, the aim of the arts being the creation of affects and percepts on a plane of composition. Philosophy, by contrast, has as its goal the creation of concepts on a plane of immanence. The arts' plane of composition is identified as a plane of the possible, whereas philosophy's plane of immanence is a plane of the virtual.[45] In *What Is Philosophy?* Deleuze and Guattari's treatment of the arts focuses almost exclusively on painting, music, and literature, with virtually no references to film, an absence explained perhaps by Deleuze's having already written at length on cinema, but perhaps also by the fact that cinema blurs the line between philosophy and the arts, a line Deleuze and Guattari are intent on sharpening in *What Is Philosophy?* This neat demarcation of philosophy from the arts seems especially challenged by the notion of the possible in *The Movement-Image* and *The Time-Image*, for the possible in those works is the dimension of creation in general, whether it be a creation in philosophical concepts or a creation in cinematic images. The possible is the domain of experimentation on the real, a zone in which possibilities are produced through disruptive critical practices, but in which, as well, the possibility of the new is anticipated as an outcome of each experimentation. The possible, thus, is the domain of an ethics and a faith common to thought in general.

The "strange thought" Deleuze finds in the philosophy of Kierkegaard and the cinema of Bresson is one that affirms an ethic of choosing to choose and a faith of belief in this world. Kierkegaard fashions a cinematic philosophy whose conceptual personae produce genuine movement within thought, leaping beyond universal reason and morality into a future of unknowable possibilities. Bresson constructs a philosophical cinema whose models are embodied spiritual automata, their speech and actions manifesting a split between words and images, between hearing and seeing, that split inducing fissures in the continuities of conventional narratives. Kierkegaard and Bresson's common ethic may have a transcendent religious dimension, but its practice promotes an immanent ethics. Choosing to choose is a mode of existence, a way of living in this world, and the faith that informs it is a belief in the possibilities of this world as well. The single aim of philosophy and cinema is to think differently, to unchain the sequences of inevitabilities governed by received opinion and belief, and then to reconnect the pieces in contingent yet necessary Markov chains. Thinking differently entails choosing to choose, adopting a way of living that allows a belief in the world's "possibilities in movements and intensities to give birth once again to new modes of existence."[46] As Deleuze and Guattari say in *What Is Philosophy?*, "it may be that believing in this world, in this life, has become our most difficult task, or the task of a mode of existence yet to be discovered on our plane of immanence today."[47]

Notes

1 Gilles Deleuze, *Cinema 2: The Time-Image*, trans. Hugh Tomlinson and Robert Galeta (Minneapolis: University of Minnesota Press, 1989), 225, *173*. Originally published in Paris by Éditions de Minuit in 1985. Page references are to the French edition, followed by the corresponding passage in the English translation in italics.

2 Gilles Deleuze, *Cinema 1: The Movement-Image*, trans. Hugh Tomlinson

and Barbara Habberjam (Minneapolis: University of Minnesota Press, 1986). The original edition was published in Paris by Éditions de Minuit in 1983.

3   Ibid., 163, 116.
4   Ibid.
5   Gilles Deleuze, *Nietzsche and Philosophy*, trans. Hugh Tomlinson (New York: Columbia University Press, 1983). Originally published as *Nietzsche et la philosophie* (Paris: Presses Universitaires de France, 1962).
6   Ibid., 42, 36.
7   Ibid.
8   Ibid.
9   Søren Kierkegaard, *Fear and Trembling/Repetition*, ed. and trans. Howard V. Hong and Edna H. Hong (Princeton, N.J.: Princeton University Press, 1983).
10 There are, of course, many different readings of Kierkegaard. My own is largely consonant with that of Alistair Hannay, *Kierkegaard* (London: Routledge & Kegan Paul, 1982); see esp. 19–89. For a very different, deconstructive reading of Kierkegaard and *Repetition*, see Roger Poole, *Kierkegaard: The Indirect Communication* (Charlottesville: University of Virginia Press, 1993), esp. 61–82.
11 Kierkegaard, *Fear and Trembling*, 62.
12 Kierkegaard, *Repetition*, 131.
13 Ibid., 149.
14 Kierkegaard, *Fear and Trembling*, 39.
15 Gilles Deleuze, *Difference and Repetition*, trans. Paul Patton (New York: Columbia University Press, 1994), 13, 6. Originally published as *Différence et répétition* (Paris: Presses Universitaires de France, 1968).
16 Deleuze, *Difference and Repetition*, 13, 6.
17 Ibid., 14, 6.
18 Ibid., 15, 7.
19 Deleuze himself makes reference to the Markov chain to describe the principle of historical succession in Foucault's philosophy. See Gilles Deleuze, *Foucault*, trans. Seán Hand (Minneapolis: University of Minnesota Press, 1988), 117. Originally published as *Foucault* (Paris: Éditions de Minuit, 1986), 86. In "Sur les principaux concepts de Michel Foucault," a text written shortly after Foucault's death in 1984 and published in *Deux régimes de fous* (Paris: Éditions de Minuit, 2003), 237, Deleuze says of Foucault's diagrams of systems of thought, "Between two diagrams, between two states of a diagram, there is a mutation, a reshaping of relations of force. This is not because anything can be linked [s'enchaîne] with anything. It's rather like successive drawings of lots, each one of which operates by chance, but in extrinsic conditions determined by the preceding drawing. It's a mixture of the aleatory and the dependent as in a Markov chain." Deleuze most likely draws his understanding of the Markov chain from

one of his favorite writers, the philosopher of biology Raymond Ruyer, who discusses Markov chains in *La Genèse des formes vivantes* (Paris: Flammarion, 1958) 170–89.

20 Deleuze, *Difference and Repetition*, 19, *10*.

21 Ibid., 18, *10*.

22 Ibid., 13, *5*.

23 Ibid., 16, *8*.

24 Kierkegaard, *Fear and Trembling*, 38.

25 Gilles Deleuze and Félix Guattari, *A Thousand Plateaus: Capitalism and Schizophrenia*, trans. Brian Massumi (Minneapolis: University of Minnesota Press, 1987), 281. Originally published as *Milles plateaux: capitalisme et schizophrénie* (Paris: Éditions de Minuit, 1980), 344.

26 Deleuze, *Movement-Image*, 160, *114*.

27 Ibid., 161, *114*.

28 Deleuze, *Deux régimes de fous*, 256–57, underlines the significance of the intolerable in Foucault's thought in a 1986 interview, saying that Foucault "was something of a *seer*. What he saw was for him intolerable.... His own ethics was one of seeing or seizing something as intolerable. It was not in the name of morality. It was his way of thinking. If thought did not go all the way to the intolerable, it was not worth the trouble of thinking at all. To think was always to think to the limit of something."

29 Deleuze, *Time-Image*, 234, *179*.

30 See Paul Schrader, *Transcendental Style in Film: Ozu, Bresson, Dreyer* (Berkeley: University of California Press, 1972), 59–108, and Jonathan Rosenbaum, "The Last Filmmaker: A Local, Interim Report," in *Robert Bresson*, ed. James Quandt (Toronto: Toronto International Film Festival Group, 1998), 21.

31 Keith Reader, *Robert Bresson* (Manchester, U.K.: Manchester University Press, 2000), 49, and Amedée Ayfre, "The Universe of Robert Bresson," trans. Elizabeth Kingsley-Rowe, in *The Films of Robert Bresson*, ed. Ian Cameron (London: Studio Vista, 1969), 21.

32 Deleuze, *Movement-Image*, 155, *109*.

33 Deleuze, *Time-Image*, 322, *247*; Robert Bresson, *Notes sur le cinématographe* (Paris: Gallimard, 1975), 62. Translated by Jonathan Griffin as *Notes on the Cinematographer* (Copenhagen: Green Integer, 1997), 62.

34 Bresson, *Notes*, 29, 32.

35 Ibid., 30, *33*.

36 Ibid., 69, *69*.

37 Ibid., 22, *25*.

38 Ibid., 29, *32*.

39 Ibid., 114, *110*.

40 Ibid., 30, *33*.

41 Ibid., 69, *69*.

42 Gilles Deleuze and Félix Guattari, *What Is Philosophy?*, trans. Hugh

Tomlinson and Graham Burchell (New York: Columbia University Press, 1994), 64. Originally published as *Qu'est-ce que la philosophie?* (Paris: Minuit, 1991), 62.

43 Ibid., 63, 64.
44 Ibid., 63, 64–65.
45 Ibid., 168, 177–78.
46 Ibid., 72, 74.
47 Ibid., 72, 75.

Part III. Becomings

8. Is a Schizoanalysis of Cinema Possible?

Ian Buchanan

> Que demande la schizo-analyse? Rien d'autre qu'un peu de vraie *relation avec le dehors*, un peu de réalité réelle.
>
> What does schizoanalysis ask? Nothing more than a bit of a *relation to the outside*, a little reality.
>
> —Gilles Deleuze and Félix Guattari, *L'Anti-Oedipe*[1]

Is a schizoanalysis of cinema possible? My instinct is to answer unreservedly, "Yes, it is possible," but reason makes me more cautious and doubtful. I cannot but be conscious of the disheartening thought that if Deleuze had wanted such a thing, surely he would have invented it himself. Certainly there is nothing more striking in Deleuze's writing than the apparent discontinuity between *Anti-Oedipus* and *A Thousand Plateaus* and the books he wrote immediately afterward, *Cinema 1: The Movement-Image* and *Cinema 2: The Time-Image*. With the exception of the concepts of "deterritorialization" and "facialization," there is very little crossover of concepts from one project to the next. There is no discussion, for example, of the body without organs of cinema, nor indeed either its abstract machine or assemblage. This is despite the fact that Deleuze and Guattari insisted in the previous books that these are the essential building blocks of all phenomena.

However, for that precise reason, we can perhaps permit ourselves to be somewhat more sanguine about the possibility of a schizoanalysis of cinema than my initial skepticism allowed. If, for Deleuze and Guattari, these three concepts—Deleuzism's own "holy trinity"—describe the essential building blocks of all phenomena (and it is clear that in their eyes, they do; as they write on the first page of *A Thousand Plateaus*, what they have to say applies to "all things" *[toute chose]*), then it is impossible for there *not* to be a body without organs, abstract machine,

135

and assemblage of cinema.[2] The real question, then, is not whether a schizoanalysis of cinema is possible—Deleuze always said questions of possibility were useless questions anyway—but rather, how can it be realized?

Along these lines, then, there are two propositions I want to advance:

1. Delirium is to schizoanalysis as dream is to psychoanalysis: as such, it is the essential touchstone for a schizoanalysis of cinema.
2. The tripartite conceptual schema of body without organs, abstract machine, and assemblage informs the basic matrix of Deleuze's account of the cinematic image: as such, it is already schizoanalytic in its conception.

My procedure in what follows is to look for functional equivalences—that is, rather than trace the lineage of specific words and images, I focus on "diagrams" that, in the manner of little machines, perform essentially the same function from one book to the next. I disagree, then, with those readings of Deleuze that insist on a discontinuity between one aspect of his work and the next. By contrast, I take the view that Deleuze's concepts are migratory (in the sense in which information systems engineers speak of the migration of data). I will first map the functional equivalences I have been able to trace connecting *Anti-Oedipus* and *A Thousand Plateaus* to *The Movement-Image* and *The Time-Image*. I will then endeavor to show the implications of this for a study of cinema. The real work to be done in this project, which obviously extends beyond the reach of this preliminary attempt, is ultimately to show how Deleuze and Guattari's system can be made operative, which is to say, put to use reading films.

Delirium Is to Schizoanalysis as Dream Is to Psychoanalysis

"Schizoanalysis proposes to reach those regions of the orphan unconscious—indeed 'beyond all law'—where the problem of Oedipus can no longer even be raised."[3] For Deleuze and Guattari, the royal road to the unconscious is not the dream, but rather, delirium. Delirium is generally regarded as a type of madness, or in the very least, an aberration of the mind that, if one is lucky, will pass quickly without leaving a scar. But we can also become quite attached to our deliriums—as J. M. Coetzee says, there is nothing more dismaying in literature than

Don Quixote's renunciation of his delirious quest, which is, in effect, a renunciation not only of the imagination itself, but of everything that made his life interesting.[4] The delirious see, hear, and feel things that to the outside observer appear "made up," a kind of fantasy or figment of the imagination, as in Don Quixote's windmills. Despite medical and psychiatric conventions to the contrary, everyday life brims with examples of a generalized acceptance of delirium. When we say, as my grandmother used to, that a goose has just walked over our grave, are we not trying to articulate the feeling of having sensed something that does not belong to this world? Or more exactly, have we not sensed something that can only be sensed, something that cannot be put into words? The Wolf-Man could feel himself becoming a wolf, although he knew very well he was not about to sprout fur and grow fangs. To the delirious, such feelings are fully real; the sensations are as gripping as they are confusing and inarticulable. The Wolf-Man's "mental distress" derived from the fact that he could not explain this feeling to his analysts, Freud and Brunswick, without it being misheard as a fantasy symptomatic of his Oedipal relation with his mother and father. He could never convey the "wolfness" of this feeling. For Freud, the wolf is the father, period. But this is not how the Wolf-Man felt about the wolves in his dream. As Deleuze and Guattari argue, his feelings were rather more complex than that.

On three quite prominent occasions, Deleuze and Guattari use examples drawn from cinema to articulate the significance of what they mean by delirium to an understanding of schizoanalysis considered primarily as a therapeutic enterprise:

> How does a delirium begin? Perhaps the cinema is able to capture the movement of madness, precisely because it is not analytical and regressive, but explores a global field of coexistence. Witness a film by Nicholas Ray [*Bigger Than Life*[5]], supposedly representing the formation of a cortisone delirium: an overworked father, a high-school teacher who works overtime for a radio-taxi service and is being treated for heart trouble. He begins to rave about the education system *in general*, the need to restore a pure *race*, the salvation of the social and moral *order*, then passes to *religion*, the timeliness of a return to the Bible, Abraham.[6]

"What the film shows so well," they continue, is that "every delirium is first of all the investment of a field that is social, economic, political, cultural, racial and racist, pedagogical and religious," and only second-arily familial or Oedipal.[7] His family is made to bear the brunt of his ravings, but they are merely the focal point for a delirium that exceeds the family on all sides and could quite easily be extended well past its present borders. "The fact has often been overlooked that the schizo indeed participates in history; he hallucinates and raves universal his-tory, and proliferates the races. All delirium is racial, which does not necessarily mean racist. It is not a matter of the regions of the body without organs 'representing' races and cultures. The full body does not represent anything at all. On the contrary, the races and cultures designate the regions on this body—that is, zones of intensities, fields of potentials."[8]

The different races are like so many circles of hell (to adapt a phrase from Deleuze and Guattari), radiating outward from a single point the schizo can never seem to escape no matter how far he travels. The second example shows this even more strongly, only now the races have been supplanted by animals:

> I recall the fine film *Willard* (1972, Daniel Mann). A "B" movie per-haps, but a fine unpopular film: unpopular because the heroes are rats.... Willard lives with his authoritarian mother in the old family house. Dreadful oedipal atmosphere. His mother orders him to destroy a litter of rats. He spares one (or two or several). After a violent argu-ment, the mother, who "resembles" a dog, dies. The house is coveted by a businessman, and Willard is in danger of losing it. He likes the principal rat he saved, Ben, who proves to be of prodigious intelligence. There is also a white female rat, Ben's companion. Willard spends all his free time with them. They multiply.[9]

Willard's relation to Ben is intriguing to Deleuze and Guattari because it cannot be contained within the prefabricated Oedipal mold. Ben is not his pet. He is as much Willard's nemesis as friend. He interrupts the Oedipalizing circuits of Willard's various halfhearted, or at any rate, half-witted, attempts to play the role of the man from the suburbs who has a nice house, a good steady job, and a pleasant girlfriend not even the most fastidious of mothers could object to. He gives over the entire basement of his house to Ben and his teeming progeny; he brings his rats to work with him; he feels ill at ease with his girlfriend, Joan, played by a more anemic than usual Sondra Locke, because he knows the rats view his relationship with her as a betrayal.

Willard's relation to the rats is ambivalent at best. He tries to contain the rats in the cellar, but it is futile. "I'm the boss here," he tells them, but they know better. The rats eat too much; they become a burden. What is more, the plainly malevolent Ben is not his favorite rat; the meeker Socrates is, but he stupidly allows Socrates to be killed. Even so, Ben exerts a strange power of fascination Willard cannot ignore. His relationship—a "demonic pact," Deleuze and Guattari call it—with Ben gives him the strength to deal with his overbearing boss, the brutish Mr. Martin, played by Ernest Borgnine, but at the same time, Willard is quite prepared to sacrifice Ben in the process. Willard says to his boss, "You made me hate myself. Well, now I like myself." With that, the rats attack and kill the boss. Willard closes the door, leaving the rats behind him—"Good-bye, Ben," he says. He then goes home and drowns all the rats in his basement. Afterward, Joan comes to his house. He tells her, "My life is changed now—two things did it: Socrates and you. Tomorrow, I'm going to start over. I'm not afraid anymore." Then he sees Ben and he knows it is all over. He shepherds Joan out the door to make ready for what we all know is the final showdown. The very walls of the house seethe with rats. There is no stopping them. The rats eat him.

Willard raises essentially the same questions as Hitchcock's *The Birds*. Hitchcock's film is more enigmatic because the animal behavior it depicts is not at all birdlike, whereas the rats in *Willard* behave more or less as we expect them to. By the same token, Melanie evinces no particular fascination for birds, and in contrast to *Willard*, we are given no inkling as to why the animals should choose to attack her. She does not provoke the birds, as Willard does the rats, nor do the birds appear preternaturally intelligent or hostile, as does Ben. For that reason, psychoanalysis has always tried to make the birds stand for something, usually something that would otherwise be invisible such as the id or superego.[10] But having said that, it has also to be acknowledged that neither Willard's behavior nor that of his rats is exactly ordinary—it, too, is peculiar enough to provoke us to wonder what is going to happen. In contrast to the psychoanalytic strategy of asking what the birds or rats stand for, Deleuze and Guattari focus on what they do. The rats, the birds, are not representations of abstractions like the id or superego; they are "populations" living in our heads. But it is not the fact that they are either birds or rats that is vital. What matters, rather, is the way they are organized. It is their swarming that is crucial, and then only insofar as that swarm draws an "arc of instability" around the subject, marking the current threshold of deterritorialization he or she is about to cross. Hitchcock's film is exemplary in this respect. The birds are first presented in their innocuous molar form: a single bird in a bird shop, when Mitch and Melanie meet; a pair of lovebirds in a cage on the drive to Bodega Bay; a solitary seagull in a clear sky when Melanie rows to Mitch's house. But all that changes quite suddenly, and for no apparent reason, the swarming molecular form emerges and the birds attack. In short, Hitchcock's *The Birds* does not depict what a delirium looks like, so much as capture what it *feels* like—its onset is sudden, the birds create radiating circles (the "arc of instability") around Melanie that she can never quite escape from, and when one group of birds stops attacking her in one place, another starts somewhere else.

What is on the screen is delirium in person—what we see is always inside somebody's head, and for that reason, it looks and feels real, even when it is not. In *The Movement-Image*, Deleuze makes this explicit. The shot acts like a consciousness, "but the sole cinematographic conscious-ness is not us, the spectator, nor the hero; it is the camera—sometimes human, sometimes inhuman, or superhuman."[11]

My third example takes this a step further. Citing at length Michel Cournot's account of the function of laughter in Charlie Chaplin's films, Deleuze and Guattari propose that cinema can also produce a delirium of the spectator.[12] Chaplin's genius, according to Cournot, was to lead the viewer outside of herself so as to cease to identify with the principal character, namely, Chaplin himself, and to begin to directly experience what he calls "the resistance of the events" that Chaplin's character encounters. We have the same surprises, fears, premonitions, and so forth, as he does because, psychotically enough, we have stepped into his position—we occupy his place in the cinematographic consciousness, namely, the moving camera. In this example, we have moved from a discussion of the content of the film to its constitution. In its ability to subsume the subject position of the hero, and also to perform inhuman acts of speed and flight, the camera's movement generalizes all move-ment and disorients us. The moving camera deterritorializes the image: we no longer see it as simply "theater" that happens to be filmed. "In other words, the essence of the cinematographic movement-image lies in extracting from vehicles or moving bodies the movement which is their common substance, or extracting from movements the mobility which is their essence."[13] We enter into cinema's phenomenological space—its "atmosphere," to use Deleuze and Guattari's term—as one enters a delirium: we cease to judge in terms of true and false, real and possible, and so on, and embrace instead its peculiar strain of *réalité réelle*. Two decades later, in *The Movement-Image*, Deleuze takes this position to its logical limit. In the discussion of framing, which we will have occasion to look at again in more detail in a moment, Deleuze says the following: "the cinematographic image is always dividual: This is because, in the final analysis, the screen, as the frame of frames, gives a common standard of measurement to things which do not have one—long shots of countryside and close-ups of the face, an astronomical system and a single drop of water—parts which do not have the same denominator of distance, relief or light. In all these senses the frame ensures a deterritorialization of the image."[14] Outside the darkened confines of the theater, only the seriously deranged could make the kinds of global comparisons routinely constructed by the cinematic image.

Cinema is delirium. This is the meaning of Bergson's thesis that the movement "as physical reality in the external world, and the image, as psychic reality in consciousness, could no longer be opposed," on which Deleuze bases his entire philosophy of cinema.[15] If cinema is delirium, we need a theory of delirium to form the basis of a schizoanalysis of cinema. And that, I suggest, is precisely what we get in *A Thousand Plateaus*. In a marvelous couple of pages, Deleuze and Guattari link the birth of psychiatry and psychoanalysis to the problems to thought posed by delirium: "in the first years of the twentieth century, psychiatry, at the height of its clinical skills, confronted the problem of nonhallucinatory delusions in which the mental integrity is retained without 'intellectual diminishment.'"[16] The great psychiatric thinkers of the period—Esquirol, Kraeplin, Sérieux, Capgras, and Clérambault—were able to identify two main groups of delusional behaviors, each with their own distinct etiologies, which Deleuze and Guattari designate as *signifying* or *passional* and *postsignifying* or *subjective*. The first regime has five key features: its onset is insidious; it has a hidden center that bears witness to endogenous forces organized around an idea (for this reason, Deleuze and Guattari also describe this particular delusion-formation as ideational, in contrast with the second type, which is active); it creates a "gliding atmosphere" capable of linking any kind of incident; it is organized in a series of constantly expanding radiating circles, which the individual must jump between (the "family," the "analyst," and so on); and last, its atmosphere can be changed by the irruption of secondary centers clustering around the principal nucleus of the "idea."

The second regime has four key features: its onset is sudden, usually triggered "by a decisive external occurrence, by a relation with the outside that is expressed more as an emotion than an idea and more as effort or action than imagination" (which is why it is described as an active, rather than ideational, delusion); instead of a "gliding atmosphere" pervading the entirety of one's existence, it operates in a precisely localized sector; and its movement is linear, rather than radiating, usually taking the form of a limited "series" or "proceeding" that comes to an end only to commence again elsewhere. The first regime, then, is an idea or thought we cannot shake (like Woody Allen, when he said, "If it is not one thing, it's your mother"), whereas the second is a path we are impelled to follow (like Samuel Beckett, when he said, "It is not as if I wanted to write"). "If we consider the two types of intact delusions," Deleuze and Guattari write, "we can say people in the first group seem to be completely mad, but aren't: President Schreber developed his radiating paranoia and relations with God in every direction, but was not mad in that he remained capable of managing his wealth wisely and distinguishing between circles. At the other pole are those who do not seem mad in any way, but are, as borne out by their sudden actions, such as quarrels, arsons, murders."[17]

Psychiatry, Deleuze and Guattari argue, was constituted by this dialectical split, pulling it in two contradictory directions at once, invidiously compelling it to plead for tolerance and open-door asylums, on one hand, and stepped-up surveillance and security, on the other. The problem is exacerbated by the fact that it is sane-looking active delusionals who are the really dangerous ones, not the insane-looking ideational delusionals who are, by contrast, quite placid. As the old saying goes, "It's always the quiet ones you have to watch out for." No wonder psychiatry has given rise to so much hostility over the years— psychiatrists either alarm us by locking up people who appear sane (but are not) or infuriate us by not locking up people who appear insane (but are not). Is it by chance, Deleuze and Guattari ask, that these two major types of delusion recapitulate the distinction between the classes: a paranoid bourgeoisie whose ideas are radiant and radiating (is this not the meaning of hegemony?) and a schizophrenic working class reduced to sporadic, highly localized actions that can but rarely impact on the suzerainty of the upper class's ideas? Activists as diverse as Susan George (from Attac) and Subcommandante Marcos (Zapatistas) have stressed, for this reason, that it is in the realm of ideas that our struggles against the predations of global capitalism really need to be fought. But ideas in this sense are the proverbial circles of hell, and the would-be revolutionary simply ends up jumping from one to another—we need to stop environmental degradation, we need more jobs, we need wage protection, we need to end third-world poverty, and so on, each idea forestalling the next—without us ever happening on the idea that could bring about a paradigm change. "All paranoiacs are not bourgeois, all passionals or monomaniacs are not proletarian," Deleuze and Guattari explain. "But God and his psychiatrists are charged with recognizing, among de facto mixes, those who preserve, even in delusion, the class-based social order, and those who sow disorder."[18]

Deleuze and Guattari give the highest priority they can to the analysis of the regime of signs. Schizoanalysis has no other object, they say. The regime of signs is what we presuppose to make meaning. I will not rehearse in detail here Deleuze and Guattari's full account of regimes of signs. Suffice it to point out two things: first, it is a conception of semiology in which the signifier does not have primacy; second, it is a conception of semiology "in which language never has universality in itself."[19] The implications for an analysis of cinema are surprising. What results, as I will explain in more detail later, is a strange kind of formalism that is at once rigorously deterministic and yet open to variation. There are other "regimes of signs," as Deleuze and Guattari label these delusion-formations, but these are the two most common, or predominant, in Western capitalist society. Each entails a way of seeing the world that is quite distinct from the other, even though it is rare to encounter such ways of seeing in their pure form. Psychoanalysis, Deleuze and Guattari argue, only recognizes one regime of signs, the signifying, and to its shame, whenever it encounters another type, it applies its own unique variety of thaumaturgy to transform it into something it recognizes. "The Wolf-Man keeps howling: Six Wolves! Seven Wolves! Freud says, How's that? Goats, you say? How interesting. Take away the goats and all you have left is a wolf, so it's your father."[20] One positive implication, however, is that like a watch that has stopped, psychoanalysis is right some of the time—the signifying regime does operate the way it says it does. The problem is that "interpretation" of the type psychoanalysis is justly famous for is a symptom of this regime of signs in full flight, rather than a pathway to a cure, hence the interminability of the so-called talking cure, which Freud himself acknowledged, not a little despairingly, toward the end of his life. Deleuze and Guattari state matters even more sternly: "nothing is ever over and done within a regime of this kind. It's made for that, it's the tragic regime of infinite debt, to which one is simultaneously debtor and creditor."[21]

The regime of signs systematizes the condition of production of the delirium—it does not so much render a delirium legible to us as reveal its consistency. We can see how it is formed and how it reproduces itself. Deleuze's cinema books propose two cinematic variants of what he and Guattari referred to as "regimes of signs": the movement-image and the time-image, each in their distinct way a theory of the condition of the production of the cinematographic image. These concepts articulate the consistency of the image under the sign of history—both of the medium itself (i.e., the history of its artistic and technical innovations) and of the world itself, as the essential backdrop of all forms of creativity. The history of cinema as Deleuze writes it—he sometimes calls it a "natural history"—fuses these two aspects of history by treating the image types (rather than specific instances of the image, about which he is always extremely judicious, just as liable to applaud as rebuke) as the best they can be in the circumstances in which they are produced: "the history of cinema is a long martyrology."[22] Deleuze himself alerts us to this convergence between the regime of signs and his history of types of cinematographic images, when he writes, "Two regimes of the image can be contrasted point by point; an organic regime and a crystalline regime, or more generally a kinetic regime and a chronic regime."[23] Here he maps out four key points of comparison and, in doing so, reveals very clearly the extent to which his thinking on cinema is indebted to his earlier work, and not just at the level of a generalized commitment to transcendental empiricism, but at the more practical and idiosyncratic level of the formal architecture of his concepts. The four ordinal points are as follows: (1) description, (2) the relation between the real and the imaginary, (3) narration, and (4) truth. They canvas, respectively, what in a more traditional cinema studies vernacular is known as setting, or the supposedly preexisting reality cinema either records or projects; sequencing or continuity (although these are not quite the right words), as the mental operation we constantly perform to make sense of the stream of images cinema presents; dramatization, or the weaving together of action and space; and truth, the conviction that what we are witnessing is really happening in the possible world of the cinema, something that the evolution of dream sequences and the like would cast into doubt.

The cinematographic regime, as I will call it, consists of these four elements in a state of dynamic interaction. Change at the level of the image occurs when one or more of these elements is pushed beyond its present limits in such a way that it risks bringing about a generalized collapse of the regime and, in doing so, opens up new "vistas of possibility," to use one Guattari's formulations. Deleuze is always quite careful to stipulate that the shift from the movement-image (which was the first form of cinematographic image to be invented) to the time-image (which was the second, and so far the only other form of cinematographic image to be invented) cannot be conceived as progress: "there is no value-judgment here, because this new regime—no less than the old one—throws up its ready-made formulas, its set procedures, its labored and empty applications, its failures, its conventional and 'second-hand' examples offered to us as masterpieces. What is interesting is the new status of the image, this new type of narration-description in so far as it initially inspires very different great authors [auteurs]."[24] Under the umbrella of these two major forms of the image, there are dozens of complex and highly original permutations, which is what gives cinema its interest. The point to be borne in mind here is that the image has a "deep structure" that functions as its immanent condition of possibility, determining what can and cannot be incorporated.

Slavoj Žižek provides a vivid illustration of what is at stake here when he asks us to imagine a pornographic sex scene inserted in the middle of *Out of Africa*. In effect, when he argues that this is impossible to conceive without radically altering the movie, he is saying that the regime of signs underpinning it is incompatible with the regime of signs we conventionally associate with pornography.[25] The actual film does not need to show "all" because its regime is constituted in such a way that everything the camera "touches" is imbued with significance; thus a "gliding atmosphere" of eroticism is established that constantly radiates outward from the idea of what might take place in the privacy of the bedroom. To show "all" would realign this heady atmosphere so that instead of radiating waves of eroticism, there would be a linear sequence leading from the first kiss to the bedroom, where the act would be consummated, and then the whole sequence would need to be restarted elsewhere. In other words, the problem is not—as Žižek supposes—that the film cannot incorporate explicit sex; rather, what it cannot incorporate is a linear sequence with a beginning, middle, and end as sex scenes inevitably tend to be. It should not be thought from this that it is always impossible to mix different regimes, because that is not the case, nor indeed that pornography is only ever filmed in one way. But it is the case that regimes can only be mixed under certain conditions. We may add, too, that what we take to be the most exciting works are very often the products of mixed regimes.[26]

Delirium is a royal road to a schizoanalysis of cinema because its perceptual regime can be formalized. In the next section, I will consider how the cinematic regime of signs is realized by looking at cinema's own "holy trinity," at least according to Deleuze, of the shot, frame, and montage. The regime of signs is a form of expression; shot, frame, and montage comprise the corresponding form of content.

Deleuze's Account of the Cinematic Image Is Already Schizoanalytic

Deleuze and Guattari's revision of psychoanalysis does not take the form of a wholesale repudiation of Freud, as most people seem to think. Their tendency, rather, is to attempt to unblock the blockages in his thought. Very often, as is the case with delirium, they are more than willing to credit him with great clinical discoveries, only then to shake their heads in disappointment that he did not realize the true nature of his insights. Their general assessment of Freud is that he understood neurosis, but psychosis escaped him. Even so, Deleuze and Guattari attribute to Freud's 1915 paper "The Unconscious" the clinical discovery of the difference between neurosis and psychosis: "Freud says that hysterics or obsessives are people capable of making a global comparison between a sock and a vagina, a scar and castration, etc. Doubtless it is at one and the same time they apprehend the object globally and perceive it as lost. Yet it would never occur to a neurotic to grasp the skin erotically as a multiplicity of pores, little spots, little scars or black holes, or to grasp the sock erotically as a multiplicity of stitches.... Comparing a sock to a vagina is OK, it's done all the time, but you'd have to be insane to compare a pure aggregate of stitches to a field of vaginas: that's what Freud says."[27]

Deleuze and Guattari describe this observation as a great clinical discovery because it clarifies the difference between the two types of pathologies known commonly as neurosis and psychosis, and because it sets the stage for their own investigations. What is at stake here is the difference between two regimes of signs—the "signifying" and "passional." In their eyes, Freud stood on the threshold of making the discovery of "the greatest art of the unconscious," namely, the art of "molecular multiplicities," but somehow he botched it. Having served him so well in so many other situations, Freud's unshakeable conviction that all "dream-thoughts" can be treated sensibly—that is, as representations of one kind or another: a sock for a vagina, a wolf for daddy, and so on—left him unable to grasp the peculiar form of action and ideation known as delirium. Although mindful of the fact that this correspondence appears to break down in the case of psychosis, Freud nonetheless pins his hopes on the power of the proper name to restore unity to thoughts and ideas that seem to be fleeing from his grasp. The Wolf-Man has an obsession with wolves, Freud thinks, but this is just a screen for his true state of mind, and all his symptoms can be explained by isolating the central fact of his passive attitude toward his father. His imperious gaze, that of the "one supposed to know," prevents him from seeing that the boy in the dream is not just looking at the wolves; they are also looking at him, or more particularly, reaching out to him: "a fibre stretches from a human to an animal, from a human or an animal to molecules, from molecules to particles, and so on to the imperceptible. Every fibre is a Universe fibre."[28]

Here Deleuze and Guattari make their single most important intervention into dream analysis. Freud, they cry, thinks that the boy of the famous dream of the five wolves in the tree is looking at the wolves. But are not the wolves also looking at him? "Freud obviously knows nothing about the fascination exerted by wolves and the meaning of their silent call, the call to become-wolf. Wolves watch, intently watch, the dreaming child; it is so much more reassuring to tell oneself that it is really the child who sees the dogs or parents in the act of making love."[29] The watching wolves could still be representations of daddy, to be sure, but to acknowledge that the wolves are watching the boy and not merely obscuring thoughts of his father via the process Freud termed the dream-work is already to insist on the importance of something Freud more or less ignores, namely, the spatial arrangement of the dream elements. The wolves are just outside the window, watching, waiting, threatening, but in an obscure manner. What are they waiting for? If they wanted to attack, why do they hesitate? Is there something holding them back? If they are not about to attack, then what is their purpose? What do they watch for? Are they perhaps waiting for someone to join them?

We see more clearly what Deleuze and Guattari are trying to do when they offer Kafka's short story, "Jackals and Arabs," as a parallel example. The Jackals, too, watch and wait, on the edge of the camp, thereby creating, as they explain, three different kinds of spaces that can be designated as follows: inside the camp, outside the camp, and the boundary between the two. The Wolf-Man's dream exhibits the same three types of spaces: inside the bedroom, outside the bedroom, and the boundary between the two. One can specify the difference between these two positions very simply: it is the difference between being inside or outside a particular space, and being an insider or an outsider. Jackals and Wolves are outsiders regardless of whether they are inside or outside the camp or bedroom, which is what makes them so fearful. It is not the topography that governs the distribution or peopling of these spaces, but the other way round: it is the distribution or peopling that creates the topography. If this were a film instead of a dream, we would say that it is the camera that creates the distribution that, in turn, creates the topography.

If we draw a diagram of the Wolf-Man's dream, taking account of where the wolves are in relation to the boy, the first thing we notice is that the boy is on the outer edge of the pack. We know he is part of the pack because the wolves are in his head; they are his people. But the fact that they are standing in the cold, hiding out in a skeletal tree in the middle of an immense barren space, tells us that his relation to them is uncertain. What sinews reach out to him to bind him to the group? How does he relate to them? Why is it so dark and cold? These are the second and third things, respectively, that we should notice about the spatial arrangement of the dream. The interesting question, then, is how does the boy in the dream feel? I do not mean how does the Wolf-Man feel? We know the answer to that, or at least, we have an answer to that—he says he felt terrified, that he was in great danger. But his fear is nameless. He halfheartedly ascribes it to a fear of being eaten, but we are no less unconvinced by that than Deleuze and Guattari. It does not ring true somehow. Our attention is drawn to what the Wolf-Man specifies as the only action in the dream—the opening of the bedroom window. This is a threshold moment in the dream: is he an insider or an outsider? Obviously, the boy is inside the four walls of his bedroom, but those walls no longer seem to contain him. He does not feel as though he belongs there. The wolves are watching him, but perhaps not as predators salivating over their prey, as he at first fears, but as compassionate outsiders who recognize their own—the Wolf-Man feels like he is part of the pack; that is where he belongs. If he is an insider at all, it is as a member of the wolf pack watching him from the tree, not the family sleeping in the bedrooms down the corridor. They are out in the cold, and so is he. But this is a giant step to make, and he hesitates. The frozen wasteland seen from his window is his plane of immanence, his body without organs. Freud makes no mention of the geography underpinning the spatial arrangement of the dream. He imbues the wolves with significance, but not the snow. In contrast, Deleuze and Guattari downplay the significance of the wolves, except to observe that they are species that hunt and live in packs, but play up the significance of the snow, or at least its icy emptiness.

Deleuze and Guattari's delirium-centered dream analysis does not ask what the wolves in the tree mean, but rather, what does this distribution of wolves on that plane tell us about the boy's state of mind? How is it working? We can observe that his mental topography and physical geography are at odds with one another. He is an insider where he is not, and an outsider where he is. His feet are in one place, and his head another. What Deleuze and Guattari describe as becoming-wolf is precisely this process of leaving one formation, where one is an insider, for another—we become-wolf to the extent that we start to feel like outsiders in human company and insiders in the company of wolves. The wolves mark the limit point of our present state of "humanity"; they are the point beyond which we are no longer the same person. This affinity does not imply that one identifies with wolves or feels in any way wolflike (which is why the designation "Wolf-Man" is really an abuse).

The space of the dream appears vast and unlimited, but in reality, it is a closed system, a regime of signs—it cannot admit any changes of detail without changing the whole. A trace of blood, a swirling leaf, tracks in the snow, even the smallest additional detail alters everything. But rather than continue to think of it in pathological terms, I want to shift the discussion back to the schizoanalysis of cinema by viewing it, experimentally, as a cinematographic image. I have said that the royal road for schizoanalysis is the delirium, not the dream, so it may appear that I am going back on my word by focusing on this example. However, I think there is good reason to plead that this is a special case of a dream that has the quality of a delirium—or as it might also be said with some justice, a delirium that took the form of a dream. As Freud notes, the dream has a "lasting sense of reality," which the Wolf-Man himself seemed to think deserved notice.[30] Freud takes this as his starting point because according to his experience, this indicates that the dream recollects in its own uniquely transfigured way some real event. We may simply say that in the manner of all deliriums, it *felt real* to the Wolf-Man—the wolves were in his head; they were alive to him, and whether they sprang from the pages of half-remembered fairy tales, they clearly had more substance, more flesh and blood, than mere figments of a dream. (The Wolf-Man would later tell Freud that he thought the opening of the window indicated that in reality, he had opened his eyes, so that what he saw in the trees belonged to his waking memory, not his dreams.)

It will be recalled that the cinematographic regime consists of the following four dynamic elements (these elements are realized through the agencies of framing, shot, and montage, which I will deal with in more detail in a moment):

1. description
2. the relation between the real and the imaginary
3. narration
4. truth

What is crucial concerning description, Deleuze says, is whether the setting stands for a "supposedly pre-existing reality" or creates its own reality or realities, which constantly give way to other realities that "contradict, displace, or modify the preceding ones."[31] It is clear that Freud treats the Wolf-Man's account as belonging to the first type. This is what Deleuze calls the *organic regime*, which implies that the reality of the dream comes from the outside, whereas Deleuze and Guattari categorize it as belonging to the second type, namely, the *crystalline regime*, which means that the reality of the dream is at once self-generating and unstable. The dream does not occur in *his* bedroom, but a bedroom, and as the window opens—which it does all by itself—the room itself seems to change nature: it is no longer *a* bedroom looking out on a frosty landscape in which there stands a tree with wolves on it, but rather, impossibly enough, *a* bedroom *in* a frosty landscape in which there stands a tree with wolves on it. If it looked like his bedroom to begin with, it was a matter of habit. Turning more directly to Deleuze's work on cinema, we may observe that the Wolf-Man's passivity is consistent, too, with the crystalline regime, which Deleuze says is the cinema of the seer *(voyant)*, not the agent *(actant)*: he does not react to his situation, but rather, he records it. His situation "outstrips his motor capacities on all sides," and, as Deleuze puts it, "makes him see and hear what is no longer subject to the rules of a response or an action."[32] His situation is patently that of the child, which, as Deleuze notes, was of central importance to the development of neorealism because in the child's motor helplessness, the child is an astute watcher and listener of what goes on around him or her. The child absorbs the world.

Quite obviously, the second element, the relation between the real and the imaginary, follows from the first. In the organic regime, the distinction between the real and imaginary is rigorously maintained—even if the film consists largely of dream sequences, there is always a perspective point of the real that serves to differentiate one kind of image from the other. The ontology of the preexisting reality is preserved, even if interrupted by "the continuity shots which establish it and by the laws which determine successions, simultaneities and permanences: it is a regime of localizable relations, actual linkages, legal, causal and logical connections."[33] There is always a consciousness in which the dream sequences can be actualized and the various illogicalities of sequencing rationalized. Think of the way the Dalí-designed sequence in Hitchcock's *Spellbound* is carefully corralled by a plot that makes it into an intelligible "truth," so there is never any doubt that what we are witnessing is a dream firmly connected to a preexisting reality. One has only to compare this to David Lynch's *Mulholland Drive* to see what happens when this model of structuration is dispensed with and the organic regime gives way to the crystalline. Here there is no overarching plot to position the dream as a dream and render it intelligible. We can no longer discern a perspective point of the real that can reliably differentiate the dream image from the supposedly real, and consequently, we find ourselves absorbed by a game of cat and mouse, in which the virtual and actual seem to be chasing each other.

In apparent contradiction of our initial findings, the Wolf-Man's dream would seem to be a clear-cut case of an organic regime, and not crystalline, as just described, inasmuch as the dream seems to be clearly differentiated from reality and firmly anchored in *his* consciousness. Yet on closer examination, our impression soon changes, and we find that our first thought is confirmed. If we follow Freud as he elicits the Wolf-Man's associated memories that supposedly "explain" the dream, we start to wonder where the dream begins and ends: we move from a picture of a rampant wolf in an illustrated book of fairy tales to flocks of fluffy white sheep on the family estate, and from there, to an epidemic in the flock, a failed attempt at a cure, and the resulting pile of sheep corpses. Then there is grandfather's story, which he cannot recall whether he had heard before or after the dream, that tells the tale of the tailor who pulls the tail of a wolf and supposedly explains the presence of the tree in the dream. As for the number of wolves in the dream, this is conveniently accounted for by a "forced" recollection of the fairy story, "The Wolf and the Seven Little Goats." Which is real? The dream or the memory it allegedly condenses? In terms of narration, the difference between the two regimes turns on whether the characters act or react to their situation. Freud clearly wants the Wolf-Man to tell a story and, in doing so, to connect all the flotsam and jetsam of "free association" he can dredge up in a logical and precise way. One could imagine how this might be filmed: you'd start with the dream image, and then, in a quite mechanical way, the camera would cut between a page torn from a fairy tale book to sheep in a paddock, and from there, to a little boy listening to his grandfather telling him a bedtime story (for added effect, an animated version of this tale might be inserted), and then back to another fairy tale, and so on. At the center of it all would be Freud, the analyst, his consciousness connecting the apparently random chain of associations and securing their coherence, in the last instance. The crystalline regime would, in contrast, be achieved by eliminating the analyst's unconscious as the center of meaning.

"A fourth point, more complex or more general, follows on from this. If we take the history of thought," Deleuze explains, "we see that time has always put the notion of truth into crisis."[34] Deleuze refers to this problem as the "crisis of contingent future": "if it is *true* that a naval battle *may* take place tomorrow, how are we to avoid one of the true following consequences: either the impossible proceeds from the possible (since, if the battle takes place, it is no longer possible that it may not take place), or that the past is not necessarily true (since the battle could not have taken place)."[35] From this, Deleuze says, a new status of narration arises—Deleuze characterizes this new possibility of narration as the "power of the false." The false is not the untrue, as such, but rather, the undecidable. In cinema, it comes into being when the virtual ceases to be a derivative of the actual and takes on a life of its own. This is the moment when the choices not made, the choices that could not be made, the choices that were never made, the fanciful, frightening, and impossible choices with which we are all confronted in everyday life, suddenly become as real to us as the choices we consciously do make. Is there a better definition of the potency of delirium?

Again, Hitchcock's *The Birds* is an instructive example. Whatever could have happened for the birds to behave that way and to start attacking people like that? Is it something in Melanie's past or in her present that makes them attack her? The false is the problematic. It is a delicate power, Deleuze says, but it is also "the only chance for art or life," by which he means it is the power of chance itself.[36] From the point of view of cinema, the key question is to ask from which direction the impetus for narrative movement comes? In the case of *The Birds*, that impelling force comes from the outside, not from within, which is undoubtedly why critics have always been ambivalent about it. The inexplicable logic of the story's development compels us to search beyond the confines of the situation for an answer. Similarly, any attempt to read the birds as symbols tends to fail because there is no consistency in the narrative—they come from nowhere, attack without reason, and cease without being halted. The impossibility of deciding why the events are taking place calls into question and literally falsifies our standard means of apprehending them. Raymond Bellour's famous shot-by-shot analysis is, in this sense, a heroic failure inasmuch as it attempts to establish a chronicle of events for a mode of narration-description that destroys the possibility of the chronicle itself. [37] Like Melanie, the Wolf-Man, too, wonders, whatever could have happened for me to start feeling this way, to feel like I am becoming a wolf?

Conclusion

We should not be surprised that the terms *body without organs, assemblage*, and *abstract machine* are not used in the film books because Deleuze made it his practice not to cling to a rigidly prescribed set of labels for his concepts—within the confines of a single volume, such as *A Thousand Plateaus*, he unapologetically uses several names for the same thing: the plane of immanence is the body without organs, the body without organs is the earth, and so on. We should, however, be very surprised if the structure of Deleuze's key concepts were not preserved in the movement between one book and the next. As Deleuze and Guattari themselves say, ideas do not die; they migrate, they change their appearance to suit the demands of their new context, but their structure, the set of preconditions underpinning them, remains intact. Whether any of the foregoing can help launch a schizoanalysis of cinema only time will tell. What I have tried to do is first of all make a direct link between cinema and schizoanalysis by highlighting the significance of delirium to both; second, I have shown how Deleuze and Guattari's reconceptualization of delirium as a "regime of signs" can be used to inaugurate a new kind of semiology of cinema not reliant on unhelpful analogies of the order that cinema is a "kind of language"; and third, I have shown that at the most microscopic level, Deleuze's anatomy of the image follows the logic of his previous books. There is much more work to be done, of course, and it is clear that this will have to concentrate on the "moving parts" of Deleuze's thought to enable us to move past a description of the cinema using schizoanalytic terms to a genuine schizoanalysis of it.

Notes

1   It is worth noting here that the English translation of this passage—"What does schizoanalysis ask? Nothing more than a bit of a *relation to the outside*, a little reality"—downplays the emphasis Deleuze and Guattari place on schizoanalysis's need for a nonfalsified, nonfantasized, that is to say, *true* relation with the outside as the *really real*. Given the centrality of delirium and, concomitantly, hallucination, to their thinking, it is perhaps not insignificant that in trying to articulate the therapeutic goal of schizo-analysis, they should be compelled to resort to a tautological locution like "*réalité réelle.*" For if the hallucination is real to the one who hallucinates, then what can be outside that but the really real? See Gilles Deleuze and Félix Guattari, *Anti-Oedipus: Capitalism and Schizophrenia 1*, trans. R. Hurley, M. Seem, and H. R. Lane (Minneapolis: University of Minnesota Press, 1977), 334.

2   "In a book, as in all things, there are lines of articulation or segmentarity, strata and territories; but also lines of flight, movements of deterritorialisa-tion and destratification." Gilles Deleuze and Félix Guattari, *A Thousand Plateaus: Capitalism and Schizophrenia*, trans. Brian Massumi (Minneapolis: University of Minnesota Press, 1987), 3.

3   Deleuze and Guattari, *Anti-Oedipus*, 81–82.

4   "Sleeping Beauty," *New York Review of Books* 53, no. 3 (2004): 4–8.

5   I must thank D. N. Rodowick for identifying this film for me.

6   Deleuze and Guattari, *Anti-Oedipus*, 274.

7   Ibid.

8   Ibid., 85.

9   Deleuze and Guattari, *A Thousand Plateaus*, 233.

10   I have treated this subject at greater length in my essay "Žižek and Deleuze," in *Traversing the Fantasy: Critical Responses to Slavoj Žižek*, ed. Geoff Boucher, Jason Glynos, and Matthew Sharpe (London: Ashgate, 2005), 69–85.

11   Gilles Deleuze, *Cinema 1: The Movement-Image*, trans. Hugh Tomlinson

and Barbara Habberjam (Minneapolis: University of Minnesota Press, 1986), 20.

12 Deleuze and Guattari, *Anti-Oedipus*, 317.

13 Deleuze, *Movement-Image*, 23.

14 Ibid., 14–15.

15 Ibid., xiv.

16 Ibid., 119.

17 Deleuze and Guattari, *A Thousand Plateaus*, 120.

18 Ibid., 121.

19 Ibid., 111–12.

20 Ibid., 38.

21 Ibid., 113.

22 Deleuze, *Movement-Image*, xiv.

23 Gilles Deleuze, *Cinema 2: The Time-Image*, trans. Hugh Tomlinson and Robert Galeta (Minneapolis: University of Minnesota Press, 1989), 126.

24 Ibid., 132. I must save for another occasion what seems to me an extremely interesting comparison to be made here between the different regimes of narration-description and Bakhtin's concept of the "chronotope." At least part of the interest of doing this would be to enrich our understanding of Bakhtin and dispel the rather simplistic rendering of the chronotope as time-space.

25 Slavoj Žižek, *Looking Awry: An Introduction to Jacques Lacan through Popular Culture* (Cambridge, Mass.: MIT Press, 1991), 111.

26 To give only one example, I would point to the original *C.S.I.*: as a crime series, the action is driven by the reactions of characters to their situation and clearly follows a pattern of linear sequences commencing and recommencing. But the central character, Grissom, has a hearing problem that is occasionally allowed to interrupt the snapping together of one sequence and another, causing, for a time, a small shimmering of radiation: he becomes childlike, hearing and seeing his world anew, observing, not acting, and a "gliding" atmosphere of significance takes over.

27 Deleuze and Guattari, *A Thousand Plateaus*, 27.

28 Ibid., 249.

29 Ibid., 28.

30 Sigmund Freud, "From the History of an Infantile Neurosis ('The Wolf Man')," in *Case Histories II: Penguin Freud Library*, ed. A. Richards, trans. J. Strachey (London: Penguin, 1990), 9:263–64.

31 Deleuze, *Time-Image*, 126.

32 Ibid., 3.

33 Ibid., 126–27.

34 Ibid., 130.

35 Ibid.

36 Ibid., 146.

37 The least one must say about *The Birds* is that one cannot say this x led to

that y; each shot, each scene, each event, is rather piled one on top of the other, x and x and x and so on. Žižek's interpretive strategy is exemplary in this regard. To make sense of the film and contrive an x-leads-to-y reading, he instructs us first of all to imagine it as film without birds. This not only serves to underscore their importance—because without them, the film becomes, as Žižek says, a boring family drama—but also confirms that the logic of their presence cannot be discerned from within. See Žižek, *Looking Awry*, 104–5.

9. Cinemasochism: Submissive Spectatorship as Unthought

Patricia MacCormack

> The masochist needs to believe he is dreaming, even when he is not.
>
> —Gilles Deleuze, *Masochism: Coldness and Cruelty*

Form, Film, and Flesh

Cinemasochism describes the openness of the spectator to images. Extending Deleuze's discussion of affect in *Cinema 1: The Movement-Image*, and particularly his chapter "Cinema, Body, Brain, and Thought" in *Cinema 2: The Time-Image*, cinemasochism asks not what the image means, but rather, what it does—the spectator begs of the image, "use me." Particularly in films that push the affect of the image to its extreme—from horror to abstract films—submission to the image beyond comprehension takes the viewer outside of film's metonymy, meaning, and time toward the kind of spatial ecstasy forged within the folding of film with embodied spectatorship. There is a risk in opening ourselves to cinematic affect, in experiencing the pain of loss of reified meaning in images. All spectators who open up to film potentially challenge their relationship to cinema in terms of gender, pleasure, and desire.

Feminist, structuralist, and psychoanalytic film theory have long been seduced by a sadistic conception of the gaze expressed through the dialectic of the phallic eye and the nonconsenting "to-be-looked-at" object. The power distribution within this dialectic of the phallic sadist and objectified masochist is not a clear binary, and its complexities are interrogated by Deleuze. Deleuze is adamant that the sadist and masochist inevitably reverse their proclivities, not as expiation for personal guilt, but as the culmination of an expiation of the larger (though also internalized) structures of prohibition and punishment associated with sadism and masochism. Beyond his claim that reversal only affirms the supremacy of the primary power, cinemasochism suggests a turn toward a nondialectical encounter with the outside or an alterity within self—the ecstasy of asignification and the experience of cinesexuality. Deleuze's "switch-hitter" sadist and masochist emphasize that one cannot be a single element of a dialectic without the possibility of becoming, or even aspiring, toward the other opposing element: not the sadist become masochist, but rather, the sadist become object of sadism and masochist become facilitator of masochism. In both turns, the subject (in film, the spectator) neither controls the gaze (it is controlled inevitably by camera, form, and affect) nor submits entirely to a passive spectatorship. In cinema, as in all art, the dialectic collapses because the object of desire—film—is technically nonvolitional and unable to adapt organically, although images are able to effectuate material changes in the spectator. Film is nonetheless multifaceted, or what Deleuze would call extensive. Images create connections in various ways and themselves experience becomings as forms proliferate their transcribable functions and meanings. Speech in talkies makes language aural—the close-up disanchors the face from the representation of personhood and thus consumes the viewer with inflections of flesh that are no longer human, but rather, pure angle, trajectory, proprioceptivity, viscosity, and saturation. These elements are all material aspects of phenomena not technically physically available in film (particularly proprioceptivity and viscosity) if it is taken as a series of represented, shadowy forms that signify rather than as affect as a material force. What is evoked in these elements, however, is the impossibility of characterizing the image as purely representative or reflective. The image is not reducible to a series of forms as "things" or nouns that mirror those of the real world, and neither is it a player using forms for function on a kinetic plateau where things "happen."

Here the spectator is externalized as a reader or observer and is affected only to the extent that the screen resonates with the already known or knowable. Deleuze collapses this dialectic in *The Time-Image*, when he writes of the interaction between that which is not the heard being understood, or the seen being transcribed, as simple signifiers and what they signify: "interactions *make themselves seen* in speech acts."[1] Deleuze considers each image as having its own unique singularity, which can refer infinitely to other planes, descriptions, or meanings.[2] Here spectator and screen themselves create a margin, interstice, inflection, or fold. The event of cinema, which can disengage us from the world, while making the everydayness of the world seem unbearable, can also present the possibility of a pure event of desire and pleasure.[3] While Deleuze's work on dramaturgy is undeniably relevant here, more important is his conception of images as occurring within series and structures that coalesce their component toward the image as a plane of intensity.

What do masochism and cinematic spectatorship share in their traditional conceptions? Both involve a contract between two entities, ritual, expectation of satisfaction, narrativized desire, and expression submitted to preestablished meanings and functions. To "read" an image exchanges its affects, replacing them with the possibility of meaning derived from prior significations. To seek pleasure in a preestablished object of desire or experience similarly encloses the intensity of pleasure as possibility. Objects are materially cut from their unique powers as they claim to reflect material objects outside of the image—signifiers *of* something else, but not possible affective energies unto themselves. Objects and patterns of desire are also philosophically forced into deference to preformed patterns, as their intensities are inflected toward resonances with the already thought, rather than bringing the spectator to a precipice of the relation between thought and unthought—not the yet to be thought, but thought in excess of the possibility of knowing. The image and its affects become unfamiliar.

Traditional material and philosophical dialectics rely on Deleuze and Guattari's three phantoms that interrupt desire as flow: "namely internal lack, higher transcendence, and apparent exteriority."[4] Inserting an image into signification defines it as lacking in itself until it is able to emerge through an established metaphor (an object defined) and metonymic structure (the relations between objects). Meaning is made apparent through the function of making it appear via something else, prior to the image as event or pleasure as rupture. The compulsion to experience images and pleasures via their emergence through transcendental meaning acknowledges and circumscribes the force of all flows that exceed lack, transcendence, and a relation to established significations.

Reading an image and defining a desire for that image through the ritual of watching and reading thus segment pleasure. In *The Time-Image*, Deleuze affirms the inexhaustibility of any one image to be created by and to create phyla of series and structure. Can we extricate cinematic pleasure from its relationship with visual and linguistic series and structure? Cinematic pleasure would here be inextricable from philosophy or "thought" (not purely libidinal or sexual). Inflecting or folding the image as intensity with the desiring spectator dissipates possibilities of thought and pleasure. Spectatorship as fold is a pure event of pleasure that transforms the self as a multifaceted configuration of flesh, film, desire, and thought. Desire shifts from being "for" a thing to desire toward a shift in the fold. Can letting go of a need to read, comprehend, or even be astonished by any image's ability to fox this need create a spectator who is purely cinesexual, where pleasure is found in all images, be they radical, abstract, or "traditional"? Most important, what is at risk in opening ourselves up to being affectuated— the spatial event of the shift in the fold? Welcoming and reflecting on the effects of events that already take place in each cinematic encounter welcomes a self otherwise.

Masochism is a traditionally perverse form of sexuality. But the event of spectatorship, as in all forms of created materiality, also perverts through its exploitation of possibilities. Even the most realistic of representations bears no clear or necessary analogous relation to the world. When cinema exploits overtly impossible situations, particularly in extreme genres, such as horror, science fiction, and abstract film, the perverse possibilities of the world are emphasized. Perversion is not expressed here through images of gore, fabulous monsters and machines, erratic lines, and color without form, but rather, because the relationship of meaning with its analogous significations in the "real" world are particularly tentative or, at best, reduced to resonances in excess of their correspondence to real forms and events. This is also true of modes of seeing elicited in certain kinetic uses of the camera, particularly where we see impossibly slowly or quickly. I have chosen to exploit the perverse because its first step requires dissolution of the self, maintaining patterns of the subject's history to guarantee future patterns of desire. At its simplest, perversion alters trajectories of self, pleasure, and relation to world. Both masochism and spectatorship pay very little attention to the dialectically opposed other as a sentient or actual other. Image and punisher are facilitators, rather than objects of desire and pleasure. Masochism thus involves "the process of turning around upon the self [which] may be regarded as a *reflexive* stage, as in obsessional neurosis ('I punish myself'), but since masochism implies a passive stage ('I am punished, I am beaten'), we must infer the existence in masochism of a particular mechanism of projection through which an external agent is made to assume the role of the subject."[5] Against the sadistic gaze, our relationship with the image is entirely submissive.

Pragmatically, we have no control over the images, the cinematography, or the events we see. Films unfurl without our intervention. At best, we only have the mediated intervention of making meaning from the images.

For this reason, the extent to which we subjugate images to meaning, or release them as flows able to affect us, is the active making-passive of the spectator as submission to cinema. The masochistic pleasure of horror films is an obvious example of forsaking the power to look for submission to the affects produced by what is seen. Similarly, avant-garde cinema requires a submission to images that disputes their reliance on deference to signification. Cinema's affect suspends power just as it suspends reality. An image's ability to exceed signification extricates it from being a shadowy or lacking version of reality, emphasizing, instead, its materiality, incarnated as an actual affective force on the self. "We should note here," Deleuze writes, "that the art of suspense always places us on the side of the victim and forces us to identify with him, whereas the gathering momentum of repetition tends to force us onto the side of the torturer and make us identify with the sadistic hero."[6]

But the image is not a subject, so with which victim do we identify in moments of submission to affect? Like the traditional masochist, the spectator sacrifices self in his willingness to be punished by cinema. This is essentially the willingness to punish the self through an encounter with images. There is no necessary contradiction in situating cinema as actively affective alongside an active spectator, only in the extent to which they both make themselves passive. This is not a dialectic, but an involution. When binary structures are dissolved, so, too, are polar and segmentarily linked correspondences of terms such as *active–passive*, *subject–object*, and *punishment–submission*. Involution is a nonnarrative consistency. It is not suspended; it *is* suspension. No binary terms means no "leading to." Suspension is desire outside of temporality, a segmentation in which the nostalgic past ensures the desired future. It creates a pure space outside. Desire and pleasure are flow, but singular flow. As Deleuze and Guattari explain, "it is claimed the masochist, like everybody else, is after pleasure but can only get it through pain and phantasms, humiliations whose function is to allay or ward off deep anxiety. This is inaccurate. The masochist's suffering is the price he must pay, not to achieve pleasure, but to untie the pseudobond between desire and pleasure as an extrinsic measure."[7]

To be *after*, to seek something that comes after, after the wait, after the suspense, necessitates a temporal trajectory of a future imagined and thus somewhat established in the present. Repetition similarly excavates the past, bringing it into the present to allow it to colonize the future. Here time contracts into what Deleuze and Guattari call the *pseudobond* between desire (a desire *for*—for pleasure, for attainment, for pain, for the dissipation of suspense) and pleasure (pleasure *in*, within a moment, or within the thing or effect of what was desired). Desire is measured by the extent to which it fulfils the expectation of pleasure. Neither term is defined by its "intrinsic" qualities. Their success is measured by their relation to preformed fantasies of satisfaction. Expectation, repetition, and narrativized desire express temporality as a series of dividuated events (equation not consistency). Nonetheless, Deleuze explains, "we must conclude that the pleasure principle, though it may rule over all, does not have the highest or final authority over all. . . . There is a residue that is irreducible to it; nothing contradicts the principle, but there remains something which falls outside of it and is not homogenous with it—something in short, *beyond*."[8]

The cinemasochist is an active unmaker of signification. This is not a presymbolic infantile situation, or even, after Kristeva, an abject semiotics, but rather, it is a pure asemiosis. Guattari speaks of the urgency through which cinema can alter all systems of discourse through asignification. Here the image creates a spatial rupture that dislodges our relation to it as part of a serialized nostalgic before and an anticipated or expected after. Similar to the legible image and the sadistic gaze (which is most often accepted as the transgressive sexuality of cinema), Guattari sees "the capitalist eros [as making] itself the accomplice of what is forbidden. This economy of transgression polarizes the desiring production in a game of mirrors that cuts it from all access to the real and catches it in phantasmatic representations."[9] Like cinema itself, capitalist Eros uses forms and desires as deferred objects of worth. Deferring objects to empty signifiers delays their affects, mirroring that reflects endlessly, concealing transgression's possible material subversions. All signifying systems from law to art play this game of delay. All exploit their capacity to endlessly refer desires and pleasures to dematerial empty economic structures. Each desire event is bled of singularity and thus the power to proliferate or differentiate.

Cinema is real, however. It is material and forcefully affective, while the world of capitalist Eros is a world-made-cinema, as reflection rather than creation. Even in cinema that adheres to the most traditional significations and patterns, there is always a residue of pleasure. This is a "cinematic" feel or a risky, excessive, asemiotic moment in which the spectator could turn toward or return from the affectivity of spectatorship in the same way that Guattari sees all representation as selecting to be either repetitive or revolutionary. Cinemasochism is therefore a becoming-masochist through becoming pure image intensity. The spectator's becoming passes through the agony of the loss of signification. This is an agony within which the minoritarian culture has had to exist ethically. Women, racial others, and perverts have all been denied signification beyond their isomorphic inferiority to the majoritarian, a violent subjugation through relatively immobile discursive systems. Isomorphism creates a myth of "two" within a binary, refusing the specificity of the second term and concealing the second term, defined only through its failure to fulfill the elements of the dominant. Woman, the nonwhite, and the homosexual man fail the default majoritarian significations of the white heterosexual man. They are not opposite and equal, but less-than and thus both unequal to and undefined independently of the majoritarian. Isomorphism also conceals the debt the dominant term owes to the minoritarian as the presence of a failed majoritarian is the condition of the majoritarian's possibility. Where Deleuze and Guattari take the most obvious failed majoritarian—woman—as the first term toward becoming, cinematically, the image as invoking force (but without signifying form or function) is the first painful moment of loss toward our voluminously joyful cinesexual becomings—a minoritarian spectatorship. Deleuze and Guattari present "woman" as the first minoritarian becoming, through which all others must pass because it is the least fixed by signification. Similarly, the cinematic image invokes force, but without a signifying form or function, and thus expresses the first painful moment of loss toward our voluminously joyful cinesexual becomings. This is an ethically risky project because, neither naming nor being named, it is the active becoming-passive of no longer controlling meaning.

The cinemasochist shows power in passivity and action in grace. The hybrid fold of film and spectatorial flesh evokes the becoming of cinema, and Deleuze and Guattari tell us that all becomings are hybrid. The image is taken out of its reflective state of forms and functions, series and structures, and is unraveled into an immanent constellation. If, as Guattari claims, "enjoyment = possession,"[10] can we allow the image to enjoy us by relinquishing our power over it? Or is giving power to the image a shift away from the power we give to the hierarchy of discursive and capitalist structures, where spectators "can only desire the objects that market production proposes to them; they must not only submit to the hierarchy but, even more, love it as such"?[11] Lacking innate force, here the spectator simply transmits the dominant ideologies through all systems, in a way that leads Lyotard to characterize the reading viewer as both "victim" and "client" of art.[12] Alternatively, in becoming-cinemasochist, the spectator expresses innate force as transmitted through the energy of the image.

As a first moment toward minoritarian cinema, can all cinema become "women's" cinema, and can we even speak of women's cinema in terms of representation? As Peggy Phelan, among others, has suggested, is *not* being represented a form of a "feminine" representing system, the asemiotic as visual invisibility?[13] What is at stake in cinemasochism, however, are excessive, rather than absent, elements of representation. A becoming-female spectator is thus close to cinemasochism. In a first move, becoming-cinemasochist might imagine the sadistic gaze as passing through the masochistic female spectator. Cinemasochism, however, does not insert itself into the cinematic system of gendered character identification. All spectators relinquish their place of power. Alternatively, when, in her essay on horror, Linda Williams equates the monster with the female look, she suggests the possibility of a becoming-monster spectator, which philosophers such as Rosi Braidotti have explored, although not in terms of film.[14] Nonetheless, film theorists such as Mulvey and Williams remain within a psychoanalytic (i.e., Lacanian–structuralist–linguistic) paradigm and hence an enjoyment = possession–desiring realm. Associations of masochism with femininity remain unsettlingly binary in their logic. A better formulation is Lyotard's emphasis that "the central problem is not the representational arrangement and its accompanying question, that of knowing how and what to represent . . . the fundamental problem is the exclusion and foreclosure of all that is judged unrepresentable because non-recurrent."[15]

There is nothing "real" about cinema. Therefore how can we express desire for the image within "real" sexual paradigms? We could just as easily assert that there is nothing "real" in sexuality that can be subsumed and known through psychoanalytic, neuroanatomical, biological, historical, or creative discourses on sexuality and desire. Nonetheless, these discourses create and are created by a social reality. The notion that cinema is alien to everyday life is arbitrary. Because of its impossible worlds, cinema presents a particular risk of offense and pleasure as well as the threat of losing the actual in the material world of the represented. Cinema may interrogate desire along unfamiliar lines, even if desire is not acknowledged as already and always unfamiliar. In fantasy or extreme gore films; abstract films that experiment with form, line, and color; or perhaps even films that only offer space for a more "feminine" spectator position, spectators must lose themselves to an event that may cause unpleasure or difficulty, or may simply confound. The viewer suffers under these images. Becoming-cinemasochist is a becoming with the image's own becomings. Like Deleuze and Guattari's call to becoming, it is neither imitation nor filiation, but alliance, that occludes the space between image as event and enfleshed spectator. The spectator's submission folds the image with her or him, thus necessitating a shift in discursive patterns beyond the actual content of the film. In this manner, we cannot be prescriptive about which films or images would be more or less appropriate for cinemasochistic explorations. Perhaps we could select more evocative films in the way that Deleuze and Guattari recommend the de- or asignified woman, animal, or music as ripe alliances for becomings. Are there films that demand more of our masochism, enforce more pain, or alienate us more readily from signification? Should we experience cinemasochism with women's films, abstract films, gore films, or films that disgust rather than seduce us? Or is cinemasochism more powerful with respect to the very films that conserve traditional economies of signification?

These are evocative and perhaps unanswerable questions, or perhaps questions that need not be answered within the scope of this chapter. In the next section, I will start to theorize the nature of the cinemasochistic relation itself, rather than exploring the two terms of *transmitter* and *spectator-becoming* as they create a relationship. Cinemasochism produces an encounter, event, or fold between and within the spectator and the image and thereby creates a space outside of time, but within the world—what Deleuze and Guattari call a *haeccetic immanence*, Blanchot a *going under*, and Foucault an *encounter with the outside*. In the following section, I will shift from Deleuze's work on film theory to sketch out some ideas inspired by reading film through Deleuze as a philosopher of desire, rather than one of cinema, and explore the concept of spectatorship through the work of other philosophers of desire such as Guattari, Blanchot, Derrida, Lyotard, and Foucault.

Cinemasochism

Viewing creates a distribution of intensities. These are not necessarily specific to the case of cinema, but they are especially sought after by the cinephile, who is enamored of the image and relishes connecting with the plane of desire of or from cinema. Cinesexuality does not describe cinema as an object of desire. It does not promise satisfaction for desire that lacks, but rather, offers an alliance that cannot help but transform the qualities and speeds of intensities of self. The desire for cinema is often incarnated as a desire before the fact, but singularities of intensity, even in repeat viewings, cannot be assured. Thinking the self as flux, convocation, and involution makes redundant a repetitive performance of desiring narratives. Although all desire is incapable of repeating itself, the desire to repeat must nonetheless acknowledge the impossibility of the drive to be satisfied. Desire can be a project of experimentation, but like becomings, it cannot be turned on and off. Desire is a continuity that changes trajectories of relations and saturations. Desire is redistribution of self and world, self in the world, the world in self, and self as world. Although pleasure cannot help but mobilize the subject, the discourse describing it may be relatively immobile and should be mobilized to acknowledge the inextricability of discourse from existence.

Beyond dialectics, cinema can be thought as involuting self and image on a libidinal plateau, twisting textures of intensity including, but not limited to, vague notions of visceral, genital, and cerebral pleasure. Although the dissipated, enfleshed self repudiates certain aspects of the body itself as signified, the explicitly fleshly or visceral body is necessarily the libidinal and the cerebral corporeal. As Deleuze suggests in his cinema books, the image affects in a way that goes beyond perception, signification, or cognition. Even when a concept emerges through the prethought—creation as recreation—there is plenitude that exceeds and escapes the limits of thought. The authority to desire the image authors and authorizes its pleasure. To address this or challenge it by desiring the licit or illicit maintains the horizon of signification. As Guattari explains,

> when it is exploited by capitalist and bureaucratic . . . powers to mould the collective imaginary, cinema topples over to the side of meaning. Yet its own effectiveness continues to depend on its pre-signifying symbolic components as well as its a-signifying ones: linkages, internal movements of visual images, colors, sounds, rhythms, gestures, speech etc. But unlike the writing and speech that for thousands of years has remained pretty much the same as a means of expression, cinema has, in a few decades, never ceased to enrich its technique. . . . The more it enlarges its scale of aesthetic intensities, the more the systems of control and censures have tried to subjugate it to signifying semiologies.[16]

Cinema's excess of signification, which Guattari sees as asignification and presignification, is not necessarily more radical or extreme than that of language. In this case, it is a question of the speed or slowness of immobilization. Similarly, the shift from silent to sound cinema, which Deleuze sees as crucial in *The Time-Image*, includes silence as its own form of language or sound. The silence of images and languages makes their libidinal intensity flow. For Lyotard, submission to this silence-pleasure is fundamental to desire. Representation and intensities that emerge only through signification dam desire and regiment it in a majoritarian system: "this silence is not blind and does not require that one make certain of what comes about through a language, even one of hands or skin. We love the language of hands or skin but here it would be unsubtle. To resort to it here would be to obey the ideology of sex. To suggest to someone: let's fuck, would truly be to treat oneself as *representing* the sexual liberation movement."[17] Lyotard does not discuss cinema in *Libidinal Economy*. However, his exploration of libidinality is explicitly visual and more resonant still with cinema—cutting the world up into minute intensities and inflections born of subtle gestures and movements as well as close-ups of skin, inorganic objects, and suchlike. This form of libidinality seems more cinematic than his work specifically on "Acinema." This is perhaps an example of sexuality as cinema, rather than a cinema that evokes sexuality.

Cinematic images are saturated along visual, aural, and linguistic planes fluid within and across each other. Cinema seems to have evolved faster than writing and speech, and it differs from other forms of art because it automates movement. This is why Guattari emphasizes linkages and movements as well as cinema's relationship with flesh. Cinema offers imaginable but otherwise unavailable worlds—fantasy worlds seen at extremes in horror films and framed worlds where giant plateaus of flesh and sound bombard the viewer on a scale that one does not experience in the intimacy of everyday life. These aspects ally cinema with actual libidinal experience that involves more than one sense and more than one world. All language, read or heard, redistributes sense so the heard or read can materially affect the self libidinally, whether it presents pornography, philosophy, or the intensity of a simple metonymic juxtaposition that trembles the subject into delirium. Cinema humbly offers one particular intervention. And in our culture, the visual seems arguably to have a particular capacity to affect the subject more violently than the text (as evinced in panic censorship). To think color, sound, saturation, and speed in text is potentially more difficult than to be exposed to and made vulnerable by a cinematic moment.

Cinesexuality is an anomalous sexuality. As Deleuze and Guattari explain, "the anomalous is neither an individual nor a species; it has only affects, it has neither familiar or subjectified feelings, nor specific or significant characteristics."[18] While all sexuality is an unnatural alliance with aspects that defy signification and defeat satisfaction, cinema intensifies the multiplicity of all libidinal alliances. Heterosexuality and homosexuality strictly define their objects to reign in the asignifiable characteristics of even the most banal sexual acts. We can ask, with what do you have sex? and the answer male or female is imagined as a stable enough term to explain sexuality. But if we answer cinema, questions proliferate beyond, rather than refer back to, a preestablished system of desire. Clearly no systemization of desire, no stratification of the body through which pleasure and desire are organized, can be anything more than tactically signified here, despite the investment culture places in regulation in this way. Male or female, all flesh and desire is beyond signification; they are asignifiable and beyond objectification, identification, and recognition. Certain film theorists have attempted to relate cinesexuality *back* to hetero and homo gender–sexual matrices. Can we relate sexuality *forward* to cinema? After all, every libidinal moment could be described as a version of cinema in its bombardment of excessive intensities in ways that are desired (in whatever way, and this does not, of course, preclude unexpected desire, etc.) but entirely unpredictable. The image is no less material, but of a different sort. Like all art, and all flesh, there are infinite and inexhaustible possible intensities that we can never know in advance. Far from suggesting that all affect is simply a re-presentation of perceived effect, I want to emphasize that all affect is a corporeal and material sensorial redistribution of energy or desire. The image is as capable of materially transforming and affecting its disciple as is the flesh of the lover, albeit perhaps through different configurations of libidinal plateaus.

Film Inside Out

> Where there is force of violence all is clear but when there is voluntary adherence, there is perhaps no more than an effect of inner violence concealed amidst the most unshakeable consent.
>
> —Maurice Blanchot, "Foucault as I Imagine Him"

Masochism should not be defined as a narrative of suffering laid down entirely in advance, nor should libidinality be oriented around waiting and the intensity of the moment before the cinematic event. Cinemasochism occludes traditional masochism in the very loose drawing up of a contract between a party desiring to exploit the openness and vulnerability required of the masochist and the facilitator of the masochistic acts and effects. Both masochism and cinemasochism express a desire to lose the self that involves an encounter of the infinite outside within the self; this is a (nonnihilistic) sacrifice of self. Deleuze points out that both sadism and masochism are a binding of Thanatos to Eros, but while sadism (especially that of early gaze theory) is exo-Thanatographic or expressed outward onto the sacred object, masochism folds Thanatos toward the self.

Similar to Blanchot's claim, through cinemasochism, there is *voluntary adherence and inner violence*, emphasizing the indiscernibility between the inside and outside. Indiscernibility suggests that redoubled (rather than dialectical) submission is infinite because it is not about a better quality or quantity of traditional masochism—it is only about infinite openness. Unlike traditional masochism, but like becoming, the seduction of images in cinemasochism is not turned on and off, nor is it repeatable in narrative and affect; rather, this seduction reverberates and mystifies the self through the force of desire, which resonates with the ritualistic act of masochism, whether through viewing or torture. Without at least the tactical signification of object and act can we ask, what, why, and how do we desire? (For example, abstract film is different, although perhaps no less libidinal, than films that offer forms.) Images cannot be wholly free of, nor wholly converted to, meaning, just as desire itself exceeds its conversion into systems, whether heterosexual, homosexual, or perverse. Foucault's sense of conversion is important here. Signifying an image requires an active conversion to an established meaning, rather than a mechanical reflection of the world. Cinemasochism resists total conversion, thereby putting signification at risk, and because the self is signified within the systems to which images are converted, the self is put at risk as well.

"This kind of symmetrical conversion," Foucault writes, "is required of the language of fiction. It must no longer be a power that tirelessly produces images and makes them shine, but rather, a power that undoes them, that lessens their overload, that infuses them with an inner transparency that illuminates them little by little until they burst and scatter into the light of the unimaginable."[19] The wonder of images folds with the viewer; it makes *us* shine. The image unravels our selves onto a plateau of intensity, bursting and scattering us. But how does the image fold into us? How do our own signified bodies open up to the image? Here masochism goes beyond the act of watching affective images. Our own capacity to affect ourselves, to exceed our own signification, becomes in the act and affect of cinematic viewing.

Bataille writes that "he who already knows cannot go beyond a known horizon."[20] The horizon of cinema is not found at the seam where screen buttresses against flesh, but at the threshold of thinking toward the unthought. Knowledge of what the images may signify, what desire may be signified there, and through which systems it is authorized is the horizon. Thought is the beyond. As D. N. Rodowick argues, "thinking or thought is defined not by what we know but by the virtual or what is unthought. To think . . . is not to interpret or to reflect but to experiment and to create. Thought is always in contact with the new, the emergent, what is in the midst of making itself . . . and finally there is 'the outside,' virtuality or an absolute relation that is in fact a non-relation: the unthought in thought."[21] The encounter between screen and spectator is not a horizon or a limit, but rather, the inflected emergence of thought that is unthought. Here the potentials of alterity proliferate within and between each term, invoking their becomings but now as becoming-imperceptible—cinema as perceived, but perception as unthinkable thought. As signified sexualized selves, we are sacrificed by folding with the outside within us. We are faced up against the image's inability, finally, to be thought. We sacrifice the fantasy of thinking the self when we open up to cinemasochism, but not in hope of thinking the new or the yet to be thought. There is no tapping into some stream of desire yet to be revealed. Desire through cinemasochism resonates again with traditional masochism in the vertigo of being faced with an unthought that cannot be thought and a desire that cannot know itself—we recede from this desire and this thought the closer we believe ourselves to be.

The presence of viewing teases out the unfathomable to show that "the invisibility of the visible is invisible."[22] Image as invisible visible event is primarily a spatial experience. The image is not defined through the representation of forms connected in causal time. The image-event ruptures intensities outward—the self is compelled into "the void where it undoes, its forms intersect to form a discourse appearing with no conclusion and no image, with no truth and no theatre, no proof, no masks, no affirmation, free of any centre . . . a discourse that constitutes its own space as the outside toward which, and outside of which it speaks. . . . But this discourse as a speech that is always outside what it says, is an incessant advance toward that whose absolutely fine-spun light has never received language."[23]

As forms related in time are undone, we cannot know what we see as we nonetheless see. Intersections of images are not narrative, and thus, without their metonymic relations, the forms themselves cannot "be." No masks of signification, no performance mirroring actual relations, but also no convertible essence in the material actual. Foucault's incessant advance moves toward something unseeable within or beneath the seen, eliciting the unseeable that is all we see, and because of which we usually use chronocentric signifying techniques of seeing and knowing. What it inevitably expresses is the unseeable within the desiring self. Rethinking masochism as suffering in the face of the outside within self rids desire of the narrative of the time to come (seen in most narratives of desire, whether masochistic or not). Or, as Bataille puts it, "at some moment I must abandon myself to chance or keep myself under control . . . without such free play the present instant is subordinated to preoccupation with the time to come."[24]

Actual and impossible, unthought desire folds the self within the infinite outside-within-itself in the face of cinema as the most indifferent of lovers. Film has a force that is not responsive. But in the encounter with absolute indifference, our flesh is no less enflamed, our desire no less transformative. As desire reveals only the impossibility of its own revelation, the self transforms beyond any project or narrative. This is why we cannot be cinemasochists in the same way that Deleuze defines masochism. The ultimate suffering comes from teetering on the brink of the abyss that is our own desire—a vacuum that is not empty, but outside, that does not exist to be thought or known, but is no less abundant for being so. Our masochistic suffering comes from the impossibility of the agony that is our own desire and the pleasure of its impossible revelation. We are open to chance, knowing we are without a chance oriented toward a result. Chance of what? Nothing, simply chance. This occurs no matter what we see, but the will to openness can be figured here as a minoritarian subjectivity.

Self-Sacrifice and Cinecstasy

> But who is this we, which is not me?
> —Gilles Deleuze and Félix Guattari, "How to Make
> Yourself a Body without Organs"

Why is cinemasochism sacrificial? Foucault claims that the outside is out of time because it shows arrival and memory as impossible in the face of an encounter, which, folding the self with its outside, folds the outside in. If self and desire form a constellation, this encounter implodes with and beyond itself. Drawn inside the image outside, the world involutes us into the inside-of-self, which is the outside-of-self in the face of the self inside the image and world. This outside-of-self does not refer to that which is outside-of-self, but rather, the outside which is *within* the self. Desire reflects here the inner experience outside of the world—the encounter as ecstasy, so often described by its intensification of pleasure as suffering or pain. But while all erotic encounters encounter the self ex-stasis—outside-of-self, yet irreducibly inside this flesh—the viewing self desires the outside of a sexual matrix that discursively replaces the self back into a temporal narrative of desire. Making the sexual act signify is an attempt to suture the minoritarian qualities of desire, and making the image signify or structuring its relations dialectically ablates the inherent infinite possibility of all spectatorial encounters. (There is always a remainder, however.) Signification cannot reveal the "unrevealable" that is the outside within ourselves. It reveals, rather, the unrevealability of desire as it (not affects, but) embodies us. Masochism, by making the self aware of its own desire to not-be (in a nonnihilistic sense to not be "as" but to "become otherwise"), emphasizes that the self is not everything, but also that it is *not everything to the self.*

The unrevealable, like the invisible, is not waiting-to-be-revealed. It is that which can never be revealed because it goes to the beyond that is thought and hence the possibility of revelation. Possession by a lover or an image is not possession by an entity outside the self, but rather, the self's possession of the outside entity as well as the inevitable possession of the self by the outside-of-self. Possession is the making apparent of the self one can never possess. I am not possessed; the one that is me is possessed—taken by that which is outside the "self." Through ecstatic encounters with the outside-of-self, the cinematic is taken outside. It does not simply pierce us to launch us on ecstatic trajectories, but also resides within us outside of its signification as a cinematic image in the world. For this reason, the image is also dead to the world, yet very much enlivened within the ecstatic cinesexual plane. It, too, is dead to signification, having become folded within an expressive outside-of-self.

Unique particulars of desire that make us love an image or cinematic sensorium like we love another are proliferated through the extent to which they take us to the outside-of-self and we take them outside of themselves. As Derrida explains, "how can another see into me, into my most secret self, without me being able to see in there myself and without my being able to see him in me? And if my secret self, that which can be revealed only to the other, to the wholly other ... is a secret that I will never reflect on, that I will never know or experience or possess as my own."[25] Implicit in "unknowing," "unthought," and "unrevealable" is the falsity of "there is something to know/think/reveal." The self cannot reflect because the self cannot know the question; there is no question and there is no answer beyond the beyond itself.

We therefore die to ourselves *as* we are dead to the world and, unable to be disclosed to the other, dead to the object of desire as a desirable corresponding object. Is the moment of desire outside of the world and the inner self the gift to the lover, the gift of the self we cannot know but give nonetheless? The self we give is not the self we know we give. The image similarly gifts itself beyond its seriality or signification. The gift cannot be made as a gift that fills a place, completes an absence, or resolves an impossibility. The gift of ecstasy knows not what it gives and gives precisely that which it cannot know. It is the gift that acknowledges that the self has nothing it can willfully give that will affect the receiver in any known way. This is why desire is risky. It must first open up to the self as unthinkable. The masochistic self does not die in its sacrificial, Bataillean sense; rather, it demands of cinema, "use me":

> The passion of passivity which stimulates this offer is not one single force, a resource of force in a battle, but it is force itself, liquidating all stases.... "Use me" is an order and a supplication, but what she demands is the abolition of the I/you relation (which is, like the master/slave relation, reversible) and also the use relation ... not let me die by your hand.... She wants you to die with her, she desires that the exclusive limits be pushed back, sweeping across all tissues, the immense tactility, the tact of whatever closes up on itself without becoming a box [dialectic spectatorship] and whatever ceaselessly extends beyond itself without becoming a conquest [desire = possession].[26]

Like Deleuze and Guattari's "woman," Lyotard here explicitly makes the collapse of the dialectic and the sacrifice of self female, thus characterizing a self that is both libidinally and actually sacrificed in majoritarian culture or one that is not granted a self to sacrifice. In this way, the cinemasochist is a feminine or feminist project, a form of becoming-woman resonant with Deleuze and Guattari's exploration of the masochist as a Body without Organs. Sacrifice of self in ecstasy could similarly be seen as a feminist turn, relinquishing signification or even conception of self.

When the outside within dissipates the self into the inside without, an infinity of folded relations are formed, and the constellation is redistributed. The solitude of ecstasy includes the other which is self and the self in the outside, or given to the outside—the gift that knows not what it gives, but can only offer the pure openness of the gifted self. Is becoming-woman or becoming-cinemasochist a gift of or toward alterity? Desire is the gift of the outside-of-self to self, without revelation or presence but no less apparent. As Derrida points out, we cannot die for the other, but only offer our own death as a gift, which "has no need of the *event of a revelation or the revelation of an event*. It needs to think the possibility of such an event but not the event itself."[27] If we can never know what we give to the other, we can only sacrifice what we know of the self in our gift.

Thus all sacrifice is masochism, and masochism is itself a gift that opens outward; it is no longer Deleuze's entirely reflexive masochism. Masochism is the gifting of self to other as the collapse between two elements and accepting the other of self that may be encountered, but not revealed. Desire gives the other of self, or the outside, to self and gives self to the risk and chance of the outside-of-self. The gift cannot be "in exchange" for something else. The gift of death in desire is the death of the subject as enclosed, hermeneutic, sexually regulated, and signified, the death that is necessarily desire. It does not exchange the "I" for a new self; it simply gifts the self which is all (as) we encounter (the we) that we cannot know. Desire folds outside in on self. The self is folded in on itself and out toward the world, becoming a crevice into which the outside slips and offering planes of self slipping outside but invisible to self. The outside-of-self is then gifted to the outside, as our thought (but not knowledge) of it is invoked by the outside. If neither the invisibility in the visible nor the unthought in desire can be known, then the outside-of-self expresses the unself or unsubject of self.

Cinemasochism embraces the impossibility of self in the face of the force of the image, without acknowledging the impossibility within all representation or signification. There is no other position in opposition to self, but the subject no less dissipates into what Guattari calls the *degree zero point of implosion*. Dissipation is violence in the sacrifice of self, or Blanchot's inner violence in the face of an unshakeable consent that makes us tremble, which Derrida characterizes as the "I which trembles in secret,"[28] for which there is no answer. The "I" is a trembling, desire a redistribution of trembling, masochism the unbearable pain within the pleasure of desire, and cinema a lover we take, a becoming alliance, an image with which we fold and to which we consent, giving the gift of self we cannot give, to die in the ecstasy of the outside-of-self.

Notes

1   Gilles Deleuze, *Cinema 2: The Time-Image*, trans. Hugh Tomlinson and Robert Galeta (Minneapolis: University of Minnesota Press, 1989), 227.
2   Ibid., 46.
3   Deleuze's preference for "desire" and Foucault's for "pleasure" must be cited here. However, it is hoped that through the course of the chapter, these terms will no longer create a necessary antagonism or divisibility. Deleuze's disdain for pleasure as a "thing" and Foucault's for desire as being "for a thing" is destabilized when "thingness" itself is no longer divisible. See Michel Foucault, "Bodies and Pleasure," trans. James Steintrager, in *More and Less*, ed. Sylvère Lotringer (New York: Semiotext(e), 2000), 238–47, and Gilles Deleuze, "Desire and Pleasure," trans. Daniel W. Smith, in *Foucault and His Interlocutors*, ed. Arnold I. Davidson (Chicago: University of Chicago Press, 1997), 183–92.
4   Gilles Deleuze and Félix Guattari, *A Thousand Plateaus: Capitalism and Schizophrenia*, trans. Brian Massumi (Minneapolis: University of Minnesota Press, 1987), 156–57.
5   Gilles Deleuze, *Masochism: Coldness and Cruelty*, trans. Jean McNeil (New York: Zone Books, 1994), 105–6.
6   Ibid., 34.
7   Deleuze and Guattari, *A Thousand Plateaus*, 155.
8   Deleuze, *Masochism*, 112.
9   Félix Guattari, *Soft Subversions*, trans. and ed. Sylvère Lotringer (New York: Semiotext(e), 1996), 152.
10   Ibid., 145.

11   Ibid.
12   Jean-François Lyotard, "Acinema," in *The Lyotard Reader* (London: Blackwell, 1989), 179.
13   Peggy Phelan, *Unmarked: The Politics of Performance* (London: Routledge, 1993).
14   See Linda Williams, "When the Woman Looks," in *Re-Vision: Essays in Feminist Film Criticism*, ed. Mary Ann Doane, Patricia Mellencamp, and Linda Williams (Los Angeles: University Publications of America, 1984), 67–82. Also see Rosi Braidotti, *Nomadic Subjects: Embodiment and Sexual Difference in Contemporary Feminist Theory* (New York: Columbia University Press, 1994), and Rosi Braidotti, "Meta(l)morphoses," *Theory, Culture and Society* 14 (1997): 67–80.
15   Jean-François Lyotard, *Libidinal Economy*, trans. Iain Hamilton (Bloomington, Ind.: Indiana University Press, 1993), 176.
16   Guattari, *Soft Subversions*, 150.
17   Lyotard, *Libidinal Economy*, 29.
18   Deleuze and Guattari, *A Thousand Plateaus*, 244.
19   Michel Foucault, *Maurice Blanchot: The Thought from Outside*, trans. Brian Massumi (New York: Zone Books, 1987), 23.
20   Georges Bataille, *Inner Experience*, trans. Leslie Anne Boldt (Albany, N.Y.: SUNY Press, 1988), 3.
21   D. N. Rodowick, *Gilles Deleuze's Time Machine* (Durham, N.C.: Duke University Press, 1997), 198.
22   Foucault, *Thought from Outside*, 24.
23   Ibid., 24–25.
24   Georges Bataille, *Eroticism*, trans. Mary Dalwood (London: Penguin, 2001), 250–51.
25   Jacques Derrida, *The Gift of Death*, trans. David Wills (Chicago: University of Chicago Press, 1992), 92.
26   Lyotard, *Libidinal Economy*, 63, 65, 66.
27   Derrida, *Gift of Death*, 49.
28   Ibid., 92.

10. Unthinkable Sex

D. N. Rodowick

For Reni Celeste

In his two books on cinema, Gilles Deleuze never mentions the concept of conceptual personae, a central concern of chapter 3 of *What Is Philosophy?* Moreover, Deleuze writes even less on questions of sexual identification. Nonetheless, my parti pris here is the following: to think the question of "gender" in relation to the time-image, we must pass through conceptual personae who may become, for their part, the unthought of sexual difference.

This is an equally curious idea since conceptual personae have only an oblique relation with either characters or cinematic identification. They are *philosophical* figures. Their oblique relation to art should not be surprising because the objective of *What Is Philosophy?* is to demonstrate the singularity of philosophy in its relations with art and science. This is why Deleuze and Guattari distinguish conceptual personae from, on one hand, *aesthetic figures*, and on the other, *psychosocial* types.

Aesthetic figures are certainly close to what one might call filmic "characters." Constructed across the bodies and voices of actors through framing, mise-en-scène, and editing, aesthetic figures produce affects and perspectives or points of view, which is to say, *percepts* in the Deleuzian sense. They are inseparable from an *agencement* or assemblage comprising blocks of sign qualities, or what Deleuze and Guattari call a "compositional plane."

No doubt the cinema also constructs psychosocial types through its aesthetic figures. These are social types in the sociological sense, as defined by Georg Simmel and others: the stranger, the excluded, the immigrant, the city dweller, and so forth. To think of these figures as stereotypes (e.g., of masculinity or femininity, hetero- or homosexuality) is equally possible. But more precisely, the raison d'être of psychosocial

types is to express the forces of territorialization and deterritorialization that constitute the social fields they occupy, thus defining their
structure and function.

Take two examples from the films of Jean-Luc Godard. Juliette in
Deux ou trois choses que je sais d'elle (1967) or Nana in *Vivre sa vie*
(1962) both comprise a psychosocial type (the prostitute) expressed as
aesthetic figures. These are two variations for showing how women are
deterritorialized from one social field (the domestic sphere) and reterritorialized on another (the street, the hotel), and how women's bodies
are territorialized by capital and so *become* commodities in response
to a desire *for* commodities. The linking of tableau in *Vivre sa vie* and
the transformations in the figure of Nana from sequence to sequence
exemplify this process: Nana is deterritorialized first from a matrimonial
coupling, and then from the store where she sells records. This is a sexual
and economic deterritorialization that is then reterritorialized on the
streets, in hotels and cafés, and so on, all through different variations
on a logic of exchange that is both semiotic and social. However, even
as Nana and Juliette figure spaces for looking on and thinking about
differing sociological dimensions, they nonetheless remain aesthetic
figures, producing intense percepts and affects according to the logic
of the time-image.

A mixture of aesthetic figures and psychosocial types, are Nana and
Juliette also conceptual personae? According to Deleuze and Guattari,
aesthetic figures, psychosocial types, and conceptual personae "refer
to each other and combine without ever merging."[1] Given the proper
conditions, then, even film might generate a series wherein one of
these figures unfolds from the others. For its part, philosophy has its
own *dramatis personae* who become conceptual, thus referring more
to mental territories than social or aesthetic ones. But as *philosophical*
figures, are conceptual personae present in film?

In *Cinema 1: The Movement-Image* and *Cinema 2: The Time-Image*,
Gilles Deleuze treats the cinema as a philosophical terrain. It has its
two planes of immanence—the movement-image and the time-image—
each with its own image of thought (organic and crystalline) and its
own concepts in the form of images and signs. For Deleuze and Guattari, philosophical expression produces a double movement: it creates
concepts, and it traces a plane of immanence or image of thought. For
Deleuze, cinematic auteurs do the same and so are indistinguishable
from philosophical authors. Both are conceptual enunciators. This is
less a biographical function than points of singularity that map a plane

of immanence through the construction of concepts. But between the creation of concepts and the mapping of a plane of immanence, "actually there is something else," write Deleuze and Guattari, "somewhat mysterious, that appears from time to time or that shows through and seems to have a hazy existence halfway between concept and preconceptual plane, passing from one to the other." This is the conceptual persona, and it is he or she "who says 'I' and launches the cogito and who also holds the subjective presuppositions or maps out the plane."[2] This could be Nicholas of Cusa's Idiot or Nietzsche's Zarathustra. But each philosopher needs his or her conceptual personae, these fluctuating figures who express the subjective presuppositions or ethos of their philosophy and, through their existence, no matter how inchoate or unstable, give life to concepts on a new plane of immanence, no matter how sketchy. Conceptual personae are the subjective presuppositions that map a plane of immanence. In this manner, they express qualities or perspectives that want to become-other, to deterritorialize toward another plane by constructing its concepts. To furnish a plane of immanence with its own concepts, to launch an image of thought, is also to express a will to become-other and to occupy another subjective milieu.

Now, in *Vivre sa vie*, one cannot simply say that Nana is a conceptual persona. Conceptual personae are not figures of representation and so, *stricto senso*, cannot be equivalent to a filmic character or a point of identification. So under what conditions can conceptual personae appear in relation to aesthetic figures?

First, it should be noted that conceptual personae are rare and difficult to distinguish: "the conceptual persona only rarely or allusively appears for himself. Nevertheless, he is there, and however nameless or subterranean, he must always be reconstituted by the reader."[3] Conceptual personae are sometimes rendered as proper names, but this is not a necessary condition because they comprise neither an identity nor a point of identification where, in Deleuze's formula from *The Time-Image*, Ego = Ego.[4] They are expressive, in fact, of a will to power. Conceptual personae manifest a nonteleological movement in which the subject wants to differentiate himself or herself in constructing new concepts or positions of identity that function as vectors for becoming.

For this reason, conceptual personae presuppose a very curious logic of enunciation. Comprising at least two points, and often several, a conceptual persona is always situated *between multiple points* of enunciation.[5] This enunciative assemblage, characterized by Deleuze in *The Movement-Image* as free indirect discourse, carries out "two

inseparable acts of subjectivation simultaneously, one of which constitutes a character in the first person, but the other of which is present
at his birth and brings him on the scene [through the camera]. There
is no mixture or average of two subjects, each belonging to a system,
but a differentiation of two correlative subjects in a system which is
itself heterogeneous."[6]

The heterogeneity of the free indirect relation, what divides it from
within, is the logic of the interstice or irrational interval. As I argue
in *Gilles Deleuze's Time Machine*, this is the key figure of the direct
time-image, sustaining all its forms of difference.[7] When connected
through irrational intervals, the elements of any given set or assemblage
are marked by incommensurable divisions that produce divergent series, which can never be resolved into a synthetic whole. In this way,
they express a power of falsification in which difference is no longer
subsumed by identity. This power connects free indirect discourse to a
process in which "the production of truth involves a series of operations
that amount to working on a material—strictly speaking, a series of
falsifications. When I work with Guattari each of us falsifies the other,
which is to say that each of us understands in his own way notions put
forward by the other. A reflective series with two terms takes shape.
And there can be several terms, or complicated branching series."[8] In
this way, Deleuze asserts that creation is fundamentally tied to the function of "intercessors," which are, in fact, the progenitors of conceptual
personae. As Deleuze explains, "whether real or imaginary, animate or
inanimate, you have to form your intercessors. It's a series. If you're not
in some series, you're lost. I need my intercessors to express myself, and
they'd never express themselves without me: you're always working in
a group, even when you seem to be on your own."[9]

There is also a close relation between free indirect discourse and
what Deleuze calls "fabulation." The indispensable condition for constructing conceptual personae in philosophy or film would thus be the
following: to make a power of the false pass as an irrational interval
between the author and the aesthetic figures he or she composes. A
falsifying current must pass between the different points of enunciation in the film. Now it could be that the author constructs a first
person discourse in relation to camera and sound. (But in fact, this
form is always already doubled because seeing and speaking, image
and sound, are constituted a priori as separate acts.) But to express a
power of the false, this discourse must pass through an intercessor that

transforms it into the discourse of an other in an act of fabulation. In this manner, intercessors give birth to concepts as seeds of thought. However, since they are divided from within by the differential relations of the irrational cut, the conceptual personae of the time-image can be neither individualized nor individualizing, for they do not "represent." They are neither figures of representation nor representative figures. At most, they can be expressed across two points of enunciation, always displaced in relation to one another by the interstice that divides them as a power of the false.

To become-other, then, one needs intercessors that function as "heteronyms" of the author, whose proper names then become pseudonyms of the personae. In this manner, conceptual personae create a subjective multiplicity that liberates themselves from the name of the author, overflowing it as virtual forces. This is a transformation of positions of enunciation, where, as Deleuze and Guattari put it,

> I am no longer myself but thought's aptitude for manifesting itself and developing across a plane that passes through me in several places. Conceptual personae have nothing to do with an abstract personification—a symbol or allegory—for they live, they insist. The philosopher is the idiosyncrasy of his conceptual personae. The destiny of the philosopher is to become his conceptual persona or personae, at the same time that these personae themselves become something other than they are historically, mythologically, or commonly (the Socrates of Plato, the Dionysus of Nietzsche, the Idiot of Nicolas of Cusa). The conceptual persona is the becoming or the subject of a philosophy, on a par with the philosopher.[10]

Call this a heteronomic enunciation, then, in which conceptual personae function as philosophical "shifters." This act of enunciation is not simply performative. It intervenes, rather, between the author and his or her intercessor, producing a sort of neutral or anonymous discourse. As Deleuze and Guattari explain, this is "a speech-act in the third person where it is always a conceptual persona who says 'I.' ... In philosophical enunciations we do not do something by saying it but produce movement by thinking it, through the intermediary of a conceptual persona. Conceptual personae are also the true agents of enunciation. "Who is 'I'?" It is always a third person."[11]

Running between author and intercessor, the conceptual persona of the time-image is divided within and from itself by time. This is a plane of identity where, in Rimbaud's beautiful phrasing, "I is an other *[Je est un autre]*," that is, in the midst of becoming or self-differentiation. And this is why the conceptual persona says "I" and not the author. But how is it possible that the subject wants or wills to become-other? That is, how can one construct a conceptual persona who calls on the powers of the false, thus expressing a will to becoming or becoming-other?

In fact, the problem of conceptual personae is also the problem of an ethos, or the creation of new modes of existence. And in this respect, the existential traits manifested in conceptual personae are very important because, as Deleuze and Guattari insist, "possibilities of life or modes of existence can be invented only on a plane of immanence that develops the power of conceptual personae."[12] Conceptual personae populate those philosophies and minor arts in which they function as constituting an ethos or style of living that does not yet exist. Still, conceptual personae persist and insist as immanent forces that want this other life. And it is in this context that one should ask, can an ethics of sexual difference be sustained by the time-image and in the other arts? How can one create new values concerning "gender" expressed as "heteronyms"—positions of subjectivity or enunciation— that elude the binary logic of sexual opposition (masculine–feminine, heterosexuality–homosexuality)? How to liberate sexual positionalities that are *unthinkable* because, no longer mastered by opposition and representation, they function as pure difference?

In this respect, little attention has been paid to how the postwar crisis of the action-image, as described by Deleuze, implies as well a crisis of sexual identification.[13] This appears forcefully in the dissolution of a certain image of masculinity characteristic of the male protagonists of French New Wave. These films and this crisis in representation challenge the subjective presuppositions of the movement-image, thus conditioning a new enunciated assemblage. As I discuss in *Reading the Figural*, the audiovisual culture of prewar societies may be characterized by a belief in organic ideologies in which concepts of democracy or socialism functioned as universals defined by a linear and teleological movement in time—the idea of history as progress or as the dialectical unfolding of a whole.[14] As expressed through the coherence of sensorimotor situations, here perceptions flow from coherent and meaningful images of the world, while extending into actions capable of transforming this world (representation). Events are linked in a teleological causality with origins and ends; opposition and conflict are resolvable through actions and are amenable to coherent solutions. Finally, the individual functions as the agent of history, representing, pars pro toto, the collective, and thus expresses the will of a people. The individual represents the collective as a differentiated image of the whole, expressive of the will of a people. The people are thus subjected to an organic representation, and the protagonist is the vehicle of this representation—the very incarnation of the destiny of a people through an organic image becoming in a linear and homogenous time.

In this manner, seven characteristics define the ethos of the movement-image and express the subjective presuppositions that populate its plane of immanence. The people are a universal subject, and this subject is implicitly masculine, with few exceptions (Pudovkin's *Mother* [1926] comes to mind). This image conforms perfectly to Laura Mulvey's account of narration and point of view, as the movements of history are reduced to actions that are distributed in active–passive relations according to the characters' sex.[15] This image also expresses a will to knowledge in which the woman often represents the negative image of truth, a negativity posing risks to the masculine hero that must be vanquished, submitted to his perspective, and transmitted to the spectator as the truth of the text. The conceptual persona of the movement-image is therefore a universal and masculine subject—the organic or synthetic image of the people—that defines a position of identity in which the subject identifies with himself in an image of the whole. Again, this is the model of Ego = Ego.

Emerging in the context of Italian neorealism and coming to fruition in the French New Wave, the direct image of time challenged this image of subjectivity. Liberated from sensorimotor situations and teleological orientations, lines of action become lines of flight, arbitrary, indeterminate, and without fixed points of departure or arrival. "It is here that the voyage-form *[la forme-balade]*," writes Deleuze, "is freed from the spatio-temporal coordinates which were left over from the old Social Realism and begins to have value for itself or as the expression of a new society, of a new pure present. . . . In these [films] we see the birth of a race of charming, moving characters who are hardly concerned by the events that happen to them . . . and experience and act out obscure events which are as poorly linked as the portion of the any-space-whatever which they traverse."[16] In the films of the French New Wave, this voyage-form has several variants: from Paris to the provinces and back (*Le beau Serge, Les cousins* [1958]); errant trajectories in the city whose value is more ethical and analytic than spatial (Rohmer's *Moral Tales* or Truffaut's *L'amour à vingt ans*, but also Agnès Varda's *Cléo de 5 à 7* [1961]); investigations with obscure ends and objectives (*Paris nous appartient* [1961] and other Rivette films); and finally, Godard and Truffaut's "*évasions*," which, as suggested by the dual senses of the French word, involve both eluding the law and escaping the constraints of everyday life (*A bout de soufflé* [1959], *Tirez sur le pianiste* [1960], *Pierrot le fou* [1965]).

Deleuze seems unaware that he foregrounds the place of the masculine protagonists here. One could conclude, then, that is it also a certain concept of masculinity that begins to fray along with the dissolution of sensorimotor situations: masculine identification is no longer supported here in conclusive actions, confident trajectories, or reliable perceptions; rather, it dissolves beneath the sign of a masochism fueled by the death drive—the endings of *A bout de souffle* and *Pierrot le fou* are excellent examples. This is also why I wanted to mention *Cléo*, in which, in presenting a series of clichés of femininity unfolding across an errant city walk, Varda extracts a new character, and a new image of woman, that will function for her as a conceptual persona.

Thus the protagonists of the French New Wave are defined by a nomadism in which the characters of the time-image wander and observe across empty and disconnected spaces. Aleatory walks replace linear actions, which construct, in turn, elliptical narratives. Because images are no longer linked by actions, space changes nature, becoming a series of disconnected any-spaces-whatever, a line broken by irrational cuts: "the interval is set free, the interstice becomes irreducible and stands on its own [*vaut pour lui-même*]."[17] Autonomous and irreducible, the interstice gives a direct or transcendental image of time perceived as false movements that no longer belong to an image and are no longer spatial. This is why I defined, in *Gilles Deleuze's Time Machine*, the interstice or direct image of time as a nonspatial perception.[18] The interstice is not spatial, nor does it represent. It is an Event, or a horizon of events on a plane of immanence from which conceptual personae may emerge. As Alain Badiou argued in an interview with *Cahiers du cinéma*,

in its fashioning of subjectivity, artistic experience plays a great role because it acts as an impregnation. There is a powerful unconscious effect in art, an effect on the general structures of desire that belong to it. . . . Some films which, ideologically, seem only to figure a romantic nihilism without any political consequence (for example, *A bout de souffle*), have a real effect . . . that aims towards other things: errance and delocalization, the fact of asking fresh questions, outside of the mediation of an institutional representation, across a character who is anything but "settled." In this sense, these films contributed to the delocalizations of '68.[19]

Here the masculine protagonists no longer function as a universal subject, the representative of a people, because "the people no longer exist, or not yet . . . *the people are missing*."[20] When the interval passes into the subject, there is no longer an identity that can return to itself, nor is there the possibility of sustaining a binary logic opposing masculinity and femininity—"I" has become an other.

"To liberate difference," wrote Foucault, "we need a thought without contradiction, without dialectic, without negation: a thought that says yes to divergence; affirmative thought whose instrument is disjunction; a thought of the multiple—of the nomadic and dispersed multiplicity that is not limited or confined by the constraints of self-similarity."[21] When the interstice or irrational interval passes within the subject, there is no longer an identity that returns to itself, nor is there the possibility of sustaining a binary logic that opposes femininity to masculinity. This is a question of comprehending how relations of sexual *difference*, rather than opposition, are expressed through conceptual personae as constructions of the direct time-image. There are at least two possibilities that are themselves intimately related: (1) operate a difference between two series, which could well be marked by sexual difference, so that they can no longer be reduced to a binary logic or simple opposition (masculine–feminine, heterosexual–homosexual), or (2) affirm a force of becoming within the sexual relation itself so that it is no longer a sexual or gendered *identification*, but becomes, rather, a question of nomad identities open to new constructions of subjectivity. Here, among the great authors of the time-image, are three exemplary cases that could serve as projects for future research:

1. Godard, from Anna Karina to Anne-Marie Mièville, the male author who needs feminine conceptual personae
2. Agnès Varda, a female author who needs feminine and heterosexual conceptual personae to make false the clichés of femininity
3. Chantal Akerman, a female author who needs conceptual personae who are both feminine and masculine (homosexual)

In the first case, one would return to *Vivre sa vie* to consider how Nana functions as a conceptual persona for Godard. Nana is the heteronym for Godard, who is no longer himself, for "Nana" is not simply a character played by Anna Karina, but rather, Karina also functions as an intercessor for Godard. This is a collaborative work comprising seven films. However, between the period of Karina and that of Anne-Marie Miéville, the status of enunciation changes profoundly.

Why is it that Godard returned so insistently to the problem of femininity, above all in its relation to the image and to the reduction of images, cinematic or otherwise, to the commodity form? At first, this is because the woman's body is the signifier for a love or fascination with the cinema, especially the American cinema. But this is not necessarily a fetishistic desire in the psychoanalytic sense because the body of the woman–actress hides a truth other than that of castration. Like the adored cinema, the body of the woman–actress is alienated within a capitalist system of exchange. They both function as commodities, and in becoming an "author," the name of Godard is rendered as a commodity as well. Otherwise, he could not continue to make films. This is why the theme of prostitution is the insistent refrain of Godard's first period. The problem is how to find a position from which to look at and to love (the woman–the cinema), a position that is no longer reducible to a system of exchange determined by the alienated structure of commodity fetishism. On the basis of a series of variations on an AB structure of repetition, what David Bordwell calls the "parametric" narration of *Vivre sa vie* aspires to transform the very structure of exchange.[22] This type of repetition includes equally the structure of the dialogue, that of shot–countershot, camera and character perspective, voice and image, but also, the relations between subject and object, those who sell and those being sold. The will of these series and variations is to liberate a new look, to multiply and vary the perspectives organized by the camera in the attempt to extract a new mode of existence for the cinema, where it is possible to look and to love in a nonalienated form.

To be sure, it is not at all certain that Godard succeeds in this project. Compare *Vivre sa vie*, for example, to the sequence in *Ici et ailleurs* (1976) where Godard and Miéville propose two different "stories" for the same images. In one, a young Arab girl recites a fiery revolutionary poem, and Godard and Miéville "speak" two alternative readings for the same image. In the second, a young Arab woman is presented first in a "masculine" version, narrated by Godard, as a pregnant revolutionary ready to sacrifice her son for the *intifada*. She is then revealed in a second version, renarrated by Mièville, as an unmarried intellectual who agreed to play a role. In this film, the voice and position of enunciation of Mièville are equal to that of Godard. But it is no longer a question of two authorial voices because Mièville and Godard have become intercessors, one for the other. This is a double enunciation that is questioned and falsified from each side and where each position disappears within or between the two voices that say "I" and "you," but always as if speaking from a third place or in the third person as an anonymous and neutral voice.

Agnès Varda presents a second case: a female author who needs feminine and heterosexual conceptual personae. Most contemporary readers of *Cléo de 5 à 7*, for example, are struck by the proliferation of clichés of femininity in the film. And rightly so, for Varda's ethos in this film is to create a new enunciative position for the *femme-auteur* by constructing a falsifying narration from these series of stereotypes. To become-cineast in a way that is other to her (male) peers in the New Wave, Varda needs the singer-Cléo as a conceptual persona, an artistic heteronym for Varda herself. The film is full of extraordinary examples of a free indirect discourse passing between camera and character, just as Deleuze describes in *The Movement-Image*. To be sure, Cléo is the double of Florence, but a double that exists as a fetishized commodity image. The problem posed by Varda is therefore how to transform this petrified image into an image of becoming and differentiation. Note, then, how Cléo is disturbed in several sequences by how her recorded voice circulates independently of her body. The turning point in the film occurs in the strange episode in which Cléo rehearses several possible new songs with her composers. Here the music of the song referred to in the film as "*Le cri d'amour*" begins in a supposedly diegetic space, then subtlety becomes nondiegetic when an orchestra joins the piano of Michel Legrand and Cléo's voice. But is the voice of Cléo direct or indirect sound? It is simultaneously her voice *and* a voice coming from elsewhere, neither direct nor indirect, but surging in an indeterminate space. Afterward, everything changes. One sees Cléo becoming-other as Varda creates a new position of enunciation for herself in relation to camera and sound.

The third case is no doubt the most interesting and the most complicated: Chantal Akerman as a feminine author whose conceptual personae are distributed across a feminine–maternal position and a masculine–homosexual one. I am thinking, in particular, of *News from Home* (1977). The fascination of this film derives from the tension between a direct discourse (camera and sound) and the voice-off in which Akerman reads her mother's letters. The style of this film owes much to Andy Warhol. Composed almost entirely of fixed framings of very long duration, the camera organizes a sort of detached voyeurism, an immobile stare on any-spaces-whatever and empty time. As for the letters, Akerman reads the text by adopting the position of her mother, thus substituting her *voice* for a maternal *writing*. Similarly, the film itself is a belated letter addressed no longer just to her mother. In this manner, the "news from home" is already a doubled and displaced communication traveling in two directions—from Brussels to New York and back again—where "home" becomes a fluctuating locality whose placement is unclear. This passage between the various spaces or points of enunciation—direct and indirect discourse, voice and writing, each spatially and temporally displaced with respect to one another— produces a strange shifting between levels of discourse. The logic of the subject here is no longer one of identification. An irrational break emerges first in the voice-off (maternal writing–filial voice; the time of reception and the time of response) and then between the voice-off and the direct images and sounds of New York. Here the mother becomes a conceptual persona, present in the voice but absent in space, that is doubled by another best characterized as a Warholian stare—this fluc- tuating presence–absence whose camera-eye presents a space in which it does not take part.[23] The two together function as virtual intercessors, not spatially present in the film, constructing a position of enunciation that is neither that of a homosexual masculinity nor that of a maternal identification. This is the construction of a "queer look" that is neither masculine nor heterosexual.

In each of these examples, difference functions in an interval that generates a free indirect discourse expressive of sexual difference, or perhaps a differentiating sex, that is no longer conditioned by opposi- tion. What the direct time-image expresses is difference as a force of becoming in the midst of mapping new territories, and these territories are populated by conceptual personae.

Notes

1   Gilles Deleuze and Félix Guattari, *What Is Philosophy?*, trans. Hugh Tomlinson and Graham Burchell (New York: Columbia University Press, 1994), 70. Originally published as *Qu'est-ce que la philosophie?* (Paris: Éditions de Minuit, 1991). Italicized page numbers in citations refer to the original text in French, indicating that I have modified the translation.

2   Ibid., 61–62, *60*.

3   Ibid., 63.

4   See Gilles Deleuze, *Cinema 2: The Time-Image*, trans. Hugh Tomlinson and Robert Galeta (Minneapolis: University of Minnesota Press, 1989), 133.

5   Consider, e.g., Alain Resnais's *L'année dernière à Marienbad* (1961), in which the conceptual persona is not double, but triple (A, X, and M), persisting in an unstable triangular figure where time is always overflowing space.

6   Gilles Deleuze, *Cinema 1: The Movement-Image*, trans. Hugh Tomlinson and Barbara Habberjam (Minneapolis: University of Minnesota Press, 1986), 73.

7   D. N. Rodowick, *Gilles Deleuze's Time Machine* (Durham, N.C.: Duke University Press, 1997).

8   Gilles Deleuze, "Mediators," in *Negotiations: 1972–1990*, trans. Martin Joughin (New York: Columbia University Press, 1995), 126. Originally published in *Pourparlers* (Paris: Éditions de Minuit, 1990).

9   Ibid., *125*, *171*.

10 Deleuze and Guattari, *What Is Philosophy?*, 64, *62*.

11 Ibid., 64–65.

12 Ibid., 73.

13 Also see my essay "Les personnages conceptuels de l'image-temps: 'gender' et l'histoire dans la Nouvelle Vague et après," *L'Esprit Créateur* 42, no. 1 (2002): 107–21. A shorter version was published online as "Unthinkable Sex: Conceptual Personae and the Time-Image," *(In)Visible Culture* 3 (2000), http://www.rochester.edu/in_visible_culture/issue3/rodowick.htm. This essay is a revised and expanded version of the English text.

14 D. N. Rodowick, *Reading the Figural, or, Philosophy after the New Media* (Durham, N.C.: Duke University Press, 2001), esp. chap. 6, "A Genealogy of Time."

15 Laura Mulvey, "Visual Pleasure and Narrative Cinema," *Screen* 16, no. 3 (1975): 6–18.

16 Deleuze, *Movement-Image*, 213.

17 Deleuze, *Time-Image*, 277, 362.

18 Rodowick, *Time Machine*, 178.

19   See E. Burdeau and F. Ramone, "Penser le surgissement de l'événement: entretien avec Alain Badiou," *Cahiers du cinéma* 68 (1998): 14.

20   Deleuze, *Time-Image*, 216.

21   Michel Foucault, "Theatrum Philosophicum," in *Language, Counter-Memory, Practice: Selected Essays and Interviews*, ed. Donald F. Bouchard (Ithaca, N.Y.: Cornell University Press, 1977), 185, 90. Published in French in *Dits et écrits*, vol. 2, ed. Daniel Defert and François Ewald (Paris: Gallimard, 1994), 75–99.

22   See David Bordwell, *Narration in the Fiction Film* (Madison: University of Wisconsin Press, 1985), 281–89.

23   I owe this idea to discussions with Sheila Murphy. See her "Lurking and Looking: Media Technologies and Cultural Convergences of Spectatorship, Voyeurism, and Surveillance" (PhD diss., University of California, Irvine, 2002).

Part IV. Experiments

11. The Strategist and the Stratigrapher

Tom Conley

Frame enlargement from *Tall in the Saddle* (Edgar Marin, 1944)

Toward the end of the ninth chapter of *Cinema 2: The Time-Image*, Gilles Deleuze speculates that modern cinema accedes to a "new visibility of things." The visibility he describes is of a character that accompanies what he calls the new and unforeseen presence of the "stratigraphic" image.[1] Taking up the rupture of the sensorimotor connection that, in the earlier regime of the movement-image, had tied the spectator's gaze to the motion of what was projected on the screen, now Deleuze sketches out what seems to be a thumbnail treatise of the *landscape* of contemporary cinema. He writes of a layered and metamorphic landscape, a landscape composed of so many deposits of time that it indicates the presence of an extremely long duration. Just as time would constitute the *real* for the historian, as something that knows neither an origin nor an ending, the landscape in contemporary cinema is shown simply to be *there*: in all of its quiddity (or "haeccity"), it is what it *is*. Because it belongs to a geological order, it embodies a time that both antedates and exceeds any presence or vestige of human labors. It resembles the places that Claude Lévi-Strauss, the "archeologist of space" (as he had described himself in *Tristes Tropiques* in 1955), recalled when he paid homage to the three "mistresses"—Marx, Freud, and geology—who had nourished him in his formative years. Geology was the mother and nursemaid of history, the muse (who might bear the name of a goddess such as "Geologia") who "assigns new meanings to the transformations of the terrestrial globe *[affecte d'un nouveau sens les transformations du globe terrestre]*."[2] Already in the writings of the ethnologist for whom Deleuze bore great admiration, the stratigraphic landscape was of a time and quality in which the organic and inorganic orders of things were of boundless force and vitality. Varying on Lévi-Strauss, Deleuze appears to be reminding us that the desert or the rocky beach, a locus classicus in treatises of the human sciences, also becomes a privileged space of cinema from its origins up to the present.

At this moment in *The Time-Image*, to find a point of view from which he is enabled to gaze on the stratigraphic landscape, indeed, to discern a new cinematic visibility of the world, Deleuze—good pedagogue that he is—feels impelled to sum up the hypotheses that had concluded *The Movement-Image*: sensorimotor linkages are attenuated and weakened; the camera begins to wander and move on its own; the principal event around which a narrative was organized now begins to proliferate; clichés become a primary matter of cinema; conspiracies that engage illicit exercise of power on a global scale are denounced. He reiterates that especially in the area where the sensorimotor regime gives way to almost purely optical and auditory situations, traditional distinctions between the subjective and objective realms are erased.[3]

Deleuze recalls these points to underscore the nature of the new and highly tactile qualities of the visual image. In the "becoming" that it embodies—as indicated by the verb that moves his sentence ahead—the visual image "becomes *[devient]*" "archeological, stratigraphic, tectonic *[archéologique, stratigraphique, tectonique]*."[4] But how can duration of this quality or order ever "become" if it had not been and become so already? In approaching an answer to the implicit question, Deleuze enumerates, according to both historical and geographical criteria, a list of authors and films in which this type of landscape is found. "These are the deserts in German cities," he notes, suggesting that he is thinking of the panoramic shots of the rubble of Berlin in Rossellini's *Germany, Year Zero*. They include "Pasolini's deserts that cause prehistory to become the abstract poetic element, the 'essence' co-present in our history, the Archean bedrock that reveals under our own an endless history,"[5] the remark here alluding perhaps to the jump cuts to arid and inhuman landscapes that we recall from *Teorema*.

Included in the list are "Antonioni's deserts," which bear the traces only of "abstract courses *[parcours abstraits]*" and which "recover the multiple fragments of a primordial couple *[recouvrent les fragments multiples d'un couple primordial]*," in most likelihood the landscapes that the originary (but also the final) couple of the world crosses in *Zabriskie Point*. Then follows "Bresson's fragmentations that march or concatenate shards of space of which each is closed on its own account": are these, we wonder, the muddy roads in *Diary of a Country Priest* that, for Deleuze, mark a strong contrast with the landscape of the woman's body in Rohmer's cinema, which "undergoes fragmentations, in most respect like fetishes," but also as fragments of a cup or the "pieces of a vase or a refracted *[irisée]* piece of pottery coming out of the sea"?[6] The reader would assume that the author is thinking of the crenellated Alpine landscape around Annecy in *Claire's Knee*, or the edge of the Norman beach and gossamer sand along the English channel in *Pauline at the Beach*, or perhaps even the evanescent green band where the sea and setting sun melt at the end of *The Green Ray*.

Whatever Deleuze may recall of these filmmakers, for him, it is Pierre Perrault who comes forward first and foremost. The inventor of direct cinema, especially in *Le pays de la terre sans arbre*, Perrault juxtaposes "geographical, cartographical and archeological images" when he tells of the eradication of the caribou herds. The philosopher goes so far as to admit that Alain Resnais merits the name "stratigrapher" when he "plunges the image into the ages of the world and variable orders of its layers."[7] But above all, Jean-Louis Straub and Danièlle Huillet are the past and present masters of these landscapes. The typically "Straubian shot" is effectively a "manual of stratigraphy," a cross section revealing little pointed lines of absent *facies* and full lines of those we continue to touch "such that the visual image amounts to the molar form of a 'rock.'"[8]

It might be said that in Deleuze's idiolect, the list that goes from Antonioni to Straub amounts to a miniature *archive* of modern cinema.

The archive, we recall from his *Foucault*, is comparable to a historical landscape, like a diorama, in which a display of the sum of the elements of the past in a given time and space has as its counterpart the *diagram*, a chart that reconfigures the elements of the archive to program things to come. The archive deals with what was in the realm of what is, while the diagram begins from what is to project what will be. The stratigraphic landscapes he finds among these filmmakers constitute archives of geological time, while they simultaneously display the virtues and powers of Bergsonian duration par excellence, a continuum that he calls a "non-chronological time grasped in its foundation."[9] The stratigraphic take would be an archive and a diagram of time past that, on one hand, becomes (in an intransitive sense), while on the other, it would be something for which the visual image is "present and past, ever present and already past, all at once at the same time."[10] Insofar as it is an archive, Deleuze's list goes from the immediate postwar era, from Rossellini's trilogy—in which cities are the sites of "any-spaces-whatsoever, an urban cancer, a dedifferentiated fabric, inhuman zones that are opposed to the determinate space of earlier realism"—running up to the 1980s.[11] The moment when the films of Straub and Huillet come forward is synchronous with the advent of an independent and minoritarian cinema whose task is to invent a public that, consciously or unconsciously, had been waiting for it. Thus understood as a *diagram*, the stratigraphic image would be the proof of the new and unexpected, indeed perplexing presence of the cinematic landscape as it can be grasped only here and now. What he calls Straub and Huillet's "manual" of stratigraphy would be a diagram, a filmic treatise aiming at transforming a visual archive into a new order of film.

For the general reader, that is, for the "ordinary" man or woman of cinema, the idea of a "new" stratigraphy becomes problematic.[12] In these pages, the landscape that Deleuze is describing includes a duration going well beyond and outside the time in which it is perceived. But paradoxically, the landscape remains within the confines of the perception that discerns its traits and qualities. The stratigraphic image causes one to think of the impossibility of being able to think about or through it in all its totality: we gaze on something so far beyond what we can assimilate of its force and virtue that we can only admire, in a sublime way, what we cannot comprehend. Yet we are able to perceive to some degree what we cannot perceive. Here it can be observed that the *diagram* of a new archeology of the image would be a different form of the landscape, in other words, a landscape seen in view of a temporality that belongs to geology. At the same time, the landscape might be said to transform the memory of a painterly tradition (from Lorrain to Catlin and Remington) into a type of ciphered picture, a map or a two-dimensional palimpsest that is no longer taken to be a space seen through a window onto the world at large.[13]

In the same context, Deleuze implies that the regime of the time-image has as its foundation the "archive" of classical cinema. Insisting on the presence of silence in contemporary cinema, he sees in both silent and experimental cinema an autonomy that the sound track gains with respect to the image track. Having dealt with the perception-image that is generally made manifest in the long shot in deep focus, especially in the tradition of the Western,[14] Deleuze observed, while citing *Winchester 73*, that the cinema of this (classical) genre lays stress at once on the character of the landscape and on the birth of our perception both of the landscape and of our perception of the landscape.[15] In moving over and through these great vistas (in part, we can add, by virtue of silence), the eyes of the viewer begin to perceive perception. Here Deleuze notes that in the regime of the movement-image, an interval is opened between the landscape and what makes it visible or perceptible. By contrast, the stratigraphic landscape of modern cinema, as opposed to that of the classical Western, no longer allows any such delay or interval. From one shot to the next, the landscape is striated with lines of different density.

But why would stratigraphy *not* be part and parcel of the Western or classical cinema? Why is it that from its origins, cinema would *not* be a site or an origin of the tectonic image? The question is raised less to impugn Deleuze's hypotheses about the character of modern cinema than to show that their breadth is of far greater reach than either his taxonomy or the *strategy* informing his choice of examples. In a general way, the reader of *The Movement-Image* or *The Time-Image* never fails to note that the major concepts belong to a rigorous and carefully conceived lexicon and that the words conveying them are no less vigorous in what they express. They are of a drive and poetic force that causes them, by virtue of their style or manner of exposition, to "become" *at once legible and visible.* Deleuze's words thus inhere in the "stratigraphic" landscape he describes, and they are to be seen and read in their own metamorphic form and tectonic movement. Sometimes they are of a sight and sound that could be called "rocky" and "pebbly," now and again both incarnating and occulting the meanings that they convey, indicate, or even, like a rebus or a riddle, embody.

Now and again, they become the very events of which they appear to be "speaking" or on which they shed light enough to make themselves seen.

The character of Deleuze's words seems to be refracted (as he would say, *irisé*) through his close reading of *The Archaeology of Knowledge* in *Foucault*. He remarks that the author of the *Archaeology* is "singularly close to contemporary cinema" because he "cracks open words and things."[16] By doing so, Foucault arrives at the limit that separates things *visible* from things *utterable* or legible. He notes that also, in his early *Raymond Roussel*, Foucault makes the same remarks: it is up to the reader the "break up, to open words."[17] And in *Foucault*, no less, Deleuze refers to Jean-Marie Straub to elucidate the meaning of the "strata or historical formations" that inform Foucault's work in general. The allusion to Straub, the very Straub who would be the author of a "manual of stratigraphy" in *The Time-Image*, causes Foucault's own idiolect to be cracked open, split, and even scattered. No less, it is he who also causes Deleuze's words to be subjected to the very analytical pressures he applies to his subject.

In *Foucault*, Deleuze formulates a major hypothesis, scaffolded from a double reading of the writings of Maurice Blanchot and Foucault, in which he states that *what is seen is never anchored in what is said.*[18] In "cracking open" Deleuze's words along the axes of seeing and speaking, the reader quickly observes that in *stratigraphy* (and in the archive of films that are implied by this term), Deleuze suggests that there exists the presence both of *stratèges* or strategists—who might be the "great authors of cinema"—and of *strategies*, perhaps what he would call a politics of film, if not, at least as is suggested in the last pages of *The Time-Image*, even a politics of film theory. Thus the task that Deleuze confers on his reader entails that of reading theory as if it were a text to be cracked open, as a text riddled with words to be split asunder, as a crosshatched and fragmented work pocked with broken signs, replete with vocables and scattered forms that are paradoxically interwoven or visible in the abstraction of an interlace. The text would be likened to a stratigraphy, an array of words, maps, and textual fragments superimposed on one another. Some are torn from a given context, others from others, the sum being a tectonic movement of the whole work in general.[19] The stake is therefore one of seeing how *strategy* resonates or is echoed in the *stratigraphic* landscape.

The first indication is found in what is meant by *archive* and *diagram*. The former would be close to the history of film and classical cinema (the regime of the movement-image) that circulates in modern works. The latter, by contrast, would be a sum of archives put to work so that cinema, at least such as it is understood here and now, might be considered from the angle of a strategic operation. Here it would be asked to what degree a stratigraphic cinema leans in the direction of the one or the other. Does it move toward the archive or toward the diagram? In *Foucault*, Deleuze takes a step that goes beyond the principle of things seen and things read or heard, but the move is especially evident in the final pages of "The Components of the Image," the final chapter of *The Time-Image*, in which Deleuze attempts to distinguish the interval, a distinguishing trait of the movement-image, from the interstice, that which identifies a total disjunction between a shot and those that precede and follow it. In the classical Western, we recall, at stake is the "drama as much of the visible and invisible as an epic of action" because the hero "imposes upon action the interval or delay of a second that allows him to see everything."[20] The *interval* connotes continuity and the matching of shots and action. Yet the landscape in which Deleuze notes the presence of the interval, in *Winchester 73*, is arguably almost entirely of a stratigraphic quality. The interval, if an interval is there, is so slight that it becomes an interstice for the simple reason that the landscape—in all its rocky nooks and crannies, the jagged shapes of its boulders and abrupt rifts of peaks and valleys—is as much to be read as to be seen.

In view of the interval, it suffices to return to the pages describing the features of a stratigraphic landscape. In a dazzling display of allusions Deleuze makes to cinema of every age and period, including that of the regime of the movement-image, he recalls first of all that the false match of two shots, or else the match made along the uncanny sight line of 180 degrees (used frequently by Fritz Lang and evident in some keynote shots in Jean Vigo's *L'Atalante*), requires a double reading of the two disjoined aspects or surfaces of the same thing or subject. In *Moses and Aaron*, in which Straub and Huillet offer autonomous shots of arid landscapes, a similar reading is required. It is qualified "as a function of the eye, a perception of perception, a perception that is grasped only through perception that the other side—the imagination, memory, or knowledge—is to be grasped. In short, what we call a reading of the visual image is its stratigraphic condition *[état stratigraphique]*.... To read is to re-link instead of linking; it means turning about, returning, instead of going directly to a place."[21] Speech seen in silent cinema (such as in intertitles, in writing found in the field of the image, in close-ups that cause the reader to read in the movement of the lips of the personages in view the grain of the words they are speaking) requires a reading of the image. Inversely, in modern cinema, speech that is read or heard "becomes independent of the visual image" and, as a result, causes the shot to become a sort of table or graph, an "archeological or rather a stratigraphic cross section."[22] When speech intervenes, he adds, it underlines how present is the sight of a space "empty of any event [vide d'événement]."[23]

Speech intervenes not as a fact, but as an act or instance of language that is so disjointed and coming from so far away that it would be an echo of itself, a sort of voice-*off-off*. There follows a new and unforeseen *distribution* of elements to be seen and uttered, or perceived and read, in ways that have little to do with the continuities of "reality" as we know them in everyday life. In the new cinema, a speech-act has no grounding. Its geography, understood as a site of the origin of an instance and of its ostensive destination, becomes entirely uncertain and improbable. Speech would be emitted from sedimentary layers of earth and from memory fossilized in rocks and boulders. It would become a kind of unwarranted sounding of the depths and deposits revealed by a geological cross section of the scene.

Here Deleuze observes that a new pedagogy of cinema is born. It derives from speech that lays stress on disjunction that is inherent to its nature. It insists—or rather, it teaches—that space is other than what is found in the intervals and contours of narrative cinema. All of a sudden, there emerges from within the highly pedagogical style of *The Time-Image* a visibility that can be seen in the graphic character of his remarks. The contradictions and undecidable elements in the new brand of cinema "do not let us merely confront what is heard and what is seen shot by shot or one after the other, in a pedagogical way: their role is to induce a system of uncouplings and interlacings that now and again determine the different moments of the present through anticipation or retrogradation, in a direct time-image, or in a series of powers, of a quality either retrogradable or progressive, under the sign of the false [sous le signe du faux]."[24]

A flash of light seems to shoot through the word *faux* and cause it break into pieces. Here the sign of the false to which Deleuze refers is rent by the emblem of Father Time, the image of the grim reaper: by the scythe or *faux* of time and by the undecided or undecidable necessity underscoring that one cannot (qu'il ne faut pas) choose between things true and false. In most likelihood, Deleuze is referring to his chapter "The Powers of the False," especially the pages in which his remarks anticipate those on stratigraphy when he reminds us that Antonioni's and Ozu's spaces cannot be explained in a spatial way because of the fact that they cannot be located. But at this very moment, and in these films, a time lacking chronology is acutely felt. It is a time of a geological duration "that produces necessarily 'anormal,' essentially 'false' movements."[25] The casual reader would say that Deleuze is attacking the underlying truth-effects of the style and form of narrative or classical cinema; that he wants to bring forward a "falsifying narration"[26] to confer on the time-image an undecidable quality; that he is aligning his analysis of cinema with Nietzschean philosophy. But the diligent reader, he or she who seeks to "crack" words "open" and to project their part toward "the limit that separates the visible from the utterable,"[27] *le faux* (i.e., what is false) becomes the double and the other of *la faux* (the icon of the finality of time). The substantive appears to display in its form, like the "I" of Rimbaud's *je est un autre*, an "other" in itself. The cutting edge of the word breaks the agreement (or the continuity) of the "masculine" article that would guarantee unilateral meaning. Its "feminine" other would belong to an unconscious in the diction that at once upsets and confirms Deleuze's pedagogy.[28]

The stratigraphic image, he adds, is such that as of now, no longer can there exist either voice-*off* or off-screen space. What we hear becomes an image in and of itself, a singular form born from a rupture or break from the visual image. Deleuze coins a polymorphous expression to explain the nature of this new cinema: sound and landscape are "no longer even two autonomous components of a single audio-visual image, as in Rossellini, but these are two 'heautonomous' *[héautonomes]* images, one visual and one sonorous, with a break, an irrational cut that splits the two."[29] An aspiration, hiatus, or interstice is seen and heard in the prefix *hé-*. It may be an unconscious interpellation that underlines how *autonomie* is transformed into its double in *héautonomie*. In the neologism, Deleuze insists that it recalls the memory of a similar form in Kant's *Critique of Judgment*. But for every student of French prosody, *hé-* and *héau-* force immediate recall of the short poem bearing one of the longest and memorable titles in Baudelaire's *Les Fleurs du Mal*. "L'héautotimoroumenos" begins thus:

> *Je te frapperai sans colère*
> *Et sans haine, comme un boucher,*
> *Comme Moïse sur le rocher!*
> *Et je ferai de ta paupière,*

Pour abreuver mon Saharah,
Jaillir les eaux de la souffrance.[30]
[I will strike you without anger
And without hate, like a butcher,
Like Moses on the boulder!
And from your eyelid I will make,
To slake the thirst of my Sahara,
Spring the waters of suffering.]

The title of the poem refers to one of Terence's comedies that designates he or she who is self-tormented, *ipse se puniens.*[31] It is impossible not to behold in Deleuze's neologism an "autonomy of oneself" or an autonomy marked by the memory of Baudelaire's arid and sandy landscape transposed on that of Straub and Huillet's *Moses and Aaron.* In Deleuze's formula, the memory of "Moïse sur le rocher" in this poem (which most students of French know by heart) is morphed into a cinematographic landscape in the same way that "mon Saharah" becomes identified both as a biblical female (Sarah) and an African desert, the locus classicus of stratigraphic cinema.[32] Kant has Baudelaire as his double, and the classic cineasts of the desert—Stroheim, Ford, Vidor, Walsh—have as their complements Straub and Huillet. The latter succeed in creating a sonorous image that is torn "from its legible support, a text, a book, letters, or documents"[33] that are foreign to it. The reader is never far from Baudelaire's tourniquet—"*Je suis la plaie et le couteau* [I am the wound and the knife]" (l. 21)—when the speech-act that enunciates the condition "resists" itself[34] and thus becomes an act of resistance, resisting its very action.

In these sentences, the speech-acts that Deleuze ascribes to Straub and Huillet would be evidence of the memories of the image of archeological and geological "cuts" or cross sections of the desert landscape. All of a sudden, stratigraphy is marked by history, perhaps for the reason that the two filmmakers embrace a Marxian politics. Either between or across the strata of the landscape, the viewer of their films would witness class struggle or, failing that, myriad conflicts among the various layers or *couches.* In accord with this line of thinking, the silent peasant who inhabits the landscape would make visible how much the decor resists the speech-act that would seek to transform the place into an event.[35] By means of acts of speech and of visibility in *Moses and Aaron,* "the telluric landscape develops an entire aesthetic power that uncovers the layers of history and the political struggles on which it is built."[36] A vital disjunction of visual and sonorous images once again refers to Blanchot's literary space, in which there is "a very exact relation of incommensurability, found not through an absence of relation," but rather, through a dissociation of visibility from audibility, each being *héautonome*, "heautonomous," with respect to the other.[37] The relation cannot be totalized. Deleuze remarks that when the visual image lacks a sonorous component, sight and sound "become two autonomous components of one audio-visual image or, still further, two heautonomous images."[38]

Given thus is a mixed and polymorphous landscape of a long duration, but also a landscape cut and divided into autonomous historical strata. Would the desert landscape, riddled with disconnected elements, be the background from which the new audiovisual creation emerges, or it is a space inhering in the "incommensurable" relation of sight and sound? The remarks in these difficult but luminous pages are inflected by Deleuze's attraction to Blanchot, which finds its origins in *Foucault*, a book of the same inspiration as *The Time-Image*, in which the broken relation of things utterable and things visible is keynote. An utterance, Deleuze notes of Foucault on speech-acts, is of a *héautonomie* in respect to visible formations.[39] Foucault, a philosopher whom he calls (in indirect homage to Rimbaud) a *voyant*,[40] has passion for seeing. Through the attention he brings to sight and sound, Foucault marks the history of philosophy in an utterly new fashion. He attends to *strata*, to "historical formations, positivities or empiricities" made of words and things.[41] The field of strata "does not necessarily refer to the past,"[42] and the knowledge that derives from their observation is constituted by a unity of strata or thresholds. The *archive*, Deleuze notes further, belongs to an audiovisual order and, as a result, is of a disjunctive character.[43] It is so disjunctive in seeing-and-speaking that "the most complete examples" are found in the films of the Straubs, in Syberberg, and in Marguerite Duras. The split or broken relation of seeing and speaking is part of Foucault's "stratum" and of strata that are transformed "at the same time."[44]

In the following chapter, "Strategies or the Non-stratified," Power (capital *P* in the text) takes the form (such is the *Panopticon*) of a *diagram*, in other words, of a presentation "of relations of forces that belong to a formation" that would be both legible and visible. At this juncture, the *diagram* is confused, as if in a verbal lap dissolve, with the concept of *strategy*. In following the line of divide between seeing and speaking, in *Foucault*, Deleuze coins a metaphor in which the diagram takes the place of the archive. "Strategies are distinguished from stratifications, just as diagrams are distinguished from archives."[45] Returning to the pages that explain what makes the one different from the other, the reader quickly discovers that the archive signifies a "history of forms" that the diagram, what he calls "a becoming of forces," will double or surpass.[46] The variable combinations of the visible and the utterable, Deleuze later adds,[47] are so many "strata" or historical formations. It avers that the diagram is made from "superimposed maps" and thus resembles a stratigraphy of geographical representations. The diagram arrogates power because it mixes the distinction or intervals between form and content or between discourse and visible forms. Unlike the archive, which merely contains other archives of various origins, the diagram is a mechanism that will program (or map out) a new reality. Instead of making an inventory of history in the manner of the archive, the diagram will open itself onto the horizon of unforeseen and unheard creativities.

The high degree of abstraction in these pages does not make it impossible for the reader to discern in the "diagram" a concept that has as its cinematic equivalent or correlative the "stratigraphic" landscape. The auteurs who are dear to Deleuze construct their films on the basis of the disjunctions they engineer among visibilities and acts of speech. Unlikely sounds perturb the places they cross (as in Bresson), while the landscapes they invent isolate and estrange every utterance in the field of the image (from Rossellini to Straub and Huillet). An archive would be a stratified landscape, and a diagram the "heautonomous effect," thanks to the uncanny quality of the landscape, which comes with our perception of the abyss opened between speaking and seeing.

Yet the strategist who constructs a diagram is the filmmaker who will restratify and recompose the archive of present time in view of a long future and of the principle of becoming. The great auteurs of cinema are no less *stratèges* or strategists insofar as they break open the lexicon of the archives of which they are inheritors, and by and large in following, copying, and redeploying them. Thus the archive, a sort of "cut" or cross section of sedimentary landscapes, would be the turf on which the great directors deploy their strategies. They create films that bring forward an impossible sense of duration by means of the way that sound riddles their archeological decors. They alter all synchrony between voice or sound and the landscape in which human expression would seem to be unwarranted.

Furthermore, it could be said that when Deleuze notes how the visual image *becomes* archeological, stratigraphic, and tectonic,[48] it becomes so because, when his words are cracked open and split, a *strategy* inheres in what he calls a cinematic *stratigraphy*. Here is where the ordinary viewer of cinema—he or she who would be affiliated with the "archive" when viewing films constructed with movement-images, and with the "diagram" when studying the great contemporary auteurs—begins to wonder where stratigraphies begin and where they end. Would it be a *strategy* to mix classical landscapes, drawn from the archive of the Western or the road movie, with landscapes of diagrammatical or tabular quality? Is it possible to discover a sense of becoming when the viewer works through and about the archive of classical directors? In other words, can classical landscapes that appear to be highly stratigraphic—the desert of *Greed*, the Monument Valley of *Stagecoach* and *The Searchers*, the great escarpments of cliff sides in *Pursued* and *Colorado Territory*, the land of rock and cactus in *Seven Men from Now* or *Winchester 73*—be turned into diagrams when the viewer displaces them from their historical niches in the history of cinema? Are they pertinent when refashioned and reformatted for the DVD and for digital transmission?

The answer would be affirmative where politics are invested into the pedagogy of cinema. If so, it seems that a strategy of a return and a reworking of the archive belongs to a tactics, a term that is visibly absent where Deleuze discusses strata and strategy. When Deleuze draws attention to the sedimentary and tectonic landscapes of film in the years stretching from the 1950s to the 1980s, he effectively becomes a tactician of film history. A sense of "tactics" (and of tact and tactility, too) is manifest when he frames his observations about the tectonic landscape under the title of "components" in the contemporary world that reach back to the beginnings of cinema.[49] Through a sublime irony, the project that would distinguish the movement-image from the time-image, presented as if it were a strategic operation, finds itself subverted by the *tactics* of his return to early cinema.

In this way, the historical overview of the stratigraphic landscape offered in the chapter "The Components of the Image" is found in the imagination of a duration that is longer than (1) the history of cinema (which counts little more than a century), and (2) the history at the basis of the founding taxonomies of *The Movement-Image* and *The Time-Image*.[50] A tactics is at stake when Deleuze mixes strata, strategy, and stratigraphy. It is evident when his words are "cracked open" or when we follow their "rhizomatic" connections and bifurcations; various crisscrossings and breakages generate new itineraries of meaning. As a result, we can observe that the stratigraphic landscape, evinced in the Western from the beginnings of cinema, becomes a site for Deleuze's most intensive work in *The Time-Image* on film and duration. The landscape figures in a historical operation that draws on the cinematic *archive* stretching from the beginnings of cinema to independent and vanguard work. It has a diagrammatical character when it includes in its image of duration not only the entire history of film, but also history tout court. If, as it has been argued previously, Deleuze is at once a strategist and a stratigrapher, his readers cannot fail to find in *The Time-Image* a tactics that bears both on the taxonomy and the history of cinema. The work both affirms and calls itself into question.

By way of a problematic conclusion, it suffices to return to the landscape shown at the beginning of this chapter. Taken from *Tall in the Saddle* (Edgar Marin, 1944), a nondescript and almost generic Western made during World War II, the shot records what might be called a classically stratified landscape. Empty of human presence, a mountain is scarred by the zigzagged road drawn up and across its western slope. The point of view of the shot is taken from what seems to be the same road on the side of a mountain from which the spectator sees the landscape in the distance. In the sequence, the voice-off of an anxious and persnickety old lady comments on what we behold. The stagecoach that Gabby Hayes has been driving over a rocky and bumpy road has come to a halt. John Wayne, the young man who is riding shotgun at his left side, has just asked his old friend if he might "spell him" by taking the reins. The old man affirms that, no, he will not hand over the reins because he will soon lead the stage down the mountain at breakneck speed. Stopping to aggravate the passengers— especially the old lady—in the compartment below, he takes vicious pleasure in hearing her complain about time being lost. Her voice-off asserts that indeed, because of the slope of the road before her eyes, the driver would do well to put the whip to the horses. Yet for all the movement of the coach that has led to this point of arrest, the sudden immobility causes the viewer to lose track both of the narrative and of the line of the road: the geology of the decor comes forward when, all of a sudden, the film stops.

No human being is visible in the shot. As if coming from nowhere, the voice-off of the old lady merely indicates the path that the stage will follow. For an instant, we begin to perceive our perception of the landscape, but in such a way that the origin of the voice, because it is *off*, might be seen located in the rock, situated halfway between the point of view of the camera (outside the doorway of the stagecoach) and the stratigraphic landscape in the distance. Thanks to what is clearly the "indirect discourse of the film,"[51] it might be said that the face we discern in the rock—which displays the eye and nose of a skull-like head in profile—is speaking. The rock bears the attributes of an inorganic face, indeed, of a fossilized person, belonging to an originary duration, who gazes on the landscape in which he or she has been residing since time immemorial. Here is where, all of a sudden, a classical image from the archive of the interval or of the movement-image is transformed into a time-image. If Valéry's celebrated *Achille immobile à grands pas* is a fitting description of this moment, then a metamorphosis takes place in an "archeological, tectonic, stratigraphic" setting and an unforeseen duration of a timeless instant, when the film immobilizes itself in its movement. At this point, the Western of 1944 theorizes itself: the archive that its landscape seems to embody in the pantheon of the Western classic becomes a diagram of duration. The classical Western turns into a manual of stratigraphy. And like Deleuze, the reader of *Tall in the Saddle* who discerns the qualities of the stratigraphy becomes a cinematic strategist.

Notes

1　Gilles Deleuze, *Cinéma 2: L'Image-temps* (Paris: Editions de Minuit, 1985), 320. Published in English as *Cinema 2: The Time-Image*, trans. Hugh Tomlinson and Robert Galeta (Minneapolis: University of Minnesota Press, 1989), 246. All translations from the French in this text and others are mine. Page references are to the French edition, followed by the corresponding passage in the English translation (in italics).

2　Claude Lévi-Strauss, *Tristes Tropiques* (Paris: Plon, 1955), 63. Published in English as *Tristes Tropiques*, trans. John Weightman and Doreen Weightman (New York: Pocket Books, 1977), 51.

3　Deleuze, *Time-Image*, 15, 7.

4　Ibid., 317, 243.

5　Ibid.

6　Ibid., 317–18, 244.

7   Deleuze, *Time-Image*, 318.

8   Ibid., 319, 245. In Ronald Bogue, *Deleuze on Cinema* (New York: Rout-
     ledge, 2003). Ronald Bogue reads and carefully resumes these pages under
     the subheading of "The Modern Lectosign" (pp. 187–94). The intent of
     the paragraphs to follow is to theorize further Bogue's valuable observa-
     tions.

9   Deleuze, *Time-Image*, 110, 82.

10   Ibid., 106, 79. Deleuze, *Time-Image*, 132, *100*, explains the point further
     when he quotes St. Augustine, an inhabitant of the North African desert,
     for whom there exists "a present of the future, a present of the present,
     [and] a present of the past" that are incrusted in an event in such a way
     that one "discovers a time inhering in the event that is composed of the
     simultaneity of these three implied presents, of the de-actualized *points
     of the present.*"

11   Gilles Deleuze, *Cinéma 1: L'Image-mouvement* (Paris: Editions de Minuit,
     1983), 286. Published in English as *Cinema 1: The Movement-Image*,
     trans. Hugh Tomlinson and Barbara Habberjam (Minneapolis: University
     of Minnesota Press, 1986), 212. Page references are to the French edition,
     followed by the corresponding passage in the English translation (in ital-
     ics).

12   The formula of the "ordinary" viewer of cinema refers to Jean Louis Schefer,
     L'Homme ordinaire du cinéma (Paris: Cahiers du cinéma / Gallimard,
     1982). Deleuze counts among the few readers of Schefer who mobilize his
     speculations in a critical sense. Thanks to *L'Homme ordinaire*, Deleuze,
     Time-Image, 343, *263*, observes that cinema is comparable to "a man-
     nequin or a machine, a mechanical man not born of the world who puts
     it into a state of suspension."

13   We can speculate that for Straub and Huillet, the landscape would be
     comparable to Rauschenberg's painting, in which, Deleuze notes, "one
     might say that the surface of the painting were no longer a window on
     the world in order to become an opaque information table on which a
     ciphered line is drawn." See Gilles Deleuze, *Le Pli: Leibniz et le Baroque*
     (Paris: Editions de Minuit, 1988), 38. Published in English as *The Fold:
     Leibniz and the Baroque*, trans. Tom Conley (Minneapolis: University of
     Minnesota Press, 1993), 27.

14   Deleuze, *Movement-Image*, 102, *69*.

15   I have dealt with perception and landscape in *Winchester 73* (by way
     of dialogue with Deleuze) at greater length in Tom Conley, "Landscape
     and Perception: On Anthony Mann," in *Landscape and Film*, ed. Martin
     Lefevre (New York: Routledge, 2006), 289–312.

16   Gilles Deleuze, *Foucault* (Paris: Editions de Minuit, 1986), 72. Published
     in English as *Foucault*, trans. Seán Hand (Minneapolis: University of Min-
     nesota Press, 1988), 65. Page references are to the French edition, followed
     by the corresponding passage in the English translation (in italics).

17 Ibid., 59, 52.

18 Ibid., 71, 64.

19 In Gilles Deleuze, *Proust and Signs*, trans. Richard Howard (New York: George Braziller, 1972), Deleuze already wrote of works whose "wholes" were of a movement and force of greater subtlety than their constituent parts. They included *À la recherche du temps perdu*, to be sure, Balzac's *La Comédie humaine*, and the jumbled sum of Leibniz's philosophical writings.

20 Deleuze, *Movement-Image*, 102, 70.

21 Deleuze, *Time-Image*, 319, 245. Here Deleuze's words are very close to Blanchot's initial pages of "Parler, ce n'est pas voir," in *L'Entretien infini* (Paris: Gallimard, 1969), 33–35, in which the author glosses *trouver* not to mean "to find," but, in respect to its etymology, "to turn and turn about," *tourner tout autour*, such that what—if anything—is found in the act of finding is that of circulating around an absent center, a center implied to be discerned in the verb itself (*trou* in *trouver*) or the hole toward which (*vers*) one turns that always appears and disappears. See Maurice Blanchot, *The Infinite Conversation*, trans. Susan Hanson (Minneapolis: University of Minnesota Press, 1993).

22 Deleuze, *Time-Image*, 320, 246.

23 Ibid., 322, 247.

24 Ibid., 326, 250.

25 Ibid., 169, 129.

26 Ibid., 171, 131.

27 Deleuze, *Foucault*, 59.

28 It is worth recalling that for poets who reach back to the early modern age, in the hidden layers of what we might call a stratigraphy of French grammar, the gender of words is fluid. In "Sur des vers de Virgile," Michel de Montaigne, *Essais*, in *Oeuvres complètes*, ed. Albert Thibaudet and Maurice Rat (Paris: Gallimard/Pléiade, 1962), 852, discusses the surplus of pleasure that make the simulacra of love far more erotic and vibrant in their Eros than love in its impoverished reality. A paper Venus is more attractive than the real being. The pleasure of sexual indifference, of the neutrality of gender, is made manifest when he remarks, "*Quand mon page fait l'amour, il l'entend* [When my page makes love he [or it?] knows it]." Is Montaigne's page the person *(le page)* or the page of paper *(la page)* on which the observation is made? It can be added that pedagogy as such and its etymology belong to an erotic nexus that is not lost on Deleuze's style. One of his remarks about the identity of homosexuality as language and as a state of things, in his "Préface à l'après-midi des faunes" (an ephemeral gay journal), makes the point marvelously clear: "*moins l'homosexualité est un état de chose, plus l'homosexualité est un mot, plus il faut la prendre au mot, assumer sa position comme spécifique, ses énoncés comme irréductibles* [the less that homosexuality is a state of

things the more homosexuality is a word, the more it must be taken as a word [*au mot* = *homo*], the more its position must be assumed as specific, its utterances as irreducible]." In *L'île déserte et autres textes* (Paris: Editions de Minuit, 2002), 398–99; emphasis mine. When homosexuality is taken at the level of the word, *au mot*, it also bears its own name, *homo*, within the word. Here Deleuze uses paronomasia to break open a common substantive in the gender wars at the time they were waged in the 1970s. See Gilles Deleuze, *Desert Islands and Other Texts (1953–1974)*, trans. Mike Taormina (New York: Semiotext(e), 2003).

29   Deleuze, *Time-Image*, 327, 251.

30   Charles Baudelaire, *Les Fleurs du Mal*, ed. Antoine Adam (Paris: Garnier, 1961), 84.

31   Lewis and Short, *A Latin Dictionary* (1879; Oxford: Clarendon Press, 1989), 845c2.

32   Deleuze's relation with deserts and desert spaces could be pursued in the context of stratigraphy. An early essay "Causes and Reasons of the Desert Island" (see n. 26) uses the abstraction of the isolated place to ground philosophical labor. In an essay on T. E. Lawrence, he remarks that the desert is the site where entities or subjective dispositions *double images* and bring to these spaces a "visionary dimension." In Gilles Deleuze, *Critique et clinique* (Paris: Editions de Minuit, 1993), 150. Published in English as *Essays Critical and Clinical*, trans. Daniel W. Smith and Michael A. Greco (Minneapolis: University of Minnesota Press, 1997), 120.

33   Deleuze, *Time-Image*, 330, 253.

34   Ibid., 331, 254.

35   Gilles Deleuze, "L'Epuisé," in *Quad* (Paris: Minuit, 1992), 72–75, remarks that an event—in this instance, speech-acts in Beckett's theater, in which video technology plays a role—creates from the place (the site of utterance) a space that it abolishes almost simultaneously.

36   Deleuze, *Time-Image*, 334, 256.

37   Ibid., 334. At stake is Maurice Blanchot, *L'Espace littéraire* (Paris: Gallimard, 1955), whose dynamics of space and visibility are later crystallized in "Parler, ce n'est pas voir" (see n. 20). Published in English as *The Space of Literature*, trans. Ann Smock (Lincoln: University of Nebraska Press, 1982).

38   Deleuze, *Time-Image*, 330, 253.

39   Deleuze, *Foucault*, 57.

40   Ibid., 58.

41   Ibid., 55.

42   Ibid., 58.

43   Ibid., 71.

44   Ibid., 70.

45   Ibid., 80.

46   Ibid., 51.

47 Ibid., 90.

48 Deleuze, *Time-Image*, 317.

49 In the thick of the discussion bearing on the time-image, Deleuze, *Time-Image*, 298, notes that "silent film engaged a division of the visible image and legible speech" in such a way that it is implied that to be visible, the silent image needs to be read, and that to be legible, speech in films made before 1930 needs to be seen. See Blanchot, *Space of Literature*.

50 Here the distinction between strategy and tactics is drawn from what Michel de Certeau makes of Greco-Roman polemology in *L'Invention du quotidian 1: Arts de faire*, ed. Luce Giard (Paris: Gallimard, 1987), published in English as *The Practice of Everyday Life*, trans. Steven F. Rendall (Berkeley: University of California Press, 1984). Strategy: "[a] Cartesian attitude, if you wish: it is an effort to delimit one's own place in a world bewitched by the invisible powers of the Other" (p. 36), in other words, a gesture of scientific, political, or military modernity. Tactics: actions that take advantage of time and of contingency that "make use of the cracks that particular conjunctions open in the surveillance of proprietary powers," and that "poach" and "create surprise in them" (p. 37). They privilege relations of places by mobilizing "a clever utilization of time, of the opportunities it presents and also of the play that it introduces into the foundations of power" (p. 39). Of note is that where Deleuze explains Foucault's *strategies* (esp. in Michel Foucault, *Surveiller et punir: Naissance de la prison* [Paris: Editions Gallimard, 1975]), Certeau qualifies them as *tactics* and describes its ways of reading once again as "poaching." In Michel de Certeau, *Histoire et psychanalyse entre science et fiction*, ed. Luce Giard (Paris: Gallimard, 1987), 46–47.

51 Deleuze, *Movement-Image*, 108–13, 74–78.

12. Pleats of Matter, Folds of the Soul

Giuliana Bruno

This chapter weaves together aspects of Gilles Deleuze's philosophy of the fold with thoughts on the texture of cinematic time-space. In addressing the fashioning of space in film, architecture, and fashion, it is especially concerned with tailoring a space for affect and with exploring the material of emotional fabrics. The starting point for this exploration of the fabrics of the visual is the recognition that Deleuze, unlike many philosophers and film theorists, gives space to the realm of affect in his work on the visual arts.

Most notably, Deleuze theorizes the notion of an "affection-image," especially in his book *Cinema 1: The Movement-Image*.[1] His first way of imaging this affect involves reading the face and pointing to the close-up as the form that makes it visible in film. Here the philosopher follows the perspective of Béla Balázs, who pioneered an understanding of affect in film in terms of microphysiognomy, offering an "animated" reading of visual life that extended from the human face to the face of things.[2] Deleuze engages the role of the face in film as a way to gather up and express affect as a complex entity. After initially suggesting that, in the first instance, the affection-image is the close-up and that the close-up is the face, he later questions the strict linkage of the face to the cinematic figure of the close-up. This critique has to be taken further: although the reading of the face is an important way to address affect in film and has a fascinating history in the visual arts, such a reading has its limitations. In limiting oneself to this perspective, one risks equating affect with the expression of passions, which is simply one side of the possible manifestations of emotional life. To map the terrain of affect on, and as, a larger surface, one needs to go beyond physiognomy, to look outside the contour of the face and avoid the restrictive enclosure of affect within the close-up. In this chapter, affect is thus to be explored as an extensive form of con*tact*: a transmission that communicates in different spaces, and does so tangibly.

In turning to a *landscape* of affects, we must first note that the face is itself a landscape. If we begin to think of the face as dermal surface, we can then move toward a more textured configuration of affective landscapes and extend their material manifestation onto a larger screen. Deleuze himself offers us this opportunity when he theorizes the face as landscape and designs its texture as surface as well as map and screen. In *A Thousand Plateaus*, he writes, with Félix Guattari, about faciality and deterritorialization: "the face is part of a surface-hole, holey surface system. . . . The face is a surface: facial traits, lines, wrinkles. . . . The face is a map. . . . The face has a correlate of great importance: the landscape. . . . Architecture positions its ensembles—houses, towns or cities, monuments or factories—to function like faces in the landscape they transform. Painting takes up the same movement but also reverses it, positioning a landscape as a face."[3]

This reading of faciality in the visual arts and architecture opens up for us a larger perspective in which to locate affect. In some way, it approaches an aspect of "the affection-image" that also emerges in one part of *The Movement-Image*, when Deleuze moves beyond the close-up and arrives at reading affect in relation to larger spaces.[4] Having established that the affect can obtain space for itself as faciality, it eventually becomes possible that it can do so even without the face and independently from the close-up. Deleuze admits that affect can become space that is no longer a specifically determined place. In this more virtual manifestation, "the affection-image" can come close to the potential space Deleuze refers to as "any-space-whatever" *(espace quelconque)*.

Deleuze defines any-space-whatever as a space that has "lost its homogeneity, that is, the principle of its metric relations or the connection of its own parts, so that the linkages can be made in an infinite number of ways."[5] In opening up this space of virtual conjunction, the locus of possibility extends to include the existence of affects. Thus, when he deploys affects in any-space-whatever, Deleuze arrives at fully recognizing the potential of space at large in creating a landscape of affects in film. His understanding of cinematic space here widens to include even "atmospheric" formations such as the play of light and shadow, the use of color, the design of empty space, the power of the void, and that movement which is nonaction.

In stressing the role of these latter spatial configurations in imaging affect, it is important to note that they are tactile. Ultimately, one could say that any-space-whatever can become the genetic element of the affection-image insofar as it involves tactile space. In relation to this notion, it is helpful to consider as well *Cinema 2: The Time-Image,* for it is here that Deleuze treats this constitutive element of the affect. The philosopher speaks of the haptic—the sense of touch—following the art historian Alois Riegl's "formula for indicating a touching that is specific to the gaze."[6] In calling attention to tactility, he recognizes the spatial component of the haptic, claiming that, in cinema, "the hand doubles its prehensile function (of object) by a connective function (of space)."[7]

In extending Deleuze's material grasp of cinema as an affective space, I wish to build on this idea of haptic spatiality and highlight the bond of film to the actual space of architecture. There is a connective closeness between architecture and film. It is an elective affinity, a sensory bond, predicated on the sense of touch. Architecture and film are both tangibly inhabited. Like a built environment, cinema is a lived space, activated by the movements of its inhabitants. As Walter Benjamin clearly put it, "buildings are appropriated . . . by touch. . . . Tactile appropriation is accomplished by habit. . . . This mode of appropriation, developed with reference to architecture . . . today [is] in the film."[8] Such closeness between architecture and film—a tactile link—is indeed "touching." It is, in other words, "moving."

As Deleuze has it, the movement-image includes the affection-image. Motion in film is not simply kinetic nor only kinesthetic. It implies more than the movement of bodies and objects as imprinted in the change of film frames and shots, the flow of camera movement, or any other kind of locomotive shift in viewpoint. Motion pictures move not only through time and space or narrative development; they move also through inner space. Film, like architecture, enables us to journey through the space of the imagination, the sites of memory, and the topography of affects. It is this inner motion, a mental itinerary, that links film to architecture and design and makes cinema the art that is closest to architecture. Architecture and film are not only sites of movement, but also "moving" sites. They are doors that create a passage between interior and exterior and windows that open this passage for exploration. In the habit of habitation, they house tangible interactions—passages of private space, itineraries of lived space. As spaces of affect, they are sites of public intimacy.

As I have argued in *Atlas of Emotion*, when movement through space is conjoined with affective movement in these sites of public intimacy, motion and emotion themselves become connected.[9] Building on this premise, this chapter continues to reflect on the mental picturing that links cinema to the spatiovisual arts to see how this interior landscape can become represented as affective fabric.[10] I aim to show that this joint world of imagination and affectivity makes itself visible as a moving architecture and, furthermore, that this world is architected with the design of the fold.

In turning to Deleuze's book *The Fold*, I will engage with one particular aspect of this work: the texture of the fold.[11] The fold emerges out of a consideration of architecture, fabrics, and other textural surfaces.[12] To introduce the fold, Deleuze interweaves the textured surfaces of Baroque architecture with philosophy and the history of science. He draws on the design of the Baroque house as it creates a "curtained" notion of the interior, which he then associates with the monadic inner figuration of Leibniz's philosophy. Reading the fold in this way, Deleuze's fashion of philosophy thus inspired me to engage an intimate cultural fabric.

In bending the notion of the fold in the direction of intimate fabrics, the main point I intend to make is that the inner world unfolds as a design. It can be not only mapped, but also "fashioned." Conversely, mental picturing finds its own form—an actual fashion—in the world of design. In other words, film, architecture, and clothing are linked here as they are "folded" in mental space. All three have the ability to communicate our interior design and to fashion a landscape of affects. They are our second skin, our sensory cloth. They house the motion of emotion. They make mood, and as we will see, a mood is a matter of motion. A mood moves. It unfolds as an ever changing space. It is driven by the tissuelike rhythm of unreeling as state of mind. Speaking of affects in this way becomes a matter of fashioning them as folds of space—that is to say, as atmospheres.

In rethinking affective navigations in this way, we will thus return to architecture, especially as it involves atmosphere. For now, it should be noted that insofar as the spatial aspect of form is concerned, the fold has had substantial impact on the creation of novel architectural space.[13] However, the fold also has been too often misunderstood in recent architectural discourse and reduced to a mere formal device: a twisted structure, a warped form, or even a gimmick. By arguing

Matidia Dressed as Aura. Statue from the theater of Sessa
Aurunca (second century B.C.).

differently in this chapter, I wish to show that in Deleuze's philosophy,
the fold is actually an elaborate mutual figuration of mind and matter.
It is the form of their transformation. Its theoretical fabric not only can
fashion affect-space but also transform emotional fabrics into moving
images. The fold can ultimately bridge the gap between the movement-
image and the time-image: it holds the potential to incorporate the flow
of temporality in the unreeling of inner space. After all, we must recall
that when the affection-image is no longer a particular, determined
space, it becomes a matter of that temporal landscape which is spiritual affect. In Deleuze's words, when "space is no longer determined,
it has become the any-space-whatever which is identical to the power
of the spirit."[14] In other words, as the fold holds the elastic texture of

moving pictures, the act of unfolding conveys a material expression of our moving inner world. It is the *fabric* of our inner landscape, the manner in which a psychic world becomes "architected" in time and expresses itself materially in the language of film, fashion, and architecture.

With this theoretical premise in mind as context, let us now take a closer look at how we actually *fashion* the self and mental life—in buildings, in clothing, and in motion pictures. We will go on a textural journey, interweaving exemplary materials, stitching together three objects of design: a tailored concept, a piece of cloth, and a strip of celluloid. We will travel from the philosophy of the fold put forth by Gilles Deleuze to the fashions of Issey Miyake and to the fabrication of moods in Wong Kar-wai's cinema. Along the way, we will unreel a sartorial archi*texture*. What follows is a play of fabrics. It is a story of pleats . . .

The Fabric of Touch and Mental Images

> The soul is what has folds and is full of folds.
> —Gilles Deleuze, *The Fold*

Every affect has a place, and reciprocally, places can unfold in an array of affects. A landscape is, ultimately, a work of the mind. Places and affects are produced jointly, in the movement of a mental projection between interior and exterior landscapes. Affects not only are makers of space, but are also themselves configured as space: they are atmospheres. To sense a mood is to be sensitive to a subtle "atmospheric" shift. In this way, motion creates emotion, and reciprocally, emotion contains a movement. It is not by chance that we say we are "moved." Emotion itself moves, and the language of emotion relies on the terminology of motion. The affect of our mood is not a static picture and cannot be reduced to optical paradigms or imaged in terms of optical devices and visual metaphors. Its language is material, made of haptic fabrics and moving atmospheres.

An interior landscape moves, creases, and folds in tangible ways. It is, in many ways, designed—woven as if it were handmade. Frames of mind can be said to be fabricated, tailored to a specific subject and suited to a particular intersubjectivity. Mental images are fashioned as cloth is—haptically, out of the texture of our world: they are pictured with the material, stretchy, malleable, creative quality of its fabric.

Emotions are produced within the fabric of what we touch and from that which touches us: we "handle" them, even when we cannot handle them. Emotional situations are touchy, indeed.

When we touch, we experience immersion and inversion fully, and reciprocity is a quality of this touch. There is a haptic rule of thumb: when we touch something or someone, we are, inevitably, touched in return. When we look, we are not necessarily being looked at, but when we touch, by the very nature of pressing our hand or any part of our body on a subject or object, we cannot escape the contact. Touch is never unidirectional, a one-way street. Touch always enables an affective return.

With this reciprocity, there is also reversibility, which is derived from the very "fabric" of touch. Reversibility is most palpable in objects of design whose main function is to be handled. It is an essential quality of the texture of cloth, and it is also an attribute of paper. A fabric has pleats and folds. Its verso, as with paper, is not the reverse, but the reversible. As it links inside and outside, the texture of the fold reveals an affective unfolding. In the architecture of sensing, reciprocal and reversible, we become connected. Touching—a foldable landscape—always communicates, mutually. It is not by chance that we say we are "in touch."

Sensing a mood is an elaborate inner process, ranging from the surface of perception to the depth of affect. As the philosopher John Dewey put it, "'sense' covers a wide range of contents: the sensory, the sensational, the sensitive, the sensible, and the sentimental, along with the sensory. It includes almost everything from bare physical and emotional shock to sense itself—that is, the meaning of things present in immediate experience."[15] It is in this layered way that meaning is formed, that signification makes "sense." The haptic sense is broadly conceived to reach out into the fabric of meaning, into the folds of experience. As fabric, it stretches wide. The sense of sensing extends from sensations to sentiments, from sensory surface to psychic sensibility. It can range from feeling motion all the way to experiencing emotions. The haptic sense drives our inner world and mental architecture. It makes this architecture move. In fact, according to contemporary neuroscience, to create mental images, we use the same neuronal paths that make up material sensory perception.[16] The self is thus "fabricated" in moving, sentient fashion. Mood itself is a process of imaging fashioned in movement. As emotions constantly unfold within us, they reciprocally shape our ever changing quotidian environment.

The Matter of the Fold

The haptic design of the emotion bears the actual materiality of the fold. As affective atmosphere, this design takes shape in our daily fashioning of space: it is an elaborate folded landscape we contend with in our lives. To grasp fully its material mental architecture and to move beyond architectural formalism, we must revisit, and get close to, the theoretical fabrication of the fold in the philosophy of Deleuze. When Deleuze speaks of the fold, he goes well beyond mere form, shape, exterior appearance, or decor. If we listen closely to his words, we can sense the actual *fabric* of the fold: "matter is clothed, with 'clothed' signifying two things: that matter is a buoyant surface, a structure endowed with an organic fabric, or that it is the very fabric or clothing, the texture enveloping."[17] The fold, in Deleuze's conception, is a textured philosophical fabrication. It has a palpable quality, a material culture, a tissuelike texture. Fold is "drapery, producing folds of air or heavy clouds; a tablecloth, with maritime or fluvial folds: jewelry that burns with folds of fire; vegetable, mushrooms, or sugared fruits caught in their earthly folds.... Matter [that] tends to flow out of the frame."[18]

This material unfolding finds correspondence in film. Indeed, in cinema, "matter" always "flows out of the frame," exactly as it does in psychic life. By way of this fold, Deleuze gives physical texture to frames of mind. He relates "the pleats of matter, and the folds in the soul."[19] In his words,

> The infinite fold separates or moves between matter and soul, the façade and the closed room, the outside and the inside. Because it is a virtuality that never stops dividing itself, the line of inflection is actualized in the soul and realized in matter.... An exterior always on the outside, an interior always on the inside. An infinite "receptivity," an infinite "spontaneity": the outer façade of reception and inner room of action.... Conciliation of the two will never be direct but necessarily harmonic, inspiring a new harmony: it is the same expression, the line, that is expressed in the elevation of the inner song of the soul, through memory or by heart, and in the extrinsic fabrication of material partitions.... Pleats of matter ... folds of the soul.[20]

What emerges from Deleuze's philosophy of the fold is a corporeal architecture that houses the materiality of spirit. Ultimately, the fold is the very "fashioning" of spirit. This is truly a sartorial philosophy:

"the fold can be recognized first of all in the textile model of the kind implied by garments. . . . Folds of clothing acquire an autonomy and a fullness *that are not simply decorative effects.* They convey the intensity of a spiritual force exerted on the body, either to turn it upside down or to stand or raise it up over and again, but in every event to turn it inside out and to mold its inner surfaces."[21] What is unfolding here is the actual movement of the affective fabric. Draped around and unreeling from Deleuze's words is an emotional bend: there, one discovers that the design of the fold fashions inner life. It is, ultimately, the very architecture of the soul. Thus conceived, the soul becomes a sartorial fabrication.

Deleuze's philosophy clearly connects folds of clothing to the fabric of psychic interiority. As it unfolds the fabrication of this latter, it unravels the matter of its spiritual power. The folds of the garment, pressing on the skin, convey an inner strength. Folds, draping the surface of our body, express and mold our inner surface. They impress matters of energy into us. The folds of pleats hold great psychic force—a transformative force. Such is the force that can turn matters inside out and outside in. In this transformative way, "pleats, please."

Unfolding Madam-T

An enticing spirit of sartorial philosophy, the fold is a geopsychic matter that is an actual element of fashion. Fashion itself can make this psychic topography visible. As the fashion designer Sonya Rykiel puts it, "it's in the fold that all comes into play. As in a dream, it rises and then hides itself, unfolding into a sun, regathering into tiny folds or falling back into tighter pleats. Open the heart of those folds. . . . The pleat is sewn to conceal inner thought. . . . It is said that everything may be read in a face, I reckon that all may be read in clothes."[22]

For Rykiel, not all can be read in the face, and the affect may be concealed in other surfaces: everything can be read in the pleats of one's clothes. The "superficial" movement of the tightly folded fabric strives to design the motion of an emotion. She is not alone in proposing this fashion. For a similar move in the same pattern, take Issey Miyake, whose pleats are a potential correlate of Deleuze's fold. If Deleuze fashions the folds of the soul as pleats of matter, Issey Miyake provides designs that materialize a philosophical spirit.

This fashion designer has reinvented and extensively practiced an ancient sculptural form that "suits" a philosophical texture. From Greek sculpture all the way to Mariano Fortuny's textile design, the fold has

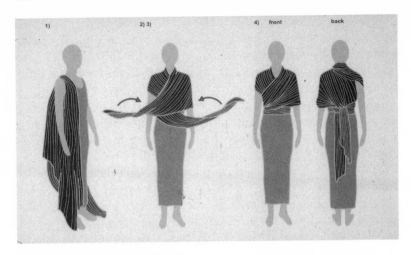

"Pleats Please": Issey Miyake, Madam-T

been a highly adaptable, sensuous form.[23] Miyake's pleats are infinite forms that reshape body space across design and visual art as they travel from fashion to art installation. These pleated garments not only shape themselves to one's body, but also mold to the wearer's own cultural and affective fabric. Think of his Madam-T. This garment unfolds as a constant transformation. First of all, you unroll it from a clear plastic tube. A piece of living, pleated, foldable fabric is in your hands: just a long strip of fabric, full of folds, and nothing more. Inside this fabric, there is a hole. Very simple. A perfect architecture.

Now, this can be your home. You step into this pleated construction. You put it on in any fashion you wish to adopt. In its foldable fabrication, Madam-T comes alive. It becomes different garments. It reshapes itself. It can be more and less than a dress: it can be a gown, a skirt, a T-shirt, a jacket, a cloak, a cape, a mantle, a shawl, a head scarf, a wrap, or any kind of draping layer in which you wish to clothe yourself. You fashion it. Every time, you do something different with it. You construct it, endlessly.

It is the very simplicity of the fold that entails its remarkable complexity. The folding construction of Madam-T is not a formal gimmick. It is an actual piece of architecture, for it is a construction to be inhabited. And like any interesting work of architecture, it gives the inhabitant an active role in fashioning it. After all, the fold of clothing is the first space you live in. You access it, as if you were entering your house, your own primary architecture. As you put it on, it suits you. It can host your soul and house your moods. Every time you unfold it, this architecture tells you who you are and how you feel, even if you do not know it.

The folds of Madam-T unconsciously bond to that "room of one's own" and to one's own cultural makeup. Fashion can reveal this kind of mapping. Remember what Nagiko said in Peter Greenaway's film *The Pillow Book*. She was a fashion model who had a habit of fashioning herself by writing on her body. This fashioning unveiled a cultural mapping: she became "a signpost to point East, West, North, and South" and claimed to have had "shoes in German, stockings in French, gloves in Hebrew, and a hat with a veil in Italian."[24] Not unlike this writing on the flesh, the folding architecture of Madam-T is a multiple, elastic cultural fabric. It can be sari as much as sarong or kimono. It can span from evening dress to casual attire. It can go back in time, becoming revival dressing, retro fantasy. Or it can be real-time you. It can be cosmopolitan minimalism or Baroque extravaganza. Actually, it can hold both these parts of you in its folds.

Sartorial Arts

Issey Miyake's pleats house a conjunction between architectural form and fashion—a textural conjunction that has a history in the movement of modernity and especially in the aesthetic of various modernist avant-gardes.[25] It was here that art, architecture, and fashion would closely interweave. Futurism, for example, was not only very interested in fashion, but also employed it as a language to redefine the very architecture of painting and the design of the city. Setting out a futurist manifesto on clothing, the artist Giacomo Balla wrote, in 1913, "We must invent futurist clothes. . . . They must be simple . . . to provide constant and novel enjoyment for our bodies. . . . The consequent merry dazzle produced by our clothes in the noisy streets which we shall have transformed into our futurist architecture will mean that everything will begin to sparkle."[26]

In Balla's conception, clothes exist in the realm of architecture because they participate in the architectonics of the city streets. Clothes and architecture are cut from the same cloth and share a specific mobility: they are actions that develop in space as lived emotion. Futurist apparel had the dynamic ability to provoke imaginative emotionality. In the conception of these artists, fashion was a way of building a new tactilism. Reinforcing the tone of the manifesto on clothes in a text he titled "Tactilism," Filippo Tommaso Marinetti wrote in 1924 of a "tactile art" as a "spiritual communication among human beings through epidermics."[27] He used X-ray vision to show that all senses are a modification of touch and considered this synesthesia "a harmony of electronic systems."[28] In his earlier "tactile tables," from 1921 (described as "voyages of hands"), he listed among the endeavors related to this haptic mode the design of rooms, furniture, clothes, roads, and theaters.[29] And to make clothes even more like rooms, Balla invented *modificanti*: literally, "modifiers." *Modificanti* were elements of variable decor one could add to one's apparel by pneumatic application. These modifiers were to be used, creatively, to change the shape of one's dress so that one might invent a new outfit at any time, according to mood.[30]

The futurist *modificante* understood the sartorial architecture of mood. Now Issey Miyake's pleats take this notion of the modifier of mood from decor and ornament to the very architecture of clothing. Madam-T is itself a *modificante*. It is a complete architecture of mood. As you continue to play with it, its mood keeps on changing, and it always surprises you. Every time, it emerges as something subtly different. In its unfolding metamorphosis, Madam-T suits your ever changing moods. It can be stark, pensive, and melancholic or playful, joyous, and frivolous. It can morph from one shade of mood to the next or go directly for the opposite affect. It can do this, filmically, in single takes, in assemblage, or in sequence. The folds can transport you from one affective atmosphere to the next. Their draping motion embodies the motion of an emotion. This is the perfect cloth to suit your soul. It shows its inner folds. It contains the force of spirit exerted on the architecture of your body, molding its inner surfaces. To fold, after all, means to envelop, embrace, and hug. It is the intensity you covet. "Pleats, please."

Addressing Inner Space

This kind of architecture, a transitory habitation, is indeed transformative. As a concept, the emotional fabric of the fold conveys a psychic leap in women's fashion. It is this leap that, years before Madam-T, the avant-garde filmmaker Maya Deren envisaged for women's clothing.[31] Deren wrote about the "Psychology of Fashion" in response to an art and fashion show curated by the architect Bernard Rudofsky at the Museum of Modern Art (MoMA) in New York in 1944–45, titled "Are Clothes Modern?" Pioneering an investigation of the relation of fashion to the visual and spatial arts, as part of the history of the human body, the show resulted in the publication of a fascinating book in 1947.[32] Questioning the relation of *mode* (fashion) and *modernité* (modernity), Rudofsky read the modernity of fashion as an evolving architecture of the body.

Maya Deren was deeply inspired by Rudofsky's show at MoMA, and the filmmaker joined the architect in conceiving of fashion as a fashioning of space. Deren was particularly concerned with women's ways of addressing dress. As an experimental filmmaker, she was able to see dressing as a form of picture making. But she understood this picture making not simply in the sense of image making, but of mental picturing. For Deren, fashion represented mental landscapes and maps of intersubjectivity, offering a transformative picturing. Fashion, she thought, could truly become an affective metaphor—that is, according to the Greek etymology, a means of transport. As she put it, among the options for fashioning the self, a "woman wishes to express, in the line of her clothes, a sense of speed and mobility."[33] She understood this quality of motion to be an emotion—a transmission of affect. "The most important role of fashion is in relation to a woman's *individual psychology*," she claimed. "First of all, a woman's clothes serve as an outlet for her creative energies. Secondly, she uses those energies to create, in reality, some image she has of herself; a method of projection of her inner attitudes ... a kind of expressionism."[34] Maya Deren was sensitive to the liminality that links attire to affective apparel, making fashion part of its landscape. In this moving, filmic sense, she activated fashion as a form of psychic life. As she related the language of fashion to the psychic register, the filmmaker provided a valuable lesson in taste. Here is her fashion advice: "the closer the outward appearance to the inner state of mind, the better dressed."[35]

Psychic Fabrics

Home of the fold, fashion resides within the reversible continuity that, rather than separating, provides a breathing membrane—a skin—to the world. Sensorially speaking, clothes come alive in (e)motion. They are physically moved, as we are, activated by our personas. Livened by kinesthetics and our spirits, clothes are the envelopes of our histories, the material residue of a corporeal passage. As such an epidermic envelopment, fashion is an interior map in reverse: a trace of the emotional address left on the outer dress in a twofold projection. First, as a chart in the negative, an affect is projected outward as if onto a screen and, in such a way, is written on the skin of the world. Next, in the transfer of dress and address, a passage to intimacy takes place. A mapping of this intimacy is liminally designed on the surface of dwelling. It unfolds on the wall, the skin, and the screen as folds of matter and pleats of the soul.

From folds of the soul to pleats of matter, emotions are designed in an elastic archi*texture*. As we have learned from psychoanalysis, reversibility and reciprocity rule in the unconscious. Unfolding from their pleated topography, affects, as we have mentioned, display the same texture as the folds that characterize paper and textile. As with these folding materials, the reverse of an emotion is only its verso, never its opposite. We tell one side of the story to reach the other side. We desire that other. We hate, hence we love. We love to hate, and we hate to love. We dream love, we mean hate. Emotions are fully transferable and reversible. They are *our* (reversible) fabric. In this way, emotions are "fashioned"—indeed, designed—as an inside out.

There is no stasis in this affective landscape, even when nothing seems to move. The life of the mind implies nonaction that is active, for as Hannah Arendt puts it, citing from Cicero, "never is a man more active than when he does nothing."[36] Only then can we watch our thoughts unfold and move by. Only in this time-space can real trans-formation occur. It is in the immobility of reflective states that we might be covering the most ground. Here, folds of the soul unreel. Our inner world moves even when we do not. After all, as we know from cinema and from dreams, motion happens most palpably as we stay still, in a state of spectatorial reverie. And then it is not just the dream image that moves. There is always movement in mental picturing. Wherever emotion is concerned, there is a picture in motion.

If the fabric of the unconscious is a picture in motion, this is because it holds the most imaginative aspect of our cognitive process. Cognition is also a moving field, when invested in mental picturing. Knowledge, whenever affected by emotion, itself moves. Mental pictures move as if they were motion pictures.[37] As recent findings from neuroscience show, "our mental composition of even a still picture—if we could watch ourselves composing in slow motion—has motion in it."[38] This view confirms how much our psychic architecture is, indeed, a cinematic language. Film fashions the motion of our thought process. As the filmmaker Sergei Eisenstein made clear in writing on filmic and architectural promenades back in the 1930s, cinematic motion follows the actual operations of the human mind.[39] Put differently, and treading on the path of the psychologist and film theorist Hugo Münsterberg, one can say that cinema can project the moving world of imagination, memory, affect, and mood because its workings are analogous to the way our mind works.[40] Motion pictures unfold mental pictures, and such pictures actually "move" us. As cinema makes manifest, we are moved when affects provide access to knowledge, when they reach into its very fabric, enacting a passage of unconscious experiences, a transfer of states of mind, feelings, and moods. The moving image is thus not only a language of mental motion, but also a language for emotion—a moody, atmospheric way to fashion affects in transmittable fabrics.

Now, if you wish to experience how this transport of the emotions really unfolds, take a look at Wong Kar-wai's work. Watch *In the Mood for Love* (2000).[41] You will be embraced in folds of affects. If you are the type of person who feels moody and has a craving for clothing, this film will suit you. If fashioning your inner self is a way of life for you, this is your movie. It will move you. The mood is so pervasive that you can smell it. This is a film of pure atmosphere, haunted by the very spirit of design.

Moods and Atmospheres

Hong Kong, sometime in the 1960s. A city melancholically suspended in time and arrested in space. The story unfolds in interiors. We are always inside, even when we are not. When the characters exit their cramped apartment building and go outside onto the street, the city feels internal. It is strangely enveloping. This Hong Kong is an inner landscape. It is an architecture of the mind. We do not know if it is a memory or a fantasy. In this film, we are wrapped in a mental atmosphere, folded in its mood. The rhythm of the editing reinforces the feeling, for it constantly folds on itself, returning to us moments that were briefly lived in the past, or perhaps only dreamed. Times are stitched together loosely, unfolding back or leaping ahead in an undulating mode—that mode known to waves, or to ... pleats.

She, played by Maggie Cheung, is a fashion addict, always dressed to the nines. She wears her best clothes even when going out to get noodles. She has a phenomenal wardrobe of different cheongsam, the enwrapping Chinese-style dress, and parades it throughout the movie. In one outfit after another, she lets us share in the lush textures of her retro attire. As in a fashion show, we come to expect the next cheongsam and revel in its luxurious fabric.

In this film where nothing happens, only the clothes change. They constitute a rhythm. In this story, frozen in time, her changes of dress are the only way we know time is actually going by. When her dress changes, a subtle, atmospheric shift occurs, a change of disposition. Clothes embody the ever changing architecture of feeling. They are a shift in mood.

The main mood of the film is love: love that is fugitive, that cannot be had: elusive, pervasive, evasive, unattainable, and intangible. A vague affair, love here has the texture of vapor, haze, or fog. Actually, it is more like mist. An "atmospheric" affair, it parallels the light rain that falls down on her. A slow drizzle envelops her as she descends the steps of the noodle shop. As she moves down the narrow staircase in slow motion, she passes him. Their elbows, their hips, their faces get close. Grazing the wall, they almost touch. They are both in the mood for love.

Their story unfolds in a continual situation of longing. It is consumed in pervasive desire. As it enrobes the characters, their consuming yearning for each other encircles us all. We are immersed in this ambience. The clothes, the sets, the editing all speak of this mood. Longing is here written on the walls. It exudes from space and makes all spaces speak of their wish for love.

This mood for love is architectural atmospherics. It drapes around the entire space, all the way from dress to address. When you look at her cheongsam, you can see the weave of the cloth reflected in the texture of the wallpaper. You can see it mirrored in the folds of the curtains. The wall itself is designed as a fabric. You stare at her cheongsam against these matching walls and notice that everything matches, even the magazine she is reading and the lampshade of the light that illuminates it. When she leans against this wall that looks like her, she is baked in the same melancholic fabric of light. When she walks outside and leans against the city walls, there is also no difference: the peeling layers of the paint on the wall reflect the textured layers that make up the fabric of her clothes. In an affective embrace, she literally melts into the walls.

In this film, fashion is an architecture. Clothes and architectural settings are part of the same spirit: they are made of the same fabric; they have the same feel. Draped and folded within a fashioned space, we are taken into a total architectonics of mood. This amorous mood is an atmosphere that is entirely fashioned, fabricated as enveloping fabric. And the mood for love has the architecture of the fold. As if to stretch the point, the lovers' eventual erotic encounter—elusive, only ambiguously alluded to, and never shown—happens behind drawn curtains, an actual architecture of the fold. In ornate visual style, the

Frame enlargement from *In the Mood for Love* (Wong Kar-Wai, 2000)

camera tracks to caress the red curtains of the hotel lobby where the lovers are meeting. The curtains move in the wind. As the fabric creases, we can feel the ruffle of their bodies embracing. We feel the embrace, even if it did not happen. We sense it, even if it was only a dream. Perhaps even more so, for it might have been a fantasy or a faded memory. The embrace unfolds in the design of an enveloping material. It is a projection of the mental architecture of the fold.

Fabrics of Time

As *In the Mood for Love* sensuously shows, architecture, fashion, and cinema all unfold as imaginative fashioners of moving images. This fashioning is a matter of folding spaces and layered fabrics. As fabrications of visual fabric, fashion, architecture, and film are archives of mental imaging, affective residues. Their form of inhabitation is the interior—the public intimacy of lived space—experienced by *habitus*. After all, *habitus*, as a mode of being, is rooted in *habitare*, dwelling. Indeed, as noted at the beginning, we inhabit space tactilely by way of habit. Now, if habit and habitation are haptically bound, *abito*, which in Italian means "dress," is an element of their connection. There is a haptic bond that links, even etymologically, sheltering to clothing the body—architecture to fashion. In fact, in Italian, the word *abito* is used for both a dress and an address. In German, too, *wand*, as both "wall" and "screen," is connected to *gewand*, meaning "garment" or "clothing."[42] In other words, one "suits" oneself to space. We address a dress just as we access a house or a movie house: as we put ourselves in them, we absorb them, and they absorb us. A dress, like a house or a film, is "consumed" in such suitable fashion. Because it is inhabited, design "wears" the marks of life, both material and mental. It enables the reversible passage of these aspects of life as it holds our being in passing. To occupy a space is, literally, to wear it. A building, like a dress, is not only worn; it wears out.

As we recognize this "wearing" fashion of dwelling, we can now see the link between *abito*, habit, and habitation as an unfolding historicity. This is an architecture of time, the actual design of duration. Indeed, design, architecture, and cinema all move with the temporal mood of history as traces of the movement of time. In particular, to use Adorno's words, "fashion is one of the ways in which historical change affects the sensory apparatus."[43] These objects of material culture are mnemonic fabrications. They hold in the pleats of their material texture the inner rhythm, the actual movement, of mental unfolding—the temporal flow of interior landscapes. Ultimately, as objects of design, architecture, fashion, and cinema design the very texture of psychic interiority.

In conclusion, as we fold our discussion back to Gilles Deleuze and hear his words on the "spirit" of the matter, we can sense the threads of a "neuroaesthetic" weave: "something bizarre about the cinema struck me: its unexpected ability to show not only behavior, but spiritual life *[la vie spirituelle]*. . . . Spiritual life isn't dream or fantasy—which were always the cinema's dead ends—but rather . . . the choice of existence. How is it that the cinema is so expert at excavating this spiritual life? . . . Cinema not only puts movement in the image, it also puts movement in the mind. Spiritual life *is* the movement of the mind. . . . The brain is the screen."[44]

Mental picturing unfolds, sensitively and affectively, as if on a cinematic screen—a screen itself made of fabric. This brain-screen makes images move as states of mind. Fashion, film, and the architectural surface are all such screens of moving pictures. Acting on images as if they were elastic, they actually fashion our inner self. After all, as even neuroscience confirms, all mental pictures possess the "creasable quality of cloth or the foldable, tearable quality of paper."[45] Inner images have a definite textural quality. It is no wonder, then, that they touch us. They are fabrics.

Being itself a fabric—a design—an inner image can be pleated. It can be folded and unfolded, bent, warped, and flexed. It can be tied and unraveled, pulled and torn apart. It can be rumpled and crumpled, wrinkled, rustled, and creased. It can envelop us, for it is embracing. It can transform us, for it is transformative. A design that moves has the alluring ability to continue to affect us. If "pleats please" us, let us have more such pleats, please.

Notes

1   Gilles Deleuze, *Cinema 1: The Movement-Image*, trans. Hugh Tomlinson and Barbara Habberjam (Minneapolis: University of Minnesota Press, 1986), esp. chaps. 6–8.

2   See Béla Balázs, *Theory of Film: Character and Growth of a New Art*, trans. Edith Bone (New York: Dover, 1970).

3   Gilles Deleuze and Félix Guattari, *A Thousand Plateaus: Capitalism and Schizophrenia*, trans. Brian Massumi (Minneapolis: University of Minnesota Press, 1987), 170–72.

4   Deleuze, *Movement-Image*, esp. chap. 7.

5   Ibid., 109.

6   Gilles Deleuze, *Cinema 2: The Time-Image*, trans. Hugh Tomlinson and Robert Galeta (Minneapolis: University of Minnesota Press, 1989), 13.

7   Ibid., 13.

8   Walter Benjamin, "The Work of Art in the Age of Mechanical Reproduction," in *Illuminations: Essays and Reflections*, ed. Hannah Arendt, trans. Harry Zohn (New York: Schocken Books, 1969), 240.

9   See Giuliana Bruno, *Atlas of Emotion: Journeys in Art, Architecture, and Film* (London: Verso, 2002).

10   This chapter, as published in this anthology, is part of my book in progress on fabrics of the visual.

11   See Gilles Deleuze, *The Fold: Leibniz and the Baroque*, trans. Tom Conley (Minneapolis: University of Minnesota Press, 1993). I do not mean to provide an exegetic account of the fold in this chapter. I am simply taking inspiration from the fold to unfold a performative writing of affect in its fashion.

12   As far as architecture is concerned, it is worth noting that Deleuze carried on a dialogue and exchange with the architect Bernard Cache, who is repeatedly referenced in Deleuze, *The Fold*. Cache's own work developed in close relation to Deleuze's philosophical teaching in his Paris seminar. See Bernard Cache, *Earth Moves: The Furnishing of Territories*, ed. Michael Speaks, trans. Anne Boyman (Cambridge, Mass.: MIT Press, 1995).

13   For a review of the impact of the fold on architectural discourse, see "Folding in Architecture," ed. Greg Lynn, special issue, *Architectural Design* 62, no. 103 (1993).

14 Deleuze, *Movement-Image*, 117.

15 John Dewey, *Art as Experience* (New York: Perigee Books, 1995), 22.

16 See, among others, Stephen Kosslyn, *Image and Brain: The Resolution of the Imagery Debate* (Cambridge, Mass.: MIT Press, 1994).

17 Deleuze, *The Fold*, 115.

18 Ibid., 122–23.

19 Ibid., 3.

20 Ibid., 35.

21 Ibid., 121–22.

22 Sonya Rykiel, "From *Celebration*," in *On Fashion*, ed. Shari Benstock and Suzanne Ferriss (New Brunswick, N.J.: Rutgers University Press, 1994), 100–3.

23 On Mariano Fortuny's pleated designs, see Anne-Marie Deschodt and Doretta Davanzo Poli, *Fortuny* (New York: Harry N. Abrams, 2001).

24 Peter Greenaway, dir., *The Pillow Book*, Columbia/Tristar Studios, 1996. Cited from the film's diaristic register.

25 On this subject, see Mark Wigley, *White Walls, Designer Dresses: The Fashioning of Modern Architecture* (Cambridge, Mass.: MIT Press, 1995).

26 Giacomo Balla, "The Futurist Manifesto on Men's Clothing," 1913, repr. in *Futurist Manifestos*, ed. Umbro Apollonio, trans. Robert Brain (London: Thames and Hudson, 1973), 132. On futurist fashion, see the exhibition catalog *Balla, futurismo tra arte e moda: Opere della Fondazione Biagiotti Cigna* (Milan: Leonardo Editore, 1998).

27 Filippo Tommaso Marinetti, "Tactilism," 1924, repr. in *Let's Murder the Moon Shine: Selected Writings*, ed. and trans. R. W. Flint (Los Angeles: Sun and Moon Classics, 1991), 119.

28 Ibid., 120.

29 Ibid., January 11, 1921.

30 Giacomo Balla, "Il vestito antineutrale," September 11, 1914, a slightly modified version of the 1913 "The Futurist Manifesto."

31 Maya Deren's unpublished manuscript "Psychology of Fashion" has been printed in Vèvè A. Clark, Millicent Hodson, and Catrina Neiman, eds., *The Legend of Maya Deren: A Documentary Biography and Collected Works*, vol. 1, part 2 (New York: Anthology Film Archives, 1988).

32 See Bernard Rudofsky, *Are Clothes Modern? An Essay on Contemporary Apparel* (Chicago: Paul Theobald, 1947).

33 Deren, "Psychology of Fashion," 436.

34 Ibid., 435.

35 Ibid.

36 Hannah Arendt, *The Life of the Mind* (New York: Harcourt, 1978), 7. In citing this sentence, she mentions that Cicero ascribed it to Cato.

37 For an introduction to this neurological point of view, see Oliver Sacks, "In the River of Consciousness," *New York Review of Books* 51, no. 1 (2004): 41–44.

38 Elaine Scarry, *Dreaming by the Book* (Princeton, N.J.: Princeton University Press, 1999), 127.

39 Sergei M. Eisenstein, "Montage and Architecture," *Assemblage* 10 (1989): 111–31. The text, published in English in this journal of architecture theory, with an introduction by Yve-Alain Bois, was written circa 1937, to be inserted in a book-length work.

40 For a pioneering articulation of this notion of affect, see Hugo Münsterberg, *The Photoplay: A Psychological Study and Other Writing*, ed. Allan Langdale (New York: Routledge, 2002). Originally published in 1916.

41 Wong Kar-wai, dir., *In the Mood for Love*, USA Films, 2000.

42 On this subject, see Gottfried Semper, *Style in the Technical and Tectonic Arts; or, Practical Aesthetics*, trans. Harry Francis Mallgrave and Michael Robinson (Los Angeles, Calif.: Getty Research Institute, 2004). First published 1860.

43 Theodor W. Adorno, *Aesthetic Theory*, trans. C. Lenhardt (London: Routledge, 1984), 255.

44 "The Brain Is the Screen: An Interview with Gilles Deleuze," in *The Brain Is the Screen: Deleuze and the Philosophy of Cinema*, ed. Gregory Flaxman (Minneapolis: University of Minnesota Press, 2000), 366. For a reading of Deleuze's film theory as neuroaesthetics, see also John Rajchman, *The Deleuze Connections* (Cambridge, Mass.: MIT Press, 2001), chap. 6.

45 Scarry, *Dreaming by the Book*, 137.

13. The Affection-Image and the Movement-Image

James Chandler

Deleuze's engagement with Bergson at the very outset of his two-part study of cinema is now widely recognized as having produced some remarkable results, both conceptual and critical. Some readers who were put off by Deleuze's work on cinema when it first appeared have gone back to it in a more receptive spirit. Others, like me, even those of us who knew much of Deleuze's other work, have recently encountered it for the first time with something like a sense of wonder. Part of the wonder in my own case is that although Deleuze makes his Bergsonian categories seem inevitable for a reconceptualization of twentieth-century cinema, it is not as though one could have begun with those categories and predicted what Deleuze would do with them. This combined sense of retrospective inevitability and prospective surprise has partly to do with the way in which Deleuze reads Bergson against himself—especially where cinema becomes an explicit topic in Bergson's writings. It has partly to do as well with the way in which Deleuze locates both Bergsonianism and the development of cinema in his own distinctive terminological framework and philosophical genealogy. The belated interest in Deleuze's Bergson-inflected account of cinema now, twenty-odd years after its publication, can surely be explained in some measure by its appositeness for—perhaps even its anticipation of—the widespread current interest in the emotions. For those of us engaged in work on, say, the history of affect, it is particularly the first of the two cinema volumes that stands out. And within that first volume, it is Deleuze's discussion of the affection-image that seems both arresting and promising.

In what follows here, I consider the Bergsonian affection-image in Deleuze's account of cinema in a number of its relationships: in its

connections with Deleuzian faciality, with Deleuze's Bergsonian movement theory, and with Deleuze's account of the *shot* as a species of
Bergsonian "mobile section." How to see the affection-image in a longer
history of affect is a question that I wish to pursue here in the context
of my own ongoing investigations into the history of the sentimental
as an aesthetic mode, its emergence in one medium and reappearance
in another. Between the *literary* sentimental tradition (established in
the mid-eighteenth century with Laurence Sterne and others) and the
cinematic sentimental tradition (established in the twentieth century
with the work of D. W. Griffith and Frank Capra), one can in fact trace
some key lines of continuity and change: conceptual, formal, stylistic.[1]
One of my central contentions in the larger project, for example, is that
the so-called classical system of film narration amounted to a kind of
technological incarnation of the eighteenth-century notion of how we
form sentiments through the process of exchanging places by means
of sympathetic imagination. Deleuze's relevance for such a project is
something that I hope to show in the course of the discussion. The
discussion itself will fall into three parts: (1) some contexts in which
I come to Deleuze's book on the movement-image, (2) what I claim
to find there, and (3) what I have tentatively begun to make of these
findings.

One key starting point for my consideration of the sentimental is
the notion of sentiment as reflected feeling. In accepting this premise, I
follow Friedrich Schiller's analysis, in the 1795 treatise *On the Naïve
and Sentimental in Poetry*, in which he distinguishes the sentimental as
the mode of mixed feelings, explaining that unlike the naive poet, the
sentimental poet reflects on his impressions. Certainly for the British
moral sense school, mid-eighteenth-century thinkers such as David
Hume and Adam Smith, whom Schiller knew well, sentiments are
indeed reflected feelings—what in Hume's technical vocabulary are
called "impressions of reflection" (as Annette Baier has convincingly
shown).[2] "*Moral* sentiments," as one can infer from Adam Smith's
influential *Theory of Moral Sentiments* (1759), are feelings reflected
by an act of sympathy in the mirror of other people's imagined points
of view. This is why the very first chapter of that book is called "Of
Sympathy." Moral sentiments, we might say, are feelings registered
through a virtual point of view. In this Scottish Enlightenment theory,
sentiments develop in the course of our daily intercourse in commercial society, whereby we each imagine ourselves sympathetically in the
place, or "case" (as Smith says), of another.[3] Their circulation helps to

form what Hume calls a "general point of view"—a concept that, as it happens, Deleuze takes some pains to explicate in his early book on subjectivity and empiricism in Hume.[4]

A key figure in any story of the history and transformation of the sentimental is Dickens, who expanded the sentimental novel into epic form and promoted its ethos to the status of a political program. Dickens is key because, in addition to developing the sentimental form in literature, he also, as Eisenstein famously demonstrated, did much to shape Griffith's new mode of film narrative.[5] My way of connecting the literary and cinematic modes of the sentimental relies on a fairly standard account of Hollywood's classical narrative system, as that system was developed by Griffith (among others) and received by the young Capra in the 1920s. This account emphasizes the well-documented coordination of new cinematographic practices: multiple angles, moving cameras, montage, and especially those techniques, such as shot–reverse-shot (and point-of-view shots more generally), that instilled the system with certain psychological principles of identification and causality. Béla Balázs and Jean Mitry—two early film historians cited by Deleuze—both tend to support this way of understanding the new classical system of the 1910s, and so have many commentators since.[6]

I take this story forward through the career of Capra as far as *It's a Wonderful Life* (1946), his self-proclaimed *summa cinematica*—a frankly sentimental film based on a novella by Dickens *(A Christmas Carol)* that places the relations between sympathy, spectatorship, and political economy at the center of its concerns. It is a film that is, in a number of ways, I believe, actually *about* the eighteenth century, even as it is about the affective powers of the new cinematic medium: much of the film, after all, consists of a "screening" of the life of George Bailey *by* a character first identified as Ben Franklin *and for* an angel who is supposed to have been born in the eighteenth century. During his first decade in filmmaking, Capra not only became an adept of classical Hollywood cinema; he also developed a well-nigh obsessive self-consciousness as a would-be auteur, a programmatic cultural agenda in a marginal studio. Capra came to understand the classical narrative system as a scheme of sympathetic identification that functioned rather in the way I described previously. He had arrived at this sense of things, I believe, by the time he finished *Mr. Deeds Goes to Town* (1935), a pivotal film for him in that it offered a kind of sentimental manifesto for his ideological turn in midcareer, a point that becomes all but explicit in Capra's autobiography.[7] Furthermore, with Gary Cooper anticipating

James Stewart's later Capra roles, *Mr. Deeds* also inaugurated Capra's cinematic reinvention of the post-Sternean "Man of Feeling" (to borrow the title of the novel Henry Mackenzie published in the wake of Sterne's work in 1771), though we do find the germ of this figure in Capra's silent work with Harry Langdon.[8] And crucially, in crafting Mr. Deeds's face-to-face encounter with the irate farmer who invades his house midway through the film, Capra markedly thematized the shot–reverse-shot technique as part of his newly developed politics of sentimental sympathy.

And just as, on this account, the literary sentimental of the eighteenth century emerged from the complex translation of a theatrical regime into a print cultural regime (as Jean-Christophe Agnew has charted it), so the cinematic sentimental of the twentieth century emerged from the complex transformation of a print-cultural regime into a cinematic regime.[9] Some such argument can partly explain, I believe, why the Capraesque sentimental mode that takes shape in the 1930s is so preoccupied with newspapers—and nowhere more clearly than in *Mr. Deeds* and its sequel, *Mr. Smith Goes to Washington* (1939). Indeed, *Mr. Smith* allegorizes the contest between print cultural and cinematic claims to represent the American public sphere, a contest that is sentimentally resolved in the face-to-face encounter between James Stewart's Mr. Smith and Harry Carey's Senate President on the verge of the film's last-minute denouement. Where the *literary* sentimental of the eighteenth century apotheosizes the face-to-face encounter at the cost of making the theatrical face virtual, the cinematic sentimental rematerializes the face, while still offering the possibility of narrative shifts in point of view.

One context, therefore, in which a turn to Deleuze's account of the affection-image seemed to make sense is shaped by these connected notions of faciality, medium, and point of view. There is, however, a second context within the history of the sentimental for my approach to or appropriation of Deleuze. This one bears indirectly on Deleuze's remarks about how what he terms the *balade* film poses a critical challenge for the action-image. But it bears more directly on those moments where Deleuze attends most closely to the mobility of the shot in the age of the movement-image, and indeed, where his account of it reaches beyond that age to invoke, among other films, Wim Wenders's *Kings of the Road* as dramatizing a certain kind of reflexivity about what Deleuze describes as cinematic vehicularity: a self-conscious association of the motion of the camera with the motion of what the camera records.

This second context has to do with the subgenre that Laurence Sterne invented in 1768, nine years after Smith's *Theory of Moral Sentiments*, and that he christened with a phrase of his own coinage, "Sentimental Journey"—a novel that transformed the writing of fiction both instantly and enduringly across England and Europe. Sterne's own text was repeatedly reprinted in English and translated into several languages, and in its wake came a multitude of titles bearing the word *sentimental* and, indeed, a host of works that identify themselves as sentimental journeys to this place or that.

One of my projects has been how to explain the impact of this book, its claim to novelty, and its place in the subsequent literary and cinematic history of the sentimental. The playful preface that Parson Yorick wrote for his travels itself already raises the question, but only in the most enigmatic possible terms. Waxing philosophical, Yorick offers a taxonomy of travelers—Simple Travelers, Vain Travelers, Splenetic Travelers—which eventually arrives at the category Sentimental Traveler. Yorick expresses concern that since both his "travels and [his] observations will be altogether of a different cast from any of [his] fore-runners," he "might have insisted upon a whole nitch [*sic*] entirely to [himself]."[10] Yorick renounces any claim to exclusive rights to the category, however, for fear that he "should break in upon the confines of the *Vain* Traveller, in wishing to draw attention towards me, till I have some better grounds for it than the mere *Novelty of my Vehicle*."[11]

It has seemed to me that if we are to register the place of this key book in the history of the sentimental, we need to come to terms with this phrase, "the mere *Novelty of my Vehicle*." What, for example, is the relation between the novelty of Sterne's vehicle and the vehicle, so to speak, of the novel? How does it matter that the preface, which, in typical Sternean fashion, comes well along in the narrative, is actually supposed to be written *in* a vehicle? The vehicle in question, moreover, is a one-person carriage suggestively called a *Désobligeant*, which is unhitched and stationed in the carriage yard in Calais, where he later enters another stationary vehicle, this time with a woman, and where many of the novel's early scenes take place, before Yorick has even managed to take to the road. The *Désobligeant* does not move forward, though it is described by passersby as moving with an agitation that seems faintly masturbatory. This episode tells us that something curious is going on with vehicles, movement, and feeling—with the relation between motion and being moved.

I have worked out at least a part of the puzzle, as I explain in the final part of this chapter, but to establish initial relevance of this problem for Deleuze, it helps to see the new sentimental journey form as a transformation of the picaresque tradition, which is more than once invoked by Sterne in reference to Cervantes. Probably the most famous and widely anthologized of the vignettes in the book, for example, the one in which Sterne's Yorick encounters the woeful shepherdess, Maria of Moulines, is introduced with the following comment: "'Tis going, I own, like the Knight of the Woeful Countenance, in quest of melancholy adventures—but I know not how it is, but I am never so perfectly conscious of the existence of a soul within me, as when I am entangled in them."[12] Yorick's emphasis on the "soul" here—his "consciousness" of it—is a key to understanding Sterne's revision of the picaresque travel story, though in ways that the reader cannot well fathom until the end of the episode.

The encounter with Maria is indeed bookended by references of this kind. Here is how Yorick narrates the conclusion of his meeting with the shepherdess, a locus classicus in the history of sentimental literature:

> I sat down close by her; and Maria let me wipe them away as they fell with my handkerchief.—I then steep'd it in my own—and then in hers—and then in mine—and then I wip'd hers again—and as I did it, I felt such indescribable emotions within me, as I am sure could not be accounted for from any combinations of matter and motion.
>
> I am positive I have a soul; nor can all the books with which the materialists have pester'd the world ever convince me of the contrary.[13]

This question of matter and motion, and the critique of the soul by the materialists, involves a set of philosophical questions born in debates of the seventeenth century, but it also, in the end, takes us closer to Deleuze's Bergsonian frame of reference, to the dynamics of the movement-image and its interval. These, too, are topics to which I return in the closing section.

Before examining Deleuze's arguments, however, I should note the strong emphasis in this encounter, as in so many in *A Sentimental Journey*, on the dynamics of sympathy and on the theatrical dimension of its expression. Like the most famous of picaros, Don Quixote, Yorick's itinerary is guided by affection. His movements respond to his being moved, and they express his capacity to go beyond himself. Unlike Don Quixote, Yorick is characterized almost exclusively by the expression of his feelings. He does little or nothing to aid this maiden in distress,

Maria of Moulines. It is as though his being moved by sympathy not only supplemented the physical movement of the picaro's journey, but actually displaced it—emotion taking the place of quest-driven motion. This is a recurring motif, indeed, a constitutive structure, in the sentimental journey: the sense of emotion coming at the point of arrested motion. The poet Wordsworth, for example, who owed far more to Sterne and the form of the sentimental journey than we normally assume, developed it to perhaps its highest pitch in his own poetry of journey and encounter.[14]

In the modernized picaresque of the sentimental journey, then, Sterne managed to develop a form in which he could figure the practice of sympathy as a kind of imaginative mobility—the capacity, as Smith had suggested, of passing into points of view not one's own. The crucial conceit of the sentimental journey form involved a paradoxical play between, on one hand, the virtual representation of sentiments occasioned by actual travel and, on the other, the actual exercise of virtual travel *in* sentiment. Sterne's great genius—and his special brand of sentimental wit—was to create a textual exercise in which these two dimensions could not finally be told apart. *A Sentimental Journey* is a book in which the literal and figurative modes are constantly changing places, with the accompanying ambiguity about "order," ordonnance, and causality that is technically associated by Sterne himself with the figure of hypallage. Modern manuals describe hypallage as the trope of switching places, but in *Tristram Shandy*, Sterne's own Walter Shandy defined it for a puzzled Uncle Toby, in vehicular terms, as "putting the cart before the horse." Like the second modality of Deleuze's affection-image—not the facialization of the close-up, but the immersion in "any spaces whatever"—the world of *A Sentimental Journey*, one might argue, is causally disjointed in that it is supersaturated with *affect*. Again, there is perhaps some resonance here with the transitional cinematic travel forms that Deleuze punningly calls *balade*. Since the French term suggests both "trip" and "ballad," it thus captures that sense of sylleptic play (between the literal and figurative levels, and between the travel and its narration) that is so prevalent in Sterne's ur-text, though in Deleuze, the space is saturated with what he calls thought or recollection. The trip-ballad form, writes Deleuze, is defined by "the slackening of the sensory-motor connections" implicit in the affection-image.[15] The "clearest aspect" of this form of "modern voyage" is that it "happens in any-space-whatever . . . in opposition to action which most often unfolded in the qualified space-time of the old realism."[16]

But this is to get ahead of ourselves. What initially drew me to Deleuze's work was his and Guattari's provocative discussion of faciality in *A Thousand Plateaus*, the analysis of how a face deterritorializes a body. What I only later discovered was that Deleuze elaborated his views on faciality and affection in *The Movement-Image*. Though Deleuze insisted that the organization of his two cinema books was not strictly historical, it is fair to say that this first volume spans the Griffith–Capra period in cinema. It is his work with the films of this period, roughly 1915–45, that leads Deleuze to articulate affection with movement and vehicularity. Deleuze's account of the conceptual structure of cinema in *The Movement-Image* has two distinct starting points, each of them candidly derived from a "commentary" on Bergson. The first is an argument centered on the conceptual status of the shot as a "mobile section," the second on the question of how the shot should be understood in relation to the Bergsonian analysis of the movement-image in its three primary varieties: perception-image, affection-image, and action-image. On my reading of Deleuze, his concept of the shot proves to have a peculiar congruence with that of the affection-image so that "moving" and "being moved" come to be thought together in highly suggestive terms.

Perhaps the simplest first approximation of what Deleuze means by the "shot" is to say that it can be defined by its way of mediating between two other practices in classical cinema: *cadrage* (or framing) and *montage*. Framing is what determines the *ensemble*, the provisionally closed set of elements that will be involved in a shot, while *montage* names the work of composing a film's shots into an unclosed whole *(un tout)*, which changes indefinitely. In its relation to the frame understood as an immobile section, the shot supplies the principle of movement. In relation to the whole produced in the work of montage, however, the shot becomes itself a *mobile* section, indicative of the changing open whole. Deleuze illustrates all this with the following scheme:

Frame as Mobile Section	Shot as Immobile Section
Shot as Movement	Cinematic Whole

In borrowing the framework of this analysis from Bergson's presentation of the movement-image in relation to the *durée*, Deleuze acknowledges that Bergson himself, ironically, regarded cinema not as the illustration of his theory, but as its technological nemesis. This, says Deleuze, is because Bergson insisted on seeing cinema as restricted to its primitive state—that is, before the advent of the shot's centrality in the 1910s—thus violating his (Bergson's) own injunction to understand things in their becoming, rather than in an arrested state and, in this case, also its primitive state.

Deleuze's second derivation from Bergson concerns the movement-image itself, its etiology and its three-part articulation. For the purposes of his analysis, Deleuze accepts Bergson's notion that the world is made up of luminous images that preexist their apprehension in the perception of living beings. Living beings are, in one sense, themselves just so many images among these others, but in another sense, they are "contingent centers" and thus introduce what Bergson calls "centers of indetermination" into the mix; that is, they introduce perception and action, the dual capacity to take in the world and respond accordingly. But since perception and action are not simultaneous, least of all in more highly developed living beings, a gap appears between them that, always following Bergson, Deleuze terms an "interval"—a state of in-betweenness. And this state is what both philosophers term the state of *affection*.[17]

If the shot, then, just *is* the cinematic movement-image, as Deleuze explicitly states, it follows from the Bergsonian framework of analysis that there are three varieties in which it appears—perception-image, affection-image, and action-image. The three kinds of movement-image, then, supply the elements with which montage does its work in assembling the whole *(le tout)*. From another angle, however, Deleuze's analysis suggests an *alignment* of the three kinds of movement-image with the three-part analysis. In *this* alignment, the perception-image corresponds to the frame, the action-image to the montage, and the affection-image to the shot (i.e., with the movement-image as such). Though Bergsonian conceptual dynamics tend to be fluid ("immanent"), these complex relationships can perhaps be suggested diagrammatically:

My interest here is in the curious symmetry between the triadic terms on the two levels. My suggestion about it, however, relies not on any explicit statement to this effect by Deleuze, but only on an implicit pattern in his analysis.[18] His account of the perception-image, for example, is couched in a marked language of *cadrage*: "the perception of a thing is the same thing related to another special image which frames it."[19] The work of cinematic framing corresponds to that of perceptual framing. Similarly, Deleuze implicitly aligns the action-image with the changing, open whole composed in montage, especially insofar as he associates the action-image with time. Sometimes he makes the association quite explicit, as when he explains that montage is "the operation which bears on the movement-images to release the whole from them, that is, the image *of* time,"[20] or again, "the only generality about montage is that it puts the cinematographic image into a relationship with the whole. . . . In this way it gives an indirect image of time."[21] (At these points, Deleuze relies on Bergson's phrasing in a way that implies a connection of perception with space and action with time, for in Bergson, "perception is master of space in the exact measure in which action is master of time."[22])

So if, roughly speaking, *cadrage* is to montage as perception is to action, what is to be said about the respective middle terms in each of these triads: the shot and the affection-image? What is the basis or principle of their apparent congruence, their occupation of analogous positions in parallel schemes? To begin with, one must recognize that both the shot and the affection-image inhabit the Bergsonian interval. The affection-image is unequivocally situated by Deleuze in the interval defined by the gap between perception and action. This, as we have seen, is quite explicit in his second commentary on Bergson.[23] The shot is similarly identified by its conceptual location between the work of framing and the work of montage. Thus, apropos Deleuze's account of decoupage, D. N. Rodowick has noted that it "determines the shot as a set of a particular kind, an interval of movement."[24]

Furthermore, on a more abstract plane, we can say that each triad corresponds to what Deleuze, speaking more generally, calls "the three Bergsonian levels: the sets and their parts; the whole which fuses with the Open or change in duration, and the movement which is established between parts or sets, but which also expresses duration. That is the change of the whole."[25] Viewed this way, it is easy enough to see *cadrage* and the perception-image as corresponding to the first level, and montage and the action-image as corresponding to the third level (which Deleuze lists second), leaving the shot and the affection-image in the position of the middle level, which here (as elsewhere in this Bergsonian system) is assigned a double operation. Its movement is one that *governs* the relation of the parts but that also *expresses* the open whole. At one point in his analysis, Deleuze articulates the double operation of the middle level (or term) in this framework in a tantalizing formulation—apropos of the movement in terms of which we should conceptualize the shot—that it "has two movements: as inseparable as the inside and the outside, as the two sides of a coin: *it is the relationship between parts and it is the state* [affection] *of the whole*."[26] In this formulation, the shot—as the middle term of the interval between *cadrage* and montage—is explicitly defined in terms of the very category that names the interval between perception and action: the category of *affection*.

Two aspects of this curious congruence between the shot and the affection-image deserve closer scrutiny. The first of these has to do with Deleuze's association of the affection-image with the face—and especially with the face as understood in Deleuze's readings of famous accounts of the close-up in Balázs, Epstein, and Eisenstein. In what sense, we might ask, is the face or the close-up shot to be seen as congruent with the shot as such? In the general Bergsonian scheme, we must recall, the consequence of having living beings among the general flux of images is that, for such beings, motion is going to be either incoming (in perception) or outgoing (in action). Our human bodily organs, accordingly, are specialized according to their role in receiving motion or generating it. Our nerves, on this view, are either *af*ferent or *ef*ferent. Bergson himself defined affection—in another passage directly cited by Deleuze—as a kind of translation point between the incoming and outgoing motions— "a kind of motor tendency on a sensitive nerve."[27]

Though Bergson does not himself associate affectivity with the face as such, Deleuze argues that the face fits the Bergsonian bill in that it is the site of sensory perception but not of organs of locomotion. It is also, of course, a widely acknowledged locus of emotional expression. In an important passage that reflects Deleuze's synthesis of Bergsonian vitalism and the close-up theory of Balázs–Epstein–Eisenstein, Deleuze lays out what he calls the "relationships between affection and movement in general," especially in respect to how perception is "translated" into action:

> The movement of translation is not merely interrupted in its direct propagation by an interval which allocates on the one hand the received movement, and on the other the executed movement, and which might

make them in a sense incommensurable. Between the two there is affection which re-establishes the relation. But, it is precisely in affection that the movement ceases to be that of translation in order to become movement of expression, that is to say quality, simple tendency stirring up an immobile element. It is not surprising that, in the image that we are, it is the face, with its relative immobility and its receptive organs, which brings to light these movements of expression while they remain most frequently buried in the rest of the body.[28]

The affection-image, on this account, is the medium of a double transformation. On one hand, it inhabits the interval in which the movement of perception along the afferent nerves is translated into the movement of action along the efferent nerves. On the other, it transforms *this very process* into a movement of expression, which might be called a different order of movement from the other two, and one most visibly registered in the expression of the face. Jean Epstein argued that a perfectly still close-up could make no sense.[29] So while the respective movements of perception and action might seem disparate enough (one from the other) to require the positing of the interval of the affections, the kind of movement generated in the transformation of the one movement into the other is itself sufficiently different from either as to produce this translative *effect*. What is this distinctive kind of movement that is "expressed" in the affection-image? And what does it have to do with the shot?

It might at first seem that any claim for congruence between the shot and the affection-image breaks down in view of Deleuze's insistence on the face as an immobile plate because he so frequently insists on the *mobility* of the shot. The shot, he tells us directly, is a mobile section of duration, though even Bergson himself failed to see it so. Deleuze explains that the mobility of the shot in the cinema dominated by the movement-image could assume a number of forms: (1) the continuous movement of the camera, (2) the continuity of a connection between two shots from fixed positions, (3) the "sequence shot" with depth of planes (as in Welles and Wyler), or (4) the sequence shot without depth (as in Dreyer's *Ordet* or *Gertrud*). But of what, in these various instances, does the "movement" of the shot consist? What qualifies it to be considered a Bergsonian "mobile section of a duration"?[30]

Deleuze, in effect, tries to answer this question with a series of analytic examples from across the history of cinema, in which a moving camera registers moving bodies—examples that turn on the question of vehicularity. One of the most fascinating of these examples is Wim Wenders's *Kings of the Road (Im Lauf der Zeit)*, a picaresque narrative featuring two male protagonists who embark on a moving exploration of media and affect. These characters are both dramatically introduced in their respective vehicles, when, at the outset, one of them drives his Volkswagen into a small pond next to which the other is shaving in the large white van in which he habitually sleeps and eats. The van carries the equipment for his work as a repairman for projection equipment in cinemas around West Germany. The man who emerges from the submerged Volkswagen is a doctor in flight from a marriage, and he joins the cinema repairman on a series of travels that eventually leads each into their respective pasts. Wenders's camera in this film is as mobile as the vehicles it shoots, and at least once in the film, he offers a near-match cut between the paired reels of a projector and the paired wheels of the van. The doctor eventually confronts his father, who, significantly for a film so reflexive about media, is ensconced with his printing machinery in a small newspaper office—a reprise, perhaps, of the media rivalries staged in 1930s newspaper films.

Kings of the Road is a film that had already come up in *A Thousand Plateaus*, but in *The Movement-Image*, it becomes for Deleuze an illustration of how a director can dramatize the movement inherent in the shot by making fungible the movements that the camera registers and the movements that the camera itself undertakes. It is in this sense that Deleuze's discussion of *Kings of the Road* sums up his argument over a series of examples from various eras of filmmaking. These include his analysis of the principle of mobility in a celebrated early sequence from Murnau's *The Last Laugh* (where the camera descends an elevator and then exits it in pursuit of its subjects), in one from Vidor's *The Crowd* (where the camera leaves the traffic of a New York street to climb an office building and pass through a high window to find the protagonist at his desk), or in the equally famous opening of Welles's *Touch of Evil* (with the crane shot that tracks a car out of a busy Mexican plaza to the point of its explosion). "What counts" in such shots, says Deleuze, "is that the mobile camera is like a *general equivalent* of all the means of locomotion that it shows or that it makes use of—aeroplane, car, boat, bicycle, foot, metro."[31]

In *Kings of the Road*, Deleuze maintains, this equivalence becomes the "soul" of the film, a way of "introducing into the cinema a particularly concrete reflection on the cinema."[32] This leads Deleuze directly into his most extended discussion of vehicularity:

In other words, the essence of the cinematographic movement-image lies in extracting from vehicles or moving bodies the movement which is their common substance, or extracting from movements the mobility which is their essence. This was what Bergson wanted: beginning from the body or moving thing to which our natural perception attaches movement as if it were a vehicle, to extract a simple colored "spot," the movement-image, which "is reduced in itself to a series of extremely rapid oscillations" and "is in reality only a movement of movements." Now, because Bergson only considered what happened in the apparatus (the homogeneous abstract movement of the procession of images) he believed the cinema to be incapable of that which the apparatus is in fact most capable, eminently capable of: the movement-image—that is, pure movement extracted from bodies or moving things. This is not an abstraction, but an emancipation.[33]

"The shot is the movement-image."[34] This much Deleuze states explicitly at the start of his discussion of vehicularity. At the same time, the movement-image is "pure movement," understood as an extraction from the moving things to which our natural perception attends, as mobility can be extracted from a vehicle. Such "movement" is both what gives the relationship of the parts of the framed set and what expresses the changes worked through in the film considered as an "open whole."

Understanding the shot in this way, the congruity of its relation to the affection-image that constitutes one of its aspects, and hence to the close-up, becomes a little easier to see. Both shot and close-up are "soullike" elements of the cinema, reflections on its central principles of operation.[35] Furthermore, both are forms of what Deleuze punningly calls "planitude"—they are planar fields with two poles, or sides. We must recall here that the French word for "shot" and "plane" are the same: *plan*. Furthermore, the "face," for Deleuze, is a *plaque*, or "plate"—and it, too, as Deleuze repeatedly insists, has two poles, "reflection" and "intensity"; in French, of course, *shot* and *close-up* have the linguistic congruence of *plan* and *gros plan*. Perhaps the most important point of similarity, though, is that both planes are really best described as meta-movements—"movements of movements," using the phrase that Deleuze cites from Bergson. Thus the fact that the affection-image is associated with an absence of locomotion may seem less significant when we recall that, like that of the shot, the movement of the affection-image is a meta-movement to begin with.

In considering how to bring the preceding observations into intelligible relation, I was initially tempted to point to the strange congruence of the shot and the affection-image—*plan* and *gros plan*—as supplying a means of reconceptualizing my account of the cinematic incarnation of sentimental spectatorship theory from the Scottish Enlightenment. My thought was that, according to that theory, the point of view from which we observe the case of another must be reversible with that case; that is, in imagining ourselves in the case of another, in a situation to which the face of the other is at least a partial index, we must imagine our case, and thus our own face, through the other's eyes as well. What might be called the "sentimentalization of the case" in Adam Smith's critique of casuistry seems to have been conceived with respect to the dynamics of the face-to-face situation and to the management and interpretation of the countenance. The sentimentalized case, one might say, makes fungible the close-up shot and what it registers.[36] For a quick illustration of this, think of the moment in that most Smithian of sentimental films, Frank Capra's *It's a Wonderful Life*, when we see for the first time James Stewart as the adult George Bailey. The frame freezes on Stewart, and an exchange takes place between a senior angel named Joseph (Ben Franklin in the original script) and a lesser angel named Clarence, who has been assigned to Bailey's case:

CLARENCE: What did you stop it for?
JOSEPH: I want you to take a good look at that face.

Clarence is moved to sympathy in a shot that registers the expressive force of the face itself, and all in a moment in which Stewart, as it happens, is measuring precisely the size of the case he wishes for his romantic adventure abroad.[37]

There are, however, serious obstacles to taking this route with Deleuze's account of the affection-image and the movement-image. It is true that one can find some suggestive remarks about faces, possible worlds, and the concept of the *autrui* in Deleuze and Guattari's later book, *What Is Philosophy?*[38] But Deleuze seems to block this sort of appropriation by his repeated rejection of the notion that the close-up is primarily about shot–reverse-shot techniques. This we recall from his use of the close-ups in Dreyer's *Joan of Arc* as a central exhibit in his account of the affection-image and his emphasis on Dreyer's refusal of eye-line matches: "Dreyer avoids the shot-reverse shot procedure which would maintain a real relation between each face and the other."[39] It might ultimately be possible to understand the congruence of *plan* and *gros plan* in such terms as I had imagined, but such an analysis would need to take account of Deleuze's exemplary use of Dreyer's techniques and the complications they entail.

A second approach—one I hinted at earlier in comments on materialist accounts of the soul—has come to seem more promising even as it has proven to be yet more circuitous. It involves our taking seriously that other great concept of the sentimental tradition, sensibility, and placing it in turn in a history that reaches back into the seventeenth-century debates about materialism and its implications for the early modern notion of the soul. Turning back again to Sterne, we might now recall that of all the chestnuts gleaned from *A Sentimental Journey* for the many anthologies with titles like "Beauties of Sterne," perhaps none appeared more often than his great paean to sensibility, occasioned by his encounter with Maria of Moulines. It runs, in part, "—Dear sensibility! source inexhausted of all that's precious in our joys, or costly in our sorrows!—all comes from thee, great—great Sensorium of the world! which vibrates, if a hair of our heads but falls upon the ground, in the remotest desert of thy creation."[40] Bearing in mind the apposition of "sensibility" with "sensorium," we can now note that in the very same year when *A Sentimental Journey* was published, 1768, Abraham Tucker defined *sensorium* in his *Light of Nature Pursued* as "that part of the body where the action of all the sensory nerves terminates, and from thence the influence of the Will first begins to operate on certain muscles."[41] More suggestively still for our genealogy of Deleuze's Bergsonian account of vehicular mobility in the cinema, the passage appears in a chapter titled "The Vehicular State."

It is too long a story to tell in full here, but the connection between, on one hand, the sensorium understood as the point of translation between motion in and motion out and, on the other, the discourse on what was known as the vehicular state has a history that reaches back to the first modern attempts to articulate something like the model that Deleuze, following Bergson, would adopt as the framework for *The Movement-Image*. Indeed, the term *sensorium* was coined in the 1640s by the Cambridge Latitudinarian Henry More in the course of his response to the new mechanist and materialist positions of Descartes, Hobbes, and Spinoza—these are positions, especially Spinoza's, in which Deleuze, of course, demonstrated long-standing interest. As early as the

1640s, we find in More the earliest mention of *sensorium* in the *Oxford English Dictionary*: "for there is first a tactuall conjunction as it were of the representative rayes of every thing, with our sensorium before we know the things ourselves."[42] And he went on, in the 1650s, to develop a theory that would be debated for a century and a half under the heading of the "vehicular hypothesis." Joseph Priestley continued the debate into the 1780s with his discussion "Of the Vehicle of the Soul" in *Disquisitions Relating to Matter and Spirit* (1782).

Designed to respond to the reductionist accounts of the soul that More found in the "new science," the vehicular hypothesis is based on the notion that the soul resides in a subtle body—a body composed of subtilized matter. This subtilized body functions as a kind of zeugma. It is at once material in relation to the soul and immaterial in relation to the rest of the body. The vehicle, on this account, is the means by which we journey onward after death. Over the course of the next decades, leading up to the time of Sterne, this vehicular hypothesis would be literalized and concretized, and often to comic effect that seems un-mistakably to have prefigured, even as early as Thomas Browne's 1690 satire of Dryden, one of Sterne's central sentimental conceits:

> *Eugenius:* There was a certain Country Gentleman, no matter for his Name, or where he lived, but he had read the *Sadducismus Triumphatus*, and was so mightily taken with Dr. *More*'s Notion of a Vehicle, that he could not rest, till he had bought him a Vehicle, call'd in *English* a Calash; so he eat and drank in his Vehicle, and slept in his Vehicle, and lay with his Wife in his Vehicle, and got an Heir Apparent upon her Virtuous body in his Vehicle; and Vehicle was his Name.[43]

Thus developed one of the key discourses in which Sterne's sub-genre of the "sentimental journey" was anticipated—one might almost say precipitated. By 1768, the year in which *Sentimental Journey* was published, Abraham Tucker could devote scores of pages of his *Light of Nature Pursued* to a dream vision of the author's passage into the afterlife by way of the vehicular. In Sterne, the vehicle becomes the means of the soul's sympathetically journeying in life as well as in the afterlife.

The vehicular hypothesis remained somewhat occulted for decades after Sterne, appearing by name in Emma Hay's Godwinian novel *The Memoirs of Emma Courtney* (1795), but mostly as a subterranean influence.[44] It is explicitly revived as well in the later Yeats, who had a more than passing interest in Henry More. Once you look for it, though, you begin to see it in some celebrated texts along the way. It is there, inevitably, in Dickens. When Mr. Marley appears face-to-face with Scrooge, and Scrooge tries to dismiss his spirit with a materialist reduction as just a bit of undigested beef, Marley replies, "If [a man's] spirit goes not forth in life, it is condemned to do so after his death."[45] The apocalypse of failed circulation in Dickens is perhaps the much discussed London panorama from the top of Todgers' Commercial Boarding House in *Martin Chuzzlewit*. Here the clogging of vehicular traffic leads to stagnant conditions emblematized in the rotting fruit that cannot make the transit from the docks to the markets. But it is perhaps in *A Tale of Two Cities* that the vehicular conceit was given freest reign. The significantly named bank agent, Mr. Lorry, offers perhaps Dickens's clearest personification of the sentimental agent, one who is associated from the start with the English mail coach. He is, of course, the good version of the British man of commerce, and the kind of emotional relay that Mr. Lorry supplies is to be set against the ominous vehicular figures of the French. In a schema borrowed from Edmund Burke, French vehicularity is represented by way of paired extremes: first, the coach of the French marquis, which kills a child under its wheels on a Paris street, and then its proletarian counterpart, the revolutionary tumbril, whose construction is glimpsed at the start of the book and whose dark purposes are revealed in the climactic final scene, when Sydney Carton, embodiment of the sentimental principle of putting yourself in the place of the other, is wheeled out to the guillotine in one.[46]

Looking ahead again to cinema and to Capra, we can register the particularly uncanny fact that the last scene of *A Sentimental Journey* (the very next vignette after the encounter with Maria of Moulines) involves a rainy night, an awkwardly shared room at an inn, and an ingeniously contrived barrier between two beds. All of this strikingly anticipates the famous sequence in Capra's first important comedy, *It Happened One Night* (1934), when Peter Warne, played by Clark Gable, hangs a blanket between his own bed and that of Elly Andrews, the young unmarried heiress played by Claudette Colbert, and christens it "The Walls of Jericho." Might we not regard this blanket as the vehicle of the very age-of-sensibility sentiments that the young lovers, whose faces are shown in alternating close-ups, project on it from their beds on either side? Can it be a coincidence that this film, taken from a short story titled "Night Bus," focuses so much of its only action on the events aboard the twentieth-century equivalent of the horse-drawn coach, or that so many other kinds of vehicles—automobiles, airplanes, motorcycles, and, at the close, the one-person helicopter (a twentieth-century *Désobligeant?*) of Warne's showy rival—come to figure so prominently in the film?[47]

My aim here has been to offer a kind of genealogy for the congruence of the affection-image and the movement-image in the first of Deleuze's cinema books. The screen itself operates much as the face does in that it registers a translative movement, though it is not itself in motion. But I have also been concerned to give a similar account of those sites that, in the affection-image, Deleuze identifies as "any spaces whatever." The production of these sites on the plane of the movement-image threatens the work of the action-image, producing those forms of displacement Deleuze calls the *balade* and *voyage*, labels that themselves bespeak a certain cultural archaism. My hope has been that the history of the translative vehicle and the sentimental journey might shed new light on the difficult Deleuzian notion of deterritorialization.[48] Late in *It Happened One Night*, we see the face of Gable/Warne, as he motors cheerfully down the road singing the faux ballad "Young People in Love Are Never Hungry." Suddenly, he passes the convoy of cars bearing Colbert/Andrews in the opposite direction, back to her father's custody, thus dashing his high spirits. His tire goes flat. The landscape is suddenly transformed—a cinematic passage that calls to mind the contrastive emotional journeys in Browning's "Childe Roland to the Dark Tower Came." We are caught up in this face, its shifting intensities and reflections, even if the deflated tire of the old jalopy gives us a too obvious hint of allegory. We can perhaps deduce from the geography that Gable/Warne is on Route 1 between Philadelphia and New York—in other words, that he is in, well, New Jersey. Yet, within the Deleuzian logic of the sentimental journey, one would have to say that he could be in any space whatever.

Notes

I would like to thank Daniel Morgan, for his valuable responses to a prior draft of this essay, and Mollie Godfrey, my graduate assistant, for help in preparing it for publication.

1   Theater has a place in this story, too, of course, and I address that briefly in "Moving Accidents: The Emergence of Sentimental Probability," in *The Age of Cultural Revolutions: Britain and France, 1750–1820* (Berkeley: University of California Press, 2002), 137–70.

2   Annette Baier, *A Progress of Sentiments: Reflections on Hume's Treatise* (Cambridge, Mass.: Harvard University Press, 1991), 180–81.

3   For more on the notion of the virtual point of view and the role of the "case," see my "The Face of the Case: Conrad, *Lord Jim*, and the Sentimental Novel," *Critical Inquiry* 33 (2007): 837–64.

4   Gilles Deleuze, *Empiricism and Subjectivity: An Essay on Hume's Theory of Human Nature*, trans. Constantin V. Boundas (New York: Columbia University Press, 1991), 40–42.

5   Sergei Eisenstein, "Dickens, Griffith and the Film Today," in *Film Form: Essays in Film Theory*, trans. Jay Leyda (New York: Harcourt Brace Jovanovich, 1949), 195–255.

6   On identificatory associations with point-of-view shots, see Béla Balázs, *Theory of the Film: Character and Growth of a New Art*, trans. Edith Bone (New York: Dover, 1970), 90–92, and Jean Mitry, *The Aesthetics and Psychology of the Cinema*, trans. Christopher King (Bloomington: Indiana University Press, 1997), 206–8. On the deployment of the new techniques of classical cinema on behalf of "psychological causality," see David Bordwell, Janet Saiger, and Kristin Thompson, *The Classical Hollywood Cinema: Film Style and Mode of Production to 1960* (New York: Routledge and Kegan Paul, 1985), 13–17.

7   Frank Capra, *The Name above the Title: An Autobiography* (New York: Macmillan, 1971), 175–76.

8   For a recent reassessment of Langdon, his craft, his childlike persona, and his relation to Capra, see Joanna E. Rapf, "Doing Nothing: Harry Langdon and the Performance of Absence," *Film Quarterly* 59 (2005): 27–35.

9   Jean-Christophe Agnew, *Worlds Apart: The Market and the Theater in Anglo-American Thought, 1550–1750* (Cambridge: Cambridge University Press, 1986), 18–56.

10   Laurence Sterne, *A Sentimental Journey* (New York: Oxford University Press, 1984), 11.

11   Ibid.

12   Ibid., 113.

13   Ibid., 114.

14 It was this kind of moment in Wordsworth that Geoffrey Hartman described as somewhat different in relation to the epitaphic admonition—*Siste viator!*—that Hartman saw at work in a series of poems from "The Solitary Reaper" to *The Prelude.* See his *Wordsworth's Poetry, 1787–1814* (New Haven, Conn.: Yale University Press, 1964).

15 Gilles Deleuze, *Cinema 2: The Time-Image,* trans. Hugh Tomlinson and Robert Galeta (Minneapolis: University of Minnesota Press, 1989), 3.

16 Gilles Deleuze, *Cinema 1: The Movement-Image,* trans. Hugh Tomlinson and Barbara Habberjam (Minneapolis: University of Minnesota Press, 1986), 208. In the course of his discussion of the *balade* form, Deleuze himself makes a literary connection to the eighteenth century—specifically to William Blake. He does not, however, cite Blake's own balladic contribution to the sentimental journey tradition—"The Mental Traveler"—a contribution that challenges its premises. See my "Blake and the Syntax of Sentiment: An Essay on 'Blaking' Understanding," in *Blake, Nation, Empire,* ed. Steve Clark and David Worrall (Basingstoke, U.K.: Palgrave, 2006), 113–29.

17 Cf. Henri Bergson, *Matter and Memory,* trans. Nancy Margaret Paul and W. Scott Palmer (London: George Allen and Unwin, 1911), 11–12.

18 In stressing the possibility of congruence between two levels here, I may be reading Deleuze somewhat against the grain. The notion of the level is always complicated in Deleuze by his commitment to the work of what Foucault calls "dis-leveling" or "*dénivillation.*" Michel Foucault, *L'Ordre du Discours* (Paris: Gallimard, 1971), 24.

19 Deleuze, *Movement-Image,* 63.

20 Ibid., 29.

21 Ibid., 55.

22 Bergson, *Matter and Memory,* as quoted in Deleuze, *Movement-Image,* 65.

23 Deleuze, *Movement-Image,* 61.

24 D. N. Rodowick, *Gilles Deleuze's Time Machine* (Durham, N.C.: Duke University Press, 1997), 49.

25 Deleuze, *Movement-Image,* 20.

26 Ibid., 19.

27 Bergson, *Matter and Memory,* 61–63, as quoted in Deleuze, *Movement-Image,* 66.

28 Deleuze, *Movement-Image,* 66.

29 "I have never understood motionless close-ups. They sacrifice their essence, which is movement. . . . The close-up, the keystone of the cinema, is the maximum expression of this photogeny of movement. When static, it verges on contradiction." Jean Epstein, "Magnification and Other Writings," trans. Stuart Liebman, *October* 3 (1977): 9–10. For two divergent recent discussions of Balázs, Epstein, and the theory of the close-up, see

Jacques Aumont, *Du Visage au Cinéma* (Paris: Seuil, 1992), 77–101, and Mary Ann Doane, "The Close-Up: Scale and Detail in the Cinema," *Differences: A Journal of Feminist Cultural Studies* 14 (2005): 89–111.

30 Deleuze, *Movement-Image*, 22. It is a question not unlike the one that Garrett Stewart poses in *Between Film and Screen: Modernism's Photo Synthesis* (Chicago: University of Chicago Press, 1999), 85–89.

31 Deleuze, *Movement-Image*, 22.

32 Ibid., 23.

33 Ibid.

34 Ibid., 22.

35 With Deleuze's claim, quoted earlier, to find the "soul" of cinema in the "general equivalence" of motion in the shot, compare Epstein's, "Magnification," 9, bold declaration: "The close-up is the soul of the cinema."

36 Not quite the same as Bazin's notion that the photographic object is the object in itself. See Daniel Morgan's discussion of "The Ontology of the Photographic Image" in "Rethinking Bazin: Ontology and Realist Aesthetics," *Critical Inquiry* 32 (2006): 443–81.

37 I have expanded on this use of the facial close-up in noncinematic contexts in "On the Face of the Case."

38 E.g., "The other is a possible world as it exists in a face that expresses it and takes shape in a language that gives it a reality." Gilles Deleuze and Félix Guattari, *What Is Philosophy?*, trans. Hugh Tomlinson and Graham Burchell (New York: Columbia University Press, 1991), 17. This is decidedly not a face in the Levinasian sense of the term.

39 Deleuze, *Movement-Image*, 107.

40 Sterne, *Sentimental Journey*, 117.

41 Abraham Tucker, *The Light of Nature Pursued*, vol. 4 (London: printed by T. Jones; sold by T. Payne, 1768), 26.

42 Henry More, *Platonica; or, A Platonicall Song of the Soul 1642* (Cambridge: R. Daniel, 1642), quoted in "Sensorium," def. a, *The Oxford English Dictionary*, 2nd ed., 1989, November 11, 2006, http://www.oed.com.

43 Thomas Brown, *The Reasons of Mr. Bays's Changing His Religion* (London: T. Bennet, 1690), 43.

44 See Mary Hays, *Memoirs of Emma Courtney*, vol. 1 (London: G. G. and J. Robinson, 1796), 177–78.

45 Charles Dickens, "A Christmas Carol," in *A Christmas Carol and Other Christmas Writings* (New York: Penguin, 2003), 47.

46 D. W. Griffith may have shown another aspect of what he owed to Dickens when he made vehicular accidents central to his own epic treatment of the French Revolution in *Orphans of the Storm* (1921).

47 For an account of this film's philosophical themes in a very different register, see Stanley Cavell's remarkable chapter "Knowledge as Transgression: *It Happened One Night*," in *Pursuits of Happiness: The Hollywood*

Comedy of Remarriage (Cambridge, Mass.: Harvard University Press, 1981), 71–109.

48   On the relevance of literary history for Deleuze's concept, and vice versa, see my "Edgeworth and Scott: The Literature of Reterritorialization," in *Repossessing the Romantic Past*, ed. Heather Glen and Paul Hamilton (Cambridge: Cambridge University Press, 2006), 119–39.

14. Becoming-Fluid: History, Corporeality, and the Musical Spectacle

Amy Herzog

In "The Mass Ornament," Siegfried Kracauer describes the spectacle of the Tiller Girls, a franchise of dance troupes that performed synchronized routines in geometrical formations. Kracauer writes, "These products of American distraction factories are no longer individual girls, but indissoluble girl clusters, whose movements are demonstrations of mathematics.... One need only glance at the screen to learn that the ornaments are composed of thousands of bodies, sexless bodies in bathing suits. The regularity of their patterns is cheered by the masses, themselves arranged by the stands in tier upon ordered tier."[1] For Kracauer, the fragmentation and abstraction of the body that takes place in the Tiller Girls performance echoes the abstract regimentation of industry. Kracauer draws a distinction in his reading of this spectacle between two levels of reality, one being the structural foundation of a given culture, the second consisting of its external "surface-level expressions."[2] The pure externality of surface-level expressions, for Kracauer, provides "unmediated access to the fundamental substance of the state of things."[3] The "girl cluster" is a prismatic ornament that exposes the logic at the heart of the capitalist *Ratio*.

Even if one is skeptical of the visual parallel that he draws between the "girl cluster" and the factory, Kracauer points to a provocative connection between aesthetics and politics, refusing to dismiss the spectacle as sheer escapism. There are a number of questions that arise from his formulation, however. Kracauer describes the body found here as sexless, but it is nevertheless always decidedly female. Moreover, the distinction that Kracauer draws between surface and depth appears entirely at odds with Deleuzian theory, which rejects understandings

259

of the real as something that exists beneath a veil of signs. But the concept of reality that Kracauer presents is far more complex than it might first appear, especially when read in light of his *Theory of Film*, for the relation between this reality and its surface is not necessarily one of resemblance or representation.

The potential correspondences and divergences between Kracauer's and Deleuze's work will unfortunately remain beyond the scope of this chapter. Yet I would like to seize on the image that Kracauer presents in this passage as a leaping off point to ask how we might think about cinematic spectacles in relation to the notion of a historical image. For Kracauer, the physical reality that film bears witness to is the base substance of that lived experience, the *Lebenswelt*. If film is to reveal physical reality, however, it does so by exposing reality's conflicted nature; like the mass ornament, the historical image makes the embedded nature of repressive social structures all the more apparent, preferring "a fragmentized whole to a false unity."[4]

Deleuze asserts that cinematic history cannot be described as a chronological evolution; neither is cinema an "aesthetic reflex," a mirror image of a historical moment. The power of the time-image, in fact, rests in its incommensurability with a teleological History; it is discontinuous, interstitial, and it serves to destabilize and falsify notions of identity and truth. The time-image, however, is exceedingly rare. How might one, then, following Deleuze, explore questions of history through films that fall short of this ideal? I am specifically interested in musicals for precisely this reason—they are popular, politically compromised works that nevertheless differ significantly from other kinds of narrative film, particularly in their nonlinear deployment of space and time.

Musical films are driven by contradictory tendencies, simultaneously verging toward creative differentiation and the repetition of the mass-produced same. Classical Hollywood musicals in particular seem irretrievably distant from the political, minoritarian cinema that Deleuze discusses in the *Cinema* books. Yet Deleuze speaks briefly of musicals in *The Time-Image*, suggesting that their flights into dance provide a potentially disruptive force, a point of "indiscernability," "an 'unhooking,' a 'discrepancy' of the action."[5]

My inquiry here will be driven by two extraordinarily different sets of examples, both of which feature highly spectacular musical ornaments. The first involves Esther Williams's musical films, which spotlight the champion swimmer in synchronized "girl cluster" extravaganzas. These films are exceptional both for the impossible otherworldliness of their musical productions and for the extreme rupture between narrative and number imposed by their watery nature. At the same time, Williams's filmography is incredibly formulaic. Fixated by design on the bathing-suited female body, these films were often thinly disguised marketing tools for swimwear, aboveground pools, and vacation destinations. Indeed, the Williams film is driven by fairly base presumptions: attractive female athletes hold a certain fascination with audiences; plots involving swimsuits allow for the maximum display of the female body; "wholesome" girls and chlorinated waters simultaneously sanitize and contain that body's threatening sexuality; and underwater photography is a profitable technological novelty.[6] As unapologetically exploitative and market-oriented films, Williams's body of work highlights the capitalist rationale at the heart of the spectacle's will to entertain.

In stark contrast, *The Hole*, by Taiwanese director Tsai Ming-liang, presents an apocalyptic vision of Taipei racked by a mysterious virus, a narrative curiously interrupted by intensely stylized musical performances. These performances, which remain unaccounted for by the "real world" of the narrative, feature the female protagonist lip-synching to songs by Grace Chang (Ge Lan), a Hong Kong musical star of the 1950s and 1960s. Tsai extends the musical's prototypical break between narrative and production number into an insurmountable gulf. The songs that invade the dystopian space of the narrative are themselves Western-style pop songs culled from frothy musicals that, much like the films of Williams, were formulaic vehicles for their female star. Grace Chang's films made few attempts to veil their celebration of capitalist ideals and Western trends, as the English translations of several of her titles indicate (*Mambo Girl* [Yang, 1957], *Air Hostess* [Yang, 1959], *Our Dream Car* [Yang, 1959]). Tsai's use of the musical spectacle is thus complex and ambiguous, suggesting at once the bankrupt abyss of industrialized urban life and the potentially deterritorializing power of the musical baubles that this world has produced.

There are several points of resonance between these films. In terms of their musical style, both feature production spectacles that are relatively autonomous. Tsai offers no immediate justification for the jarring insertion of musical numbers, and while several of Williams's films involve the production of a water ballet, the link between narrative and number is so preposterous that these justifications are rendered completely hollow.[7] Both *The Hole* and the Williams film prominently feature the spectacle of the female body, and as distinct from the more anonymous girl cluster, combine elements of abstraction with the fetishization of the singular star. Perhaps most significantly, water plays a critical role in each, utterly transforming the temporal and spatial planes along which they unfold.

Clearly there are even larger distinctions between these examples, particularly in terms of their historical and political contexts. My objective in reading these works alongside one another is not to map an evolution of the musical, nor to posit Tsai as a simple corrective to the more conservative Williams-style musical. I am more interested in the ways in which these films are part of an ongoing process of de- and reterritorialization. One articulation may amplify tensions that the other seeks to resolve, yet each articulation is also intrinsically linked to the other. My project here, then, rather than reflecting directly on Deleuze, will be an attempt to think through him, using his work on cinema and history to bring to light some of the affinities between these works.

Deleuze's reading of the Berkeleyesque production number, which draws on language very similar to Kracauer's, suggests that it is in part the impersonality of the spectacle that makes these compositions so evocative: "in Berkeley, the multiplied and reflected girls form an enchanted proletariat whose bodies, legs and faces are the parts of a great transformational machine: the 'shapes' are like kaleidoscopic views which contract and dilate in an earthly or watery space . . . turning around the vertical axis and changing into each other to end up as pure abstractions."[8] Deleuze sees the multiplications that occur in the kaleidoscopic image as a type of "implied dream," a dream-image not bound by the narrative rationalization of a dreamer whose reverie we witness. In the musical, the dance is our dream, and the movement between dream world and "reality" is, to greater or lesser degrees, open and ambiguous. The significance of the musical number rests in its rupturing of the sensorimotor situations that define the movement-image. While the dream-image does not attain the state of pure virtuality and indiscernibility that, for Deleuze, defines the time-image, it does mark a significant movement in that direction. Within the musical spectacle, the actions of the individual are subsumed by the indeterminate and depersonalized movements of the world.

Nevertheless it is not abstraction alone that gives the spectacle access to this larger movement. As Deleuze notes, even when "the dancer or couple retain an individuality as creative source of movement . . . what counts is the way in which the dancer's individual genius . . . moves from a personal motivity to a supra-personal element, to a movement of world that the dance will outline."[9] The power of the innovative musical is to reveal a "plurality of worlds," juxtaposed and unresolved. The ostensible problem-solving function of the number (a song that fixes a narrative conflict) is entirely secondary to this movement of world that subsumes individual agency. Like the elaborate conveyer belts that move Berkeley's chorines, even the solo performer becomes a puppet for the forces that flow through her. Thus Williams, as a swimmer pulled by the movements of water and music, becomes an avatar and the catalyst for our shift between various planes and registers.

Given its propensity for the irrational, there is little concern within the musical to reconcretize imaginary events within an everyday world, at least not in one that is realistically believable. While two distinct registers of fantasy and reality most often exist, the joy of the musical emanates from their conflation and confusion. The Williams spectacle, in particular, is governed by an excessive objectification of the human—here, always female—body, surpassing the standard "singing and dancing" number in its dissolution of logical spatiotemporal coordinates.

How are we to make sense of "reality" or "history," then, in this context? Clearly such fantastical formulations are inextricably linked to the historical moments in which they are produced, conditions that play a large role in shaping the worlds these films dream. Yet Deleuze's concept of the dream-image poses a significant challenge to our commonsensical understandings of history. Deleuze invokes Bergson in the *Cinema* books to supplant chronological history with a temporality that is eternally splitting into the past and the indefinite future. Rather than a timeline, we are confronted by coexistent, incommensurate sheets of the past. The distinctions between movement-images, recollection-images, dream-images, and time-images center on this question of temporality, each containing varied "pressures" of time. Neither time nor history can be represented. Instead, cinema at its most creative seeks to resist the entombing of a fixed History, opposing it with time as difference and the never ending processes of becoming.

It is essential to understand Deleuze's theorization of history in the context of his larger work, particularly his rereading of Nietzsche. Deleuze's, and Foucault's, formulation of a Nietzschean genealogical history is especially relevant here, suggesting a complex interplay between philosophy, history, and art.

For Foucault, a genealogical approach to history refuses to search for points of origin and refutes any universalizing notions of "truth." Because it opposes a sweeping History, the practice of effective history demands a new means of perceiving and conceptualizing, a "historical sense" that counters the pillars of Platonic history (reality, identity, and truth) with parody, dissociation, and the powers of the false.[10] Genealogical history thus destabilizes the teleology of metahistories by unearthing multiple and contradictory points of emergence. Rather than a hermetic, unified narrative, the descent that this genealogy traces is continually branching, open to chance and the accidental.

The modality of the genealogical critique plays a central role in Deleuze's work on cinema, even when it is not directly acknowledged as such. He does not, however, approach the cinema as a historical object to be analyzed; rather, the cinema is a creative process that can act to excavate, to provoke, to make the previously imperceptible perceptible. Engagement with the cinema becomes a means of generating new thought, of rethinking history. The question is how to understand the modality by which a film operates. Does the film structure its sonic and visual elements according to associative links, or through differentiation and incommensurability? Does it build its narrative through chronological progressions or through discontinuities and chance? Is identity asserted as a unified whole, or is it dissociated, contradictory, and multiple? Does the film aspire to speak the truth, or does it wage a battle against universals through fiction and fabulation? These are the questions that lie at the heart of the distinction between the movement-image and the time-image.

The movie musical as a genre seems designed to toy with an indiscernibility between the present and past, the virtual and actual. Its images ripple outward with no conceivable sensorimotor motivation. The musical spectacle introduces a profound discontinuity into the chronological flow of the film, a stuttering in which causal associations are replaced by dissociation and impossibility. And the image of time that the musical spectacle offers exists in fluid layers of simultaneous present–past–future. Yet in the process of their actualization, the disturbances that occur in the musical appear to be of a distinctly identifiable sort. Discrepancies, discontinuities, and falsifications proliferate in the Esther Williams film, but certain reconciliations are also at work. In *Neptune's Daughter*, for example, the teleology of the heterosexual romance not only frames the dream, but springs forth directly—in the case of Ricardo Montalban, quite literally—from its any-space-whatever.

The significance of these types of intrusions goes beyond that of a narrative linkage. The melding of economic and sexual interests in *Neptune's Daughter*, namely, the blatant marketing of the swimsuit as commodity (the film prominently features Cole bathing suits and even

Frame enlargement from *Million Dollar Mermaid* (Mervyn LeRoy, 1952)

posters used by Cole in actual magazine advertisements), culminates in a convenient display of Williams's body and a catalog of suits all inextricably linked to one another in a "happy ending."[11] Such "material" concerns not only fix the dream-image temporally within the narrative timeline, but also significantly color the fantasies that they offer us by repressing difference and imposing cohesive models of identity.

The female musical star is capitalism's ornament par excellence. Her body, whether multiplied or singular, is displayed as a surface of contradiction and fascination that is ultimately unified and contained by the twinned metanarratives of capitalism and heteronormativity. There is no doubt that the dream-image of the musical spectacle is almost invariably encapsulated within these types of universalizing frameworks. That said, one might still legitimately question how successful or complete this encapsulation is.

There is indeed something decidedly and delightfully perverse about musicals. The absolute excesses of the spectacle can, in this context, be read as implicit, if incomplete, affronts to heteronormative demands.[12] When the female body becomes the site for the musical's complex negotiations, these performances rely on a specular apparatus that tends to affirm objectifying presumptions about femininity.[13] Yet in the process, femininity itself is exposed as conflicted and performative. To pose this dilemma in slightly different terms, the image of the "girl cluster" shares much in common with the modality of the *tableau vivant*. Like the *tableau vivant*, the Berkeleyesque spectacle obscures the distinction between motion and stillness, surface and depth, object and living being. Space, time, and scale are unhinged from the axis of linear causality. The female form in the musical spectacle becomes a sheer surface, an empty mask. The gestures it offers are decidedly contradictory, appearing to be obsessed with the female body as a sexual object, yet eradicating any sensuality or eroticism through abstraction.[14]

"We know nothing about a body," Deleuze and Guattari write, "until we know what it can do, in other words, what its affects are, how they can or cannot enter into composition with other affects, with the affects of another body, either to destroy that body or to be destroyed by it, either to exchange actions and passions with it or to join with it in composing a more powerful body."[15] Williams is a hybrid figure, marked by an extreme rupture between her "wet" and "dry" incarnations. In the space of the underwater performance, Williams enters into a relation with water, an assemblage that multiplies her form and opens it to new paths of movement. There is a viscosity to the aquatic spectacle that opposes and permeates boundaries. Female corporeality and water become a musical machine that introduces discontinuity into the ideological space of the narrative, forcing time and space to enter into new types of configurations. Given their tendencies toward the specularization of the molar identity of woman, however, Esther Williams's becomings retreat and are recuperated before they are fully set into motion. Yet perhaps we can read this fluid-corporeality as a refrainlike pattern, one that reemerges, radically transformed, within the films of Tsai Ming-liang.

Tsai's films are about bodies, bodies adrift in urban landscapes and the architectural bodies that comprise the city itself. Time is a palpable presence in his work, frozen into long blocks of suspended duration. Characters are ceaselessly waiting and consumed with the drudgery of monotonous, bodily tasks (eating, sleeping, peeing, vomiting, masturbating). The landscape of Taipei that Tsai presents is a labyrinth of banality and hollow consumption. Empty corridors of shops, video arcades, food courts, movie theaters, and massage parlors are interspersed with elevators and escalators that go nowhere. Tsai's films are marked by distinct and persistent repetition, obsessed with the specific speeds and slownesses of the everyday. We see the same actors, in particular, his muse Lee Kang-sheng, appearing in scenarios that resonate strangely with subtle shifts in content and context.[16] The spaces of the city are similarly addressed in patient detail, and particular types of spaces recur consistently. Nothing ever happens beyond the slow revolutions of these interdependent yet isolated elements.[17]

Tsai's films are noticeably devoid of scored music, which he perhaps avoids due to its artifice, with one primary exception: his 1998 musical, *The Hole*.[18] The film opens seven days before the end of the millennium, and the city of Taipei is devastated by a mysterious illness. Victims of this "Taiwan fever" begin to behave like cockroaches, scurrying across the floor and hiding in moist, dark corners, a becoming-insect that apparently leads to an irretrievable loss of identity. Though the illness is apparently spread through the secretions of roaches, garbage and water services are being discontinued in the quarantined areas, perhaps in an effort to force residents to leave. Throughout this crisis, Taipei is besieged by a ceaseless, torrential rain. The film takes place entirely within the confines of a large public-housing complex, where several residents remain despite an evacuation. The nameless "man upstairs" (Lee Kang-sheng) works in a small grocery stand in a corridor of shuttered shops within the apartment building, futilely, it seems, for his only interaction each day is with a stray cat he feeds in the hallway.

Beneath the man's apartment, the apartment of "the woman downstairs" (Yang Kuei-mei) is plagued by horrific flooding. A plumber searching for the source of the leak leaves a massive hole between their apartments. The hole becomes a vexed threshold throughout the film, a voyeuristic peephole and a passageway for sounds, dirt, fluids, scents, and insects. The relationship between the man and the woman remains anonymous, and somewhat antagonistic, throughout the majority of the film, despite a deepening fascination with one other. This fascination, which remains ambiguously asexual, appears to be born purely from their mutual alienation and boredom as well as from their eruptions into each other's spaces through the hole. The woman vainly attempts to maintain the boundaries of her porous apartment as it falls to pieces around her. She stockpiles giant bags of toilet paper to stem the flow of water, which appears to be seeping in through every wall. The man's apartment is utterly dry, yet his actions have deleterious effects downstairs. When he turns on his faucet, the woman's tap water stops running, and his toilet leaks into her bathroom. The flows through the hole from his apartment are even more pointed, and at times antagonistic. On the first evening after the hole appears, he arrives home drunk and vomits through the opening. The next day, he sits on his floor and watches the woman until he is hit in the face with a cloud of insecticide. The woman attempts several prophylactic measures to seal the hole; she calls several plumbers and covers the hole with packing tape. These attempts are each impeded to some degree by the man. He pretends not to be home when the plumber rings his bell, and he pours water onto the tape from above to loosen the adhesive. His intentions in both instances are unexplained.

These exchanges are interspersed with five musical spectacles featuring the woman lip-synching Grace Chang songs. In each case, there is some indirect trigger for the flight into song (the sight of a cockroach, a volley of indirect glances over a balcony). There are thematic connections between the songs and the narrative context, as well; a visceral sneeze, for example, launches into the song "Achoo Cha Cha," in which the singer describes her allergic response to the marriage proposals of her many suitors. These links are always somewhat tenuous, however, and are never resolved. Tsai, in an interview, attributes the musical sequences to the "interior world" of the woman, yet at the same time, they do not consistently begin or end at her provocation, nor do they appear to reflect what we might call her personal desires.[19] While Tsai focuses a great deal of attention on the intimate actions of his characters, there is little in his work to suggest that the surface of the body belies a divisible interior.[20] Indeed, the richness of the corporeality he presents resists notions of a mind–body split. The musical sequences in *The Hole* may be fantasies, but given their ambiguous relation to the remainder of the film, it may be more productive to view them as dreams-in-general, collective dream-images born from the connections between human bodies and the bodies of the spaces they occupy. Tsai himself complicates psychological readings of the musical spectacle when he states that "on another level, the musical numbers are weapons I use to confront the environment at the end of the millennium."[21]

Tsai uses the musical spectacle to activate a complex interaction between real and fantastic spaces. These might not fully achieve what Deleuze would call a circuit between an actual image and its virtual counterpart, as elements of the musical fantasy suggest direct associations with the tropes of Hollywood and Hong Kong musicals, in general, and with the icon of Grace Chang, in particular. Yet the circulation that occurs here comes far closer to that state than the typical musical film would allow. The key distinction is that in *The Hole*, the musical number is an intervention that arises from the real, but rather than departing from it altogether, the spectacle serves to penetrate and transform that real space, creating a zone of indeterminacy where the real is falsified

Frame enlargement from *The Hole (Dong)* (Tsai Ming-liang, 1998)

and burlesqued. Each musical number takes place within the cramped and dingy passageways of the apartment complex. Stairways and corridors are modified into stage sets; spotlights appear, and everyday objects, such as strips of plastic sheeting and fire extinguishers, become props for the dance. Yet the power and joyfulness of these spectacles springs from their failure to metamorphose convincingly. The apartment complex remains bleak and stifling; Yang's costumes are fantastically vivid, yet the overall visual effect is always just slightly off, as if the mise-en-scène aspires to something far grander than it is able to achieve. This effect is furthered by the obviousness of Yang's lip-synching and by the awkward choreography.

The first musical number encapsulates many of the tensions that drive the film as a whole. Inside her dark apartment, Yang is applying egg whites to her face, while listening to the radio. The announcer drones on for an inordinate time, shifting breezily from an update on the epidemic to an insipid report on how best to cook instant noodles. Yang stands silently in the middle of her living room, her face upturned as she waits for her facial to dry, when she is struck in the face by falling dirt. She gasps in horror as she watches a cockroach crawl out of the hole and into her apartment. The scene cuts abruptly to a long shot of the marble lobby of the apartment building. The elevator doors open to reveal Yang in a spangled evening dress and an elaborate

red-feathered headdress. The battered beige laminate walls of the elevator that we saw earlier are now covered in black and illuminated by
tiny white lights that blink off and on in clusters. Yang begins to sing
and dance to a Latin-themed Chang song, "Calypso," lit by a strong
circular spotlight. The camera begins a slow dolly across the floor of
the lobby, revealing the broken doors on the mailboxes, the dirty walls,
and the obvious artifice of the homemade light panels inside the elevator as it approaches.

Yang mimes Chang's voice with enthusiasm as she dances inside the
tiny elevator with abundant sensuality. The lyrics of the song describe
the exuberant joy of singing the calypso, which Yang further enacts
through her movements. Whereas her appearance earlier, captured off
guard within the intimate space of her apartment, had been somewhat
dowdy and unpretentious, here Yang is stunningly groomed in a slinky
dress slit to her upper thigh. Yet as the song shifts to a puzzling verse in
which Chang compares her joyful dance to that of a "proud rooster,"
Yang begins jerking her head and flapping her elbows, movements
that render her feathered headpiece suddenly ridiculous. Throughout
the entire number, Yang remains within the confines of the cramped
elevator. The emotional outpouring of the song reverberates sharply
against the harshness of the space that confines it. "I twist and I turn
with endless pleasure," Chang's voice coos, "to forget my hard day of
endless labors." The sweet and somewhat futile hopefulness of this
sentiment is echoed by the tensions contained by their visualization,
the constriction and banality of the setting confronted by the abundant
aspirations of Yang's performance. After reaching the elevator, the camera
begins to pull back slowly. The overhead lights in the lobby are now
extinguished, and Yang is isolated within the spotlight. The elevator
doors close as the song ends, and the spotlight darkens. The next cut
returns abruptly to the harsh florescent lighting of the "real" lobby, as
this same elevator, no longer filled with twinkling lights, now opens to
reveal the drunken body of Lee passed out on the floor.

The self-conscious nature of Tsai's musical numbers results in an
unusual combination of understatement and excess. While the insertion of these performances into the narrative is more abrupt than in
canonical musical films, perhaps these numbers echo more organically
the actual experience of listening to pop music—the strange confluence
of drama and spectacle with the banality of the everyday. Music trans-
ports and extends us, yet always within the same walls, which remain
oblivious to our transformation. If the musical spectacle, as Kracauer

suggests, makes visible the contradictions inherent in the physical world, Tsai's musical numbers seem highly attuned to these paradoxes.

The connection between *The Hole* and the types of spectacles found in the Esther Williams film is certainly not direct. Yet if we were to speak of the specularization of the female musical star as a type of refrain, there are some resonances between the two bodies of work. In each case, the singular female body is displayed as an object of fascination, marked by multiplicity, hybridity, and permeability, subsumed in reactive environments. Williams and Yang (as well as Grace Chang) are objects of fascination, yet their sexuality is distilled, contained, and indirectly expressed. The musical spectacles in *The Hole* and in the Williams film are sonically strange, taking place in hermetic bubbles disconnected from the "real world."

Indeed the contradictions that exist in *The Hole*'s musical sequences highlight the problematic tensions found in a Williams-style or Chang-style film. Music is an ambiguous entity in this formulation. It takes part in the construction of the female body as spectacle and commodity through its lyrics, compositions, and the physical performance. The Grace Chang songs selected for these scenes exhibit a strange combination of overt Western musical structures and Mandarin lyrics and phrasing. The "Calypso" number plays with a popular fascination with "exotic Latin culture" in the 1950s, filtered through the Hong Kong Cathay studio's fascination with the exotic United States, further confusing notions of location, culture, and the commodification of style. If Tsai presents music as a counterbalance to the destructive forces at work in our culture, he is careful to demonstrate the interdependence of these elements. The joys of the musical spectacles he presents are never fully divorced from their banal points of emergence, and the escape they gesture toward is never complete.

Whereas the Williams spectacle ultimately respects, and even fetishizes, the boundaries of the female body as a unified entity, Tsai uses every tool at his disposal to dissolve distinctions between interior and exterior. If the woman who appears in the musical numbers is a spectacular double of the woman downstairs, her body is metamorphosed on another level, as well. Coupled with these periodic flights into musical fantasy, the woman is gradually undergoing a much darker process of becoming. She begins exhibiting flu symptoms—hence the sneeze that launches her into the "Achoo Cha Cha"—and immediately recognizes that she has been infected with Taiwan fever. This instant reflects the intersection of a number of simultaneous movements articulated through the conjoined bodies of the woman and her environment. She is multiplied through her musical double at the same time that her body is wracked with illness and begins the process of becoming-insect. The flooding that crumbles her walls, too, is one and the same with the forces that have penetrated her own fragile surface.

The woman's relationship with her apartment is so tightly woven that the differences between them are indistinguishable. This is not merely a case in which the environment serves as a metaphor for her inner state. The permeability of the apartment's ceiling and walls allows for the damp conditions and roach infestation that very literally make her ill. Moreover, the bodies of the apartment, of the complex, and of the city itself bear the marks of the historical conditions that brought them into being—the by-products of a technological, aspiring capitalist state that has overextended itself. The alienation being expressed here is very specific to contemporary Taiwan; the context of its strained relations with China, Japan, and the West; and the fallout of its economic boom. Rain and disease are present here as the very tangible results of housing crises, massive environmental problems, and more general class inequities. Disease forges a link between the physical body and the body of the city—a thematic refrain that can be mapped throughout Tsai's larger body of work (especially his 1997 film *The River* and his 1995 television documentary about young, gay, HIV-positive men).

The woman's body, too, is born from this history; her flaws and weaknesses, her flows and movements are all part of the nexus of forces that define a cultural moment. The alliance that is formed between the woman and her building is a dark and desperate one. The woman's attempt to preserve her boundaries is a battle for her survival. The flooding and disintegration of her home becomes that much more tragic. In one of the more poignant illustrations of her shared becoming with her building, the woman engages in an erotic telephone conversation. As she languidly pulls down sheets of wallpaper, she tells the listener, "I'm stripping . . . I'm undressing myself."

The presence of water as a dominating theme in Tsai's films points to a more global connection between bodies and spaces. Rain, rivers, and bodily fluids permeate all types of divergent bodies, eradicating the distinctions between them. Rain is an invading force, fallout from the excesses of industrialization. Water flows from people, as well, in the form of tears, which express absolute alienation, and piss, which, in its excessive presence in Tsai's films, often suggests drunkenness, fear, and illness. The woman in *The Hole* succumbs to her infection, scuttling across her wet floor on her hands and knees, drowning, in effect, in her own apartment. This is the becoming-fluid of Esther Williams through the looking glass: the water that is the surfeit of Taipei's material condition painfully disintegrates her body and her identity.[22]

If Tsai's musical presents a historical-image, it can be located precisely within his reformulation of the body as open to the outside.[23] For Foucault, the body is central to any genealogical critique. "History becomes 'effective,'" he writes, "to the degree that it introduces discontinuity into our very being—as it divides our emotions, dramatizes our instincts, multiplies our body and sets it against itself."[24] Rather than seeking the false objectivity of historical distance, the genealogical approach examines that which is closest, the details of everyday existence. The body is shaped by social conditions, transected by vectors of power, while at the same time remaining a potent site for resistance. One can read the descent of history through the excesses and anachronisms that mark both the bodies of beings and the bodies of spaces. The body is never a mere living fossil, however, but a conglomeration of contradictory forces that actively destroy that body. "Descent," Foucault writes, "attaches itself to the body. It inscribes itself in the nervous system, in temperament, in the digestive apparatus. . . . The body is the inscribed surface of events . . . , the locus of a dissociated Self . . . and a volume in perpetual disintegration."[25]

Deleuze and Guattari's description of becoming-other is similarly rooted in corporeality. It involves the meeting of disparate entities who form an alliance toward the realization of some goal. Becomings reassemble the core components of these molar identities, the very specificity of their bodies, forming "unnatural" unions that rupture, transect, and take flight from those stable positions. Becoming is transitory, but it is never imaginary. In their articulation of this process, Deleuze and Guattari propose a model of descent not driven by heredity, but by heterogeneous assemblages: "we oppose epidemic to filiation," Deleuze and Guattari write, ". . . peopling by contagion to sexual reproduction. . . . The difference is that contagion . . . involves terms that are entirely heterogeneous: for example, a human being, an animal, and a bacterium. . . . These combinations are neither genetic nor structural; they are interkingdoms, unnatural participations."[26]

The excesses and infections articulated through the body, while inducing illness and suffering, at the same time pose a threat to the unity of the larger system. Elizabeth Grosz writes about Bataille's formulation of excess that "dirt, disorder, contagion, expenditure, filth, immoderation—

and above all, shit—exceed the proper. . . . If the world of . . . regulated production, constitutes an economy . . . a world of exchange, use, and expedience, then there is an excess, a remainder, an uncontained element . . . an economy of excremental proliferations."[27]

Disease, filth, rain, insects, and abandoned architectural spaces are the uncontained elements within the economy of *The Hole*. The resistance they present, however, is far from transcendent. They mutate the body through illness, through flooding, painful acts of becoming-insect and becoming-fluid that push the body to its absolute limits. While many of the things bodies can do relate to the suffering of "excremental proliferations," the body also acts as a conduit or catalyst for movement and transformation. Eleanor Kaufman writes of Klossowski's work on Nietzsche, "The experience of the body in its extreme states (sex, sickness) provides access to an otherwise inaccessible realm of lucidity, one where the distinction between body and thought, between matter and energy, is momentarily suspended."[28] I would like to suggest that the musical body, the body engaged in the ornamental excesses of performance, enters into another type of extreme state. While this state is obviously quite distinct from that of sex or illness, the body-in-music posits another type of becoming, one that explores the limitations of corporeality, dissolves distinctions between interior and exterior, and forges new alliances between the bodies of living beings, objects, and environments.

Tsai combines a proliferation of irresolvable corporeal processes (becoming-insect, becoming-building, becoming-fluid, becoming–Grace Chang) within the singular figure of the woman downstairs. Her multiplied and impossible body bears the marks of history, yet it is also a site of emergence. That the destruction of the woman's body is accompanied by her more ecstatic musical multiplications results in a highly paradoxical formulation—we find here two simultaneous movements, one toward infestation, dissolution, and death, and the other toward music and pleasure. The hole in this context can be read not as a lack, but as a site of exchange; encounters are not governed by a moral mandate, but by chance and proximity, the creation of unnatural couplings, an ethics of alterity.[29]

In the finale of the film, the woman has been fully transformed by the virus. She crawls madly about the perimeter of her apartment, finally burying herself beneath a heap of tissue paper. The man upstairs, who has been watching, attempts to rouse her from her hiding place; he sobs uncontrollably. A hand descends from the hole, offering a glass of water and then lifting the woman upward. The final musical number begins, upstairs, where the couple dance. "I don't care who you are," Chang sings, "just hold me close." The film closes with a postscript from Tsai: "in the year 2000, we are grateful that we still have Grace Chang's songs to comfort us."

The hope that this ending might inspire is uncharacteristic for Tsai. The woman's rescue appears literally transcendent. To call Chang's songs comforting, too, is perhaps to suggest that music is a temporary (and ultimately futile) escape from the disease and alienation that define our contemporary condition. It is not necessary, however, to read the music here as merely escapist. The pleasure Chang's songs provide is not disconnected from historical reality, nor is it necessarily regressive, the soothing repetition of familiar formulas, false identities, and the certainty of a happy ending. Music here is created by the same system that destroys the body, but it also refuses to be contained. The culture industry, in the process of churning out pop songs and films, generates excesses and by-products that, while colored by their origins, are not necessarily faithful to them. Popular music, as one of those by-products, bears the marks of its historical genesis within the structures of commodity culture. It relies on formulas and clichés that repeatedly assert the fixity of gendered and raced identities. Yet popular music is also irreverent and irrepressible, generating contradictions and differences that seep through the borders of those identities. Unpredictable, fickle, and elusive, music—and film—are nevertheless powerful forces that, when actively engaged with, can provoke transformation, disrupting and destabilizing unified models of time, space, and identity.

Deleuze is careful to stress the contingent nature of becoming-other, which is necessarily embedded within the molarized bodies and systems that sustain life. If an entity is to resist death, it must continually engage in cycles of de- and reterritorialization. Becoming as such will never be fully divorced from territorialized existence, nor should it, if it is to maintain any real political viability. Tsai similarly links the destructive becomings of infection with the productive becomings of music. The error here would be to read either illness or the musical spectacle as a finale, for neither side can "win" without destroying the conditions necessary for existence itself.

For Nietzsche, if survival in the modern world is possible, the destructive thrust of the historical drive must be accompanied by the force of creation and a movement toward the future. He posits history as the "antithesis" of art, for history has only the power to destroy illusions and has no capacity to construct.[30] Art fabricates illusions, and these illusions may contribute to the metanarratives of a universalizing History. But when art is guided by an incisive perceptiveness, when it grasps the details of existence outside of obscuring generalizations, art can generate productive illusions. In concert, then, with genealogical history, the creative tendencies of art penetrate the minutiae that history unearths and, propelled by a similar resistance to teleological narratives, begin the work of crafting a new means of existence. Nietzsche writes,

> If the value of a drama lay solely in its conclusion, the drama itself would be merely the most wearisome and indirect way possible of reaching this goal; and so I hope that the significance of history will not be thought to lie in its general propositions, as if these were the flower and fruit of the whole endeavour, but that its value will be seen to consist in its taking a familiar, perhaps commonplace theme, an everyday melody, and composing inspired variations on it, enhancing it, elevating it to a comprehensive symbol, and thus disclosing in the original theme a whole world of profundity, power, and beauty.[31]

The musical spectacle, as a historical image, has the potential to serve a similar function. Rather than escaping from its material conditions, the spectacle excavates the excesses and detritus that a more proper history would leave buried. Through its musicality, the spectacle keys into the durations of the everyday, transforming them into suspended refrains. These refrains, like a cracked crystal, lay bare the strata of the past contained in the present, while rending that present open, at the same time, to the forces of the future.

Notes

1   Siegfried Kracauer, *The Mass Ornament: Weimar Essays*, trans. Thomas Y. Levin (Cambridge, Mass.: Harvard University Press, 1995), 75–76.
2   Ibid., 75.
3   Ibid.
4   Siegfried Kracauer, *Theory of Film* (New York: Oxford University Press, 1960), 149. As D. N. Rodowick notes, "the very forces that tend to paralyze social life, to reify it and give it the form of an object, are simultaneously, for Kracauer, the forces that energize it and generate in the *Lebenswelt* the constant possibility of unforeseen, even revolutionary, potentialities." See his *Reading the Figural, or Philosophy after the New Media* (Durham, N.C.: Duke University Press, 2001), 164.

5   Gilles Deleuze, *Cinema 2: The Time-Image*, trans. Hugh Tomlinson and Robert Galeta (Minneapolis: University of Minnesota Press, 1989), 64, 67.

6   See Catherine Williamson, "Swimming Pools, Movie Stars: The Celebrity Body in the Post-war Marketplace," *Camera Obscura* 38 (1996): 4–29, and Esther Williams with Digby Diehl, *Million Dollar Mermaid* (New York: Simon and Schuster, 1999).

7   Williams's work is not unique in this as I would locate this tendency, to greater or lesser degrees, in all backstage musicals, particularly in the impossible fluid spaces of the Busby Berkeley–style performance.

8   Deleuze, *Time-Image*, 60–61.

9   Ibid., 61.

10 Michel Foucault, "Nietzsche, Genealogy, History," in *Language, Counter-Memory, Practice: Selected Essays and Interviews*, trans. Donald F. Bouchard and Sherry Simon (Ithaca, N.Y.: Cornell University Press, 1977), 162.

11 See Williamson, "Swimming Pools," for a thorough account of the cross-marketing strategies attached to Esther Williams as an icon.

12 See Matthew Tinkcom, "'Working Like a Homosexual': Camp Visual Codes and the Labor of Gay Subjects in the MGM Freed Unit," *Cinema Journal* 35, no. 2 (1996): 24–42, and Leonard J. Leff, "'Come on Home with Me': *42nd Street* and the Gay Male World of the 1930s," *Cinema Journal* 39, no. 1 (1999): 3–22. See also D. A. Miller, *Place for Us: Essay on the Broadway Musical* (Cambridge, Mass.: Harvard University Press, 1998).

13 See Lucy Fischer, "The Image of Woman," and Lucy Fischer, "Designing Women: Art Deco, the Musical, and the Female Body," in *Music and Cinema*, ed. James Buhler, Caryl Flinn, and David Neumeyer (Hanover, N.H.: Wesleyan University Press, 2000), 295–315; see also Patricia Mellencamp, "Sexual Economics: *Gold Diggers of 1933*," Pamela Robertson, "Feminist Camp in *Gold Diggers of 1933*," and Linda Mizejewski, "Beautiful White Bodies," all anthologized in *Hollywood Musicals: The Film Reader*, ed. Steven Cohan (New York: Routledge, 2002).

14 This contradictory image of femininity clearly resonates with larger feminist debates about Deleuze's treatment of gender and sexuality, particularly Deleuze and Guattari's formulation of "becoming-woman." While I am not able to elaborate on these complex debates within this chapter, my argument is indebted to theorists such as Dorothea Olkowski and Elizabeth Grosz, who find clear correspondences between Deleuze and Guattari's work on becoming and feminist projects.

15 Gilles Deleuze and Félix Guattari, *A Thousand Plateaus: Capitalism and Schizophrenia*, trans. Brian Massumi (Minneapolis: University of Minnesota Press, 1987), 257.

16 See Tsai's director's notes included in the DVD edition of *What Time Is It There?* (Wellspring Media, 2004). Lee's nickname, Hsaio Kang, is used as his character name in several films, and the apartment interior the films repeatedly return to is his family's actual apartment in Taipei.

17 Many of these observations are echoed in Jean-Pierre Rehm, Olivier Jo-
yard, Danièle Rivière, and Tsai Ming-liang, *Tsaï Ming-liang*, trans. J. Ames
Hodges and Andrew Rothwell (Paris: Editions Dis Voir, 1999).

18 *Rebels of the Neon God*, Tsai's first feature film, has a recurrent, minimalist musical theme, a score that apparently was added at the insistence of
a producer. See Danièle Rivière, "Scouting," an interview with Tsai Ming-
liang, trans. Andrew Rothwell, in Hodges et al., *Tsaï Ming-liang*, 111.

19 David Walsh, interview with Tsai Ming-liang, *World Socialist*, October
7, 1998, June 6, 2003, http://www.wsws.org/arts/1998/oct1998/tsai-o07.
shtml.

20 Tsai, in a later interview, describes his work as limited to the surface of
the body: "but more and more now I think that my observation can only
be restricted to appearances, and never reach the inner character." Rivière,
"Scouting," 83.

21 Walsh, interview.

22 Perhaps it is not anecdotal to note here that *la fuite* of *la ligne de fuite*
can refer to a flight as well as to a leak. See John Rajchman, *The Deleuze
Connections* (Cambridge, Mass.: MIT Press, 2000), 12.

23 Rey Chow, "A Pain in the Neck, a Scene of 'Incest,' and Other Enigmas
of an Allegorical Cinema: Tsai Ming-liang's *The River*," *CR: The New
Centennial Review* 4, no. 1 (2004): 123–42, speaks in very similar terms
about *The River*: "I would propose that what Tsai has undertaken is a
production of discursivity, one that is not exactly geared toward a cen-
tralizable and thus summarizable logic, but that operates in the manner
of an archeological excavation. What is being excavated? The *remnants
of social relations*, which are presented by Tsai as *images with little or no
interiority*—in the form of bodies, gestures, movements, and looks."

24 Foucault, "Nietzsche," 154.

25 Ibid., 147–48.

26 Deleuze and Guattari, *Thousand Plateaus*, 241–42.

27 Elizabeth Grosz, *Architecture from the Outside: Essays on Virtual and
Real Space* (Cambridge, Mass.: MIT Press, 2001), 153. Grosz reads these
superfluous and unnecessary excesses in the context of architecture, positing excess and ornamentality—those things that serve no clear functional
purpose—as potential strategies for rethinking notions of space, and for
building spaces that would resist repressive systems. Grosz reads Bataille
with and against Irigaray in her theorization of "architectures of excess,"
contrasting Irigaray's femininity with Bataille's excrementality as an alternate excess that architecture fails to contain. While I am unable to pursue
this line of questioning here, Grosz's formulation suggests a provocative
means of reading the gendered nature of the excesses produced within the
space of the musical, and *The Hole*, in particular.

28 Eleanor Kaufman, "Klossowski or Thoughts-Becoming," in *Becomings:*

Explorations in Time, Memory, and Futures, ed. Elizabeth Grosz (Ithaca, N.Y.: Cornell University Press, 1999), 151.

29 I am also particularly interested in the correlations between *The Hole* and Tsai's *The River*. Here, the body of the male lead is infected through his encounter with water, and he is ravaged by an unexplainable pain in his neck, a pain that cripples and contorts his body. There is no musical comfort to be found in *The River*, however, and the boy's journey leads him to a far darker site of exchange—an incestuous encounter with his own father.

30 See Friedrich Nietzsche, "On the Uses and Disadvantages of History for Life," in *Untimely Meditations*, ed. Daniel Breazeale, trans. R. J. Hollingdale (Cambridge: Cambridge University Press, 1997), 95.

31 Ibid., 92–93.

Part V. Futures

15. Deleuze's Time, or How the Cinematic Changes Our Idea of Art

John Rajchman

After the War

How does the cinematic change our idea of art? Citing Paul Valery, Walter Benjamin begins his great 1934 essay on mechanical reproduction with this question. The problem was not so much whether cinema is an art, the so-called seventh one, but how, starting in the nineteenth century, it helped transform what we think art is, and in particular, how one thinks in the arts or with the arts. For Benjamin already, the problem of the cinematic was inseparable from the whole question, at once aesthetic and political, of how one thinks with the new mass industrial audiovisual means of film and projection.

We might think of Deleuze as taking up this question again after World War II, when there arose not simply a new cinema in France, but also new styles of thinking—a new "image of thought." The "upheaval in general sensibility" that followed the war would lead to "new dispositions of thought."[1] Filmmakers invented new ways of thinking with film and projection at the same time as others, in other domains, started to invent related ideas, creating a whole new zone of interference and exchange. Deleuze's two volumes on cinema are a monumental attempt to see the new European cinema in terms of this constellation, to isolate the notions of image, space, and time they involved, and so show the distinctive ways filmmakers took part in this larger mutation in thought.

Even though Deleuze wrote his study of cinema in the 1980s, the basic philosophical notions he uses go back to his 1956 essay on the problem of difference in Bergson, written at a time when Alain Resnais was making documentaries like his great study of Van Gogh's suicide as well as, of course, *Night and Fog*. These films would play a key role in Deleuze's analysis of cinema and, in particular, for the principle that "the cinematographic image is never in the present."[2] Deleuze thought Resnais had perhaps gone the furthest in this principle, for in his documentaries, as well as in the fiction-films he would go on to make, we find not only new kinds of images, but also a new function for them: that of rendering a past, at once indeterminate and violent, irreducible to anyone's memory, any *prise de conscience.*

The war is thus a dividing point not only for Deleuze's inventory of new signs and images in cinematic thinking, but also, at the same time, for his sense of a particular problem in postwar philosophy and in his philosophy: the problem of the peculiar "time that takes thought."[3] In effect, cinema makes visible the problem philosophy developed at the same time, for which Deleuze himself would try to work out a new logic of "events" and their sense. If, especially in France, postwar cinema developed in tandem with postwar philosophy, following its peculiar twists and turns through psychoanalysis and structuralism, it was because, Deleuze suggests, postwar cinema was itself an original audiovisual way of thinking—a peculiar relation of thought to *aisthesis*, a whole aesthetics. That is why the great filmmakers needed to be confronted not simply with writers or painters, but also, at the same time, with thinkers and questions of thought. The signs and images they invented involved a new sense of what a creative image is and what it means to think. Even the crisis in cinema brought on by television, and then by digital images, had to be posed on this aesthetic level as a problem of images that do not force us to think, or that keep us from thinking, as with the "presentifying" tendencies Deleuze saw in most television.[4] "What I call Ideas are images that make one think," Deleuze declared at the start of his study.[5] To write about cinema was to identify these images and to examine the larger "apparatuses" or *dispositifs* through which cinema manages to pose them.[6] The problem of the new televisual-digital regime must be analyzed in this way and not simply "media-logically," as, more generally, in Deleuze's approach to the question of technology and, in particular, to the problems of information and control to which his study of cinema led him. For machines, unlike simple mechanisms, always have an indeterminate sensory or aesthetic component through which they participate in larger fields, larger sorts of arrangements of our senses, our bodies and brains. Cinema is a way of having ideas with images that introduces a new "psychomechanics," a new way of affecting us and our nervous systems. Central to this arrangement was the invention of new determinations of space and time as forms of sensibility in relation to thinking. At the heart of Deleuze's analysis of cinematic images and their *dispositifs*, we find the problem of a determination of a time no longer defined by succession (past, present, future), of a space no longer defined by simultaneity (distinct elements in closed or framed space), and of a permanence no longer based in eternity (instead given as a form of a complex variation).[7] Such were the new sorts of images that postwar filmmakers gave us to think with, and with which they started to work themselves.

Deleuze, then, might have responded to Valery's question in the following way. Cinema changed the idea of art because of the new ways it invented to show or render movement and time, participating in a distinctive manner in a larger aesthetics of duration, connected not simply with new technologies or new forces, but also with new ways of thinking, new questions and paradoxes, new political uses. Across all the arts, whether "expanded" or not, we see these changes, these new sorts of determinations of space and time, this larger aesthetics, in which filmmaking, starting in its early spaces, and with its early means, would play a key role.[8] As earlier with Walter Benjamin, there was a Kantian element in this aesthetic field, but one that comes from Deleuze's new reading of Kant or his new idea of the sense in which we are still Kantian. Indeed, the crucial distinction between time and movement elaborated in the books on cinema is first introduced in *Difference and Repetition*, in which Deleuze proposes to see as central to Kant's revolution the problem of a "time out of joint." Later, Deleuze would declare that the war offered cinema the condition to effectuate its own Kantian revolution in a much shorter interval, its own audiovisual way of freeing the idea of time from subordination to any prior movement, any extensive space.[9]

Kant had already taken space and time as forms of intuition or as a priori conditions of an *aisthesis*, or of what he already called "sensibilia." The forms of sensation are thus distinct from the categories of the understanding and can only be linked to them through the workings of a mysterious "schematism" or through the "productive imagination." What matters for Deleuze is the independence of these forms from the understanding and not the way they figure in a unified consciousness. In freeing time from its subordination to the identities of movement in a closed world, and in associating it with forces or virtualities of another sort, the great postwar filmmakers would thus free the forms of sensibilia themselves from any such schematic link with the understanding, making them, instead, a matter of artistic experimentation or invention in relation to another kind of thinking—precisely that of "ideas." The "time that takes thought" would be freed from categories of causality or even teleology; the postwar filmmakers would link it, instead, to a whole new relation to character, milieu, space, and action. What is new in Kant for Deleuze, then, is how, with the disjunction between our sensibilia and our categories for understanding substance or causality, there arises a new experimental zone where other sorts of determinations of space and time (as when, in music or literature, one "occupies without measuring" a sensory milieu) are linked to ideas.[10] Dostoevsky's "Idiot," for example, not only moves in a much altered novelistic space and time, but in the process, is also obliged to think, just because there are no schemata to govern his actions—a situation Deleuze sees Kurosawa later exploring in cinema. The cinematic lies in the distinctive ways filmmakers invented to disjoin the forms of sensation from the understanding, using them, instead, to give us "ideas" and so new "personae" in thinking, like the Idiot. We see this, for example, in Deleuze's demonstration of how Marguerite Duras or Straub-Huillet turned the disjunction between sound and visual images into a veritable "idea in cinema," a whole new exploration of the peculiar postwar intersection of "stories without places" and "places without stories."[11] Indeed, it is precisely this sort of "nonrelation" between what we see and what we say that shows why it is so misleading to think of cinema as language, rather than as a "signaletic material." Deleuze was no textualist or narratologist; the signs and images he finds in cinema are given by no theory of language or code; rather, in each case, they are the result of a singular invention. Even in literature, he thought we should look not to linguistics or narratology, but rather, to the ways great writers invent a "foreign language" in our language, tied up with the invention of new percepts and affects, as with the "complicated time" in Proust, or the "crack-up" of the characters in Fitzgerald, or their peculiar relation to a "secret past" in Henry James's short stories, later exploited in film by Joseph Mankiewicz. The cinematic, in short, is this strange, great complex of signs and images that filmmakers invented to explore the problem that arises when space and time, regarded as forms of our sensibilia, are disjoined from the schemata that tie them to our understanding and are linked, instead, to another kind of thinking, governed by logic not of propositions and truths, but of the sense (and non-sense) of what is happening to us.

Deleuze's study of cinema was his attempt to elaborate this problem at once philosophical and aesthetic. He saw filmmakers as developing an original way of exploring what Kant called the "paradox of inner sense," or of the peculiar way we can be said to be "in time"—a problem in which he thought Resnais had gone further than Proust or Bergson. The question of the sense in which we are "in time" was, of course, also a central one in modern philosophy; in his books on film, Deleuze takes up this issue by contrasting the ways Husserl and Bergson each formulate it in relation to science and mathematics. Husserl still imagined the forms of space and time as being centered in a consciousness, whereas Bergson offered a new idea of image freed from this assumption, closer to the way filmmakers explore acentered spaces prior to anyone's point of view. The cinematic is found in images that make visible or palpable this "acentered" condition or that "sensibilize" us to it. The images in cinema are thus forms that explore a strange sort of movement in our lives that is irreducible to translation in extended space, the lines of which are freed from starting and ending points, instead tracing trajectories, at once fictive and real, in indeterminate milieus; they thus call for a time or a duration based not in chronology and succession, but rather, in an interlocking topology or overlapping seriality. That is how cinema posed the question of how we actually think, how we are oriented and disoriented in thinking, in our lives, our relations with ourselves, and to one another. In *Cinema 1* and *Cinema 2*, Deleuze tried to analyze how, through the possibilities of camera movement, framing, editing, and projecting, cinema would invent a whole new "psychomechanical" way to make visible such times and spaces in our worlds, situations, or milieus, prior to (and immanent in) our conscious selves as individuals or groups.

The principle that "the cinematographic image is never in the present," for which Deleuze would find such a striking application in the troubling "sheets of time" in *Night and Fog*, was thus part of a larger transformation in the very idea of image itself in all the arts, in painting, photography, or literature as well as new practices that would break away from such traditional media. We know, for example, that Soviet cinema would be seen to play a key role in the process in the 1920s and 1930s that Walter Benjamin analyzed in the avant-garde when he spoke of the new function of author as producer.[12] At the same time, the principle of "not being in the present" was a philosophical matter that concerned the very concept of image and the way it presents things before they are represented for a unified subject or consciousness. Deleuze's conception of "images" in cinema breaks from the idea that they are inner representations in our minds or brains, linking them, instead, with new questions explored in neurology and psychology—fields of knowledge, including especially psychoanalysis, with which cinema would have so many relations throughout the nineteenth and twentieth centuries.[13] To introduce movement and time into the very idea of image was inseparable from a long neuroscientific literature of how images figure in our bodies or brains, or in the ideas of consciousness and unconsciousness, in which the new memory sciences played a key role, as, for example, in Deleuze's discussion of Pierre Janet. Indeed, that is how the "cinematic," regarded as a way of thinking with the forms of sensibilia, could be seen to extract itself from the great stupefying explosion of images in our lives that mechanical reproduction facilitated (before the "control" of the postwar information-type machines) with its cliché pictures and ordered words and its relations with propaganda or advertising. If, as Deleuze proposes, the invention of a cinematic sensibilia arises from the crisis in psychology concerning the status of image, it is developed through and within the new industrial mass means that we see, at the same time, in the psychological or social sciences.

In philosophy, already in the 1920s, Martin Heidegger had shown how time and the problem of "inner sense" were central to the Kantian enterprise and to his own attempt to move beyond its still metaphysical enclosure. But Deleuze's writings on difference in Bergson suggested a fresh way of taking up the question of time, which moves away from Heidegger's idea of a constitutive finitude or the "*Dasein*" of a *Volk* disclosed in and through the work of art. Deleuze tried to develop an ungrounded element in the kind of time and movement the cinematic image makes visible. In cinema, as in philosophy, he discovers something at once inhuman and vital. It is already to be seen in the kind of movement Vertov explored through the intervals in his editing or "montage," or with the ability of the camera to capture "acentered" worlds with "indeterminate" zones, for example, in Orson Welles. He tried to work out an original notion of world the way it appears, closer to Liebnizian perspectivism than to Husserlian grounding in a life-world, with which cinema would be peculiarly concerned. Cinema not only invents images; it surrounds them with a world—a world that, for Deleuze, has become light or deterritorialized, irreducible to our "being-there."

We are thus "in time" in a peculiar way, irreducible to the familiar division between subjective (or lived) and objective (or clocked) time. The problem is, rather, how we are affected by time and "affect ourselves through it" at once objectively and subjectively; it is the problem of time itself as this uncontrollable potential in who we are or may become. The function of cinematic images is to show the workings of this time in our lives and our worlds. That is why the time-images in cinema are ones that defeat the presumed coincidence of subjective and objective images on which a whole tradition of story or narrative has rested; rather, such relations between space and viewing are undone as description of space frees itself from the presumption of a single objective viewpoint, and the form of narration frees itself from domination of a single narrative voice, as if in a free, indirect style. The forms of description and narration, in other words, depend on the role of mobility and indetermination in the images, and so with the sense and non-sense of what is happening. In Bergson (as well as in the Russian city of Vertov's *Man with a Movie Camera*), Deleuze finds a multiple, moving universe in which things appear without appearing as such *to* anyone, or to any one point of view. He finds images that make visible a world that cannot be united or made fully present to our conscious selves, the sense of which is nevertheless unfolded in time, through movement and the forms of sensibilia that are images. It is such a world of illumination without revelation that would later be taken up in time-image cinema. The topological superposition of "sheets of time" in Resnais shows, in particular, in a vivid way, the sense in which a terrible past coexists with the present, in a manner irreducible to flashbacks or conscious recollection, rendering the present uncertain, forcing us to think, dispossessing us of our ability to say "I" or "We." Time is no longer either a matter of Man's finitude or of God's infinite understanding—neither humanist nor salvationist, it is directly linked to questions of life and death themselves.[14]

In exploring how, through the means available to it, cinema makes sensible this kind of time in worlds, Deleuze thus develops an original view of space and time as forms of sensibilia that cause us to think. He frees those forms from their Kantian subordination to what he saw as the two great functions played by the philosophical idea of the subject—the functions of "consciousness" and "individualization."[15] The world that cinema shows us is an impersonal (or "pre-personal") world prior to consciousness and individualization. In this way, cinema takes part in Deleuze's larger attempt to put the question of "a life" in the place of the classical notion of the subject or the self—a life that contrasts precisely with "*the* life of the corresponding individual," as with the conscious self, yet remains as a concrete question and possibility for our bodies, as for our brains.[16] Thus the *espaces quelconques*, or "any-spaces-whatever," that Deleuze isolates especially in postwar cinema (as well as in "structural film") involve spatial and temporal distributions that are indeterminate, or *quelconque*, just in the sense that they precede the supposed unities of conscious selfhood, or of static, grouped, definite, or definable individuality, exposing worlds, situations, or milieus prior to them. Indeed, that is why any-spaces-whatever are populated with a new, less definite kind of character and action that requires a new art of indefinite description, realistic without being naturalistic. Cinema thus maps the workings of a time once preindividual and unconscious. Deleuze offers an inventory of images that show this time, irreducible to destiny, providence, causality, or predictability, even statistical or probabilistic, which nevertheless affects us in ways we do not normally perceive. Such is the sort of time given by series and juxtapositions (rather than succession) and by indeterminate spaces of displacements and departures (rather than a "situated" intersubjectivity or world). It is the kind of temporality that requires a change in nature of belief—a turn to a more pragmatist belief-in-the-world, without need for salvation or historical destiny.

We see this time already in *Night and Fog*. Resnais's juxtapositions of a past shown through black-and-white archival materials, with a present given by cinematic mapping of mental spaces (in color and with his famous tracking shots of the peculiar mental spaces of the concentration camps), and with the uncertain future given through Cayrol's famous voice-over, thus form an early dramatic part in the constitution of cinema as a postwar kind of audiovisual thinking. If, as Deleuze argues, in this great documentary, we can see the sum of the different ways of avoiding "the piety of the recollection image," it is because of the way image and thinking discover in it a new relation to the past and the way it figures in the present. The aim is no longer to recapture or recollect the past in a consciousness, individual or collective, which would have succeeded it, but on the contrary, to prevent any such closure within private memory or public commemoration, showing, rather, the sense in which it is still at work in the present. This function that affects fiction as well as documentary, undoing the usual distinctions between the two, forms part of the new "realism" in postwar cinema that Deleuze contrasts with an earlier naturalism. Indeed, Resnais would go on in his great fiction films to explore this past coiled within the present that seems to haunt our banal lives like a terrible secret; he would explore how it forces his characters to think, as if they had come back from the dead, moving about in a world without salvation or redemption, providence, or phenomenological grounding. He would thus pose a

new question, at once philosophical and cinematic, in which, across
a whole range of arts and practices, Deleuze sought to introduce into
the very idea of an image what it means to think in and with images
in a mass industrial society.

Cinema Today

Today it would seem that the situation of cinema is no longer quite
what it was for Deleuze in 1984, any more than it was for Walter
Benjamin in 1934. Cinema is no longer alone; it no longer has the key
role that fell to it between silent film and television. It forms part of
a larger complex of images and spaces, where it discovers new roles
to play, geared to altered geographies and responding to new forces
on a global scale—Deleuze now belongs to World rather than simply
European cinema. As with anything new, there is nostalgic talk of a
"postcinematic" condition. The history of film has itself become a
matter not simply of preservation and distribution, but also of an art
of obsolescence that looks back to what it has been, as if illustrating
Marshall McLuan's old dictum that when a technological medium
is over, it is turned into an art. Deleuze himself tried to resist such
nostalgia back in 1984, when there was already much talk of a crisis
of cinema. His quarrel with Godard on the last pages of *Cinema 2* is
one indication. The crisis meant not death of cinema (its corpse to be
put into edited *histories* in melancholic anticipation of a more hopeful
time), but rather, new possibilities inseparable from the larger fate of
the kind of aesthetic thinking Deleuze had tried precisely to work out
in cinema. The time had come to ask not simply, what is cinema? but
also, and more importantly, what is philosophy? The great filmmakers
had used new technical means to invent a mode of an audiovisual way
of thinking, which formed part of a larger aesthetic, to which it then
seemed important for Deleuze to turn. What in fact does it mean to
"have an idea" in and with the arts, in relation to other arts and other
practices? This is the larger problem that Deleuze would go on to explore, together with Félix Guattari, in *What Is Philosophy?*

This problem of "thinking in and with the arts" is already to be
found in Deleuze's treatment of the abstract, experimental, or expanded
cinema traditions, which tried to use filmic techniques in ways closer to
the practices of the visual arts. While Deleuze does not focus on these
traditions, what he does say is suggestive. He was drawn to Artaud's
enthusiasm in the 1930s for silent film (as seen in his own role in Carl
Dreyer's great *Joan of Arc*), when he argued for the superiority of such

works with respect to an abstract cinema still content to ape developments in painting as too "cerebral." Artaud thought that the peculiar "witchcraft" of silent film was much closer to the "cruelty" in gesture and word that he was seeking in the theater, and Deleuze sees this idea as part of a larger invention of "theatricality" peculiar to cinema, as seen in "bodily attitudes" and their relation to time, explored in different ways in many arts. Abstract and experimental film figures in Deleuze's study when, not content to imitate what other arts are doing, it takes part in the ways the cinematic changes our ideas of theater or art, as Deleuze thought was the case for structural film in its relations with the "perception-image."[17] In other words, abstract film is not abstract in a simple modernist or self-referential sense, but rather, in the ways it experiments with the very spatiotemporal conditions of sensibilia and thought themselves that the great postwar filmmakers exploited for their own purposes, and in that sense, it is quite concrete. Indeed, the very term *espaces quelconques*, which Deleuze develops in a striking way, for example, in his discussion of Antonioni, derives from experimental film. It is not hard to imagine extending the problem of empty, disconnected spaces that Deleuze already sees in another way in Bresson to a range of other arts and art practices around the same time as structural film. Rather than a stark opposition between narrative and abstract work, there is an exchange or connection made on the basis of common exploration of forms of sensibility, explored at the same time in different ways in many arts at once. It is perhaps something like this larger exchange that we see today in a situation in which cinema no longer dominates or in which it is no longer alone. What, then, would it mean to take up Deleuze's idea of the cinematic today, in altered circumstances, in relation to current or contemporary questions and to new wars and kinds of war? What role might cinema and philosophy yet play in a situation that some have perhaps been too quick to characterize as "postcinematic" and "posttheoretical"?

I would like to look at how this question might be formulated in relation to the visual arts. How did the cinematic, regarded as a postwar *dispositif* to render the workings of time, help transform the very idea of the "visual" in the visual arts? And in what ways does it continue to be involved in the new "conditions of visibility" of today? No doubt, this is itself a complex question, with several parts that go off in a number of directions. First, there is the whole question of how to think with movement- and time-images. In what ways have they changed our understanding of what might be called "unmoving pictures"? How do questions of time and movement change the very idea or sense of images in painting, photography, or drawing as well as our ways of seeing and talking about such things? Such questions have been explored in a variety of domains: in Eisenstein's discussion of Asian scroll paintings as well as the Corbusian "architectural promenade"; with the study of movement in Klee's *Pedagogical Sketchbooks* or with Duchamp's gestalt-defeating Rotoreliefs and his descending nude; and in another way, in certain practices of kinetic art or in futurism. More recently, they have been taken up by Yves Michaud in his analysis of Aby Warburg's *Atlas* and his related Beaubourg theme show about "Images on the Move."[18] Deleuze himself develops this question, of course, through his account of how Francis Bacon renders the forces of time in relation to figures through the asignifying zones of possibility in the "pictorial facts."

Even Deleuze's treatment of the "expanded" sensibilities in structural film in terms of "molecular perception" and the role of drugs can itself be read along these lines, or again in his account of the peculiar bodily, sexed, or gendered theatricality of duration explored not simply by Andy Warhol, but also by Chantal Akerman, whose encounter with the experimentations in art and film in New York in the 1960s helped determine her own approach to questions of time in cinema and, later, in her installations. At the same time, there is perhaps something peculiarly "Asian" in the fixed frame and long duration, which Deleuze works out in Ozu, to be found in the early cinema techniques to which Warhol returned, and more generally, in the priority Deleuze accords time with respect to narration; indeed, Wu Hung has recently argued for a kind of protocinematic sense in Asian hand scroll paintings.[19] We find a related strategy in Deleuze's own treatment of the encounters of cinema with old masters' painting, as, for example, the striking pages in *The Time-Image* in which Deleuze connects the problem of depth of field in Orson Welles's invention of time-images to the decenterings of space in the Baroque, as read by Heinrich Wofflin. There are also many references to modernist painting, as, for example, with the way the whole problem of the "inhuman" in Cezanne's sensations would be taken up in turn by Vertov and the Kinoks, or again, in the way that close-ups and affection-images in Eisenstein's films may be analyzed in terms of the questions of pathos or "faciality"—a key point of encounter with Deleuze's book on Francis Bacon, who himself was struck by images from *Battleship Potemkin* in his effort to paint the scream, not the horror.

A context and impetus today for going back to look at such encounters of cinema with the visual arts is the wave of interest in moving pictures in art-spaces today. Assisted by technical and distribution
possibilities that appeared only after Deleuze wrote his cinema books,
filmmakers and artists now have a new exhibition arena outside the
traditional darkened room of the movie theater or familial televisual
viewing-spaces. Raymond Bellour and Giuliana Bruno have each analyzed the role of the actual room and its architecture in such practices and
in their relation to earlier forms or *dispositifs* of image-installation.[20] Let
me add to their analyses two brief remarks about how Deleuze's general
picture of having ideas in cinema might be used in these circumstances.
First, there is the issue of how the new uses of art-spaces to exhibit time
intersect with larger questions of movement and time themselves that
Deleuze develops in relation to postwar cinema; it is perhaps significant
that while Deleuze wrote nothing about such practices, his work remains
popular among certain artists working with them, for example, Pierre
Huyghe. On the other hand, these practices are tied up with the larger
process through which "contemporary" came to be distinguished from
"modern" art or art-practices. Visual art and art-spaces played key
roles in the 1960s in a series of attempts to free the idea of art from
a series of distinctions in which it had seemed enclosed—from traditional media and skills, from studio production, and from exhibition
in "white cube" spaces as well as from traditional divisions of art from
mass or popular culture, from critical discourse, or from information
or everyday life. Cinema participated in these movements, in Robert
Smithson's questions of site and nonsite, the violence of Matta-Clark's
"anarchitecture," or in another way, in Hélio Oiticica's interventions.
Current work must also be understood in relation to such changes. In
contrast to, say, Godard (who is still making great films), Pierre Huyghe
uses film as part of a range of practices similar to the ways in which
he uses Japanese manga images, introduces advertising signs in urban
spaces, or orchestrates participation in parades.

Deleuze had posed the question of projection in terms of the larger
dispositif of camera movement, framing, and editing as they appear in the
early history of film and are then transformed. He was interested in how
projection-practices, along with editing and framing, freed themselves
from the conventions of "natural perception" (and from the mimetic
conception of projection itself) to invent new sorts of images affecting
our nervous systems. We see that from the start, there is a sense in which
the screen was less an illusionist window or ersatz classical stage than

a moving frame with an "out-of-frame" that allows movement and time to be rendered in new ways that would move beyond the conceptions of space in classical painting or theater, or suggest alternatives to them. Thus Deleuze argues that the relation of cinema to a classical theater-space (and "theatricality") is poorly posed as a matter of a loss of, or substitution for, live presence; rather, we find a new *dispositif* for creating images and spaces (and so of "having ideas") with links or interferences with one another, which are connected to the two great efforts in theater to create new kinds of image and space—Artaud's theater of cruelty and Brecht's epic theater, each of which are related to the cinematic exploration of time in "bodily attitudes."[21] Using the techniques of shooting, editing, and projecting, cinema found a peculiar way to undercut the divisions between objective and subjective viewpoints, or between the sound- and image-space, to explore other spaces and times, which, even in darkened rooms, can strike our nervous systems in ways that are just as intense or cruel as live performances themselves, which can often seem rather more predictable. If we try, then, to set current practices in a larger history of "theatrical uses" of exhibition-spaces, we need to include the whole problem in terms of the question of "images that force us to think," which Deleuze worked out in postwar cinema.

The darkened room of theatrical cinema might be seen, then, as one highly successful *dispositif* in a larger history of image installation, itself conceived in terms of different ways of thinking in the arts. In this role, it became a laboratory to fabricate creative images—images to free our brains from patterns of clichés or order-words, which in turn serve to control our perceptions and affects, reducing them to easily identifiable opinions. Just as the filmic image is not, for Deleuze, a code or a language, but rather, an original way of expressing times and spaces that cannot be contained in natural perception or affection, so filmic-space, even in the darkened room, is more than a simple story-and-illusion apparatus. It is rather a *dispositif* that introduces a new "psychomechanics" that directly affects the brain, as Eisenstein and then Artaud imagined, and to which Jean-Louis Scheffer would later attest in his picture of the postwar cinema goer. The cinematic "autonomization" of images offered new ways to think, and to make visible, the role of time and space in thinking, and, indeed, it is just from this angle that Deleuze takes up the question of cinema as a mass, industrial art. Deleuze himself had already analyzed the whole question of rendering a "complicated time" in signs and images in relation to a new kind of "intelligence" learned without prior method—an intelligence that always "comes after" through encounters that force us to think—in his study of "signs" in the Proustian novel.[22] But when the same sort of problem (and notion of sign) is transferred, via the cinematic, to mass society, this kind of artistic intelligence encounters at the same time new enemies and rivals and must be inserted into new circuits. It must also contend with a new conception of the public (typified in TV ratings), a "statistical public" characterized by a whole new professionalization of vision and a new massive machine of control over what we can see and say, and so think and do. In this way, Deleuze argues that, after the war, Syberberg goes beyond Walter Benjamin's preoccupations with mechanical reproduction and aura to ask, more generally, how cinema can create relations or arrangements of seeing, saying, and acting irreducible to larger arrangements of information, communication, and its publics.[23] It is also why he thinks the history of cinema is a long "martyrology" in the struggle to create new images, and why there is so often in cinema the dramatization of a conspiracy against this attempt—an ongoing battle with the institutional forces of mediocrity in which an encounter with the visual arts or visual art-spaces can offer one avenue of escape. The problem of cinema as mass art, "postindustrial" as well as "industrial," is not simply a matter of the role that the cinematic *dispositif* figures in changing technical machines of production and reception; at the same time, it has to with the very idea of "mass" itself—to the changing relations between having ideas and "collective arrangements of enunciation," and hence between intellectuals and the masses. What is distinctive for postwar time-image cinema for Deleuze, in this regard, is a new political principle, seen in altered relations between filmmakers and their actors and publics. Unlike the "mass-subject" of an Eisensteinian epic or the "subjected masses" of a Leni Riefenstahl rally, or the much calculated numbers of a Hollywood blockbuster, the problem Deleuze associates with "thinking with cinema"—and in a singular way, thinking with time-image cinema—is that "the people are missing"; they must yet be invented along with making the film itself. In his analysis of the new relations of directors to actors—as well as to their publics—in "minority" and "third world" cinema, Deleuze tries to work out these changes, at once aesthetic and political. His sense of Straub-Huillet as great "political" filmmakers is a striking case of this view, as is his account of how the very idea of "minority" breaks open the whole genre of ethnographic and documentary films toward new aesthetic forms, beyond the fiction-document division. "Mass" becomes indeterminate, irreducible to "class," at the same time as there arises new ways of making it visible. We might imagine extending this idea to the global situation of the cinematic today, where, for example, beyond the division of fiction and documentary, artists or filmmakers invent images to get at "events" where an often violent, indeterminate past is tied up with the "fabulation" of peoples irreducible to fixed classes or groups, or related religious divisions or "clashes of civilization," moving in and across borders. Deleuze's study of postwar cinema may be read as a kind of aesthetic workbook for the question of the multiplication of such situations in cinema and in their relation with the visual arts and visual art-spaces.

New Analyses

How, then, does cinematic change our idea of art? What would it mean to take up this question again today in new situations, for example, in relation to transformations in the visual arts? What role might theory or philosophy yet play with respect to notions of art to which the cinematic might be linked? To what kinds of new uses might we put his larger problem of "showing time" through images that "cause us to think"? In what ways, in the process, might we refashion the larger postwar image of thought that underlies Deleuze's analysis? One side of such questions concerns the style of analysis Deleuze forges in these volumes.

In the first place, there is a question of method. While Deleuze's books range over the entire history of cinema since the late nineteenth century, and are shot through with many historical, technical, social, and political arguments, they are not themselves history books or the books of an historian. They have another selective aim: to extract from the generality of films those singular nonlinguistic signs and images invented by great filmmakers to express time or movement in our own situations, milieus, or worlds. They are thus not ahistorical; rather, they are abstract in another way, tied not to eternity, but with the present and new problems, at once artistic and philosophical, brought with it. It seems important to preserve this experimental aesthetic zone of questioning with which history is linked but to which it is not reduced.

In Deleuze's case, the new problems intersect in an increasingly complex spiral around the questions of time and thinking that link postwar cinema to philosophy (and the "theory" to which it gave rise). In this way, the war itself becomes more than an event in historical, legal, or religious discourses. It becomes, at the same time, an "aesthetic" matter—a turning point in the very nature of the images and having ideas in which the cinematic would play a key role, especially, but not exclusively, in France. Thus the war—*this* war (with its mass destruction, its shame, the terrible secrets it left within and with respect to official histories)—figured in postwar cinema not simply in the manner in which Paul Virilio analyzes it as a "field of vision" or as a technological and propaganda machine, anticipating the real-time wars of today, but precisely as the kind of upheaval in sensibility that called for the invention of new "dispositions of thought." Cinema would play a key role in the invention of a postwar aesthetic, exploring the ways a violent and indeterminate past figures in our very psyches, the very way we think in the early films of Resnais, for example, in the Boulogne-Algeria relations of *Muriel* as well as, of course, in *Hiroshima Mon Amour*.[24] For along with camps, the questions of decolonization that the war brought with it belonged to that aspect of the past with which cinema was concerned. Beyond his work with Marguerite Duras, this is what links Resnais, in documentary and fiction, to the larger sort of question developed in literature by Maurice Blanchot, who had his own sense of "not-being-in-the-present," tied up with the disaster that would befall the very possibility of friendship in thought or of the "philia" in philosophy. The philosophical concepts Deleuze forges in cinema (the new sense of the image itself in its relations with fact, truth, and "realism" as well as ourselves, our bodies and brains, characters, and situations, the new spaces they inhabit, no longer governed by sensorimotor schemata, the new relation of thinking to history or narrative) no doubt come from this situation; they are not reduced to it. Indeed, that is one reason why Deleuze insisted that the overlapping inventions and problems that he was trying to get at "in cinema" nevertheless had to be fabricated independently of it and its history, in relation to other practices and inventions yet to come. To extract the peculiar kinds of philosophical invention that Deleuze called "concepts" is to give them a life of their own, as indeed with the many earlier philosophical inventions that, apart from Bergson, Deleuze himself mobilizes in the course of his study. Theory departs from history in this way just when it ceases to be a reflective metadiscipline (as still with Kant) and instead becomes a source of new questions, encounters, interferences, and exchanges, which cast older problems in a new light. That is what Deleuze seems to have in mind when he declares that "the life and survival" of cinema lies in its struggles with the informational regime of control he feared, and which constituted a new rival to the very activity of thinking.

Deleuze's film books are thus not themselves narratives, and to take up the problems or concepts that they work out in cinema does not require that one insert oneself in any one story or history. They can be (and, indeed, have already been) used in many different ones. Not a history of cinema, Deleuze's film books are rather "montage books" of a roving philosophical spirit that tries to introduce into the criticism (or reading) of film something of the collage approach and the "stratigraphic time" that Deleuze had worked out for the history of philosophies, as in his famous image of a "nomad" style of thinking. He thought there no more exists an intrinsic narrative in the history of the arts than in the history of philosophy, whose melancholy themes have long tended to overdetermine what Deleuze took to be the false problem of the "end of art" (or "the end of philosophy"). Part of the force of fabricating concepts "in cinema" for uses outside of it was precisely to free them from the sort of intrinsic or internalizing history, or with the sense that cinema is a fixed language or medium whose only critical gesture would be to examine itself. The critical relation of the fabrication of concepts to the present is of a different sort. It is more a matter of introducing new histories into given ones. It supposes that there exist situations in which the usual stories no longer suffice, and where monolithic histories start to break off into many complicated paths. In this respect, the cinema books continue the strategy of many overlapping "rubrics" that Deleuze adopts in his study of Francis Bacon, each going off in different directions, with sometimes unrecognized precursors and unforeseen applications, such that (in one such rubric) he can declare that each new painter recapitulates the history of painting in his or her own way. Against the search for a single great story or history in art or philosophy, reflected in the great nineteenth-century European dream of a great encyclopedic Library or Museum containing all words and images in ordered sequence, Deleuze opposed a new sort of pedagogy of images and concepts to complexify the present, disrupting its classificatory presuppositions in a process from which the invention of new kinds of images and thoughts is always emerging.

Deleuze adopts two interrelated principles in his cinema books to exemplify this approach. The first says that "all criticism is comparative," and one must thus examine the cinematic in its larger overlaps with other arts and practices since there is "no work that doesn't have its continuation or its beginning in others."[25] The second, found in the last sentences of his study, asserts that "it is on the level of interferences with many practices that things happen, beings, images, concepts, all kinds of events."[26] Together, they encapsulate a preoccupation in Deleuze's writings in the 1980s with a reactive moment associated with the idea of "postmodernism," in which, as if unable to create any further movement, thinking would retreat back into metareflection or meta-art, or else ironic reappropriations of past inventions. The notion of "interferences and resonances" worked out in this analysis of the signs and images of cinema, and then developed in *What Is Philosophy?*, may even be regarded as a kind of antidote to this tendency, an attempt to get things moving again, to suggest sequences in which the cinematic might yet be inserted—"we all need our interceders," he declared.[27]

Deleuze's study of cinema is itself filled with such interferences and overlaps with many disciplines and practices such that the cinematic lies precisely in the peculiarities of the way film figures in larger complexes, at once aesthetic, social, technical, or political. When Deleuze calls postwar cinema "modern," he thus does not mean "modernist," here as elsewhere, a derivative sequence or problem in his great problem of signs and images in the arts. He does not at all see modern cinema as a melancholy retreat, turning in on itself in the face of kitsch. Its relation to "clichés," its forms of abstraction, are of a different kind, linked rather to making visible new zones of space and time, and the new kinds of characters who inhabit them, using the *dispositifs* of mass industrial society. That is why the problem of "metacinema" does not mean much to him, and why he is at such pains to distinguish the problem of the time-image from a simple opposition between narrative and nonnarrative film, and to insist that the cinema's signs and images do not form a code or language that would be distinguished from others in some epic effort at differentiation and purification. Bazin had spoken of an "impurity" peculiar to cinema or the ways it turns to literature, or the visual arts, or again to architecture or popular culture, for ideas to create its images. Deleuze extends this idea to include relations with philosophy or theory itself, as well as sciences or techniques, as part of a larger image of thought. In the place of Kant's "reflexive" idea of critique, Deleuze wanted to substitute a "creative" one, in which the forms of sensibility that are space and time are themselves thrown open to experimentation across many different disciplines at once.[28] Deleuze adopted Paul Klee's Bauhaus principle "to make visible" as a watchword for this process, and he associated with a question in painting that Delaunay formulated when he declared, "Cezanne broke the fruit-dish; too bad the Cubists sewed it up again."[29] It is just in this sense that for the signs and images of cinema—for its logic, its peculiar manner of thinking with images—there preexists "no determination technical or applied," not even a culturalist or medialogical one; the signs and images must be precisely invented in a long and often difficult process.[30] For in having an idea in cinema, there preexists no fixed sphere of competence, only available means and an inchoate necessity. As in any domain, an idea in cinema is something rare, given through many trials, moving back and forth, with many dead-ends, where one sometimes looks to other arts or disciplines for inspiration. The encounters across the arts, or through ideas in the arts, are not themselves governed by fixed models, analogies, or morphologies, but rather, through the peculiar ways one invents to develop ideas, often through sensory means or in sensory spaces and time. It is not all as if "contents" in each art could just be shuttled around from one "form" or medium to the next. However, in making such invention possible, *dispositifs*, like the cinematic, are distinguished as something more than "media," or technical supports, or means of transmitting and receiving information; they are, rather, ways of disposing our senses in such a way as to enable thinking or to make ideas possible. The cinematic *dispositif* Deleuze isolates in postwar cinema made possible the invention of new ways, beyond informing (through documentation) or narrating (through traditional characters and stories), to get at the those events we cannot make present through merely informing or narrating, or which require the invention of new kinds of "image" that undo the classical division between the two. That is why it is so misleading to imagine that new kinds of *dispositif* simply take over or replace those of older ones. While it used new audiovisual technical means, the new cinema was not an attempt to supplant the book or the Guttenberg galaxy, as a hasty reading of McLuan might suggest. It was a way of taking up the problems in the "new novel" to create a "new cinema," a way of linking creative ideas in books with those in darkened rooms. It was a way of breaking through the "*sensus communis*" supposed by our cliché-governed habits of thought, not only for the characters, but also for filmmakers and spectators. For this is something "dissensual" in the Ideas that force us to think. That is why the new cinema led to the emergence of a new public, the virtual audience that Serge Daney thought involved the critical "supplement" of a sort that Deleuze thought critical thought should continue in relation to new conditions of informational control.[31] One is thus at some distance from the kind of communicational model of the public and public space, which Kluge and Negri would challenge in Habermas in their search for another kind of "public sphere." In the place of a communicational sociability, Deleuze was interested in the ways filmmakers exploited the disjunctions of sound and image to expose another idea, developed philosophically by Simmel or Bakhtin. Indeed, we find this notion already in Deleuze's analysis of "wordly signs" in Proust, to which he returns in the passages in *What Is Philosophy?* where he is concerned more generally with contrasting thinking and communication.[32] We might imagine extending this analysis of "sociability" in cinema or literature to the way it helps create a new sociability in the ways we think and think together—one for which the principle might be developed from Deleuze's notion of a "people-yet-to-come" as a presupposition of philosophy and art, and so their relations with one another.

How, then, does the cinematic change our idea of art? In looking at Deleuze's answer to this question from a number of different angles, we may start to better see the ways his conception of the cinematic fits with a larger series of transformations in the arts, and of the idea of art, still with us today. These transformations suggest new zones for pursuing cinema's possibilities, and perhaps, as well, for playing in new ways the singular game of art and thinking for which Deleuze offered a larger aesthetic frame for pursuing his investigations and developing his ideas twenty years ago.

Notes

1   Such are the words that struck Gilles Deleuze in his "Correspondence with Dionys Mascolo," in *Two Regimes of Madness* (New York: Semiotext(e), 2006), 327. They are also suggestive for his larger encounter with Blanchot and Duras.

2   Deleuze explicates this principle of the cinematographic image introduced in Gilles Deleuze, *Cinema 2: The Time-Image*, trans. Hugh Tomlinson and Robert Galeta (Minneapolis: University of Minnesota Press, 1989), 105–16, and in Deleuze, *Two Regimes of Madness*, 290–91.

3   Gilles Deleuze, *Différence et répétition* (Paris: Presses Universitaires de France, 1968), 216; my translation. Page references are to the French edition, followed by the corresponding page numbers in italics from the English translation, *Difference and Repetition*, trans. Paul Patton (New York: Columbia University Press, 1994), *166*. At the end of his discussion of "the image of thought," Deleuze captures with these words, "time into thought," the argument he elaborates throughout his study of cinema and the larger idea of "aesthetics" it involves. Kant plays a key role in this turn; see n. 7.

4   Deleuze, *Two Regimes of Madness*, 291. Deleuze's view of the way television tends to "presentify" everything is not simply a question of its broadcast medium; indeed, one of Deleuze's first writings on cinema is his discussion of Godard's television work. The link between "present" and "live" is nevertheless important, as found today, e.g., in so-called reality TV.

5   Ibid.

6   In this chapter, I retain the French term *dispositif* for the manner in which cinematic space is put together. The sense of the term is part of the larger question of the "regimes" of speaking and seeing Deleuze extracts from Foucault in Gilles Deleuze, "What Is a *Dispositif?*," in *Two Regimes of Madness*, 338–48. In cinema theory, it might be said to belong to a series of notions of the "cinematic apparatus" that descend from Marx, who stressed the ways in which automated production involves not simply forces, but also relations of production (or what Deleuze would call a technical-social machine). One variant is to be found in the Brechtian idea of *Umfunktionierung* that Walter Benjamin developed, through which an author, more than a genius-fabricator of useless or autonomous works, becomes a "producer," whose work alters the larger apparatus of production and distribution in which it finds itself, posing the problem of the link between "collectivization" of the means of production and the control of the party. (See n. 12.) Another is the notion of "apparatus" that Baudry took over from Althusser's analysis of ideologies, where it is connected to an organization of gazes in the reproduction of social roles. Deleuze starts, instead, from a notion of "machine," in which desire functions not as prothesis or projection of an inner state, but as itself a kind of program at work in larger sociotechnical arrangements, the function of which is to undo the usual controllable connections, for which he is cites many artistic examples, notably Kurt Schwitter's *Merzbau*; see Félix Guattari, "Balance Sheet-Program for Desiring Machines," in *Chaosophy* (New York: Semiotext(e), 1995), 123–50. With this example, one is close to the problem of cinema as a kind of "installation," as in the debates about how cinema went into the light of the gallery out of its darkened-room *dispositif*. In this case, the cinema hall or gallery is "architecture," just when architecture itself is seen in terms of a given *dispositif*—the darkened room itself deriving from a theatrical *dispositif* transformed by opera, the first modern mass form. Thus, e.g., when Roland Barthes stresses that "cinema" refers to a place as well as what is shown in it, he opposes the eroticism of that place to the awful familial setting of the television set; Roland Barthes, "On Leaving the Cinema," in *The Rustle of Language* (New York: Farrar, Straus, and Giroux, 1986), 345–349. And when, in *Les Mots*, Sartre stresses the "democratic" appeal of the cinema hall to the hierarchical organization of the bourgeois theater, it is to explain the source of his enthusiasm for it. To see such spaces as *dispositifs* is to see them as arrangements of sensibilia, which in turn can be analyzed in terms of their

relation to what forces us to think. By that criterion, many darkened-room experiences are more intense than their equivalents in galleries.

7   See Gilles Deleuze, "On Four Poetic Formulas," in *Essays Critical and Clinical*, trans. Daniel W. Smith and Michael A. Greco (Minneapolis: University of Minnesota Press, 1997), 28–29. For Deleuze, Kant introduces the distinction between time and movement developed in and through the cinema volumes. The distinction is first introduced in Deleuze, *Difference and Repetition*, 118, 86, in passages devoted to the problem of introducing "time into thought," and later, Deleuze, ibid., 130, 98, already develops the consequences for the notion of "aesthetics" he puts into practice in his analysis of cinema. Prior to Bergson, Kant remains the central philosophical figure for Deleuze's film aesthetic, to the point where he declares that Bergson himself was much closer to Kant than he allowed. "On Four Poetic Formulas" itself resumes the new lecture course Deleuze gave on Kant in 1978, which runs through his larger aesthetic enterprise in the 1980s and which directly concerns the "paradox of inner sense" Kant himself elaborates in *Opus Postumum* (New York: Cambridge University Press, 1993).

8   In an essay on "La chambre," which takes off from Deleuze's analysis of the room in Samuel Beckett's *Film*, Raymond Bellour suggests one way of linking the problem of the "room" in cinema to the room in which it is shown in "the other cinema" of film and video installation. Raymond Bellour, "La chambre," in *L'Entre-images 2: Mots, Images* (Paris: POL, 1999), 281–316.

9   Deleuze, *Two Regimes of Madness*, 252.

10 Ibid., 292.

11 Deleuze, *Time-Image*, 257; translation modified. Deleuze draws here on Youssef Ishaghpour's detailed analysis of Duras in *D'une image à l'autre* (Paris: Editions Denoël/Gonthier, 1982), 225–98.

12 Walter Benjamin, "The Author as Producer," in *Reflections*, trans. Edmund Jephcott (New York: Harcourt Brace Jovanovich, 1978), 220–38. See also Sergei Tret'iakov's own essay "Our Cinema," *October* 118 (2006): 27; originally published 1928. There is something in the *Umfunktionierung* characteristic of author as producer that is akin to Foucault's analysis of the individualizing function of authorship and his own attempts to get out of it. An important difference, however, concerns the way the problem of power in Foucault is purposefully posed in a way irreducible to any party control. Deleuze relates this problem in Vertov to a new "materialism of the eye." See François Zourabichvili, "The Eye of Montage: Dziga Vertov and Bergsonian Materialism," in *The Brain Is the Screen*, ed. Gregory Flaxman (Minneapolis: University of Minnesota Press, 2000), 141–49.

13 In an analysis influenced by Deleuze, Jonathan Crary, *Suspensions of Perception* (Cambridge, Mass.: MIT Press, 2001), 347, discusses Vertov and Cezanne in relation to the neuroscientific question of "attention."

14 Deleuze develops this view as an original approach to questions of biology and technology in the appendix to his book *Foucault*, trans. Séan Hand (Minneapolis: University of Minnesota Press, 1988), 124–32. Daniel Birnbaum returns to this idea in his attempt to see Doug Aitken as part of an unwritten "*Cinema 3*" in contemporary art. See Daniel Birnbaum, *Chronology* (New York: Lucas and Sternberg, 2005), 49–55.

15 Deleuze, *Two Regimes of Madness*, 253.

16 Ibid., 386. The notion of an "impersonal yet singular life" figures in Bellour's conception of "the room." (See n. 8.)

17 *Cinéma 1: L'image-mouvement* (Paris: Éditions de Minuit, 1983) 122; published in English as *Cinema 1: The Movement-Image*, trans. Hugh Tomlinson and Barbara Habberjam (Minneapolis: University of Minnesota Press, 1989), 84–85. Deleuze amusingly suggests one sense in which the "expansion" in structural as well as expanded cinema was related to the "expansion of consciousness" in drugs, as part of the larger "community," rather unlike the Soviet case, with which these American experiments were linked.

18 Phillippe-Alain Michaud, *Aby Warburg and the Image in Motion* (New York: Zone Books, 2005), 278–91; Phillippe-Alain Michaud, *The Movement of Images* (New York: Zone Books, 2006).

19 Wu Hung, "The Painted Screen," *Critical Inquiry* 23, no. 1 (1996): 37–79. The idea is developed further in Wu Hung, *The Double Screen: Medium and Representation in Chinese Painting* (Chicago: University of Chicago Press, 1997).

20 Raymond Bellour, "Of an Other Cinema," in *Black Box Illuminated*, ed. Sara Arrhenius, Magdalena Malm, and Cristina Ricupero (Stockholm: Nordic Institute for Contemporary Art, 2004), 39–58. Giuliana Bruno extends an analysis begun in her *Atlas of Emotion* (New York: Verso, 2002) in *Public Intimacy: Architecture and the Visual Arts* (Cambridge, Mass.: MIT Press, 2007).

21 Deleuze draws on Roland Barthes's, *Image, Music, Text* (New York: Hall and Wang, 1977) analysis of Eisenstein and the Brechtian "gest" in developing his analysis of "bodily attitudes" in cinema, as seen, e.g., in Cassavetes's *Faces*, while he sees Carmelo Bene as closer to Artaud. Ceremonial or everyday "bodily attitudes" are time-images because the body shows through them the workings of time irreducible to plot or subject matter. See Deleuze, *Time-Image*, 189–203.

22 Gilles Deleuze, *Proust and Signs*, trans. Richard Howard (New York: George Braziller, 1972), 5–7. Deleuze introduces in this study the question of the implications of "showing time" for what he calls, for the first time, "the image of thought."

23 Deleuze discusses the problem of information in relation to Syberberg in "What Is a Creative Act?," in *Two Regimes of Madness*, 322. Here Deleuze presents in terms of cinema the question of "control" that he would later

set out more generally in his essay "Postscript on Control Societies," in *Negotiations*, trans. Martin Joughin (New York: Columbia University Press, 1995), 177–82.

24   Paul Virilio, *War and Cinema: The Logistics of Perception*, trans. P. Camiler (New York: Verso, 1989). In a larger discussion of these same themes, Virilio says that the paradox of the documentary treatment of war starting with Rossellini's *Rome, Open City* is one that has "haunted me since I was born. . . . In 1959, *Hiroshima Mon Amour* provoked an upheaval comparable to the one caused by Seurat or Cezanne in the Impressionist period," he declares. Paul Virilio, *Politics of the Very Worst* (New York: Semiotext(e), 1999), 29. The film is exemplary of the way artists use technologies to "diverge" from the larger functions of propaganda or advertising.

25   Gilles Deleuze, "The Brain Is the Screen," in *Two Regimes of Madness*, 284; translation modified.

26   Deleuze, *Time-Image*, 280.

27   "Intercesseurs" is translated as "Mediators" in the essay by that title in *Negotiations*, 121–34.

28   "The limit common to all of these series of interventions . . . is space-time. All of these disciplines communicate at the level of something that never emerges for its own sake, but is engaged in every creative discipline: the formation of space-times." Deleuze, *Two Regimes of Madness*, 315.

29   Deleuze, *Foucault*, 52–53.

30   Deleuze, *Time-Image*, 280.

31   See "Letter to Serge Daney: Optimism, Pessmism, and Voyage," *Negotiations* 72. Here the function of "a little bit of art and thinking" is contrasted with the public as social consensus and the way it figures in the larger issue of information and control.

32   See *What is Philosophy?*, trans. Hugh Tomlinson and Graham Burchell (New York: Columbia University Press, 1994) 87–88. Here the problem of a "sociability" in thought in opposition to Imperial power is seen as the start of a problem of "philia" in philosophy, taken up later through notions of "fraternity," or "solidarity" in relation to capitalism, and hence to Blanchot's attempt to rethink notions of "community" and "communism" after the disaster of the War.

16. Immanent Images: Photography after Mobility

Damian Sutton

Photography has a singular life in the philosophy of Deleuze. At first glance, it is one of the building blocks of cinema—as the photogram—with a limited life of its own in comparison to its centrality to the cinematic image and its two different manifestations: the movement-image and the time-image. The movement-image is, of course, hugely reliant on the particular characteristics of the still image. Two photographs, side by side, account for one of the most important specificities of the cinema as a medium: its ability to modulate time and space through editing these two together. Indeed, the movement-image relies on the immobility of the photograph; it gives movement back to the photographic image. Most of the early examples of editing and montage—especially those of Eisenstein and Griffith—are based on this principle. If one were to examine a strip of projection film from *October* (1927) or *The Lonely Villa* (1909) and zoom in on any one of the many cuts that have made them archetypes of cinematic narration, one would see at the nexus of each cut two distinct still images—photographs—on whose juxtaposition the whole of the sequence, and often the whole of the film, relies.

Yet if the task of this book is to return to Deleuze's *Cinema* books and reconsider them in the light of cinema in the intervening years, we must also ask, what has happened to the photograph? The change that has occurred in photography far exceeds changes in cinema in the same time frame, and the practice of photography has left the strip of frames behind. While cinema has yet to make more than a few forays into truly digital production, the number of digital photographic images taken outstrips traditional film and paper photography. This does not mean that photography is dead—far from it. The current expansion of cell phone use in the United States and across the world, for example, is inextricably linked to its "bundling" with digital camera technology and offers an unprecedented public access to photographic technology. Because of this, the focus of attention in photography is now required to shift from its image to its *use*. In the United Kingdom, cell phones are routinely called "mobile phones," which, on the surface, more readily identifies the handset with the emerging culture of mobility identified by sociologists as a result of our information age. Yet, while technology, such as the cell phone and the Internet, may seem as far removed from the photograph as one could possibly get, cell phone photography extends and continues a practice of photography located in the personal and domestic that has existed since the first days of the daguerreotype.

Paul Levinson, in his book on the cell phone revolution, identifies it as a direct descendent of the pocket technology of the Kodak camera. Not only did the Kodak place production in the hands of what would otherwise be consumers, but also it more firmly established the pocket as a "vector" of media technology than did the keepsake daguerreotype or ambrotype.[1] Elsewhere, John Urry has demonstrated how instrumental photography was in the development of modern society and the dominance of visuality, and in particular, how they continue to have an effect in the new culture of mobility: "there is an increased mediatisation of the visual sense, especially involving the move from the printing press to electronic modes of representation, and from the camera . . . to the circulation of digital images from around and beyond the earth."[2]

Photography has always had a role in social mobility as well a visual mobility of its own. The movement of cameras in society occurs even while images become more repetitive and culturally coded by the sharing of meanings and values through consumption and use. In contemporary visual culture, Web sites such as Buzznet, Textamerica, and Mobog, and especially photo-sharing sites, such as Photobucket and Flickr, allow the easy transfer of digital images from camera to online album, effectively gifted to the public. Most important, connections are made and agreements in meaning are encouraged and tested through the referral of images by keyword tagging and space left for comments. The photograph is thus already inherently mobile, even though culture seeks to fix the photograph's technology, object, and meanings to render it immobile.

How does this different understanding of mobility fit with the immobility on which cinema and Deleuze's philosophy rely so heavily? We can, of course, argue simply that *social* mobility is not the same mobility of which Deleuze speaks. Throughout Deleuze's work, the photograph is used as an example of the *wrong* sort of image to represent time, space, and especially immanence: the life of the world that can only be expressed through the traces that it leaves behind. However, this would be a reductive approach that belies the usefulness of Deleuze's philosophy, if not also his tendency to draw culture with a broad brush. So much of Deleuze's philosophy, and his work with Félix Guattari, is interested in the creation of order and the development of hierarchical culture. This is what gives extraordinary value to Deleuze's first book on cinema. So often reduced to a footnote accompanying studies of the more influential work on the time-image, the work on the movement-image is nonetheless a glimpse of the immanence of life as it is organized into a sensorimotor schema, the chronologic of time and space to which we have been habituated. That photography is instrumental to Deleuze's philosophy is evident from the first few pages, and it is difficult to see how a different character of the photograph can emerge. However, in the intervening years, the technological changes in photography mean that the new sets of photography, the new movement-images of this visual culture, are still to be formed, and in this gathering or hardening, we might yet see a glimpse of immanence ourselves. This might be expressed in the relation that individuals and their photographs have with the world and with time—imagined through the photograph's mobility, rather than its immobility. So what can Deleuze's philosophy of the movement-image tell us about the mobility of the photograph?

The Immobile Photograph

In cinema, mobility begins at the stage when the camera moves, or when the shot, as a slice of space, is connected to other shots to inherit as a sequence "movement and duration."[3] This *inheritance* is the movement of the film in the camera, as the still images run through the machine. This is a photographic mobility only in that it can exploit the suggestion of captured movement in each image. The mobility given to it by montage or the mobile camera is specifically cinematic, and the difference is made very clear: "cinema does not give us an image to which movement is added, it immediately gives us a movement-image. It does give us a section, but a section which is mobile, not an immobile section + abstract movement."[4] Here Deleuze makes his famous challenge to Henri Bergson's suggestion of perception as a kind of cinematograph of the mind. For Bergson, perception creates the illusion of movement, just as cinema does, by "stringing" together "snapshots, as it were, of the passing reality."[5] For Deleuze, of course, it is this illusion that is the key, the specificity of cinema. Even so, the conceptual reduction of the photograph and its relation to cinema remains in both, and not only relies on the central immobility of the photograph, but also on the particular singularity created by this immobility. The photograph is immobile until it is put into sequence by cinema. This is why Deleuze refers, at one stage, to "Muybridge's equidistant snapshots" to announce the privileged instant of the photograph, which can be used to comprehend time really only by luck, such as when all four of a horse's hooves are off the ground while in midgallop.[6] The locomotion sequences created by Muybridge and his contemporaries famously anticipate cinema but, most important, they seem retrospectively to desire cinema's invention.

Yet in his understanding of the photograph, Deleuze is only following that most central orthodoxy of photographic thought—the slice or time and space created by the photograph and preserved as if in amber. This is the result of the influence of André Bazin. Bazin's cinema theory developed over a series of essays and was published in various collections under the title *What Is Cinema?* Throughout, Bazin compares cinema to photography as one compares a son's achievements to the father's failure. Cinema is able to do what photography cannot through its realization of photography's latent potential. Deleuze seizes on perhaps the sharpest dissymmetry in Bazin, when the latter describes photography as "a feeble technique in the sense that its instantaneity compels it to capture time only piecemeal," in comparison to cinema, which molds the object "as it exists in time."[7] This cements in Deleuze's philosophy of cinema an approach to the internal equilibrium of the photograph as creating an "immobile section," one so different to the modulation created by the cinematic shot as a "variable, continuous, temporal mould."[8] The fact of the photograph's salvation in cinema is never clearer in that while photography gives to cinema the transparency of the process, cinema takes photography to a new, previously unexplored dimension through the mechanism of the filmstrip and the camera/projector. However, for Deleuze, cinema's advance on photography's base means more than adding time to the photograph—the movement-image can do this, in making the immobile section of time (the photograph) a mobile section (shot) by creating succession. To do so creates larger and larger sets of images—sets of movements and episodes of time—within the

Whole of time and space. Deleuze detects a different kind of cinema in the time-image, one that is much more than a process of addition or succession and that is able to represent the totality of time through the experience of an unfolding duration.

The time-image makes time and the experience of time a central device of narration, and it relies on the photograph's poverty to do so. Deleuze, for example, refers to the still life compositions of Ozu, the deep focus of Welles, and to this we might add the symmetry of Kubrick or the asymmetry of Snow. In these situations, cinema not only effaces the still frames of which it is composed, but transcends them through direct reference or confrontation. For example, the "potential space" of Michael Snow's *Wavelength* (1967), a forty-five-minute film made in an apparently continuous single-shot zoom across a room, is hinted at in the photograph of a wave at sea, petrified and rendered immoveable, that the zoom finally rests on.[9] The zoom is able to "map" the space because the photograph is unable to render space without a direct but haphazard transcription.

It helps here to return to a slightly earlier point in Deleuze's philosophy, in particular, his work with Félix Guattari on *A Thousand Plateaus*, originally written in 1980 as the second part of their mammoth work *Capitalism and Schizophrenia*. In *A Thousand Plateaus*, the limits of photography are expressed through its all-too-faithful capture of time and space. This adheres to the principles of transparency for which the technology is famous but is nevertheless guided by a consciousness in the taking of pictures. The photograph is used as an example of a *tracing*, a term that is also used by Bazin.[10] The photography is a tracing that "begins by selecting or isolating, by artificial means such as colorations or other restrictive procedures, what it intends to reproduce."[11] In understanding space, time, identity—*life itself*—photography is an unnatural apprehension or means to a comprehension because it cannot capture or represent the change that life involves. Deleuze and Guattari are not suggesting that photography lacks succession or is limited through the photograph's lack of connection with larger sets of images or other mechanisms, as in cinema. Instead, Deleuze and Guattari treat the photograph, in this brief allusion, as a singular image comparable to drawing, focusing, in particular, on the difference between tracing and map. For Deleuze and Guattari, the limit of the photograph is in its self-sufficiency and superimposed "competence"—it allows few ways, or only one way in. The map, on the other hand, "is open and connectable in all of its dimensions; it is detachable, reversible, susceptible to constant modification. It can be torn, reversed, adapted to any kind of mounting, reworked by an individual, group, or social formation. . . . A map has multiple entryways, as opposed to the tracing, which always comes back 'to the same.'" [12] As a tracing, the photograph cannot possibly represent the mutability of identity. We may understand the photograph in terms of purely light and shadow, or we may understand it through the interpretations we make. Deleuze and Guattari describe it through everything that it is not. Later, when Deleuze turns to cinema, it is only as cinema that the photographic image is given any capacity to *involve*. When the cinematic image as a time-image deliberates on the stilled image either through the freeze frame, the long take, deep focus, or the still life/landscape, time is added to the image as intensive, rather than as extensive. The stilled image becomes a map of time in the way that it is "oriented toward an experimentation in contact with the real" [13]: its confrontation with the experience of time, in its rendering of the process of cinema, creates so many involutions of subjectivity as the image waits for the cut. As we wait for the cut, we wait for a release from the glimpse of time that can burn or blind.

The decisive part that the stilled or contemplative image has to play in Deleuze's philosophy of cinema consolidates photography's more general philosophical role as one of the chief *piloti* of both cinema's technology and its theory. And when we consider the continued importance of Deleuze's work on cinema, we see the position of photography in relation to cinema as incontrovertible and unlikely to change. In this sense, the photograph is instrumental in what Deleuze calls the civilization of the image, which "constantly sinks to the state of cliché: because it is introduced to sensory-motor linkages." [14] We can ascertain here a sense of the photograph as a result of repetitive ideas guiding the production of photographs: the snapshot, the decisive moment, and so on. For so many years, the call among artists and professionals was to think or "see" photographically, echoing the practice of "straight" photography—Ansel Adams, Edward Weston, and Group f.64. For Weston, "seeing photographically" had a literal meaning. The technology of photography, which so often cannot be corrected after exposure, requires of the operative a preemption, to the extent that the finished print must be anticipated and "created in full before the film is exposed." [15] For Weston, not to think or see photographically is to allow important images to occur only by accident. So the trained photographic act—and we must remember that this lies at the heart of even the most avant-garde filmmakers—is always a game played with the risk that any attempt to challenge the powers of cinema always contains the possibility that it will simply "resuscitate the cliché" of a culture of the photographic image.[16] For Deleuze, cinema is one of the arts for whom this risk is a possibility that lurks in any creative act—"resemblance haunts the work of art," as he later suggests with Guattari.[17] In photography, the memory of the photograph instructs the creative act, telling it how to arrest action, how to suspend time, how to create the sensorimotor link. For Deleuze, the photograph is one step above the most clichéd of cinematic images, such as when an attempt to linger on a still life, a landscape, a face, only produces a cloying homage or triteness. Thus the already redundant image is only "at best a photo," even though it remains to be explored as "the first dimension of an image that never stops growing in dimensions."[18]

The Mobile Photograph

Much of the theory of photography central to Bazin and Deleuze relies on the photograph as a mythical entity of immobility; it immobilizes but is also itself immobile because it is most commonly associated with the snapshot as a tracing of life or as a resemblance of life created for remembrance. As such, it is required to be fixed and constant against the ongoing tumult of life itself, just as it is *required* to be immobile in the cinematic apparatus. Cinema's mobility relies on what the photograph appears to represent and what it appears to be: fixity of time and a fixture of space. In two specific ways, the photograph cannot move, and cinema cures this twofold paralysis. Yet photography is mobile in ways that do not entirely fit the caricature on which the philosophy of the *Cinema* books is based. A different, qualitative mobility has existed with the photograph since its invention, from the pocket-sized daguerreotype to *cartes-de-visite* that could be bought off barrows at railway stations or presented as visiting cards of the gentry. The photograph that appears in our newspapers or subway advertisements is similarly mobile, an image *everywhere* that more directly becomes an *anywhere* in the sense that anywhere we look, we see photographs that refuse to stay put. They follow us or insist, by repetition and reproduction, on a constant presence that relies on their evanescence. A self-portrait of the artist Robert Mapplethorpe, used as an advertisement for a retrospective exhibition and seen at a bus shelter or on a subway, may appear, at the outset, the very image of stasis. It is a black-and-white, crystal clear image, a studio portrait of the artist with a cigarette at his lips and an ectoplasm of smoke above his head that can now only ever refer to his later tragic death. The capture of the smoke and the neoclassical style of the image (which both flirts with razor sharp critique of "classical" photography and risks falling into that cliché itself) exist in photography's mythology of immobility. Yet *this photograph*, the object itself, rather than the image it reproduces, will change, be torn down, be covered over, be defaced, or be forgotten. However, it will also reappear when we turn a corner or turn a page, whether we visit the exhibition and see the "real thing" or not. This is a different mobility of the photograph, but one no less a part of the photograph's role in the civilization of the image than the immobility so often associated with photography. This is a mobility most clearly expressed in recent times in the digital cell phone photograph, whose movement through the world—from expression through image to deletion—is a mobility of images not related to an object or objects, but to a series of projections and translations of thoughts, ideas, remembrances, and conjectures.

Through its technological connection with communications—in particular, the cell phone and the Internet—the photograph has become reaffirmed in its role as surrogate or metaphor for processes of perception and memory, and the creation of identity (personal and public) that relies on these. At the same time, the proliferation of photographic images has its own strange relationship with time and space. For though a photograph is a slice of space and time that still seems to be a privileged instant (if we continue to follow that most popular of paradigms), as the civilization of the image grows, then the possibility of a photography of *everything* seems to grow with it. We cannot say that a photograph exists of everything and from every vantage point, but that individual photographs begin to relate to a whole that promises any image from any point.

Deleuze's critique of Bergson, central to the philosophy of the movement-image, is based on this idea. For Bergson, photography, as a model for perception, cannot hope to apprehend reality because reality is always changing and is without a point of anchorage, save an imagined or "deduced" one.[19] Alternatively, Deleuze proffers cinema as genuinely without such an anchorage or central supposition of intellection, viewing it instead as a promise of the "infinite set of all images [that] constitutes a kind of plane of immanence."[20] Although, in 1907, Bergson dismissed the early forms of cinema to which he had been exposed, he had already left the tools of Deleuze's analysis in his earlier work on perception and memory—*Matter and Memory*, from 1896. This earlier work provides for Deleuze and for us Bergson's most powerful use of photography as a model for perception, "as a kind of photographic view of things." Instead, Bergson attests that the "photograph" to be perceived is "already taken, already developed in the heart of things and in all points of space."[21] For Deleuze, this is perhaps Bergson's most important contribution to a philosophy of immanence. The conceptual understanding of life itself is a ground for our perception: the plane of immanence is "the universe as cinema in itself, a metacinema."[22]

From this, Deleuze develops his concept of the "any-instant-whatever" that is so crucial to the movement that cinema provides for photography.[23] Yet it is still at this stage, in the first few pages of *Cinema 1*, that Deleuze offers the best illumination to cast on the mobility of photography. In his argument, Deleuze relates photography to cinema's automatism and the mechanism that creates the equidistant images on the filmstrip. This is the legacy of Muybridge and, of course, represents one of the key challenges of the cinematic process. Cinema exists in the relation between the equidistant, privileged instants as a string of photograms so that "one constructs a Whole, one assumes that all is given, while movement only occurs if the whole is neither given nor giveable."[24] The importance of the infinite set of images on the plane of immanence is in the promise of the Whole. The illusion of movement in cinema comes from the relation between images we see, but real movement cannot be seen and is only promised. There can never be a photographic plate on which to expose the images of the whole, Bergson suggests, and our "'zones of indetermination' play in some sort the part of the screen."[25] For Deleuze, the time-image is just such a zone of indetermination, a point that the image reaches when, through its confrontation with time, change, memory, and so on, it offers a glimpse of the time that movement cannot express. This is the most important aspect of Deleuze's *Cinema* books, and because of the brilliance of this philosophy of the time-image, the developmental aspects are often overlooked. In fact, they offer a way of understanding the relational aspects of photography, first in establishing the photograph in relation to the any-instant-whatever and, second, in revealing the mobility of photography as a relation to the whole, and a trace or shadow of the whole left on the plane of immanence. The sociologists John Urry and Mimi Sheller have suggested that the convergence of new technologies is embodied in the new media screen, which can tile over or switch between the cinema, television, and, of course, the Web.[26] The new screen performs all or most of these functions, stripping each of its defining characteristics (the auditorium, the living room, the office) in a physical convergence that mirrors the digital one. The plasma screen in the home, the LCD projector in the classroom, and the high-resolution flat screen in the office have all been joined by the scrolling screen of the cell phone or Web photograph album. As the technologies of the screen converge, they edge closer to the missing photographic plate that Bergson described.

Mobile Users

There can be little doubt that from 2003 to 2005, digital photography, and especially that of the camera phone, reshaped the landscape of photographic practice. An increasing rate of growth of camera phone sales led to industry predictions of 298 million units worldwide by 2007, rising to 656 million by 2008.[27] Most important, however, as many as 29 billion images worldwide were expected to have been taken on camera phones in 2004, the gadget's first full year.[28] By 2005, predictions had risen to 40 million per year for cell phones alone, with digital cameras themselves expected to account for much greater use.[29] Even so, camera phone sales outstripped conventional digital stills camera sales by four to one.[30] These statistics illustrate the effect that cell phone culture is having on consumption and on the approaches to consumption adopted by sociology and cultural studies, a drive kept up by technological innovation intended to keep phone users renewing their handsets. The built-in camera is one of these, and probably the most successful, with a heavy marketing emphasis made on picture messaging. While this type of commodity "progress" fits easily into the buying patterns that might be expected of the discerning consumer, the cell phone is one of the few leisure commodities that is also sold on the "legitimate" notion of necessity. The idea of having a cell phone on hand for personal safety as well as the perceived need for immediate and reliable person-to-person communication mean that it has assumed a place in contemporary culture as a "lifeline."[31]

Despite this take-up of camera phones, early figures showed that in October 2004 (eighteen months after their introduction in Japan), users were not sending picture messages at the volumes that had been expected. The reasons for this may ultimately be very practical—a sporadic adoption of camera phones meant that one could not guarantee, in the early days, that picture messages sent could be received by others. Similarly, downloading images onto a home computer and distributing them by e-mail could avoid the relatively high cost of picture messaging altogether.[32] This is what ultimately led to the development of mobile weblogging ("moblogging") sites and photo-sharing sites. These are enabled by direct file transfer, while in some cases, users choose simply to keep the images on the handset—perusing them in quiet moments or gathering friends around to show them off.

When the Internet first established itself as a tool of cultural connections, users interacted mostly through text. Sherry Turkle's groundbreaking study of Internet sociality, *Life on the Screen*, focused on text-based applications as media for the development of the social self, one that was multiple and integrated but whose multiplicity relied on communication. The Internet thus gave electronic evidence that "one's identity emerges from whom one knows, one's associations and connections."[33] As the Web became established, most committed users built their Web sites themselves, focusing on the architecture of the Web space with applications such as Adobe's Dreamweaver, Microsoft FrontPage, and so on. In this sense, any mobility to a Web site was "added" by links to other sites so that a so-called webring of sites with a common theme formed a kind of immobile section of the Web. The situation has been made mobile by the development of blogging software—personal content management systems as Web-based applications. Web domains, such as MySpace, offer a basic format set by the site owners with a range of available templates; only the Web page's text and image content are authored and edited by the user and visitors. Digital photographs, in particular, give weblogs and sharing sites a movement of immobile sections made mobile through their connection with other sites, other blogs. Users are just as likely, perhaps more, to navigate across to other sites by clicking on images, rather than text links.

For sites such as Flickr, perhaps the most popular photo-sharing site to emerge, this is also reflected in the use of tagging, in which images are given textual handles to make them easier to search and which encourage a free association, as tags often relate in only a tangential way to the image. This type of nonlinear movement from site to site or image to image is one of the reasons Deleuze and Guattari's anti-hierarchical concept of the rhizome has been adopted by many new media exponents, influencing the creation and maintenance of major arts and intellectual Web sites and Web groups such as nettime.org and rhizome.org. Mobility in these terms is expressed through qualitative movements: serendipity in surfing, tangential links, and the sensation of never being able to reach the end of the Web. The Web is rhizomorphic, in Deleuze–Guattari terms, in that it is "composed not of units but dimensions, or rather directions in motion. It has neither beginning nor end, but always a middle from which it grows and overspills."[34] Thus one of the key elements of Flickr's functionality is the random show of recent public images that appear alongside a user's own. Curiosity and desire, expressed through clicking on the images, instigates detours within the growing Flickr database. The result is that users become acquainted with images as parts of overlapping sets, whose connections are created by social associations, image tags, or simply by frequency of links and date of posting. Sets and subsets can also be viewed using a slideshow application, which cycles through the images from a user's page (or a pool of user pages) on demand. The flicker of the computer or cell phone screen is overlaid by a different flicker, a new "cinema" of personal experiences. Just as still frames ran vertically through the projector on their celluloid track, so these images run vertically as users scroll through their experiences and the experiences of others made public. Flickr is a commercial Web site that reflects the wider relationship of the Web's images to each other and the Whole of visual culture. In turn, the Web only serves as a reflection of the civilization of the image, in which photographs are traces made on the plane of immanence, a universe of images flickering away as a metacinema.

Mobile Subjects

The centrality of evanescence in photography cannot be overestimated. The photograph is constantly disappearing, whether it is in the visual culture of reproduction and replacement, as we have seen, or in the "tentative" nature of the digital photograph, which José Van Dijck has described as representing "a new type of materiality, a limbo between remembering and forgetting, where images may sit pending their erasure or materialization."[35] Now stored on a chip or card and seemingly fragile in their lack of tangibility, digital images thus seem far removed from paper and celluloid, even though, in advertising and editorial photography as well as cinema, the photograph itself has always had a short life. In this way, digital photographic culture mimics the mobility of cinema it its instant forgetting of images as they pass through the gate of the camera/projector. The movement-image is created when the images connected by the machine are forgotten in favor of the movement that is provoked. Similarly, the mobility of the photograph is created in part by the qualitative change of forgetting, as billboards are replaced or pages are turned. We need to forget each image as we scan across a gallery wall, yet each image cannot help but add to the one before it and the one after. Photographs require connection to make sense, connection with viewer or addressee as well as connection with text and other images on a wider scale.

Yet, ultimately, the photograph is always a result of the break in connection—it is always the subject of an unrequited gaze. A person photographed does not stare out at the viewer, but rather, into the camera lens, even though it is precisely the reverse that seems to be the case. Still, most photographs are placed in such rigid context—the editorial, the commercial, the familial—that it is rare that the photograph as an any-instant-whatever is left unconnected. Perhaps this is why the portrait that stares back is so powerful when it is disconnected, in part, from its context. We might be affected by a family portrait, a model's pose, or a political poster, but this effect is created by a logical connection between perception and action—we see and we know how to react (to weep, to vote). However, when the context is partly removed, when we do not know how but are nonetheless moved to act, this is the photograph as "affection-image."[36] Unknown or otherwise disconnected photographs are an excellent example of this indetermination created by the apparent absence of either subject or object. For Deleuze, affection is the quality of mobility that exists or "occupies the interval" between perception and "hesitant action."[37] We exist as subjects—centers of indetermination—but have "specialized one of our facets or certain of our points into receptive organs at the price of condemning them to immobility."[38] This explains Bergson's organ of perception as a "photographic view of things," which is directly translated by Deleuze onto the photograph. The civilization of the cliché is the social result of this specialization, and photography is one of its mechanisms. This is why so many photographs exist as part of immobile sections or sets: photographs are created in the image of other photographs, connected in chains of communication that rely on a logic of perception and action.

When one aspect of this chain is missing, it does not mean that affection escapes or becomes unpredictable. For example, Roland Barthes's greatest discovery was not the way that communication seeks to "counter the terror of uncertain signs," although he is most commonly praised for this.[39] Instead, by the time he wrote *Camera Lucida*, Barthes had come to appreciate the ways in which the photograph's depiction of time and place became more, not less, effective when the chains of signification were broken. If a photograph loses something of its context, or appears to lose its addressee, it does not put subjectivity and objectivity into crisis or cause them to collapse as distinctions. On the contrary, it rolls up subject and object to coincide with each other, to create a paralyzing self-consciousness. This is the effect of what Barthes called the *punctum*, the element of a photograph that arrests the viewer. Barthes explains how incidental the details are of photographs that have this effect, but in reality, what they all share is their removal from the normal situation of viewing—it is a picture of his mother before he was born that provokes an intellectual collapse for Barthes and the youthful beauty of Lewis Payne that prevents his reduction to a footnote in history. "*He is going to die.* I read at the same time: *This will be and this has been*": the knowledge of the boy's impending execution causes, for Barthes, a collapse of his sense of past and future.[40] But it is really a rolling together of subject and object that affects Barthes in this way. The boy's eyes disconnect the image from the history of the presidential assassination in which he was a plotter; he has attracted Barthes's desire in his outward stare. In so many ways, it is an affection-image, but this is mostly because it addresses the viewer, and yet, at the same time, cannot possibly do so.

Mobile Identities

If we return finally to the new life of photography, we can see how the nature of its address is so crucial to its mobility. Blogging, especially photo-blogging, is not a person-to-person activity. Few of these sites and pages involve prolonged conversations. Instead, they are addressed not to a single respondent, but rather, to potential respondents whose number can run to hundreds of millions.[41] This is why so many photo-sharing sites are highly self-conscious conversations between the user and the unknowable viewer or visitor and, in this way, why they become diaries or chronicles of the user's public and private selves. Photo-sharing pages emphasize an awareness of the widespread cultural shift toward a networked visual culture. Many of the personal diaries remain acutely focused on the user's sense of individuality as opposed to what they see as the homogeneous, global network. Rather than being the agent in a quest for uncovering and maturing multiple, mutable identities, as Turkle's study of Internet users suggested, these pages rely on the tentative creation of identity that is projected outward as a narrative. At the same time, there is an insistence that certain photographs must be taken, because the event—Christmas, Thanksgiving, a political demonstration—is one that will touch so many people so personally, and they will share *our* sentiments. Unlike the family album of old, the moblog does not elide the banal and the everyday, the unthought, from personal history, but instead, immanence is its fabric. The fact that these images are often repetitive, fragmentary, and even boring in their tracing of the minutiae of life is significant in itself. In the absence of the culturally ratified times and spaces that defined the modern self, and as the boundaries of public and private, work and leisure, local and global give way to an unstable mobility, the cell phone and its ability to represent the self might be described as a *lifeline* in more ways than one.

A central facet of the growth of the Internet and the technologies of connection has been their profound effect on identity and the destabilization of the individual as a social atom. On one hand, the noospheric impulse to see connections as creating a shared global political consciousness reflects the urge to frame the social from a perspective of this collective identity. On the other hand, Urry and Sheller see a fragmented individual who has emerged in contemporary society. If, as Anthony Giddens famously suggests, the self in late modernity is an *autobiography* of development that establishes "zones of personal time" (daily routines, communal time), these zones themselves are dissipating and becoming flows, while the boundaries of personal, private, and public space are becoming less and less clear.[42] For Urry and Sheller, Giddens's "autobiography" of the self has to be rewritten to include mobility in its plot. Software innovations, such as Web mail and Internet banking, are technologies of mobility in that they release the self from any geographical center of their social and financial worlds. This increased mobility is reflected in persons that cease to be embodied in a particular time, space, or even body, and who instead leave "traces of their selves in informational space" to be accessed from acentered locations.[43] A defining action for such persons is the daily "self-retrieval" (of e-mail, of interesting news items, of sports results) carried out in front of a screen that reflects their life back to them. The self in the mobile society is a flickering self that flashes from screen to screen over wide distances, or, in the case of instant messengers and e-mail lists, many screens at once. Camera phone images now add to this retrieval, underscoring the ephemerality of this fleeting present. Where the *Kodak moment* has come to represent temporary hiatus, copresence, and the special, the *Nokia moment* seeks to stretch this sense of the momentous until it elevates the mundane or attenuates the notion of photographic opportunity.

This is a different collapse of past and present, having more to do with the projection of identity characteristic of the affection-image. In these cases, photographs are creative images of time that relate more to the production of meaning through reading our own images, in an awareness of how the imagined viewer will understand and interrogate them. Here photographs are not accurate records of a past event, but are instead projections made of various interpretations of the present for the future that will look back on them. In the same way that photographs are images of an individual identity in relation to a Whole of the global, so they are also images of a specific, personal time in relation to the Whole of duration. In this sense, photographs offer a more complex relationship with time than is presented in Deleuze's account. In viewing cinema, "we constitute a continuum of fragments of different ages; we make use of transformations which take place between two sheets to constitute a sheet of transformation . . . a kind of transverse continuity."[44] Sheets of the past—recollections—are in this sense like the photograms or still images on the filmstrip, and it is the mobile translation from one image to another that creates a third, dynamic image. This is the movement-image. The photograph is no different—a sheet of transformation between the various sheets of the past that makes up an interpretation of the image. The mobile identity of contemporary culture—given shape and texture by new media technologies—is mobile because the photograph is already mobile, and it is for this reason that the culture has been drawn once more to the photograph, and not the other way around. This is the reason for our newfound interest in the photograph, even in the face of the much publicized "death of photography" that the development of digital imaging seemed to herald.

Deleuze often presents the photograph as a singular immobile tracing, and yet the philosophy of the *Cinema* books as well as his work with Guattari suggest that we see the photograph as mobile and multitudinous. As the abundance of photographs on the Web suggests, many images are profligate and repetitive attestations of individuality in a homogeneous culture: pictures of Thanksgiving turkeys and Christmas trees, of teenagers preening and posing, pictures taken through mall windows or windshields, pictures of the computer station or bedroom, pictures of new travel and new experiences as well as the self-consciously mundane sights of daily life. In this sense, we are really seeing the creation of new movement-images as new and wider sets are created. For example, if we were to take all the photographs shot through car windshields, we would have the basis of an enormous movement-image and more, because while we are witnessing the creation of a civilization of the cliché, we are also afforded a glimpse of immanence—the life from which these formations are created. This is photography as afterimage, the retinal halo created by staring at images for far too long. But it is also the afterimage as the plane of immanence, the "black screen" on which is left a halo of life itself.

Notes

1   Paul Levinson, *Cellphone: The Story of the World's Most Mobile Medium and How It Has Transformed Everything!* (New York: Palgrave/Macmillan, 2004), 21.

2   John Urry, *Sociology beyond Societies: Mobilities for the Twenty-first Century* (London: Routledge, 2000), 83.

3   Gilles Deleuze, *Cinema 1: The Movement-Image*, trans. Hugh Tomlinson and Barbara Habberjam (Minneapolis: University of Minnesota Press, 1997), 25.

4   Ibid., 2.

5   Henri Bergson, *Creative Evolution*, trans. Arthur Mitchell (London: Macmillan, 1911), 323.

6   Deleuze, *Movement-Image*, 5.

7   André Bazin, *What Is Cinema?*, trans. Hugh Gray (Berkeley: University of California Press, 1974), 96–97.

8   Deleuze, *Movement-Image*, 24.

9   Ibid., 122.

10 André Bazin, *Qu'est-ce que le cinéma?* (Paris: Les Éditions du Cerf, 1984), 151, writes, "*Non point l'image d'un objet ou d'un être, mais bien plus exactement sa trace.*" This is translated by Hugh Gray, in Bazin, *What Is Cinema*, 96, as "In no sense is it the image of an object or person, more correctly it is its tracing."

11 Gilles Deleuze and Félix Guattari, *A Thousand Plateaus: Capitalism and Schizophrenia*, trans. Brian Massumi (Minneapolis: University of Minnesota Press, 1987), 13.

12 Ibid., 12.

13 Ibid.

14 Gilles Deleuze, *Cinema 2: The Time-Image*, trans. Hugh Tomlinson and Robert Galeta (Minneapolis: University of Minnesota Press, 1994), 21.

15 Edward Weston, "Seeing Photographically," in *Classic Essays on Photography*, ed. Alan Trachtenberg (New Haven, Conn.: Leete's Island Books, 1980), 172.

16   Deleuze, *Time-Image*, 22.
17   Gilles Deleuze and Félix Guattari, *What Is Philosophy?*, trans. Hugh Tomlinson and Graham Burchell (New York: Columbia University Press, 1994), 166.
18   Deleuze, *Time-Image*, 22.
19   Deleuze, *Movement-Image*, 57.
20   Ibid., 58–59.
21   Henri Bergson, *Matter and Memory*, trans. Nancy Margaret Paul and W. Scott Palmer (New York: Zone Books, 1996), 38.
22   Deleuze, *Movement-Image*, 59.
23   Ibid., 5.
24   Ibid., 7.
25   Bergson, *Matter and Memory*, 38–39.
26   See Mimi Sheller and John Urry, "Mobile Transformations of 'Public' and 'Private' Life," *Theory, Culture, and Society* 20, no. 3 (2003): 120, and Urry, *Sociology beyond Societies*, 90.
27   "Are Camera Phones Really Worth All the Effort?," April 25, 2004, http://www.ewirelessnews.com/Features/33/Are-camera-phones-really-worth-all-the-effort.html.
28   "Worldwide Camera Phone Sales to Reach Nearly 150 Million in 2004, Capturing 29 Billion Digital Images," Business Wire, March 11, 2004, http://www.findarticles.com/p/articles/mi_m0EIN/is_2004_March_11/ai_114125589.
29   "Study: Camera Phones Boosting Digital Camera Sales," *PC Magazine*, August 2005, http://www.findarticles.com/p/articles/mi_zdpcm/is_200508/ai_n14909764.
30   "Strategy Analytics: Camera Phone Sales Surge to 257 Million Units Worldwide in 2004; 68 Million Digital Still Cameras Sold Globally Last Year," Business Wire, April 14, 2005, http://www.findarticles.com/p/articles/mi_m0EIN/is_2005_April_14/ai_n13608842.
31   Terhi-Anna Wilska, "Mobile Phone Use as Part of Young People's Consumption Styles," *Journal of Consumer Policy* 26, no. 4 (2003): 448–49.
32   Shelley Emling, "Cell Phone Photos Get Shot but Seldom Sent," *International Herald Tribune*, October 4, 2004, http://www.iht.com/articles/541779.html.
33   Sherry Turkle, *Life on the Screen: Identity in the Age of the Internet* (London: Wiedenfeld and Nicholson, 1996), 258.
34   Deleuze and Guattari, *Thousand Plateaus*, 21.
35   José Van Dijck, "From Shoebox to Performative Agent: The Computer as Personal Memory Machine," *New Media and Society* 7, no. 3 (2005): 325.
36   Deleuze, *Movement-Image*, 65.
37   Ibid.
38   Ibid.

39   Roland Barthes, "The Rhetoric of the Image," in *Image, Music, Text* (London: Fontana, 1977), 39.

40   Roland Barthes, *Camera Lucida*, trans. Richard Howard (New York: Hill and Wang, 1981), 96.

41   Rohan Samarajiva and Peter Shields, "Telecommunication Networks as Social Space: Implications for Research and Policy and an Exemplar," *Media, Culture, and Society* 19, no. 4 (1997): 543.

42   Anthony Giddens, *Modernity and Self-Identity: Self and Society in the Late Modern Age* (Oxford: Blackwell, 1991), 77.

43   Sheller and Urry, "Mobile Transformations," 116.

44   Deleuze, *Time-Image*, 123.

17. Cimnemonics versus Digitime

Garrett Stewart

One large question hovering over the Time@20 conference concerned what the advent of the digital might have done to the Deleuzian time-image. My more specific question is why answers should seem, in the decade since the 1995 centenary of motion pictures, to lie in a certain international drift toward not only a postfilmic image, but a postreal-ist narrative—varying the conference title, call it Digitime@10. Space permits only a cursory glance at the transatlantic (to say nothing of the Pacific Rim) axis of this trend. On one side, there is the European uncanny of temporal disjunction, ethical coincidence, and erotic te-lepathy, all couched in the repeatedly elegiac dimension of the filmic medium's self-conscious memory-effects. On the other side is what I would call the ontological gothic in recent Hollywood productions, determined at the level of plot either by laws of electronic virtuality or supernatural afterlife.[1]

Though digital technique may not be prominent in the European variants of this trend, their pervasive tension between virtual and actual would seem to owe a diffuse cultural debt to the global ambience of networked presence and interactive transmission as much as to adjusted geopolitical formations and alliances. Such elements of the fantastic as intergenerational or transnational doubling, metempsychosis, and telekinesis thus reflect a generalized dispersion of psychic space across personal as well as national borders. At times, too, these European films of the fantastic can even recruit digital figuration quite directly. In Tom Tykwer's posthumous treatment of Krzysztof Kieślowski's script for *Heaven* (2002), the film opens, before any recognizable cinematography per se, with the computerized landscape of virtual reality in an undermotivated prologue recorded from within a digital flight simulator. Given the ensuing escape plot, this opening offers the electronic matrix of a fled tangible reality. It is just this instigating matrix, then, that comes back to haunt its terrorist lovers, under lethal police fire, in the hallucinated mortal transcendence of a closing helicopter liftoff. Even without technological virtuality, however, narratives from as early as Kieślowski's own *Double Life of Veronique* (1991) through the French films *He Loves Me ... He Loves Me Not* (2002) and *Swimming Pool* (2003) have to do with an uncanny doubling or transference of personality whose vectors transgress, at times national, at times mortal, limits—sometimes both together. In their American counterparts, especially the fantasies of temporal escapism on which I will be concentrating, a curious further question arises. Even when contextualized in a youth culture saturated by commercial electronics at every turn, why are so many recent films, despite their obvious digital enhancement at the level of technique, concerned in their plots with a *non*-electronic virtuality? By what cultural displacements would this be likely to occur?

Before pursuing even some tentative answers, it is important to clarify the poles of screen production. With recent films of preternatural duration and redoubling, one is invited to update Tzvetan Todorov's influential definition of the fantastic for this new cultural field. Broad distinctions are apparent between those Hollywood narratives that find their eventual plot explanation in the "marvelous," whether technological or supernatural, and European films that seek resolution in the "uncanny."[2] The former determination is most blatant in those trick endings that render "unreal"—even when not explicitly digital—the whole spatiotemporal grounding of an elapsed plot. In contrast to this Hollywood cinema of either virtual or specifically ghostly illusion, and the warps of time that result, are the proliferating European plots of amnesia, déjà vu, telepathic transference, crisscrossed destinies, apparitional nostalgia, and the like—and their allegorization of media itself—from late Kieślowski down through Pedro Almodóvor or Michael Haneke. The Euro-American distinction tends to divide, at the plot level, between a dubious epistemology of time in flux and its evacuated ontology, with a film like David Lynch's *Mulholland Drive* (2001) coming closest, perhaps, to straddling the transatlantic tonal divide. Whereas in European plots, the autonomous agency of a protagonist may seem ambiguously invaded by spectral others, in recent American cinema of the "twist finish," heroes may turn out to *be* their own spectral others: either the digital figments of someone else's computer program or already their own ghosts, deluded into thinking themselves still alive.

My *premise* is that such narratives are not likely to detach entirely from their own material base. They need not be divorced in analysis, therefore, from the sedimentations of a media archaeology that could help assess the drift toward the digital from within a previously filmic cinema. My *hypothesis* is that screen plots of the last decade continue to address cinema's partial derivation from—and once total constitution by—the photomechanical imprint, even while (and often quite directly because) the photogram is lately eroded or replaced by the pixel. It is at this level that my previous work, initiated under the influence, in fact, of Raymond Bellour on Max Ophuls—work on the remediation of photography by cinema—was bound to depart from the assumptions of Gilles Deleuze on screen movement.[3] I inevitably sided with Bergson, instead, on the inherent artifice of serial projection, rather than with Deleuze's relaxation into the ubiquitous plane of immanence, where (for him) what you see is what you get. Since my tested assumption was that moving pictures never entirely forget that they begin, both historically and in each new projection, with the very act of moving pictures, rather than with the pictured motion that results, the question necessarily remained—one question, at least—just what impact the digital hybrid of recent screen imaging might have on new narrative parameters of temporality and presence.

However one comes at this question, it is clear that photomechanical indexicality persists as an issue within plots of the mysterious and unreal. On the Hollywood end of the spectrum, photography anchors (in however evacuated a fashion) the ontological gothic in either of its two common forms: science fiction in the virtual worlds mold (from *Johnny Mnemonic* [1995] through *The Thirteenth Floor* [1999]) or supernatural thrillers (from *Jacob's Ladder* [1990] to *The Sixth Sense* [1999]). In such narrative formats, where the hero is either artificial or already dead to begin with, the photographic index of an inhabited body is often a touchstone of this crisis. In *Dark City* (1998) as well as *The Thirteenth Floor*—and with a precedent in the dubious maternal photograph of the cyborg in *Blade Runner* (1983)—the plot turns on false photographic witness: the record of a supposed past that is only part of an encompassing digital simulacrum. On the supernatural side of Hollywood's latest ontological twists, there are, for instance, the multiple flares, orbs, or auras in the serial photographs of the psychic boy hero of *The Sixth Sense*. And, in an equal clue to a related trick ending (exposing another posthumous protagonist), there are the inspected books of Victorian mortuary photographs in *The Others* (2001). With its inherent overtones of a spectral uncanny, photography—if its own existence is not simulated by virtuality in the first place—can either index the preternatural or embalm the mortal. Then, too, in Continental production, the eerie lifelikeness of photography, in its mourning work, is also a guiding erotic motif from *The Double Life of Veronique* (1991) through such later multinational productions as Julio Medem's *Lovers of the Arctic Circle* (1998) and Raul Ruiz's Proust film *Time Regained* (1999) to François Ozon's *Swimming Pool* (2003) and Pedro Almodóvar's *Bad Education* (2004).

Cinema thus sustains its photogrammatic imaginary even in residual form. Hedged round by the culture of electronic imaging, the single mechanical imprint within a cinematic plot helps in this way to calibrate the strangely entwined medial and narrative shift into the postfilmic and the postrealist alike. And this includes the altered treatment of human temporality often entailed by such innovations. In the very structure of their stories, many such films seem intrigued, from the immaterial ground up, by the technological parameters of an optic field in which change now occurs over time from *within* the frame rather than without, by electronic mutation rather than mechanical succession. Exposure time gives way to compositing time. Weighing the narrative repercussions of this sends one back to Deleuze's second volume with new urgency. Sudden electronic possibilities of the screen image—"untheorized" by the early 1980s—induce for Deleuze not a forecast, but instead, a review of cinema's postwar transformations: "we do not claim to be producing an analysis of the new images . . . but only to indicate certain effects whose relation to the cinematographic image remains to be determined."[4] It turns out that Deleuze is never more forthright about the photographic basis of film than when articulating its contrast with the digital. Unlike binary imaging, cinematography depends on representational units that he now stresses as "superimposable,"[5] separable and successive, whereas the video or computer image is instead "reversible."[6] Intervals and interstices have been altogether replaced by the flux and reflux of internal conversions. In prewar cinema, intervallic movement was not simply measured by elapsed time in an empirical sense. More abstractly, for Deleuze, time became the very "measure of movement."[7] Motion was thus the indirect image of time. As the movement-image slipped from prominence in the stasis or introversion of postwar cinema (this is all part of Deleuze's summary "Conclusion"), time came to be imaged more directly. What, then, about time—and its tempi, no longer its s/pacing—in postcinematographic screen practice?

This is where Deleuze's evocation of the 1980s shift in medium, sketchy as it is, knows to bear down. The time of the image is no longer segmental, incremental, sequential. In the postfilmic image, no single picture precedes the one we see—or follows from it. All is determined by internal interchange.[8] Between luminous flicker and digital fleck, between whisked-away imprint and whiplash linear pinpoint or convertible pixel, lies the framed optic differential that makes either for cellular transit or fragmental transformation. Filmic cinema times its frames, clocks them in lockstep. Instead, the video or digital image frames its internal changes over time. No longer a nexus or file of *whole* rectangles, the electronic frame becomes, when digitized, more like a weightless single easel for pixel tessellations, binary bit by bit, block by microblock. Once this is recognized (acknowledged, if not exactly seen), what then for narrative cinema? What matter? Where, that is to ask, does this very different timing of the image—between mechanical procession and electronic process—come to matter on screen?

Answers are everywhere lately, tentative and various. Not a sprocketed drop of frames past the aperture, but a coded phasing in and phasing out of the graphic grid; not an ocular rhythm at the threshold of perception, but an algorithm beneath it: such is the divergent mediation that screen storytelling may tacitly contend with, even when not taking it up directly as plot. Aberrations of fantastic temporality, whether telekinetic, recursive, reversible, proleptic, or any combination thereof—in plots in which the present is melted or dismembered before the eyes of its own occupant—make for images in which morphing, not so much of human agents, but of whole captured spaces, tends to replace superimposition as the reigning time-lapse function. In such films, via a strategic interplay between medium and theme, transformation replaces the routine frame line of mere spatiotemporal transit.

As it happens, the difference between sequence and intrinsic refiguration may well seem a reductive version, more like a travesty, of Deleuze's distinction within classic cinema between the movement-image and the time-image. For it is under the spell of the latter, of postwar temporal imaging, that the spectator, according to Deleuze, waits to see what will happen across the effect of a given image—what will occur *in* the image itself or *to* its attentive viewing—rather than waiting to see what image will happen next.[9] We, of course, need to beware. Any facile parallel between the stratified and elusive mutations of the time-image in Deleuze and the inherent flux of electronic registration is not only a superficial, but a potentially misleading one. Here one can well return to that brief concluding reflection on the digital advent in *The Time-Image*—and to the passage's prophetic final simile. Deleuze has established that the digital image can alter in any direction across its own frame. This happens not by accessing off-frame space, whether inferring it or moving to include it next. There is "no outside" to electronic images, "any more than they are internalized in a whole"[10]—as, for instance, in a conception of the strip as the vanishing frame line of a sequential narrative projection. As his striking comparative analogy succinctly puts it, "the shot itself is less like an eye than an overloaded brain endlessly absorbing information"[11]—less, say, like *Man with a Movie Camera* (2003) than like Hal the cyclops-lensed computer in *2001: A Space Odyssey* (1968). It is the premise of this chapter, once again, that few theoretical aperçus about media technology are likely to go unnarrated by contemporary film. Even the French science fiction thriller *City of Lost Children* (1995) pictures such a detached brain's need for an optical prosthesis by figuring its evil "mastermind" as a disembodied cranium suspended in a fish tank. By being still humanoid, though, this brain needs an old-fashioned, wood-mounted camera lens for its contact with the outside world.

Otherwise, the brain, folded entirely on itself, would not see at all; it would just process. The meeting ground of being and time would, in this way, surrender the necessity of any ocular focal point, any Albertian myth of the "window."[12] Memory, when construed as sheer information processing, needs no figurative recourse to mind's eye as opposed to cognitive scan, so that the open question remains, for Deleuze, whether electronic transmission or generation thus "spoils" the time-image—as image—or instead "relaunches" it.[13] In this way, the fading hegemony of the cinematograph—as gradually eclipsed by what one might term the electrograph—presses new questions even about films with no interest in brandishing their computer-graphic presti/digitations. To think of the screen image as a brain pattern, rather than an eye view, might well revise the entire apparatus-based monocular logistics of the point-of-view shot—might, and in recent cinema, often does. The advent of the electrograph cannot help but lead, in connection with the time-image, to an inquiry into the "psychological automata"[14] that such images serve to narrate, for instance, in Hollywood cinema. How is plot thus correlated with the "electronic automatism"[15] of its own manifestation? Inquiry would look, for instance, to the digitally implanted (or otherwise virtual) memories of cyborgs, out-of-body agents, posthumous self-specters, autonomous laser holograms, computer simulants, schizophrenic time travelers—the whole cast of noncharacters in the postmodern fantastic. At the same time, it would survey their counterparts, for European cinema, in transnational doppelgangers, erotic revenants, the blurred embodied thresholds of past and present, the whole magicalized horizon of the real. In both filmmaking practices, and even when the means of recording is still predominantly photomechanical, recent plots often tap a new latitude in screen mediation for their own most striking optics and metamorphoses.

Le temps retrouvé, to coin a phrase, versus time framed as sheer indiscriminate duration: that is the polarized psychosomatics of temporality that tends to be manifested at one and the same time around the medial watershed of a postfilmic cinema and the transatlantic divide of the new narrative fantastic. In 2004, these discernible trends may be thought to have reached their separate apogees in the mnemonic eroticism of Almodóvar's autobiographic reverie *Bad Education* (2004) and the mechanical reduction of retrospect itself to electronic implant in the dystopian Hollywood thriller, Omar Naim's *The Final Cut* (2004).[16] In one melodramatic narrative, a director recovers his own homosexual boyhood through the imagined filming of a typescript screenplay that becomes, through layers of superimposition from scene to scene, the very film we are watching. In the other science fiction plot, a video brain implant is able to record every instant of a subject's life, in relentless point-of-view shots, for eventual disk transfer, mortuary editing, and public rescreening at a precontracted "rememory" service.

In each case, once cinematographically, once digitally, medium and memory collapse on each other as the sheer apparatus of time framed. Each film has familiar enough antecedents, of course, respectively, in high modernism (think *8½* [1963]) and in the whole spectrum of metafilmic science fiction (with its prognosticated *optical* futures).[17] Embedded more specifically in the continuing Hollywood subgenre of the temporal fantastic and its ontological subterfuges, a single recent example can stand for the way in which, with far more narrative license than in either *Bad Education* or *The Final Cut*, time has been systematically denaturalized by current plot trends. *The Butterfly Effect* (2003) builds on the cult success of *Donnie Darko* (2001), where the time travel of a schizophrenic hero amounts to the heroic acceptance (for the good of those his absence enables) of his own narrowly escaped previous death. All *The Butterfly Effect* needs to generate a new plot is the willed *alteration* of past time, rather than merely the willing acquiescence in an already elapsed and alternative past.

Its hero suffers, it seems, a genetic case of psychosis inherited from his father, who thought that he could use photographs in a secret album to hallucinate his way back into the past to redirect the course of his own repeatedly ill-fated history. The son, instead, has used his written diaries, rather than images, for a similar retroactivation of the past. Repeatedly, we have seen the lines of his script give way, by digitized blur, to a full-screen cinematic image of some past trauma that he can thus edit out, redirecting his fate, until things go wrong again—and yet again. Cornered at last in the psychiatric ward, with his diaries confiscated—and as if inspired by his father's comparable photographic fetish, of which he has just learned—he turns instead to sixteen-millimeter home movies to summon up and then surgically alter his past. These involve shots of the original backyard picnic where he met the neighbor girl who was gradually to enthrall him—and whose life he inadvertently ruined. By the digital rustle and whoosh of a shrinking image plane, he is suddenly vacuumed into the time of record, emerging by reverse shot into his own englobing (thirty-five-millimeter) past.

By way of this newly afforded interface, this fantastic *temportation*, he once and for all scares the girl off, threatening the life of both her and her family. Heroically, he thereby foregoes his own history, his own time with her, for her own eventual good. But that was not the original plan. Before the studio executives talked the director out of it, the film was to end with the same revisionary and digitally figured plunge into the filmic past—so far, so good—but this time into a further mediated recess. What would have followed repeats at first the same digital effect from the theatrical version, sending the oscillating image of the hero funneling at warp speed into the past, but this time into a yet more primal scene: the actual moment of his birth. The interface between fled present and embedding past is made clear by the full-screen image of his mother smiling on the hospital gurney in the delivery room—as our own perspective worms inward for its streaked focus on the pregnant belly. It is this optic field of recovered immanence—and fetal imminence—that is then invaded and violated by retroactive desire.

Shifting focus toward the splotchy frame-within-the frame of the ultrasound monitor (its real-time tracery descendent from Marey's own precinematic invention of the electrocardiogram), we watch the open-eyed decision of the prenatal body to strangle itself with its own umbilical chord. Not just kissing off the girl next door, but denying both her and your own mother your very existence, this eradicating gesture passes beyond all figurative or nonfantastic versions of the Oedipal in a literal return to the womb. And it does so by boring straight through the middle of a low-resolution home movie in the new temporal equivalent of the cosmic zoom, telescoping time, rather than space, in a precipitous lunge. The very layers of remediation are themselves the point. For are not the continuous trace methods of fetal imaging perhaps now the last place where the image of the human body, before emerging into—let alone retroactively invaded by—agency, can come before us without suspicion of either editing, simulation, or enhancement? In biological rather than technological terms, here is the gestated rather than generated image, tangibility in the making, morphology before morphing. Otherwise, in the fantasy plots of any number of screen fictions, the lived body is no longer rooted in space from moment to irreversible moment. The Deleuzian dialectic between the movement-image and the time-image has imploded on a kind of perverse synthesis, in which time itself has become mobile, a matter of framed exchange, rather than immersive duration.

But there is a further wrinkle to the mystique of temportation and its psychobiographical reroutings in *The Butterfly Effect*. We viewers get to see the originally shot ending, of course—how else?—only from the DVD remediation of this partly digitalized cinematic artifact. Such a "bonus feature" file thus constitutes the final scene's own alternate textual reality. Is it far-fetched to detect in this commercial phenomenon a self-mirroring case of "parallel worlds" domesticated within the very paratext (as Genette would call it) of cinema's new distribution channels? Narrative is always recognized as shaping expectations for the imagined arc of our lives. In just this sense, the young hero of *The Butterfly Effect* might well have cut his eye teeth on just such a digital model of roads not taken, parallel destinies, virtualities unactualized, as has brought us this particular alternative to his own plot's closure. The either-or logic of the videodisc supplement has, in this way, been implicitly thematized by fantastic plotting.

With its optical layering both through ultrasound tracing and digitally transfigured sixteen-millimeter home movies, how is this mediated temporal evasion (and revision) to be compared to the very different virtualization of memory in European cinema? Toward this end, I would like call to the witness stand, anonymously for the moment, a study that can be profitably subpoenaed out of all identifying historical context for the sheer heuristic use of an overlapping paradigm it quietly deploys. In ways directly relevant to the films we are canvassing, the double binary of this template involves at once national trends and representational modes. Like the present essay, a little noted turn of the influential work in question divides film's treatment of temporal limit cases and their ambivalent metaphysical horizons between "European humanism" and "American science fiction." (Within my own loosened sense of the latter category, broadened to a more general fantastic, it is, of course, easy to make room in the Hollywood sector not just for what Todorov would call the "instrumental marvelous" of posthuman technologies, but for the ontological gothics of posthumous agency, as well.)

Written during the sudden global upsurge in video and digital mediation, the precursor study to which I allude is concerned, on its own terms, with the "emergence" of new temporal models across all modes of screen narration. Both European and American cinema of this period, in their equivalent break from normative realism, are notable for a detachment of agency from its spatiotemporal surround, with a new distance installed between perception and somatic engagement. Actors within a spectacle have been transformed into spectators of their own programmed actions, with a new premium thus placed on virtuality. In the aftermath of a character's autonomous "I," subjectivity is more commonly overseen than internalized. Dismantling the old paradigm of an image medium with which only the spectator, not its narrated participants, had to *will* an identification, "it is now that the identification is actually inverted: the character has become a kind of viewer," and this of a reality in which "the imaginary and the real have become indiscernible"—or in other words, indistinguishable from each other. One result is that plot is no longer stabilized by temporal progression. According to the broadly ranging analysis prosecuted in these terms, the "new cinema"—as innovative as it is involuntarily caught up in historical change—has arrived at a point of temporal crisis where "chronos is sickness itself." What this amounts to is an undermining, one might say, of the chronological by the chronic.

A directly imaged temporality of this sort "is the phantom which has always haunted the cinema," the study is quick to admit, but "now"—and the point is *suddenly*—cinema has found a way "to give a body to this phantom" in a whole new mode in which, "if virtual is opposed to actual, it is not opposed to real, far from it." In all of this, whether in European cinema's new fantasy-imbued humanism or in "American science fiction," a massive decentering of the psyche has been not so much effected overnight as belatedly recognized. For it is now, and manifestly, "we who are internal to time, not the other way round," with subjectivity relativized and dispersed across a duration not wholly its own. Though this recognition, along with the new modes of perception it brings in tow, is inevitably alienating at first, it is in the long run the only way of "restoring our belief" in a world otherwise removed from us by mediation.

The argument I am paraphrasing so sketchily is, of course, that of Gilles Deleuze.[18] But he concludes his second volume, as we know, with an explicit demurral. He is not really speaking of the "new images" at all, "tele" and "numerical." In what I have just been quoting, his filmic "new," his "now," is already backdated to a modernist moment that may—or may not—extend to include them. For he has been talking all along, even with his emphasis on virtuality and spectatorial mediation, not about computer-generated images and their virtual reality plots, but about a cinema from Rosselini through Resnais, Hitchcock through Kubrick, in which the indirect image of time derived from action cinema, or in other words, from the movement-image, has been displaced by the direct time-image. Temporality is entirely reconfigured in the editing room. Succession yields place to a more radical and irrational seriality, the motivated to the arbitrary splice, the montage juncture to the irrational cut. His main evidence thus precedes mine often by half a century. Yet in his remarks on films from *Last Year at Marienbad* (1961) to *2001: A Space Odyssey*, from elegiac virtuality to an apocalypse of temporal cognition in the "world brain," Deleuze anticipates everything the current spectator must contend with. This is especially clear when his analysis brings home, avant la lettre, the many interlocking ways in which the metaphysical problematic that divides European humanism from American science fiction is with us even yet. Though strained almost beyond recognition in some cases, its operations still remain within the conceptual precincts of a subjectivity that, while bereft of constitutive action, has become a pure spectation suspended in a time it can no longer call its own.

Deleuze on the overthrow of logical succession in screen editing by the irrational series might resemble the latest *Screen* article on Christopher Nolan's *Memento* (2000) or Gaspar Noé's *Irréversible* (2002)—except that he is in fact speaking of Straub-Huillet and Godard. In remarking on the discontinuities of virtuality's "new" editing style, with its retroactive divergences in the time frames of action, memory, and conjecture, Deleuze suggests that "the forking points are very often so imperceptible that they cannot be revealed until after their occurrence, to an attentive memory."[19] In this, though, his evidence is not what would come first to the contemporary spectator's mind. He is not referencing that rash of alternate-world plots and "forking-path" narratives so familiar lately to screen viewers. He is not thinking of *Sliding Doors* (1998) or *Run Lola Run* (1998) or *Swimming Pool*, or the science fiction premonitions of *Minority Report* (2002). He is thinking of Welles and Fellini. At the same time, the "attentive memory" that he finds requisite for the spectator is often displaced onto characterization as a deciphering function of lived time, so that plot agents struggle heroically to retain and decipher the very shapes of time. Characters themselves become not just viewers of their lives, but sleuths of its elusive crossroads in the throes of virtual replay. It is in this sense that Deleuze's grasp of the high modernist moment of postwar cinema quite strikingly anticipates the trick solutions and retroactive adequations of much more recent films. These are plot devices as well as visual figurations common not only to the ontological gothic of American thrillers, but to the mnemonic uncanny of humanist fantasy, with its erosion of mental borders and its preternatural relays of consciousness.

Deleuze emphasizes the way the "mental world of a character" becomes "so filled up with other proliferating characters" that psychic autonomy breaks down—"hence the importance of the telepath."[20] To say so does not require, of course, any reference to the oracle in *The Matrix* (1999), the clairvoyant child in *The Sixth Sense*, the blind medium at the séance in *The Others* (2001), or even the child's eponymous telepathy as far back as *The Shining* (1980). Nor, at the pole of Continental humanism, does Deleuze need to cite the reanimated mummy and his human prosthesis in the telekinetic androgyne, Ishmael, in Bergman's *Fanny and Alexander* (1982), nor the uncanny transference across the parallel-universe divide of *The Double Life of Veronique*, nor the more recent transnational telepathy of the Hungarian–French immigration allegory *Simon the Magician* (1999), in which the overcoming of linguistic estrangement is itself mystified as paranormal contact. Deleuze's case in point is instead the performance-artist mind reader in Fellini's *8½*. Writing of a temporality that floats anchorless in "any-space-whatever"[21] does not lead Deleuze to the arbitrary digital simulations of science fiction "virtual reality" in technological form, but rather, to the anonymity and anomie of postwar urban settings. In identifying the "brain-city couple"[22] of self-absorbed metropolitan consciousness, he does not intend to evoke films like *Dark City* or *The Thirteenth Floor*, nor any of that spate of recent films which all but thematize the screen optic as closer to neural imaging than to a photographic shot, but instead the work of Rosselini and Antonioni.

Moreover, in drawing on Bergson's interest in déjà vu and "paramnesia"[23] to typify the modern perturbations of this dysfunctional brain space, Deleuze is not evoking in part, with a two-decade clairvoyance of his own, the plot twist of 2004's *The Forgotten*. But you cannot tell this from just reading him. For in that recent supernatural gothic, a mother whose son has been abducted by aliens, with even his photographic and video traces erased by extraterrestrial electronics, is half tricked (along with us) into believing, for the first hour or so, that an extreme case of the psychological "uncanny," rather than a tabloid case of the technological "marvelous" (Todorov's wavering, definitive poles of the fantastic genre again), is at play and that she has simply fantasized the boy. In evidence here is a not uncommon symptom, says a psychiatrist in league with the aliens, of "paramnesia." If one were to believe him in this case, as regards this imputed fantasy, time is warped by forgetting the merely virtual status of what never was.

Elsewhere, Deleuze writes of the inseparable fold between the virtual and the actual in that form of crystalline apparition called the "mirror image," commenting that it is "as if" a "photo or a postcard came to life."[24] With Zanussi's *The Structure of Crystals*[25] in view, he makes his point without needing to mention the animated wall photo of Julio Medem's *The Red Squirrel* (1996), which bursts to life out of its past tense index to provide a present tense clue, nor the comparable moments of the photographic uncanny in Medem's subsequent *Lovers of the Arctic Circle*, nor the four-dimensional stereo card involving the magic dimension of time itself as well as depth in Raul Ruiz's version of the Proustian time-image for *Time Regained*—so that a binocular toy gives way to point-of-view animation. Nor does Deleuze need us to recall, on the other hand, the transfigured photographs as registers of death and its eerie reversals (images of family members disappearing or remanifested within the frame, according to the vagaries of time travel or supernatural intervention) in fantasy plots from *Back to the Future* (1985) through *Frequency* (1999) to *The Forgotten*.

Noting, as Deleuze does, how the widespread break from continuity editing into the irrational cut, when exaggerated yet further into a blank white screen, offers "no longer a lacuna"[26] that can be forded, or leaped across, Deleuze is not invoking the final escape from Lacuna Corporation in *Eternal Sunshine of the Spotless Mind* (2003), with its digital loop operating to trace the recursive snowbound flight of the principals, but the sheer disposition of narrative time in Bresson and Techiné. When he insists that time manifests itself most directly on screen by layered, tectonic, stratigraphic space, he is not speaking of the planar downloads of electronic virtuality in current Hollywood, nor of the "sheets" of the past in the metaphysical double loops of the latest European uncanny. But he *might* be. When he paraphrases the hero's "I am not dead because I have not seen my life pass before me,"[27] he does not allude to films in this mode from *Jacob's Ladder* through *The Sixth Sense* and *Vanilla Sky* (2001) to *The Jacket* (2005). He has in view the 1980 *Slow Motion* by Godard. Writing of a cinema in which "there are no more flashbacks, but rather feedbacks and failed feedbacks," he is not speaking of "American science fiction" over the last decade, since for him the playback in question needs "no special machinery."[28] Nor does he have in mind, instead, the fateful recurrences and psychic overlaps in European films of the doubled or split subject. He points instead to the "newness" of a cinema like the nouvelle vague. When he therefore sees modern cinema as having "killed the flashback"[29] through the more direct presencing of memory as virtual, rather than its compart/mentalized storage as past, his reference is not either to the mortally split temporality of *The Double Life of Veronique* or to the electronic sado-porn archive of *Strange Days* (1995), but to anything on the spectrum from Bergman's *Persona* to Resnais's *Providence*.

No need, indeed no chance, to adduce that 2005 European summa of low-tech feedback in the *unheimlich* home videos of Haneke's *Caché*, where a hidden camera forces the protagonist to replay the uneventful comings and goings of his mundane diurnal round in order—even before confrontation with his repressed colonial other—not merely to be unsettled by surveillance, but, allegorically, to see himself through it at last.[30] Real time is alienated from within by its own virtualization in replay. No way for Deleuze to include this reference, yet no way to exclude it from the widening orbit of the time-image under hypermediation. When Deleuze elsewhere stresses how the "crystalline" aspect of film, composing its temporal prism, allows us to "witness the birth of memory, as function of the future,"[31] it isn't *Caché*'s final nightmare memory from a fixated and internalized point of view that gives him his best evidence.[32] Neither does he have in mind the time loop plots of an alternate past in embryo. Nor is he alluding more specifically to the hallucinated futures seeded in the death-moment images of many a trick plot from *La Jetée* (1962) to its remake as *Twelve Monkeys* (1995). His point of reference is the proleptic structure of the flashback in the Roman historical epics of Joseph Mankiewicz (*Julius Caesar* and *Cleopatra*).

Commenting on the way cinema, defined as a mechanical automatism in its own right, "confronts automata, not accidentally, but
fundamentally,"³³ Deleuze means this as a gloss on the idea of cinema
as "spiritual automaton."³⁴ True, he does not instance in this light the
electronic ghosts in the machine of the *Matrix* trilogy or the "pre-cog"
zombies in *Minority Report* (2002), not *A.I.* (2001) or *I, Robot* (2004),
but rather, Dreyer's *Gertrud* and the sleepwalkers of Antonioni. But
the tracks of interpretation are firmly laid. Or say that he has read the
"lectosigns" (his term) of these more recent films in a precognizant
vocabulary all his own. Again and again, cinema since the modernist
zenith of the time-image has found ways to literalize, parody, or further
instrumentalize the conceits of temporality as the operable deceits of
the actual in a new virtual real. Such, I have been suggesting, is the
cinema of either the elegiac uncanny or the instrumental marvelous, as
divided most often between European psyche and Hollywood *technē*.

Perhaps no film from the American side of things sums up this
tendency more fully than the most recent arrival in the ranks of this
subgenre cycle. Here is a narrative that casts back across more than a
decade's worth of derivative experiment to the death-moment fantasy
of *Jacob's Ladder* (1991), in which an irradiant lyricism rescues plot
from a gruesome and lethal nightmare. But this new, recycled version
of wartime trauma, death, and restitution, *The Jacket* (2005) is also
a film that breaks back into the constitution of its own visual conditions to find there the tropes of its own final time-image. *The Jacket*
is directed as his first mainstream feature by experimental filmmaker
John Maybury, whose avant-garde debts are fully renegotiated only in
the closing frames. At the start, the hero is shot dead in the first Gulf
War in a mélange of video jump cuts and color bleeds ("I was twenty-
seven years old the first time I died," we hear in voice-over). He is then
slain again with another bullet by a stateside psychopath after his
unaccountable survival from the battle wound. He has been living on
(out of his body, we later realize) to make something meaningful of a
life already lost. In the end, time travel becomes only a metaphor for
an appeasing deathbed projection.

From five minutes in, the entire narrative is a plotting of the sheerly
virtual. And once more, its embodied fantasy is ballasted by the photomechanical index. Far into his own unlived and ultimately canceled
future, the hero discovers a photograph of the same young girl, in the
keep of her grown alcoholic self, to whom he had once been of help,
just before his second gunshot death. His ability to join the woman in

this revisable future, and to move back with her into her own past to correct its errors, is facilitated—and, as we later recognize, *figured*—by his being strapped into the title straitjacket. It is under this constraint, yet with a drug-induced release into fantasy, that he is entombed in a morguelike wall of coffins on the orders of a sadistic psychiatrist who is trying to cure him of his delusions of rebirth. Unlike the hero of *The Butterfly Effect*, Jack in *The Jacket* does not have to arrange his own death to accomplish this. Like Donnie Darko, he has merely to accept its ex post facto revelation. As we in the audience come to do, he has to recognize that the straitening constraint of his nightly crypt, also his only source of liberation into the power of time travel, is exactly the burial place it looks like, each coffin awaiting its corpse—and what dreams may come. The whole plot has thus been laid out, suspended with him, in an interment from which only *fantasy* can extricate the mind's eye.

Unique to this otherwise formulaic false-survivor plot, however, is what follows after its de rigueur digitizations. But even these are designed to resist the predictable equation between electronic ingenuity and existential transport. In the director's allergy to the typical "tunnel shot" of a film like *The Thirteenth Floor*, or any such time-travel variant of the cosmic zoom, everything is played out instead (he and his technicians are explicit about this in an interview on the DVD supplement) across the surface of the hero's iris. The requisite boring through time is thus rendered ocular and uncanny (visionary), rather than strictly marvelous (technological). As the hero tries to strain free from his nocturnal coffin, the camera enters the veined avenues of his vision per se, at which point we revert by graphic association to the film's liminal shot. For well in advance of his first death, *The Jacket* has opened with infrared digital telescopy through the crosshairs of a bomber's targeting system. And it is these same gun sight markers that appear faintly superimposed over numerous iris close-ups in the subsequent fantasy sequences.[35] Everything passes, so to say, under the sign (and optical sights), the recurrent stigmata, of death.

Having exploited the digital to figure the hero's posthumous desire, Maybury thus returns, in marking his hero's death, to cinema's own origins not in spectacle, but in visibility per se. After all the coruscating effects rippling in maelstrom across the optical lozenge of the dead or dying mind's eye—those localized visionary equivalents of the temporal zoom, by which the subject's will to life is catapulted by turns back into his own impossibly outlived past and into his own unachievable

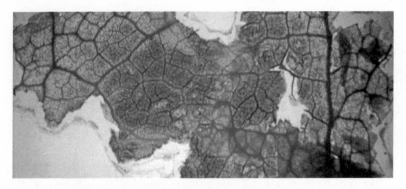

Frame enlargement from *The Jacket* (John Maybury, 2005)

future—after all this, some ocular relief is needed. Throwing over entirely its digital bravura, *The Jacket*'s final credits do nothing but project the very things of the world that death leaves behind. Unlike a host of science fiction time travelers since *Johnny Mnemonic*, though much in the mode of fantastic temportation, Jack has not been jacking in to an electronically aided fantasy. The computerized virtuality of digital editing has instead emblemized, rather than actually staged, his mind's own electrochemistry. As if finally to disinfect its time-images from all taint of virtual reality, however, even by cultural association, Maybury's film drives in closure all the way back to the prenarrative logic of optical impress itself, outside of signification and even before photomechanical transcription. Bazin's sense of photography as the "mummy complex" is trumped here by a departed world itself fossilized in light.

In its postnarrative backlighting, this visual effect nonetheless hinges on the last turn of plot. After the hero's belatedly accepted death is symbolized by a blinding light flooding from behind him—available to him only in the symbolic rearview mirror of his getaway car—the equally backlit but no longer representational end titles begin flashing by. In their flickering scroll of separate handmade frames, they offer the ultimate serialized homage to real, rather than virtual, presence. Associations rapidly coalesce around these remains of the material day. For what has been designed for this exit footage is a rolling epiphany of the organic and the found: the real. What we see are filigreed botanical and inorganic shapes flattened directly onto celluloid: a running index of the world materialized by illumination alone. In an archaeological sense, this is a return toward the original "photogram" of light writing—before the chemical print, and well before the redubbed photogram cells of mechanical cinema. Yet Maybury's closing effect also offers a quite explicit homage, not to prephotographic tracing in general, but to Stan Brakhage's *Mothlight* (1963), one of the quintessential films of the American avant-garde. Such an optical allusion to Brakhage's renowned spool of nonphotographic projection also stands in for a broader film-historical motive—nostalgic, ironic, or both—on Maybury's part. Long before the postfilmic advent of digitization, and in an antithetical sense, Brakhage's "movie" was a case of cinema without recorded film. In closing off Maybury's fantasy plot of strictly virtual existence and its digital evocations, the final prephotographic strip of *The Jacket* looks even further back, however, than to the American experimental cinema—or even than to the nineteenth century's "writing in light." From the cusp of the postfilmic, the film's final visual kinesis calls up the late-coming place of cinematography itself in a longer history of indexical tracing and its projected imaging that runs back through magic lanterns and shadow puppets to the metaphysical paradigm of Plato's cave. At the same time, however, and in the flicker of their discrete succession, these bits and pieces of an otherwise organic continuum, these arrested remnants of lived time, offer an emblem of a life died, and died again, at twenty-four frames a second. And more than this, too. Here at the end of Maybury's film is an action of the track so completely divorced from the movement-image, from the representation of the moving world, that its default to the time-image is unusually pure and need not pass through the virtual at all on its way to the real. It goes straight back to the actual.

In stark contrast to this closing leader in *The Jacket*, we may recall the hyperbolic "flicker effect" that chokes off Gaspar Noé's *Irréversible* three years earlier. Indulged there, at the overall plot level, is a play with temporality that is closer, as was *Memento* two years before, to the strictly structural anomalies of such European experiments as *Run Lola Run* (three parallel variants of the same plot) or 2003's *He Loves Me . . . He Loves Me Not* (with a suicide scene rewound all the way back to the film's first shot to initiate an alternate plotline). For all its marginal fantasy elements concerned with premonition and second sight, Noé's film bears only an antithetical relation to the Hollywood thrillers of temportation in the mode of the ontological gothic. Its time-images operate predominantly at the level of *syuzhet*, not *fabula*, structure, not event. Yet it is the violence of the latter that seems to torque and distort the former, wrenching it out of sequence. The whole point, captured by Noé's title, is that lived time (as opposed to its account) is never portable, never convertible, always irreversible. There is a devastation that cannot be escaped or transformed, even when a plot backs away from it in narrative time (savage murder, then the preceding lethal rape for which it is a revenge, then the former erotic happiness of the couple destroyed by this chain of events).

Irréversible ends with the supererogatory tag line "Time Destroys Everything," after we have seen the "good times" we know always and already to be doomed. Just before this last bludgeoning explicitness, a revolving overhead shot follows for more than a minute the rotation of a lawn sprinkler in an idyllic (and long lost) park scene—clockwise, temporally inexorable—until, with the disembodied point of view tilting skyward to a darkening cosmic backdrop, the image is interrupted, for the last endless minute or so, by blinding strobe flashes so stark as to induce mild ocular trauma. Suddenly stripping bare its own pretext in a happier time, the film becomes again just what it was to begin with in its violent manhunt and murder, if in a different key: a rush of images literally intolerable to watch. In interviews, the director has said that he meant this last registration of pure piercing duration to suggest that time is itself frightening. By contrast with the elegiac evocation of Brakhage's flickering spooled traces at the lyrical end of *The Jacket*, in *Irréversible*, time frames become again framed time, isolated, denatured, reified, and traumatic. Hence the contrast between such digitally applied or amplified scopic assault and the primitive flicker effect: a hyperbolic prevention of the seen versus its rudiments in a facilitating intermittence.

Exceptions only reaffirm the norm. In between blinding lacunae and projected slices of the real lie moving pictures as cinema knew them for a century. This is why a resistance to Deleuze on the score of movement's projected immanence only confirms the regime of the time-image at a deeper level. It is not just that the most definitive time-images on screen derive from the immediate default of the movement-image—freeze frame or altered motion, for instance. That alone would intercept Deleuze's model at an unexpected material depth. But there is something more. It is that cinema, conceived filmically, can be construed as time-image *tout court*. And this is so not at all because cinema samples and extracts the continuous duration of movement. Between protension and retention stretches the waver of tension per se. Cinematography images time because it must continually—rather than continuously—work to resynthesize the gestalt of the now from the pending and the elapsed, the going and the coming of succession itself. It may be that the digital array does serve, as Deleuze speculates, in one way or another either to "spoil" or "relaunch" the time-image: perhaps as a model of cognition in the grips of the virtual. If so, the time warps of what I have called temportation narratives might be one extreme exacerbation of this emergent cognitive model: brain scan, rather than shot.

Be that as it may, what the electronic algorithm cannot do is figure the very rhythm of surrender that is time passing. Whatever process is glimpsed by digitime, it is not duration in its successive progress. By contrast, the filmic differential is always a kind of optical and temporal portmanteau. That is what I meant by the abutment and inextricable lexical overlap of the term *cimnemonics*. To reverse the sentimental cliché to which the virtual in Deleuze can too easily be reduced, the point is not that cinema, like lived time, is memory in the making. Under the rule of cinematographic speed, of retentive evanescence, or in other words, under the impact of movement's own *virtuality* on screen, the memory trace is instead *time in the making*, time coming forth as image, where what you see is what you lose.

Something of this is what Bernard Stiegler, drawing from Heidegger's *Being and Time*, sees as the technics of duration itself, leading as it does to temporality's institution in cinema.[36] To capture this insight in the most compressed fashion, one would want to retain, as we will see his translators doing in a moment, Stiegler's typographic deconstructions of two linked Heideggerean terms: the pro/gram of pre/cedence. This is a vocabulary concerned with exactly that oscillation of retention and protention that delineates time itself as a strictly differential now. For Stiegler, the conceptual terms are in place well before he moves on, in his (untranslated) third volume, *Le Temps du cinéma*, to the sweeping modern paradigm of temporality afforded by the discrete succession of the filmic chain. And it is just such terms that are implicitly recapitulated by the divergent tropes of closure, epistemological versus ontological again, of *Irréversible* and *The Jacket*, decades after the unutterably greater modernist films of the Deleuzian time-image. One narrative recoiling back in time from a telos of violence we know to be ineluctable, one projecting forward from slaughter into a fantasy of embodied reparation, each ends in an oblique photogrammatic parable: intermittence versus index, marked respectively, and beyond the normal limits of cinema, by the stroboscopic and the prephotographic.

Each film, as film, thus testifies in extremis, and under unusual technical duress, to Steigler's pervasive sense that *Dasein*, Being in Time, is manifested nowhere more cogently than in the serial support of cinematic projection. For this is where, in Steigler's etymology and orthography both, the temporal "pro(gram)" is always one that "precedes Death,"[37] giving in to it before it arrives, materializing it on the cusp of a previous disappearance. So with the (photo)gram and its elided fatal fixity. Here once more, in screen projection, is time embalmed, change mummified, but only because it takes the form of death captured in execution twenty-four guillotine strokes per second. Here—to cast the matter in yet another typographic emblem—is duration not only navigated but inhabited as the sliding apprehension of *the/n/ow*. By any other name, this is the enduring time-image that electronic generation may well be busy reconfiguring against the residual mediation of a still filmic cinema and its motorized still frames.

Notes

1 This rough-hewn contrast in Euro-American film narrative over the last decade or so has organized two recent essays of mine, where many of the films mentioned here get a fuller discussion—and with extensive illustrations: "Crediting the Liminal: Text, Paratext, Metatext," in *Limina/Film's Thresholds*, ed. Veronica Innocenti and Valentina Re (Gorizia, Italy: Forum, 2004), 51–76, and "Frame/d Time: A Photogrammar of the Fantastic," in *Stillness and Time: Photography and the Moving Image*, ed. David Greene and Joanna Lowry (Brighton, U.K.: Photoworks/Photoforum, 2006). Parts of the present chapter are drawn from my book *Framed Time: Toward a Postfilmic Cinema* (Chicago: University of Chicago Press, 2007).

2 See Tzvetan Todorov, *The Fantastic: A Structural Approach to a Literary Genre*, trans. Richard Howard (Ithaca, N.Y.: Cornell University Press, 1975), in which the "Definition of the Fantastic" in the second chapter is followed by an exfoliated discussion of its poles in the third, "The Uncanny and the Marvelous," with a decisive schema for the whole genre spectrum given on p. 44.

3 Garrett Stewart, *Between Film and Screen: Modernism's Photo Synthesis* (Chicago: University of Chicago Press, 1999). For the debt to Bellour, see esp. pp. 39–40; for the critique of Deleuze on Bergson's dismissal of cinema, see esp. pp. 86–87, 144–48, including D. N. Rodowick's similar resistance to this turn of argument in Deleuze, p. 348n10, citing D. N. Rodowick, *Gilles Deleuze's Time Machine* (Durham, N.C.: Duke University Press, 1997), 22.

4 Gilles Deleuze, *Cinema 2: The Time-Image*, trans. Hugh Tomlinson and Robert Galeta (Minneapolis: University of Minnesota Press, 1989), 265–66.

5 Ibid., 265.

6   Ibid., 267.
7   Ibid., 271.
8   With reference especially to previous work by Lev Manovich, *The Language of New Media* (Cambridge, Mass.: MIT Press, 2001), this revolutionary aspect of the digital field, in its links to the "sequential scanning" of radar, rather than to the enchainment of cinematography, is reviewed by Mark B. N. Hansen, *New Philosophy for New Media* (Cambridge, Mass.: MIT Press, 2004), 8–9.
9   Deleuze remarks that in postwar modernism "the viewer's problem becomes 'What is there to see in the image' (and not now 'What are we going to see in the next image')." Deleuze, *Time-Image*, 272.
10   Ibid., 265.
11   Ibid., 267.
12   Ibid., 265.
13   Ibid., 267.
14   Ibid., 266.
15   Ibid., 265.
16   I discuss these two films in detail, and in view of Deleuze, in "Vitagraphic Time," for a special issue on "Narrative Cinema as an Autobiographical Act" in *Biography* 29, no. 1 (2006): 161–94.
17   On the metafilmic dimension of science fiction, see the fifth chapter, "The Photographic Regress of Science Fiction Film," in Stewart, *Between Film and Screen*, 189–224.
18   An omnibus citation to Deleuze, *The Time-Image*, for those Deleuzian emphases given out of context here: on "the division of western cinema into European humanism and American science fiction," a distinction in which Deleuze follows Antonioni, see Deleuze, *Time-Image*, 17 (see also n. 8); on the new media images, "video" and "numerical," 265; on the modernist character as spectator, 3; on the indiscernible borders between imaginary and real, 7; on time as malady, where there is "no other sickness but the chronic," 24; on the pure time-image come back as "phantom" to haunt postwar cinema after the decline of action and movement, with the result that virtual and real are no longer opposed, 24; on the Bergsonian containment of the subject by time, rather than vice versa, 82; and on film's power to restore our belief in the world through its virtual images, 172.
19   Ibid., 50.
20   Ibid., 2, 8.
21   Ibid., 5.
22   Ibid., 267.
23   Ibid., 79.
24   Ibid., 68.
25   Ibid., 70.
26   Ibid., 213.
27   Ibid., 68.

28 Ibid., 266.

29 Ibid., 278.

30 Haneke's film relentlessly dissects the failure of national "double occupancy" that Thomas Elsaesser (writing just before its appearance) poses as a partly utopian alternative to "Fortress Europe" and that appears in the plots of so many hyphenated national film productions. By contrast with the "ImpersoNations" of resolutely national cinema in an earlier chapter, see Thomas Elsaesser, "Double Occupancy and Small Adjustments: Space, Place, and Politics in the New European Cinema since the 1990s," in *European Cinema: Face to Face with Hollywood* (Amsterdam: Amsterdam University Press, 2005), 108–30. What he understands as the inevitably homeless and deterritorialized European consciousness—the always diasporic and orphaned sharing of a contestable fatherland—is exactly what the bourgeois Frenchman in Haneke's film cannot bear in the stepbrotherhood (the Algerian boy's adoption) that he has prevented as a child. He thus refuses the "mutual interferences" (p. 126) between subject and other that Elsaesser finds a film like *Amélie* designed to allegorize in the mode of the fantastic (p. 127), and he does so, as TV star of a literary talk show, precisely as a gatekeeper of high French culture, whose nationalist investments, country by country, Elsaesser sees television and film otherwise working to "dis-articulate" (pp. 114–15).

31 Deleuze, *Time-Image*, 59.

32 After all the surveillance cameras from which the hero's drugged final sleep is meant as respite, his reliving of the past (the banishment of the unwanted colonial other) is focalized through a static camera at the far back of the fateful family barn. As such, this fixated point of view is a highly charged allegorical version of what Edward Branigan calls "projecting a camera"—or in other words (to remotivate his general cognitive theory) a politically implicated version of screen viewing at large, which by its optical nature always tethers the experience of a moving picture to its focal imaging. See Edward Branigan, *Projecting a Camera: Language-Games in Film Theory* (New York: Routledge, 2006). In *Caché*'s plot and technique at once, the revenge of the video regime has succeeded. Even in his unconscious, Haneke's protagonist has "projected" his own repressed guilt as an unrelenting apparatus of record.

33 Deleuze, *Time-Image*, 263.

34 Ibid.

35 As at the end of *Syriana* from the same year, so at the opening of *The Jacket*. In the former's last scene, we think we are the primary spectators of an electoral motorcade, by the normal dispensation of narrative cinematography—only for the high-angle shot, pulling further back in disclosure, to display the image remediated on a bank of digital monitors in satellite transmission. Providential narrative and its impersonal point-of-view shots—the suggestion may run with both films—is never

far from the comparable (high-tech) unnaturalness of aerial surveillance as well as the electronically aided violence of gun sight annihilation. In the new global unconscious of televisual mediation, death is always only an eye line match away. Or say that the logic of a searchable database (and satellite download) like that of Google Earth—in this sense, the everyday interactive variant of screen spectacle's cosmic zoom—is reversed in such a case from magic cartography to the electrographic mechanism of stealth targeting.

36 Bernard Stiegler, *Technics and Time, 1: The Fault of Epimetheus*, trans. Richard Beardsworth and George Collins (Stanford, Calif.: Stanford University Press, 1998), 216.

37 Ibid.

18. Time @ Cinema's Future: New Media Art and the Thought of Temporality

Timothy Murray

> The future ain't what it used to be.
> —Yogi Berra

What will have been the result of looking back to Deleuze's cinema books from twenty years forward or looking forward from Deleuze's cinema books twenty years into the future? One response could be paradoxical, one that verges on nostalgia for the future past of cinema: the future ain't what it used to be. Another would entail a project of retrospective thought as a critical activity that toggles between past and future, one that positions us smack within the crystal of cinematic subjectivity, within what Deleuze calls the paradoxical commonplace of time. Time's crystal, or the crystallization of time, constitutes the structural paradox of temporality, its activation of passing presents, in which one moment goes, while another comes to shape the future, all the while preventing the past from falling into the inaccessible depths of the totally obscure.[1] Deleuze consistently attributes his celebration of the paradoxical commonplace of passing presents to the project of Henri Bergson by building his notion of the time crystal around Bergson's belief that time itself is subjectivity. Rather than arguing that the subject creates time through thought, Deleuze joins with Bergson in maintaining that the subject is *in* time (as *in* fantasy). Deleuze's approach to cinema is guided by his rather simple formula of cinematic time, or time's subjectivity: "it is in the present that we make a memory, in order to make use of it in the future when the present will be past."[2] Put similarly also some twenty years ago by Jean-François Lyotard, in contemplating the paradoxical event of time within the environment of new technology's expansion, "because it is absolute, the presenting present cannot be grasped: it is *not yet* or *no longer* present. It is always too soon or too late to grasp

351

presentation itself and present it. Such is the specific and paradoxical constitution of the event. . . . The event testifies that the self is essentially passible to a recurrent alterity."[3]

The body or shape of time, the event within which we find ourselves, is itself something of a phantom oscillating between the not yet and no longer, virtual but graspable in the actual. Deleuze insists that this phantom has been fundamental to cinema, haunting it and its spectators, until the arrival, that is, of "modern cinema," which has given form to the virtual image of time. The time of cinema always already awaits its passing actualization in the future present of modern cinema.

Future Cinema and the Split of Time

Future cinema and the split of time: these two themes, which find voice in Deleuze's second volume, *The Time-Image*, are what seem to have seized the attention of philosophers and the imagination of film specialists in the twenty years since the arrival of the cinema books. To some extent, we can situate the explosive contemplation of time with the coming and passing of the new millennium. Recall, for example, how the blockbuster exhibition, "Le temps, vite!," with which the Centre Pompidou ushered in the year 2000, was designed to lead the spectators through a concluding installation space, *The Future of Time*. This show was accompanied by a flood of timely writing: for J.-B. Pontalis, *Ce temps qui ne passe pas*; Georges Didi-Huberman writes *Devant le temps*; André Green finds himself ruminating on *Le temps éclaté*; while in the United States, Mary Ann Doane reflects on *The Emergence of Cinematic Time*, which has recently been followed by Elizabeth Grosz's *The Nick of Time* and preceded by *Cinema Futures . . . The Screen Arts in the Digital Age*, a collection edited by Thomas Elsaesser and Kay Hoffman.[4] These books on the thought of time arrived in fortuitous conjunction with two major exhibitions that solicit us to contemplate the place of Deleuze's "modern cinema" now that it, too, seems to have passed into the future. The massive 2003 exhibition at the ZKM in Karlsruhe, Germany, Future Cinema, curated by Jeffrey Shaw and Peter Weibel, was followed by a more focused and elegant show in Lille, France, "Cinémas du futur," which was curated by Richard Castelli for the festival Lille 2004.[5]

The emergence of time in these many reflections and exhibitions provides something of a paradoxical commonplace for consideration of Deleuze's acknowledgment of, yet relative discomfort with, the movement of his cherished "modern cinema" into the future of "future cinema"

Renate Ferro, *Screen Memory* (2004)

itself. I am referring to his passionate remarks, concluding *Cinema 2*, on the rapid acceleration of developments in electronic and digital media. His acknowledgment of the potentiality of video and digital cinema remains tempered by his affectionate ties to the philosophical vigor of cinema. "The modern configuration of the automaton is the correlate of an electronic automatism. The electronic image, that this, the tele and video image, the numerical image coming into being, either had to transform cinema or to replace it, to mark its death."[6] In an interesting way, Deleuze positions new media at the interval of cinematic time, as the carrier of both cinema's passing and its future. On the other hand, the electronic future carries for him a certain threat of deadening violence against his most cherished aspects of cinematic thought. "It is the time-image which calls on an original regime of images and signs, before electronics spoils it or, in contrast, relaunches it."[7]

It is hardly worth debating that digital technology and sensibilities deriving from new media have transformed the cinematic image, its space, and perhaps even its time. Consider, for instance, the multimedia installation of Renate Ferro, *Screen Memory* (2004), in which footage of family Super 8 film, shot in the 1950s, is digitized, reserialized, and

silently in different sequences on the facade of a miniature

projected silently in different sequences on the facade of a miniature building.[8] The footage plays on the amateurism of the patriarchal control of the camera and its contrast with the domestic activities of the play and the labor it records. At the same time, the placement of the homelike structure casts gigantic shadows onto the dissipating footage that spills onto the adjoining walls. Sound does fill this space, but it is precisely the sound of the Super 8 projector eating and tearing the brittle film as it passes through the sprockets, one final time, for digitization. To transfer this film of the past into the numerical future requires its literal wasting in the present of artistic production. The installation doubly complicates the Deleuzian celebration of the cinematic screen, moreover, by luring visitors across the threshold of the structural shell, where sensors illuminate a miniature table, set for tea. Inside, the visitors listen to the soft sounds of the artist's competing narratives not about cinema itself, but rather, about memories of the primal scene of domestic work and familial jouissance that transfer the passing of cinema into the register of other places, other screens. Screened are memories marked by the differences of gender, authority, and popular culture, as they are registered particularly by clustered groupings of visitors, some hailing from the moment of the Super 8 projector and the Buick Super Riviera, others from the more recent era of the Super 8 Motel and the digital Super Hero. Here, too, inside and outside, the visitors' bodies disrupt the enveloping projections to insert themselves phantasmatically into the fabric or screen of the installation. The purity of cinema, even in its lowly amateur guise, is sullied by the silhouette, carriage, and subtle interactivity of the viewers. While Ferro certainly places cinema's subjects in the space and place of time, and obviously transfers the stock of cinema into the digital future, she does so with artistic indifference to the ontological and even literal preservation of the very stuff of cinema. When cinema here crosses into the numerical code of archivization, its figure and ground shift in rather colossal ways. Ferro's multimedia installation, which is rather fundamental from a computing standpoint, works to highlight the extent to which even basic convolutions of electronic and digital media easily violate the conventions of the screen and alter the spectatorial habits of the cinematic viewer. *Screen Memory* can be said to exemplify how Deleuze's concern about the impact of electronic and new media on the thought of "modern cinema" seems to go in two directions, one back toward ontology, the other forward toward the uncertain valance of the "future" itself.

Du Zhenjun, *I Erase Your Trace* (2001)

To some extent, Deleuze seems to share a certain defensive identification with the ontology of cinema that similarly haunts practitioners
and theorists faced with the dissolution of its historical purity. This is
voiced no more poignantly than by Mary Ann Doane in *The Emergence
of Cinematic Time*: "a certain nostalgia for cinema precedes its 'death.'
One doesn't—and can't—love the televisual or the digital in quite the
same way. . . . It is arguable that cinephilia could not be revised at this
juncture were the cinema not threatened by the accelerating development of new electronic and digital forms of media."⁹ In a particularly
combative line concluding *The Time-Image*, Deleuze transforms Doane's
threatened nostalgia for the romance or love of cinema into the more
forceful, agonistic discourse of a philosopher confronted with the even
higher stakes of the end of time's crystal itself: "the life or afterlife of
cinema depends on its internal struggle with informatics."¹⁰ These
rather urgent words of resistance are written paradoxically by the
same philosopher with whom so many artists and theorists frequently
dialogue to articulate notions of a "philosophy after the new media."¹¹
Readers who cherish *Cinema 2* for its elaboration of the virtual may
have shared my surprise on first falling on these combative passages
at the very moment when a more committed embrace seemed possible,
if not logical, of the many faces of new media. For could not Deleuze
have recognized more unequivocally in the emergent new media a shift
in the principal variables of time and rhythm for which, in *The Fold:
Leibniz and the Baroque*, he welcomes the electronic experimentations
of Boulez and Stockhausen?

It is almost as if his book is haunted by the kind of anxious recurrence
of the temporal phantom staged by the Chinese new media artist, Du
Zhenjun, in his interactive installation *I Erase Your Trace* (2001).¹² In
this computer-driven piece, visitors are invited to walk across a platform

whose surface doubles as the screen of cinematic projection. The visitors' footsteps trigger sensors that activate a computerized program of hyperactive avatars, who clean away the traces of the visitors' footsteps. Every time another step is taken, the avatars reappear with the same passionate momentum in an effort to wipe clean the historical screen of cinema. If considered from the logic of cinema's internal strife with digitality, it is almost as if the avatars are struggling to wipe away the traces of analog visitation itself and to efface the corporeal specters of cinema's passing presents. The movement of passing presents summons back the virtual future with a vengeance. Each step into the "not yet" summons the possibility of the "no longer." While *I Erase Your Trace* could be read as a paragon of resistance to the analogical, it can be understood just as easily as a celebration of the interpellation of the virtual and its complex interface with the actual. It is almost as if Du engages in the Deleuzian logic of time's paradoxical doubling, one that contrasts the presents that "pass and are replaced" with an emergence from the scene that "launches itself towards a future, creates this future as a bursting of life."[13] In Du's work, the virtual and its paradoxical reality seem to spring out of nowhere, in sync with the advance of the curious spectator, one who roams the exhibition space in search of, as Richard Castelli might say, the "*cinémas du futur.*"

To better appreciate Deleuze's other motivation for his struggle against new media, we need to exercise caution, however, about how to gauge the valence of *future* in its cinematic context. For some theoreticians of new media, the notion of "future cinema" would be understood as merely a metaphor for something much more concrete, say, the place of cinema in cyber or virtual space. Lev Manovich, for example, emphasizes what he considers to be a fundamental characteristic of cinema in the digital era, the shift from time to space: "film montage introduced a new paradigm—creating an effect of presence in a virtual world by joining different images of time. Temporal montage became the dominant paradigm for the visual simulation of nonexistent spaces. As the examples of digital composing for film and Virtual Sets applications for television demonstrate, the computer era introduces a different paradigm. This paradigm is concerned not with time, but with space."[14]

It could be argued that Deleuze dialogues futuristically with Manovich when he contexualizes his concluding defense of cinema at the end of *Cinema 2* in relation to what he calls "this complexity of informational space."[15] In speaking admirably of the films of Syberberg, he commends the nontotalizable complexity that surpasses individual psychology, while rending impossible any sense of a spatial "whole." In view of Deleuze's emphasis on cinematic thought as what surpasses the totalizable subject, D. N. Rodowick has even praised Deleuze as "a cartographer of thought."[16] But Rodowick does so based on his appreciation for how Deleuze insists that such nontotalizable complexity finds its representation not so much in spatialized or even subjective terms, as in machinic ones—automata:

> To be a cartographer of thought for either the movement or time-image means tracing out their distinct planes of immanence, their concepts relating movement and time to thought, and the noosigns each gives rise to as particular *raccordements* of concepts and signs. Only in this way will we understand what new powers of thought arise. . . . The spiritual automaton is machinic thought, but this means that the cinema is less a technology than a *téchne* or *poesis*.[17]

Deleuze's concern over the potential dilution of "modern cinema" does not pertain to the digitalized transformation of space, perhaps a consideration more pertinent to the rise of classical cinema's movement-image, but with its potential transformation of our investment in the thought of time itself. It is to protect the very stakes of time and the spiritual automaton as machinic thought that Deleuze circles his cinematic wagons.

Particularly at issue is the shifting valence of the *future* in the age of electronic imagery and automated information. The future of "future cinema" is nothing close to being parodically metaphorical to Deleuze, but rather constitutes the fundamental machinic constituent of new informatics itself. It is the very replication of information in relation to its anchorage in the pull of the future that, he cautions, ultimately renders its pervasive automation radically ineffective: "information plays on its ineffectiveness in order to establish its power, its very power is to be ineffective, and thereby all the more dangerous."[18] A helpful elaboration of such a concern with the dangerously numbing accumulation of information for information's sake is provided in a related context by Lyotard's *The Inhuman: Reflections on Time*, a book Lyotard composed in the wake of his 1985 launching of the first major new media exhibition at the Centre Pompidou, "Les immatériaux." (It is notable that Lyotard was conceptualizing an exhibition of electronic arts at the same moment that Deleuze, his colleague at the University of Paris at Vincennes, was celebrating modern cinema.) In the chapter "Time Today," which is explicitly concerned with the unrealized potential of informatics, Lyotard focuses his analysis on information culture's privileging of the future at the expense, say, of what Deleuze calls cinema's passing presents. Lyotard joins Deleuze in reflecting on the increasing "complexification" of new technology, whose drive is the incessant recombination of information processing and data synthesis:

> As is clearly shown by the development of the techno-scientific system, technology and the culture associated with it are under a necessity to pursue their rise.... The human race is, so to speak, "pulled forward" by this process without possessing the slightest capacity for mastering it.... The growth of techno-scientific systems ... means neutralizing more events. What is already known cannot, in principle, be experienced as an event. Consequently, if one wants to control a process, the best way of so doing is to subordinate the present to what is (still) called the "future," since in these conditions the "future" will be predetermined and the present itself will cease opening onto an uncertain and contingent "afterwards." Better: what comes "after" the "now" will have to come "before" it. In as much as a monad in thus saturating its memory is stocking the future, the present loses its privilege of being an ungraspable point from which, however, time should always distribute itself between the "not yet" of the future and the "no longer" of the past.[19]

Deleuze joins Lyotard in wanting to short-circuit the pull of computational complexification to reinvest in the cinematic interval of the passing presents, between the "too early" and the "too late."

In this struggle against the informatic pull of the future, Deleuze has something greater in mind than the simple preservation of the historical promise of temporal montage, as Manovich would have it. When Manovich contrasts montage with new media, he limits montage to the logics of its articulation of the alteration of the state of the whole, which Deleuze identifies with the movement-image. In Rodowick's concise terms, "first, montage in or across movement-images is a logic of juxtaposition, connection, and linkage. Here time unfolds within movement like the cascading sections of a Jacob's ladder. The whole is given as addition (n + I ...) and time is reduced to a succession of presents.... Second, this means that the image of the whole, no matter how infinitely large or infinitesimally small, can always be given.... Thus the cinematic movement-image presents its indirect images of time through the forms or Ideas of montage."[20] Much more important to Deleuze's concerns about new media is what he calls their need to remain open to the cinematic imperative of the "*montrage*" of time.[21] This is what "brings together the before and the after in a becoming, instead of separating them; its paradox is to introduce an enduring interval in the moment itself."[22] Crucial to this concept of the interval is not its logical relation to the whole, but rather, its philosophical force as irreducible and autonomous as the *montrage* of becoming.

Privileging the force of the fissure, the interval is indifferent to the succession of images and the chains of association attributed to montage. Here the whole ("*le tout*") of cinematic ontology ("*tout cinéma de l'Etre = est*") undergoes a mutation to become the constitutive "*et*," the "*entre-deux*" of image and time.[23] Initially articulated by Deleuze in a 1976 discussion of Godard's *Ici et ailleurs*, in *Cahiers du cinéma*, the "and" resists the ontological grounding of the copula to be "neither one thing nor the other, it's always in between, between two things; it's the borderline, there's always a border, a line of flight or flow, only we don't see it, because it's the least perceptible of things. And yet it's along this line of flight that things come to pass, becomings evolve, revolutions take shape."[24] Running counter to the rationality of montage's juxtaposition and connection, this line of flight is what Deleuze lauds as an "irrational interval." Its irrationality can be said to lie in its incompossibility with the spatial perception, linear logic of the whole, and the ordering of time. I stress incompossibility as the notion that Deleuze takes from Leibniz to understand elements of thought and art that can fail to converge, while still not negating or rendering each other impossible. Rather than either converging or remaining impossible for each other, rather than being either included or excluded, they stand in paradoxical relation to one another as divergent and coexistent: as "incompossible."[25] The effect is both to rethink cinema's grounding in montage as the consequential flow of time, to release narration from its bondage to the truth-claim (making way for fabulation), and to insert the force of "incompossible presents" into the thought of time and its montrage.[26] This opens philosophy to the imperceptible frontiers of the "irrational interval." "What the irrational interval gives," suggests Rodowick, "is a nonspatial perception—not space but force, the force of time as change interrupting repetition with difference and parceling succession into series."[27]

Precisely the efficacy of the spiritual automaton and the irrational interval are what Deleuze fears may be muted but ultimately hopes can be delivered with equal or ideally more intensity by the new media. This leads us to rethink the question central to this chapter. Wherein lies the "future" in the art of new media? Might there be a way in which informatics combines with the artistic performance of the digital archive to reinvigorate the placeholder of the "future" itself, particularly in relation to the complexification of its informational present? In discussing various developments of the naissant numeric cinematics, which Deleuze calls "the corollary of the modern figure of the automata," can we come to an appreciation of what he hoped might lead to its energetic transformation of cinema, rather than simply its marking of the passing of cinema? Put otherwise, how might the very life of cinema depend fundamentally on an internal struggle with the stuff of informatics, on the becoming of artistic interactivity at the behest of the future?

In the context of new media art, I propose that we consider the form or event of the irrational interval in relation to a series of incompossible events: *archival intensities, interactivities, coded automatons*, and *the returns of the future*. As extensions of the time-image, its fabulations and its irrational intervals, the new media image capitalizes on the complexification of information science and culture by mixing and matching its softwares and hardwares, while it experiments with the crystalized density of the digital point in a way that foregrounds the extended frontiers of virtual reality (as that event of the virtual touching on the actual). A far too rapid concluding tour of a series of incompossible new media projects should make evident the lively and productive response of the new media community to Deleuze's charge that it receive and respond to the virtual as an energetic field of what has yet to be thought or registered.

Archival Intensities

Multiple modes of existence abound in the interactive, database installations of the Australian artist Jill Scott, one of the digital pioneers of what I call "archival intensity." Scott's complex new media events call on the sites of history, the projects of science, and the various possibilities of multimedia to solicit users to participate collectively in her new media environments. One of her richest installations looks directly into the future from the split perspectives of multiple characters who hail from different moments of twentieth-century time. *Frontiers of*

Utopia, mounted in 1995 and installed permanently in the ZKM in Karlsruhe, exemplifies what Scott calls her "hybrid environments." In this piece, which questions the idealism of Margaret Mead's notion of transmigratory culture, the users have the option of interacting with eight reconstructed characters: Emma (as in the anarchist Emma Goldman), Mary (a rural sociologist in Paraguay), Margaret (a secretary in a New York design firm), Pearl (an Australian aboriginal poet), Maria (a Yugoslavian hippy), Gillian (a Marxist radical student), Ki (a Chinese physicist), and Zira (a new age programmer). Users can access the lives of these women from four terminals geared to the 1900s, 1930s, 1960s, and 1990s. Rather than pursuing Ferro's strategy of collapsing the experience of time on the screen-memory of a cinematic construction made dense by its singularity, Scott provides her users with access to the viewpoints and historical artifacts important to these women, who possess different political viewpoints from across the globe and from different moments spanning the century that marks the history of cinema. Users are able to manipulate touch screens and interactive suitcases to hear the viewpoints of the characters and to peruse artifacts, news items, and memories crucial to their time periods.

Adding to the complexity of this very early new media installation is a touch screen that depicts all the women gathered together at a dinner table, à la Judy Chicago. Viewers are able to touch the characters' faces to catalyze sets of conversations between two women from different eras, locales, and imaginaries. One of my favorite exchanges is between Emma, the 1930s anarchist, and Zira, the 1990s programmer:

> ZIRA: We have to implement a system, otherwise the planet will die.
> EMMA: No rules for the hungry.
> ZIRA: The problem is too big now. In the nineties we suffer from massive overpopulation.
> EMMA: The only answer is to educate the women.
> ZIRA: Exactly for that we need a system.

What Scott's *Frontiers of Utopia* makes clear to its diverse users gathered together in struggle with the *differends* of history is that complexification itself, the ever expanding system of technology, with its mixture of archival matters and database materials, does not provide the sole answer to dilemmas of the future. While her title certainly acknowledges the pull of the future, the magnetism of her interactive objects faces the user with the enigmatic interval of passing presents. The magnetic interfaces of Scott's suitcases, which permit the users to touch keys to material icons that catalyze conflicting narratives about their historical particularity, ground the new cinematic experience in the incomposable archives of time and space. The result is what I appreciate as a dynamic staging of Deleuze's cherished paradox of split memory, "a memory for two people, or a memory for several."[28] Constructing "undecidable alternatives" inscribed literally on the tablecloth of history (*"entre nappes de passé"*), Scott far exceeds the representation of the incomposable "world-memory" so admired by Deleuze in the cinema of Alain Resnais: "the different levels of past no longer relate to a single character, a single family, or a single group, but to quite different characters as to unconnected places which make up a world-memory."[29]

Interactivities

Of course, key to the enactment of undecidable alternatives is an aesthetic practice committed to the unpredictabilities of interactivity, a practice that both solicits the user to respond to a set of predetermined choices and gives itself over to the user's momentary staging of a work whose algorithms leave it incomplete. In "The Relation-Image," one of the most thoughtful contributions to the gargantuan catalog coming out of the ZKM Future Cinema exhibition, the French new media artist Jean-Louis Boissier reflects on the aesthetic of interactivity shaping his experiments with new media, since the days when he designed the electronic interfaces for Lyotard's *Les Immatériaux*, and culminating more recently in a decadelong digital encounter with the works of Jean-Jacques Rousseau. During that time, Boissier created interactive installations of *Confessions* and *Rêveries* and developed an interactive electronic version of Rousseau that was published by Gallimard. Characteristic of this project is Boissier's experimentation with video inserts of particularly fetishistic moments of the text, with re-creations of the motion and movement inherent in the Rousseauesque narrative as well as with digital reflections on the interval of time itself. The result is an aesthetic project indebted to Boissier's particular theorization of interactivity as it dialogues with the cinema books of Deleuze:

> If we can imagine *relation* as a form, we can conceive of a relation-image capable of being produced by a new type of perspective. To that

perspective which refers to optics can be added a dimension relating to relational behavior. Within this interactive perspective, interactivity holds the position held by geometry in optical perspective. We could go so far as to say that, if perspective is that by which we can capture or construct a visual representation, interactive perspective is equally capable of seizing *[saisir]* or modeling relations. This interactive perspective projects relationships into a relational space.[30]

In *Moments de Jean-Jacques Rousseau*, the reader of the text is transformed into an interactive participant of touch and sight as she moves in and out of the historical past, the current moment, and the future reconfiguration of the texts, as the interactive tracking morphs the text into hypertextual fragments. Two structural features are particularly fascinating in how they overlap. One is Boissier's insistence on experimenting with hardware and software that permits the viewer of video to move horizontally and vertically, and thus in and out of time and focus:

> For all the sequences in *Moments*, I placed a digital camera onto a motorized panoramic head, which I had built with sufficient precision in the degrees of rotation as to achieve just such an interactive panorama. As the starting and ending positions were precisely marked during shooting, the image sequences submit themselves naturally to visual on-screen development, to looping, and to internal bifurcations. It is this equivalence of the movement with the human gaze *[du regard]*, by controlling the movement of the image, that the reader explores each sequence.[31]

Within the video sequence itself, Boissier cuts one frame out of ten, resulting in what Mary Ann Doane seems to regret as an acknowledgment of "the temporal lapse, the lost time inherent in the cinematic representation of movement."[32] But rather than marshalling the cut as what Doane calls an ellipsis through which "time becomes delimitable, commodifiable, objectlike,"[33] Boissier stages the cut as time's irrational interval itself, that which give rise neither to objects nor to commodities, but rather, to concepts, relations, and events. Thus the other structural device crucial to *Moments* is the user's interactive fractalization of text, through which time and thought are channeled to dwell in the interval of incompossibility itself. Crucial to Boissier's project is the interface of computing and interaction as the virtual ground giving rise to the poesis or thought of new media art: "in a computer cinema, the logical relation to the Real is not canceled or diminished, but rather transformed, emphasized. . . . The various domains of interactivity open up this variability . . . an interactive object's degree of openness is linked . . . to its increasing perfection [complexification] in the management of its internal relations . . . being able to respond to the demands of external interactions and to the mutations of its environment."[34] While Boissier provides his users with the option of inhabiting the intervals of history, of moving between the here while etching a virtual hypertext of the future, other artists have seized on the internal relations of the computing machine to situate the user more solidly in the shifting intervals of passing presents.

Take the simple Internet art project *Expand*, by Shu Leah Cheang, the self-proclaimed deterritorialized Internet artist, the global creator without a local address. Published in the "NetNoise" issue of *CTHEORY Multimedia, Expand* appropriates footage from Cheang's sci-fi porn film *I.K.U.* to mount the interval of digital frames versus cinema frames: thirty frames per digital second, thirty frames per cinema sequence.[35] The yellow dial intersecting the image strip permits the user to move back and forth in time and movement between and within particular eroticized image-times, catalyzed independent image and sound tracks in the style of the noosigns. By turning the Internet interface into something of a manual scratch device, Cheang permits the user to expand the narrative in shuffling mode. The project is framed by Cheang's political resistance to the male technodrive of digital complexification in dialogue with the early 1990s new media feminist collective, VNS Matrix. Cheang writes that she wishes to *Expand* VNS Matrix's mantra "The clitoris is a direct line to the matrix" by claiming that "The Pussy is the matrix":

> I am looking at a wireless digital mobile present with no portal to channel us; built in memory flash and gigabyte hard drive as delivered at birth; genetic mutation for the ALL NEW GEN. The merge is complete. We ride on the fantasy. Living comfortably with the monster within, I assign my body as a self-programmed, self-generative sexual unit. This body functions with an operating system that requires version update and memory upgrade. The unlikely future has come and gone. The retro future could be the next comeback.[36]

While Cheang's net.art depends on the retro-future fantasy of the self-generative sexual unit, the Japanese artist Masayuki Akamatsu takes for his digital subject the transferential split of time itself. In his installation *Time Machine!*, the user who approaches the console of this piece has his image captured by a video camera and transferred onto a projection facing him.[37] The image itself then becomes pixelated, extended, multiplied, and inverted in relation to the user's manipulation of a trackball. A turn to the left travels the image back into time, where it seems to split into a kind of unconscious free fall. The presence of the moment here gives way to the fracture and dislocation of time travel—a state previously known to man only through the unconscious or through literary and cinematic fiction. A turn to the left travels the image back to the future, into the present. Exhibited here, however, is a present whose image structure never appears to be constant; through pixelated imagery that moves right, into the future, it remains open to the vicissitudes of the video image's instantiation in time and the subject's entrapment in the doublings of time itself. Ask yourself if you are not witnessing something of a digital image crystal that embodies what Deleuze calls the most fundamental operation of time: "time has to split itself in two at each moment as present and past, which differ from each other in nature, or, what amounts to the same thing, it has to split the present in two heterogeneous directions, one of which is launched toward the future while the other falls into the past."[38] To be "in" the machinic state of time, in this sense, is to be always confronted with the touch, turn, vision, and thought of the interval as the recombinant turning of time.

Coded Automatons

It should be no surprise, however, that such machinic display would be cited by many philosophers of cinema not as a sign of cinema's lasting into the future, but rather, of its ontological passing in the present. One philosopher who has written elegantly on Deleuze's cinema books sets his sight directly on digital autopresentation as a procedure that threatens the promise of cinematic memory. Recalling Deleuze's expressions of digital ambivalence, Jacques Rancière warns that "information is not memory. It is not for memory that it accumulates; it labors only for its own profit. And this profit is that everything is immediately forgotten for the affirmation of the sole abstract truth of the present and that it affirms its power as the only thing up to this truth. The reign of the informational present rejects out of hand, as unreal, what is other than homogeneous process and what's indifferent to its autopresentation."[39] This is precisely the same sort of logic with which Deleuze voices his caution about informational culture at the conclusion of *Cinema 2*. To Deleuze, the autopresentation of new media threatens the liveness of cinematic automata that invigorates modern cinema with a new spirit. What he calls the new electronic automatism threatens to dissolve the cinematic inspiration of dreams and mystery into the neutral zone of random information bits indiscriminately traversing the wired membrane of gawkers and insomniacs.

Yet, Deleuze is not ready to abandon the allure of a newly constituted cinematic object, one that is in perpetual flux on the data screen, through which a new image can spring up from any point of the preceding image. Losing its directional privilege, the organization of cinematic space moves out of the theater into the fractal zones of high-speed ports, mobile computing, global positioning interfaces, and more frequently, embedded information chips. Here the admiration for the colossal cinematic screen gives over to the allure of the miniaturized information tablet, an opaque surface carrying instantaneous downloads through which the sacrality of cinema's givens are forever rendered obsolete: "inform replacing nature, and the brain-city, the third eye, replacing the eyes of nature."[40]

No artists have staged the newly coded automaton better than Mark Hansen and Ben Rubin in their collaborative project, *Listening Post*. In this hypnotic installation, which takes on a speed and life of its own, the artists display worded bits of information gleaned by data collection software that "crawls" the Web and listens to active chat rooms and online forums, news groups, and communication channels. Reaping snippets of language from the glossalia of global chat and the world memory of passing presents, the artists stream them in a series of information snapshots that flow through an interconnected grid of some 230 miniature LED screens. Here cinematic motion shows itself as the coded automaton of the passing presents of the new data archive, the NetNoise of hits, chat, traffic, instant messaging, and Web sampling. An automated voice reads some snippets aloud in a way that reenlivens Deleuze's cherished split of pure sound from cinematic image. Is the sounding a repetition of quotation or a sounding of generated digitext separated from the installation's whir and hiss of the movement of data bits?

Mark Hansen and Ben Rubin, *Listening Post* (2002)

In the eerily greenish hues of *Listening Post*, information *is* memory, pace Rancière, but of the kind literally suspended in the interval of time's code. As Tim Griffin so eloquently describes this enlivening digital memory archive, "the daily cycle of human rhythms becomes discernable across time zones, with domestic discussions often turning up in the morning, while politics and sex dominate the discussions at night. Over the course of weeks, one discerns a cultural subconscious. The currents of opinion and attention today, for example, might surround questions of war abroad, or ruminations on security issues at home, which accumulate like so many drops of rain."[41] Does not this performative grid of so many interconnected screens and sites bring to life the very kind of automatism that Deleuze identifies as the soul of modern cinema? Is this not an electronic resurgence of what he describes as "the material automatism of images which produces from the outside a thought which it imposes, as the unthinkable in our intellectual automatism"?[42] Might not the software generators that archive the intellectual automata inhabiting the wired membranes of online data culture be themselves the new source of the surging thought of the irrational interval? Does not *Listening Post* appropriate, while resisting, the flattening drive of information's surveillance to cast it in the glow of electronic Nature anew? This is the resistant interval, as D. N. Rodowick so elegantly puts it, "that restores a belief in the virtual as a site where choice has yet to be determined, a reservoir of unthought yet immanent possibilities and modes of existence. In this respect, the utopian aspect of philosophy and art is the perpetuation of a memory of resistance. This is a resistance to habitual repetition—a time that is calculated, rationalized, and reified. But it is also resistance to all forms of commerce or exchange, whether in the form of communication or that of commodities."[43]

The Returns of the Future

Put otherwise, the utopian aspect of a philosophy of resistance might be what engages the future, the avant-garde, as more than the habitual repetition of the "pull forward" of the technoscientific system. Rodowick's reminder that resistant thought is utopian requires us to return, if only very briefly, to the future, to the question of Future Cinema's future. Could we imagine a Future Cinema in which the pull of the future itself might give rise to thought exceeding the irrational interval of the passing present? Might there be a strategy of digital performance in which the machinic itself, as data automaton and screen of thought, now saturates its memory by stocking the future, to rekindle the phrase of Lyotard, by thus losing its privilege of being an ungraspable point from which, however, time should always distribute itself between the "not yet" of the future and the "no longer" of the past? What might Deleuze have had to say, for instance, about the interface with cinema of accelerating developments in affective computing, artificial intelligence, and interactive virtual bots? I am thinking of the kinds of interactive agents existing as, say, Lynn Hershman's "Agent Ruby" and Stelarc's "Prosthetic Head." These are interactive Web and prosthetic beings who are programmed to interact with the viewer through text and Web recognition software. Both beings respond to the interlocutor in uncanny ways, based on their response to conversations in the passing present. What is particularly innovative about both beings is how they are programmed as open systems—they do more than perform the archive of the past. Their performance is contingent on the archive of the future because their responses become more complex and sophisticated as they interact with successive visitors in the future.

The unpredictable future, as something of a new irrational interval in the present, one that marks the "not still" of the present and the "no longer" of the past, may well be programmed to engage in resistance to any habitual repetition of Future Cinema. I would like to conclude by turning to one such installation, *n-cha(n)t* (2001) by the Canadian artist David Rokeby, which aligns the future resistance of the coded archive with the world-memory of interactive computing. For this project, Rokeby installs a series of interconnected computers and monitors, from 6 to 12, that respond to user presence through sensors and microphones. When the computer's sensor acknowledges the presence of the user, its video image will solicit verbal interaction with the user, who then joins others in the room by speaking phrases into the microphone. This public, interactive performance is rendered strangely private because the microphone works to deaden sound by incorporating it into its system, rather than amplifying it via speakers to others in the room. Emphasizing a theoretical shift crucial to many of the artistic projects I discuss in *Digital Baroque: Temporal Folds, New Media, and the Memory of Cinema*, Rokeby hereby stages a digital dynamics of scansion, rather than a cinematic performance of projection.

What is more, the phrases uttered by the speaker interact with those internalized bits spoken by others to create something of a new emergent language, a new recombinant generator of what might come to be . . . thought. "What each computer speaks is meaningless in itself," says Rokeby. "Taken together, these phrases chart the trajectory of an unfolding narrative of communication . . . shared non-sense shimmering with a sense of meaning."[44] What is crucial to this constantly evolving installation, and what I wish to leave open for further development in my book in progress, *Immaterial Archives: Curatorial Instabilities @ New Media Art*, is that its performance remains dependent on the return of the future. It requires interaction with anticipated human interlocutors, who themselves, as thoughtful agents of the event, constitute the "pull" of the informational future in the irrational digital interval between retro-futures. This is something of a marvelous retooling of the Deleuzian *montrage*, based, you will recall, on "the bringing together of before and the after in a becoming." The paradox of the new retro-future is that "the after" is now inscribed as "the archival," one awaiting the data of the future for the sake of Rokeby's unfolding narrative of communication. *n-cha(n)t* also screens, on many levels, the new automatism's giving over to will, to the pull of the future, "put to the service of powerful, obscure, condensed will to art, aspiring to deploy itself through involuntary movements which none the less do not restrict it."[45] What continues to be at play, although with a numerical difference, is the enduring interval of cinema's internal struggle with the temporality of informatics. Crucial to this concept of the interval is not its logical relation to the whole, but rather, its philosophical force as the irreducible *montage* of becoming. Might not this be the networked ground of the *n-cha(n)*ted thought of future cinema itself?

Notes

1   A longer version of this chapter concludes my book, *Digital Baroque: New Media Art and Cinematic Folds* (Minneapolis: University of Minnesota Press, 2008). In this book, I argue that the paradoxical play of temporality lies at the crux of the intersection of cinema and new media art.

2   Gilles Deleuze, *Cinema 2: The Time-Image*, trans. Hugh Tomlinson and Robert Galeta (Minneapolis: University of Minnesota Press, 1989), 52.

3   Jean-François Lyotard, *The Inhuman: Reflections on Time*, trans. Geoffrey Bennington and Rachel Bowlby (Stanford, Calif.: Stanford University Press, 1991), 59.

4   J.-B. Pontalis, *Ce temps qui ne passe pas* (Paris: Gallimard, 1997); Georges Didi-Huberman, *Devant le temps* (Paris: Editions de Minuit, 2000); André Green, *Le temps éclaté* (Paris: Editions de Minuit, 2000); Mary Ann Doane, *The Emergence of Cinematic Time: Modernity, Contingency, the Archive* (Cambridge, Mass.: Harvard University Press, 2002); Elizabeth Grosz, *The Nick of Time: Politics, Evolution, and the Untimely* (Durham, N.C.: Duke University Press, 2004); Thomas Elsaesser and Kay Hoffman, eds., *Cinema Futures: Cain, Abel or Cable? The Screen Arts in the Digital Age* (Amsterdam: Amsterdam University Press, 1998).

5   Jeffrey Shaw and Peter Weibel, *Future Cinema: The Cinematic Imaginary after Film* (Cambridge, Mass.: MIT Press, 2003); Richard Castelli, *Cinémas du futur* (Lille, France: BAI/Lille, 2004).

6   Deleuze, *Time-Image*, 265.

7   Ibid., 267.

8   Renate Ferro, *Screen Memory*, http://www.aap.cornell.edu/aapweb/galleries/galleries-past-exhibits/galleries-past-frameset.htm.

9   Doane, *Emergence of Cinematic Time*, 228.

10   Deleuze, *Time-Image*, 270.

11   This is the term coined by one of Deleuze's most thoughtful readers; D. N. Rodowick, *Reading the Figural, or, Philosophy after the New Media* (Durham, N.C.: Duke University Press, 2001).

12 Du Zhenjun, *I Erase Your Trace*, http://membres.lycos.fr/duzhenjun/; *La leçon d'anatomie du docteur Du Zhenjun* (Rennes, France: Ecole des Beaux Arts de Rennes, 2001).

13 Deleuze, *Time-Image*, 87–88.

14 Lev Manovich, *The Language of New Media* (Cambridge, Mass.: MIT Press, 2001), 154–55.

15 Deleuze, *Time-Image*, 269.

16 D. N. Rodowick, *Gilles Deleuze's Time Machine* (Durham, N.C.: Duke University Press, 1997), 174.

17 Ibid., 175.

18 Deleuze, *Time-Image*, 269.

19 Lyotard, *The Inhuman*, 64–65.

20 Rodowick, *Time Machine*, 53.

21 Deleuze, *Time-Image*, 59.

22 Ibid., 155.

23 Ibid., 235.

24 Gilles Deleuze, *Negotiations, 1972–1990*, trans. Martin Joughin (New York: Columbia University Press, 1995), 45.

25 Deleuze, *Time-Image*, 130.

26 For further discussion of the importance of this notion to "incompossibility" to new media art, see Timothy Murray, "Digital Incompossibility: Cruising the Haze of the Electronic Threshold," *CTHEORY: Theory, Technology, and Culture* 23, no. 1–2, Article 77 (2000), http://www.ctheory.net/articles.aspx?id=121.

27 Rodowick, *Time Machine*, 178.

28 Deleuze, *Time-Image*, 116.

29 Ibid., 116–17.

30 Jean-Louis Boissier, "The Relation-Image," in Shaw and Weibel, *Future Cinema*, 403.

31 Ibid., 401.

32 Doane, *Emergence of Cinematic Time*, 214.

33 Ibid., 218.

34 Boissier, "Relation-Image," 405.

35 Shu Leah Cheang, *Expand*, http://ctheorymultimedia.cornell.edu/art/4.09/.

36 Shu Leah Cheang, "E-mail Exchange with Geert Lovink, 29 December, 2000," http://www.nettime.org/Lists-Archives/nettime-l-0012/msg00140.html.

37 Masayuki Akamatsu, *Time Machine!*, http://vision.mdg.human.nagoya-u.ac.jp/isea/program/E/artists/a438.html.

38 Deleuze, *Time-Image*, 81.

39 Jacques Rancière, *La fable cinématographique* (Paris: Seuil, 2001), 202; my translation.

40 Deleuze, *Time-Image*, 265.

41   Tim Griffin, *Listening Post* (New York: Whitney Museum of American Art, 2002).

42   Deleuze, *Time-Image*, 179.

43   Rodowick, *Time Machine*, 204.

44   Su Ditta, ed., *David Rokeby* (Oakville, Ont.: Oakville Galleries, 2004), 37.

45   Deleuze, *Time-Image*, 266. This results in something like an artistic resurgence of the enlivening aspects of what Arthur Kroker calls "the will to technology"; Arthur Kroker, *The Will to Technology and the Culture of Nihilism: Heidegger, Nietzsche, and Marx* (Toronto, Ont.: University of Toronto Press, 2004).

Publication History

Chapter 1 combines in translation Raymond Bellour, "L'image de la pensée: art ou philosophie, ou au-delà?," *Magazine Littéraire* 406 (February 2002): 42–43, and Raymond Bellour, "Michaux, Deleuze," in *Gilles Deleuze, une vie philosophique*, ed. Eric Alliez (Paris: Les Empêcheurs de penser en rond, 1998), 537–44.

Chapter 2 was previously published as *CiNéMAS* 16, nos. 2–3 (2007): 12–31; it appears here in translation for the first time.

Some material in chapter 5 was previously published as Dorothea Olkowski, *The Universal (in the Realm of the Sensible): Beyond Continental Philosophy* (New York: Columbia University Press, 2007).

Chapter 7 was previously published as *CiNéMAS* 16, nos. 2–3 (2007): 32–52; it appears here in translation for the first time.

Chapter 8 was previously published as *CiNéMAS* 16, nos. 2–3 (2007): 116–45.

Chapter 10 was previously published as D. N. Rodowick, "Unthinkable Sex: Conceptual Personae and the Time-Image," *(In)Visible Culture* 3 (2000), http://www.rochester.edu/in_visible_culture/issue3/rodowick.htm.

Chapter 11 was previously published as *CiNéMAS* 16, nos. 2–3 (2007): 74–94; it appears here in translation for the first time.

An earlier version of chapter 12 was published in *Log* 1 (Fall 2003): 113–22.

Chapter 15 was previously published as John Rajchman, "Deleuze's Time, or How the Cinematic Changes Our Idea of Art," in *Art and the Moving Image: A Critical Reader*, ed. Tanya Leighton (London: Tate, 2008), 307–27.

Chapter 17 is adapted from chapter 5 of Garrett Stewart, *Framed Time: Toward a Postfilmic Cinema* (Chicago: University of Chicago Press, 2007), 165–205.

Chapter 18 was previously published in Timothy Murray, *Digital Baroque: New Media Art and Cinematic Folds* (Minneapolis: University of Minnesota Press, 2008), 238–60.

Contributors

Raymond Bellour is director of research emeritus at the Centre Nationale de Recherches Scientifiques in Paris and a cofounder, with the late Serge Daney, of the influential critical review *Trafic*. Known for his work on the theory and criticism of cinema, photography, video, and installation art, he is also widely respected for his studies of literature, including the Brontë sisters, Alice James, Alexandre Dumas, and Henri Michaux. Editor of the Pléiade edition of Michaux's collected works, his most recent books include *Partages de l'ombre, texts* (2002), *L'Entre-Images* (1990), *L'Entre-Images 2* (1999), *The Analysis of Film* (2000), and *Le corps du cinéma* (2009).

Ronald Bogue is distinguished research professor of comparative literature at the University of Georgia. He is the author of *Deleuze on Cinema* (2003).

Giuliana Bruno is professor of visual and environmental studies at Harvard University. She the author of *Atlas of Emotion: Journeys in Art, Architecture, and Film* (2002), winner of the 2004 Kraszna-Krausz Award for "the world's best book on the moving image," and *Streetwalking on a Ruined Map* (1993), winner of the 1993 Kovács Prize from the Society for Cinema and Media Studies for best book in film studies. She is coeditor of *Off Screen: Women and Film in Italy* (1988). Her newest book, *Public Intimacy: Architecture and the Visual Arts*, was published in 2007.

Ian Buchanan is professor of critical and cultural theory at Cardiff University. He is the founding editor of *Deleuze Studies*.

James Chandler is Barbara E. and Richard J. Franke Distinguished Service Professor of English and Cinema and Media Studies at the University of Chicago, where he also serves as director of the Franke Institute for the Humanities. His publications include *England in 1819: The Politics of Literary Culture and the Case of Romantic Historicism* (1998) and *Wordsworth's Second Nature: A Study of the Poetry and Politics* (1984). He is coeditor of *Questions of Evidence* (1992), *Romantic Metropolis* (2005), and *The Cambridge Companion to Romantic Poetry* (forthcoming). He is currently completing work on the *Cambridge History of British Romantic Literature* and a book about the history of the sentimental mode in literature and cinema.

Tom Conley is Lowell Professor of Romance Languages and Visual and Environmental Studies at Harvard University. His books include *Film Hieroglyphs* (Minnesota, 1991 and 2006), *Cartographic Cinema* (Minnesota, 2007), *The Self-Made Map* (Minnesota, 1996), and *The Graphic Unconscious in Early Modern French Writing* (1992). In the 1980s, he was also a frequent contributor to *Hors Cadre*, the journal of film theory under the direction of Marie-Claire Ropars-Wuilleumier.

Amy Herzog is assistant professor of media studies at Queens College, City University of New York, where she teaches courses on film theory and popular music. She is the author of *Dreams of Difference, Songs of the Same: The Musical Moment in Film* (Minnesota, 2009).

András Bálint Kovács is head of the Film Department at Eötvös Loránd University, Budapest, and director of the National Audiovisual Archive. He has also served as artistic advisor for Béla Tarr's production company and taught in several other universities, including Université de la Nouvelle Sorbonne in Paris and the University of Stockholm. A translator of Deleuze's cinema books into Hungarian, his single-authored books include *Les mondes d'Andrej Tarkovsky* (1987), *Metropolis, Paris (On German Expressionism and the French New Wave)* (1992), *Tarkovszkij* (1997), *Film and Narration* (1997), *Collection of Essays* (2002), and *Trends in Modern Cinema* (2005). His latest book, *Screening Modernism: European Art Cinema, 1950–1980*, was published in 2008.

Patricia MacCormack is senior lecturer in English, communication, film, and media at Anglia Ruskin University, Cambridge. She has published extensively in the areas of the visceral dimension of cinema, corporeality, the posthuman, queer theory, feminism, ethics, and continental philosophy. Her particular interests lie in the work of Guattari, Deleuze, Lyotard, Foucault, Blanchot, Irigaray, Rancière, and Serres. Recent work on perversion, masochism, body modification, non-huMan rights, polysexuality, and the ethics of becoming has appeared in *Body and Society*, *Women: A Cultural Review*, *Thirdspace*, *Rhizomes*, *Queering the Non/Human*, and *Theory, Culture, and Society*. She is the author of *Cinesexuality* (2008) and coeditor, with Ian Buchanan, of *The Schizoanalysis of Cinema* (2008). She is currently writing a book on posthuman ethics.

Timothy Murray is curator of the Rose Goldsen Archive of New Media Art, director of the Society for the Humanities, and professor of comparative literature and English at Cornell University. His curatorial work has included projects for CTHEORY MULTIMEDIA, low-fi.org, and metamute.org. He has edited special issues on film and new media for *Wide Angle* and *Sites*. His books include *Digital Baroque: New Media Art and Cinematic Folds* (Minnesota, 2008), *Drama Trauma: Specters of Race and Sexuality in Performance, Video, and Art* (1997), *Like a Film: Ideological Fantasy on Camera, Screen, and Canvas* (1993), and, as editor, *Masochism, Mimesis, and Mime: The Politics of Theatricality in Contemporary French Thought* (1997).

Dorothea Olkowski is chair and professor of philosophy at the University of Colorado, Colorado Springs. She is the author of *The Universal (in the Realm of the Sensible)* (2007) and *Gilles Deleuze and the Ruin of Representation* (1999). She is the coeditor of *Feminist Interpretations of Merleau-Ponty* (2006) and three other edited collections on Merleau-Ponty, and she has edited or coedited two books of feminist philosophy: *Resistance, Flight, Creation: Feminist Enactments of French Philosophy* (2000) and *The Other: Feminist Reflections in Ethics* (2007).

John Rajchman is adjunct professor and director of MA Programs in Art History and Archaeology at Columbia University. His books include, most recently, *The Deleuze Connections* (2000) and *Constructions* (1998).

D. N. Rodowick is professor of visual and environmental studies as well as director of graduate studies in film and visual studies at Harvard University. Author of many essays and books on philosophy and film theory, his recent publications include *The Virtual Life of Film* (2007), *Reading the Figural, or Philosophy after the New Media* (2001), *Gilles Deleuze's Time Machine* (1997), and *An Elegy for Theory* (forthcoming).

Marie-Claire Ropars-Wuilleumier was, before her untimely passing in 2007, emeritus professor of French literature at University of Paris VIII. Along with Hélène Cixous, Roger Dadoun, Gilles Deleuze, Lucette Finas, Jean-François Lyotard, Gisèle Mathieu-Castellani, and others, she was a founder of Paris VIII, established in the wake of the events of May 1968. Noted for her pathbreaking studies of the intersections between philosophy, literature, and film, her many publications include *Écrire l'espace* (2002), *L'idée d'image* (1995), *Écraniques: le film du texte* (1990), *Le Texte divisé: essai sur l'écriture filmique* (1981), *L'Écran de la mémoire* (1971), and *De la littérature au cinéma: genèse d'une écriture* (1970). She was also one of the founders and editors of *Hors Cadre*, one of the most important contemporary French journals of film and theory, and editor in chief of the Presses Universitaires de Vincennes.

Garrett Stewart, James O. Freedman Professor of Letters at the University of Iowa, after several books on Victorian fiction, is the author most recently of *Between Film and Screen: Modernism's Photo Synthesis* (1999), *The Look of Reading: Book, Painting, Text* (2006), and *Framed Time: Toward a Postfilmic Cinema* (2007).

Damian Sutton is lecturer in historical and critical studies at Glasgow School of Art. He is the author of *Photography, Cinema, Memory: The Crystal Image of Time* (Minnesota, 2009) and is coeditor of *The State of the Real: Aesthetics in the Digital Age* (2007). He has published essays on photography, cinema, new media, memory, and trauma studies. He is currently developing research into new conceptual approaches to design and cinema as well as photography and time.

Melinda Szaloky is acting assistant professor at the University of California, Santa Barbara. Her articles on film theory and philosophy, silent film history, genre, and transnational cinemas and media have been published in edited collections as well as in *Cinema Journal*, *Film History*, *CiNéMAS*, and the *New Review of Film and Television Studies*.

Index

104–6; cinemasochism and, 157; delirium and schizoanalysis of film in, 140–41; ethics discussed in, 98, 115; faciality in, 242; *femme-auteur* discussed in, 187; fourth dimension discussed in, 72n86; Kant discussed in, 48, 67; Kierkegaard discussed in, 121; philosophy as art in, 128–29; philosophy of the fold in, 213–31; photography discussed in, 315; psychomechanical cinema in, 287, 295–96; shot mobility discussed in, 247–48; stratigraphic landscape in, 197–207

Cinema 2: Time-Image, The (Deleuze), xiii–xv, xviii, xx–xxii; on aesthetic and psychosocial figures, 178–80; aesthetic reflection in, 66–67; Bresson discussed in, 124–25; cinemasochism and, 157–60, 167–68; cinematic philosophy in, 115–16; crisis in belief in, 107–9; digital imaging technology in, 332–40, 348n18, 353; ethics discussed in, 98, 115; future cinema and split of time in, 352–70; Godard discussed in, 291; informational culture discussed in, 366–68; Kierkegaard discussed in, 121, 123; musical films discussed in, 260–76; "outside" discussed in, 15–28; painting discussed in, 293; philosophy as art in, 128–29; philosophy of the fold in, 215; photography and, 315–23, 332–40; psychomechanical cinema in, 287, 295–96; stratigraphic landscape in, 194–207; transcendentalism in, 55, 68n7; visibility of things discussed in, 193–94

Cinema Futures . . . The Screen Arts

in the Digital Age (Elsaesser and Hoffman), 352

"Cinémas du futur" exhibition, 352

cinemasochism, 157–75; self-sacrifice and cinecstasy, 172–75; sexuality and, 160, 164–68

cinematic history: modern technology and, 291–302; in musical films, 260, 263–76

Cities of Words (Cavell), 99

City of Lost Children (film), 332

Claire's Knee (film), 195

Cléo de 5 à 7 (film), 184, 187

Cleopatra (film), 340

close-up: affection-image and, 245–53, 255n29, 256n35; philosophy of the fold and cinematic technique of, 213–31

Cocteau, Jean, 53

coded automatons, digital imaging technology and, 365–68

Coetzee, J. M., 136–37

Colbert, Claudette, 252

Colorado Territory (film), 205

conceptual art, evolution of, 43–44

conceptual personae, 127–29; aesthetic versus psychosocial figures and, 177–82, 189n5

Confessions (Augustine), 23

Confessions (interactive installation), 362

Conley, Tom, xxi, 193–207

consciousness, Kant's discussion of, 57–60, 289–90

Contesting Tears (Cavell), 99

Cooper, Gary, 237–38

Copernican revolution (Kant), cinematic theory and, 55–60

Corbusier (Charles-Édouard Jeanneret-Gris), 293

Cournot, Michel, 140

Critique magazine, 26

Critique of Judgment (Kant), 49, 64, 67, 201

MacCormack, Patricia, xx–xxi, 157–75

Mackenzie, Henry, 238

Madam-T garment, philosophy of the fold and, 221–24

Magritte, René, 20–21, 39

Mallarmé, Stéphane, 9, 41

Mambo Girl (song), 261

Mankiewicz, Joseph, 286, 340

"Man of Feeling," Capra's use of, 238

Manovich, Lev, 356–58

Man with a Movie Camera (film), 289, 332

Mapplethorpe, Robert, 311–12

Marinetti, Filippo Tommaso, 223–24

Markov chain, cinema and philosophy and, 122–23, 126–29, 130n19

Martin Chuzzlewit (Dickens), 252

Marx, Karl, 194

Marxist ideology: Kant and, 71n79; stratigraphic landscape of film and, 202–3

masochism, Deleuze's discussion of, 127, 157–61, 169–71, 174–75. *See also* cinemasochism

"Mass Ornament, The" (Kracauer), 259

materiality of the fold, haptic design and, 220–21

mathematics, motion in context of, 93n37

Matrix, The (film), 338, 341

Matta-Clark, Gordon, 294

Matter and Memory (Bergson), 314–15

"Maurice Blanchot: The Thought from Outside" (Foucault), 20

Maybury, John, 341–44

McLuan, Marshall, 291, 301

Mead, Margaret, 361

Medem, Julio, 330, 339

Melville, Herman, 12n19

Memento (film), 337, 344

Memoirs of Emma Courtney, The (Hay), 251–52

memory, cinematic movement and, 89–91, 314–15

Merleau-Ponty, Maurice, 82–87, 92nn22–23, 93n27

Metz, Christian, 53–54, 63, 70n55

Michaud, Yves, 293

Michaux, Henri, xviii, 6–11

Miéville, Anne-Marie, 185–87

Million Dollar Mermaid (film), 265

minoritarian culture: cinemasochism and, 163–64; musical films and, 260–61

Minority Report (film), 338, 341

Mitry, Jean, 237

Miyake, Issey, xxi, 218, 222–24

mobility, photography and, 308–23

modern art: Deleuze's discussion of, 293–94; Eco's discussion of, 32–44

modern cinema: crisis in belief and, 107–9; Deleuze's discussion of, 291–302, 356–70

modernity: ethics of cinema and, 109–12; photography and identity and, 321–23

modificanti, philosophy of the fold and, 224

Moments de Jean-Jacques Rousseau (interactive installation), 362–64

Montaigne, Michel de, 109n28

Montalban, Ricardo, 264

montrage, Deleuze's discussion of, 242–43, 356–59, 369–70

moods, philosophy of the fold and, 227–31

morality, ethics of cinema and, 101–3, 112

moral sentiment, eighteenth-century theory of, 236–37

Moral Tales (film), 184